Course Booklet

Introduction to Networks

cisco.com

Cisco | **Networking Academy**
Mind Wide Open

ciscopress.com

Introduction to Networks Course Booklet

Printed in the United States of America

First Printing   July 2013

Library of Congress Control Number: 2013944487

ISBN-13: 978-1-58713-311-4

ISBN-10: 1-58713-311-3

Warning and Disclaimer

This book is designed to provide information about Introduction to Networks. Every effort has been made to make this book as complete and as accurate as possible, but no warranty or fitness is implied.

The information is provided on an "as is" basis. The authors, Cisco Press, and Cisco Systems, Inc. shall have neither liability nor responsibility to any person or entity with respect to any loss or damages arising from the information contained in this book or from the use of the discs or programs that may accompany it.

The opinions expressed in this book belong to the author and are not necessarily those of Cisco Systems, Inc.

Publisher
Paul Boger

Associate Publisher
Dave Dusthimer

Business Operations Manager, Cisco Press
Jan Cornelssen

Executive Editor
Mary Beth Ray

Managing Editor
Sandra Schroeder

Project Editor
Seth Kerney

Editorial Assistant
Vanessa Evans

Cover Designer
Louisa Adair

Interior Designer
Mark Shirar

Composition
Bronkella Publishing, LLC

Trademark Acknowledgments

All terms mentioned in this book that are known to be trademarks or service marks have been appropriately capitalized. Cisco Press or Cisco Systems, Inc., cannot attest to the accuracy of this information. Use of a term in this book should not be regarded as affecting the validity of any trademark or service mark.

Feedback Information

At Cisco Press, our goal is to create in-depth technical books of the highest quality and value. Each book is crafted with care and precision, undergoing rigorous development that involves the unique expertise of members from the professional technical community.

Readers' feedback is a natural continuation of this process. If you have any comments regarding how we could improve the quality of this book, or otherwise alter it to better suit your needs, you can contact us through email at feedback@ciscopress.com. Please make sure to include the book title and ISBN in your message.

We greatly appreciate your assistance.

Americas Headquarters	Asia Pacific Headquarters	Europe Headquarters
Cisco Systems, Inc.	Cisco Systems (USA) Pte. Ltd.	Cisco Systems International BV
San Jose, CA	Singapore	Amsterdam, The Netherlands

Cisco has more than 200 offices worldwide. Addresses, phone numbers, and fax numbers are listed on the Cisco Website at **www.cisco.com/go/offices.**

CCDE, CCENT, Cisco Eos, Cisco HealthPresence, the Cisco logo, Cisco Lumin, Cisco Nexus, Cisco StadiumVision, Cisco TelePresence, Cisco WebEx, DCE, and Welcome to the Human Network are trademarks; Changing the Way We Work, Live, Play, and Learn and Cisco Store are service marks; and Access Registrar, Aironet, AsyncOS, Bringing the Meeting To You, Catalyst, CCDA, CCDP, CCIE, CCIP, CCNA, CCNP, CCSP, CCVP, Cisco, the Cisco Certified Internetwork Expert logo, Cisco IOS, Cisco Press, Cisco Systems, Cisco Systems Capital, the Cisco Systems logo, Cisco Unity, Collaboration Without Limitation, EtherFast, EtherSwitch, Event Center, Fast Step, Follow Me Browsing, FormShare, GigaDrive, HomeLink, Internet Quotient, IOS, iPhone, iQuick Study, IronPort, the IronPort logo, LightStream, Linksys, MediaTone, MeetingPlace, MeetingPlace Chime Sound, MGX, Networkers, Networking Academy, Network Registrar, PCNow, PIX, PowerPanels, ProConnect, ScriptShare, SenderBase, SMARTnet, Spectrum Expert, StackWise, The Fastest Way to Increase Your Internet Quotient, TransPath, WebEx, and the WebEx logo are registered trademarks of Cisco Systems, Inc. and/or its affiliates in the United States and certain other countries.

All other trademarks mentioned in this document or website are the property of their respective owners. The use of the word partner does not imply a partnership relationship between Cisco and any other company. (0812R)

Contents at a Glance

Contents

Command Syntax Conventions

The conventions used to present command syntax in this book are the same conventions used in the IOS Command Reference. The Command Reference describes these conventions as follows:

- **Boldface** indicates commands and keywords that are entered literally as shown. In actual configuration examples and output (not general command syntax), boldface indicates commands that are manually input by the user (such as a **show** command).

- *Italic* indicates arguments for which you supply actual values.

- Vertical bars (|) separate alternative, mutually exclusive elements.

- Square brackets ([ ]) indicate an optional element.

- Braces ({ }) indicate a required choice.

- Braces within brackets ([{ }]) indicate a required choice within an optional element.

About This Course Booklet

Your Cisco Networking Academy Course Booklet is designed as a study resource you can easily read, highlight, and review on the go, wherever the Internet is not available or practical:

- The text is extracted directly, word-for-word, from the online course so you can highlight important points and take notes in the "Your Chapter Notes" section.

- Headings with the exact page correlations provide a quick reference to the online course for your classroom discussions and exam preparation.

- An icon system directs you to the online curriculum to take full advantage of the images imbedded within the Networking Academy online course interface and reminds you to perform the labs, Class activities, Interactive activities, Packet Tracer activities, and chapter quizzes and exams.

The *Course Booklet* is a basic, economical paper-based resource to help you succeed with the Cisco Networking Academy online course.

Companion Guide

Looking for more than the online curriculum? The Companion Guide is fully aligned to Networking Academy's online course chapters and offers additional book-based pedagogy to reinforce key concepts, enhance student comprehension, and promote retention. Using this full-fledged textbook, students can focus scarce study time, organize review for quizzes and exams, and get the day-to-day reference answers they're looking for.

The Companion Guide also offers instructors additional opportunities to assign take-home reading or vocabulary homework, helping students prepare more for in-class lab work and discussions.

Available in print and all major eBook formats (Book: 9781587133169   eBook: 9780133475449)

Course Introduction

0.0 Welcome to Introduction to Networks

0.0.1 Message to the Student

0.0.1.1 Welcome

Welcome to the CCNA Introduction to Networks course. The goal of this course is to introduce you to fundamental networking concepts and technologies. These online course materials will assist you in developing the skills necessary to plan and implement small networks across a range of applications. The specific skills covered in each chapter are described at the start of each chapter.

You can use your smart phone, tablet, laptop, or desktop to access your course, participate in discussions with your instructor, view your grades, read or review text, and practice using interactive media. However, some media are complex and must be viewed on a PC, as well as Packet Tracer activities, quizzes, and exams.

Refer to
Online Course
for Illustration

0.0.1.2 A Global Community

When you participate in the Networking Academy, you are joining a global community linked by common goals and technologies. Schools, colleges, universities, and other entities in over 160 countries participate in the program. A visualization of the global Networking Academy community is available at http://www.academynetspace.com.

Look for the Cisco Networking Academy official site on Facebook© and LinkedIn©. The Facebook site is where you can meet and engage with other Networking Academy students from around the world. The Cisco Networking Academy LinkedIn site connects you with job postings, and you can see how others are effectively communicating their skills.

Refer to
Online Course
for Illustration

0.0.1.3 More Than Just Information

The NetSpace learning environment is an important part of the overall course experience for students and instructors in the Networking Academy. These online course materials include course text and related interactive media, Packet Tracer simulation activities, real equipment labs, remote access labs, and many different types of quizzes. All of these materials provide important feedback to help you assess your progress throughout the course.

The material in this course encompasses a broad range of technologies that facilitate how people work, live, play, and learn by communicating with voice, video, and other data. Networking and the internet affect people differently in different parts of the world. Although we have worked with instructors from around the world to create these materials, it is important that you work with your instructor and fellow students to make the material in this course applicable to your local situation.

Refer to
Online Course
for Illustration

0.0.1.4   How We Teach

E-doing is a design philosophy that applies the principle that people learn best by doing. The curriculum includes embedded, highly interactive e-doing activities to help stimulate learning, increase knowledge retention, and make the whole learning experience much richer – and that makes understanding the content much easier.

Refer to
Online Course
for Illustration

0.0.1.5   Practice Leads to Mastery

In a typical lesson, after learning about a topic for the first time, you will check your understanding with some interactive media items. If there are new commands to learn, you will practice them with the Syntax Checker before using the commands to configure or troubleshoot a network in Packet Tracer, the Networking Academy network simulation tool. Next, you will do practice activities on real equipment in your classroom or accessed remotely over the internet.

Packet Tracer can also provide additional practice any time by creating your own activities or you may want to competitively test your skills with classmates in multi-user games. Packet Tracer skills assessments and skills integration labs give you rich feedback on the skills you are able to demonstrate and are great practice for chapter, checkpoint, and final exams.

Refer to
Online Course
for Illustration

0.0.1.6   Mind Wide Open

An important goal in education is to enrich you, the student, by expanding what you know and can do. It is important to realize, however, that the instructional materials and the instructor can only facilitate the process. You must make the commitment yourself to learn new skills. The following pages share a few suggestions to help you learn and prepare for transitioning your new skills to the workplace.

Refer to
Online Course
for Illustration

0.0.1.7   Engineering Journals

Professionals in the networking field often keep Engineering Journals in which they write down the things they observe and learn such as how to use protocols and commands. Keeping an Engineering Journal creates a reference you can use at work in your ICT job. Writing is one way to reinforce your learning – along with Reading, Seeing, and Practicing.

A sample entry for implementing a technology could include the necessary software commands, the purpose of the commands, command variables, and a topology diagram indicating the context for using the commands to configure the technology.

Refer to
Online Course
for Illustration

0.0.1.8   Explore the World of Networking

Packet Tracer is a networking learning tool that supports a wide range of physical and logical simulations. It also provides visualization tools to help you understand the internal workings of a network.

The pre-made Packet Tracer activities consist of network simulations, games, activities, and challenges that provide a broad range of learning experiences. These tools will help you develop an understanding of how data flows in a network.

Refer to
Online Course
for Illustration

0.0.1.9   Create Your Own Worlds

You can also use Packet Tracer to create your own experiments and networking scenarios. We hope that, over time, you consider using Packet Tracer - not only for experiencing the pre-built activities, but also to become an author, explorer, and experimenter.

The online course materials have embedded Packet Tracer activities that will launch on computers running Windows® operating systems, if Packet Tracer is installed. This integration may also work on other operating systems using Windows emulation.

Refer to
Online Course
for Illustration

0.0.1.10   How Packet Tracer Helps Master Concepts

Educational Games

Packet Tracer Multi-User games enable you or a team to compete with other students to see who can accurately complete a series of networking tasks the fastest. It is an excellent way to practice the skills you are learning in Packet Tracer activities and hands-on labs.

Cisco Aspire is a single-player, standalone strategic simulation game. Players test their networking skills by completing contracts in a virtual city. The Networking Academy Edition is specifically designed to help you prepare for the CCENT certification exam. It also incorporates business and communication skills ICT employers seek in job candidates.

Performance-Based Assessments

The Networking Academy performance-based assessments have you do Packet Tracer activities like you have been doing all along, only now integrated with an online assessment engine that will automatically score your results and provide you with immediate feedback. This feedback helps you to more accurately identify the knowledge and skills you have mastered and where you need more practice. There are also questions on chapter quizzes and exams that use Packet Tracer activities to give you additional feedback on your progress.

Refer to
Online Course
for Illustration

0.0.1.11   Course Overview

As the course title states, the focus of this course is on learning the fundamentals of networking. In this course, you will learn both the practical and conceptual skills that build the foundation for understanding basic networking. You will do the following:

- examine human versus network communication and see the parallels between them
- be introduced to the two major models used to plan and implement networks: OSI and TCP/IP
- gain an understanding of the "layered" approach to networks
- examine the OSI and TCP/IP layers in detail to understand their functions and services
- become familiar with the various network devices and network addressing schemes
- discover the types of media used to carry data across the network

By the end of this course, you will be able to build simple LANs, perform basic configurations for routers and switches, and implement IP addressing schemes.

Refer to
Online Course
for Illustration

0.1   Navigating the Course

0.1.1   Control Your Experience

0.1.1.1   Course GUI Tutorial

Your Chapter Notes

Exploring the Network

1.0 Exploring the Network

1.0.1.1 Introduction

We now stand at a critical turning point in the use of technology to extend and empower our ability to communicate. The globalization of the Internet has succeeded faster than anyone could have imagined. The manner in which social, commercial, political and personal interactions occur is rapidly changing to keep up with the evolution of this global network. In the next stage of our development, innovators will use the Internet as a starting point for their efforts - creating new products and services specifically designed to take advantage of the network capabilities. As developers push the limits of what is possible, the capabilities of the interconnected networks that form the Internet will play an increasing role in the success of these projects.

This chapter introduces the platform of data networks upon which our social and business relationships increasingly depend. The material lays the groundwork for exploring the services, technologies, and issues encountered by network professionals as they design, build, and maintain the modern network.

> Refer to
> **Lab Activity**
> for this chapter

1.0.1.2 Class Activity - Draw Your Concept of the Internet

Welcome to a new component of our Networking Academy curriculum: Modeling Activities! You will find them at the beginning and end of each chapter.

Some activities can be completed individually (at home or in class), and some will require group or learning-community interaction. Your instructor will be facilitating so that you can obtain the most from these introductory activities.

These activities will help you enhance your understanding by providing an opportunity to visualize some of the abstract concepts that you will be learning in this course. Be creative and enjoy these activities!

Here is your first modeling activity:

Draw Your Concept of the Internet

Draw and label a map of the Internet as you interpret it now. Include your home or school/university location and its respective cabling, equipment, devices, etc. Some items you may wish to include:

- Devices/Equipment
- Media (cabling)
- Link Addresses or Names

- Sources & Destinations
- Internet Service Providers

Upon completion, be sure to save your work in a hard-copy format, as it will be used for future reference at the end of this chapter. If it is an electronic document, save it to a server location provided by your instructor. Be prepared to share and explain your work in class.

For an example to get you started, please visit http://www.kk.org/internet-mapping/.

Refer to
Online Course
for Illustration

1.1   Globally Connected

1.1.1   Networking Today

1.1.1.1   Networks in Our Daily Lives

Among all of the essentials for human existence, the need to interact with others ranks just below our need to sustain life. Communication is almost as important to us as our reliance on air, water, food, and shelter.

The methods that we use to communicate are constantly changing and evolving. Whereas we were once limited to face-to-face interactions, breakthroughs in technology have significantly extended the reach of our communications. From cave paintings to the printing press to radio and television, each new development has improved and enhanced our ability to connect and communicate with others.

The creation and interconnection of robust data networks has had a profound effect on communication, and has become the new platform on which modern communications occur.

In today's world, through the use of networks, we are connected like never before. People with ideas can communicate instantly with others to make those ideas a reality. News events and discoveries are known worldwide in seconds. Individuals can even connect and play games with friends separated by oceans and continents.

Networks connect people and promote unregulated communication. Everyone can connect, share, and make a difference.

1.1.1.2   Technology Then and Now

Imagine a world without the Internet. No more Google, YouTube, instant messaging, Facebook, Wikipedia, online gaming, Netflix, iTunes, and easy access to current information. No more price comparison websites, avoiding lines by shopping online, or quickly looking up phone numbers and map directions to various locations at the click of a finger. How different would our lives be without all of this? That was the world we lived in just 15 to 20 years ago. But over the years, data networks have slowly expanded and been repurposed to improve the quality of life for people everywhere.

In the course of a day, resources that are available through the Internet can help you:

- Post and share your photographs, home videos, and experiences with friends or with the world.
- Access and submit school work.

- Communicate with friends, family, and peers using email, instant messaging, or Internet phone calls.

- Watch videos, movies, or television episodes on demand.

- Play online games with friends.

- Decide what to wear using online current weather conditions.

- Find the least congested route to your destination, displaying weather and traffic video from webcams.

- Check your bank balance and pay bills electronically.

Innovators are figuring out ways to use the Internet more every day. As developers push the limits of what is possible, the capabilities of the Internet and the role the Internet plays in our lives will expand broader and broader. Consider the changes that have happened over the last 25 years, as depicted in the figure. Now consider what changes will happen within the next 25 years. This future holds the Internet of Everything (IoE).

The IoE is bringing together people, process, data, and things to make networked connections more relevant and valuable. It is turning information into actions that create new capabilities, richer experiences, and unprecedented economic opportunity for individuals, businesses, and countries.

What else do you think we will be able to do using the network as the platform?

Refer to
Online Course
for Illustration

1.1.1.3   The Global Community

Advancements in networking technologies are perhaps the most significant change agents in the world today. They are helping to create a world in which national borders, geographic distances, and physical limitations become less relevant, and present ever-diminishing obstacles.

The Internet has changed the manner in which social, commercial, political, and personal interactions occur. The immediate nature of communications over the Internet encourages the creation of global communities. Global communities allow for social interaction that is independent of location or time zone. The creation of online communities for the exchange of ideas and information has the potential to increase productivity opportunities across the globe.

Cisco refers to this as the human network. The human network centers on the impact of the Internet and networks on people and businesses.

How has the human network affected you?

Refer to
Online Course
for Illustration

1.1.1.4   Networks Support the Way We Learn

Networks and the Internet have changed everything we do, from the way we learn, to the way we communicate, to how we work, and even how we play.

Changing the way we learn

Communication, collaboration, and engagement are fundamental building blocks of education. Institutions are continually striving to enhance these processes to maximize the dissemination of knowledge. Traditional learning methods provide primarily two sources of expertise from which the student can obtain information: the textbook and the instructor. These two sources are limited, both in the format and the timing of the presentation.

Networks have changed the way we learn. Robust and reliable networks support and enrich student learning experiences. They deliver learning material in a wide range of formats including interactive activities, assessments, and feedback. As shown in Figure 1, networks now:

- Support the creation of virtual classrooms

- Provide on-demand video

- Enable collaborative learning spaces

- Enable mobile learning

Access to high quality instruction is no longer restricted to students living in proximity to where that instruction is being delivered. Online distance learning has removed geographic barriers and improved student opportunity. Online (e-learning) courses can now be delivered over a network. These courses can contain data (text, links), voice, and video available to the students at any time from any place. Online discussion groups and message boards enable a student to collaborate with the instructor, with other students in the class, or even with students across the world. Blended courses can combine instructor-led classes with online courseware to provide the best of both delivery methods. Figure 2 is a video about the ways that the classroom has expanded.

In addition to the benefits for the student, networks have improved the management and administration of courses as well. Some of these online functions include student enrollment, assessment delivery, and progress tracking.

Refer to
Online Course
for Illustration

1.1.1.5   Networks Support the Way We Communicate

Changing the way we communicate

The globalization of the Internet has ushered in new forms of communication that empower individuals to create information that can be accessed by a global audience.

Some forms of communication include:

- **Instant Messaging (IM) / Texting** – IM and texting both enable instant real-time communication between two or more people. Many IM and texting applications incorporate features such as file transfer. IM applications can offer additional features such as voice and video communication.

- **Social Media** – Social media consists of interactive websites where people and communities create and share user-generated content with friends, family, peers, and the world.

- **Collaboration Tools** - Collaboration tools give people the opportunity to work together on shared documents. Without the constraints of location or time zone, individuals connected to a shared system can speak to each other, often across real-time interactive video. Across the network they can share text and graphics, and edit documents together. With collaboration tools always available, organizations can move quickly to share information and pursue goals. The broad distribution of data networks means that people in remote locations can contribute on an equal basis with people at the heart of large population centers.

- **Weblogs (blogs)** - Weblogs are web pages that are easy to update and edit. Unlike commercial websites, which are created by professional communications experts, blogs give anyone a means to communicate their thoughts to a global audience without technical knowledge of web design. There are blogs on nearly every topic one can think of, and communities of people often form around popular blog authors.

- **Wikis** - Wikis are web pages that groups of people can edit and view together. Whereas a blog is more of an individual, personal journal, a wiki is a group creation. As such, it may be subject to more extensive review and editing. Like blogs, wikis can be created in stages, and by anyone, without the sponsorship of a major commercial enterprise. Wikipedia has become a comprehensive resource - an online encyclopedia - of publicly-contributed topics. Private organizations and individuals can also build their own wikis to capture collected knowledge on a particular subject. Many businesses use wikis as their internal collaboration tool. With the global Internet, people of all walks of life can participate in wikis and add their own perspectives and knowledge to a shared resource.

- **Podcasting** - Podcasting is an audio-based medium that originally enabled people to record audio and convert it for use. Podcasting allows people to deliver their recordings to a wide audience. The audio file is placed on a website (or blog or wiki) where others can download it and play the recording on their computers, laptops, and other mobile devices.

- **Peer-to-Peer (P2P) File Sharing** – Peer-to-Peer file sharing allows people to share files with each other without having to store and download them from a central server. The user joins the P2P network by simply installing the P2P software. This lets them locate and share files with others in the P2P network. The widespread digitization of media files, such as music and video files has increased the interest in P2P file sharing. P2P file sharing has not been embraced by everyone. Many people are concerned about violating the laws of copyrighted materials.

What other sites or tools do you use to share your thoughts?

Refer to
Online Course
for Illustration

1.1.1.6   Networks Support the Way We Work

Changing the way we work

In the business world, data networks were initially used by businesses to internally record and manage financial information, customer information, and employee payroll systems. These business networks evolved to enable the transmission of many different types of information services, including email, video, messaging, and telephony.

The use of networks to provide efficient and cost-effective employee training is increasing in acceptance. Online learning opportunities can decrease time-consuming and costly travel yet still ensure that all employees are adequately trained to perform their jobs in a safe and productive manner.

There are many success stories illustrating innovative ways networks are being used to make us more successful in the workplace. Some of these scenarios are available through the Cisco web site at http://www.cisco.com.

Refer to
Online Course
for Illustration

1.1.1.7   Networks Support the Way We Play

Changing the way we play

The widespread adoption of the Internet by the entertainment and travel industries enhances the ability to enjoy and share many forms of recreation, regardless of location. It is possible to explore places interactively that previously we could only dream of visiting, as well as preview the actual destinations before making a trip. Travelers can post the details and photographs from their adventures online for others to view.

In addition, the Internet is used for traditional forms of entertainment. We listen to recording artists, preview or view motion pictures, read entire books, and download material for future offline access. Live sporting events and concerts can be experienced as they are happening, or recorded and viewed on demand.

Networks enable the creation of new forms of entertainment, such as online games. Players participate in any kind of online competition that game designers can imagine. We compete with friends and foes around the world in the same manner as if they were in the same room.

Even offline activities are enhanced using network collaboration services. Global communities of interest have grown rapidly. We share common experiences and hobbies well beyond our local neighborhood, city, or region. Sports fans share opinions and facts about their favorite teams. Collectors display prized collections and get expert feedback about them.

Online markets and auction sites provide the opportunity to buy, sell, and trade all types of merchandise.

Whatever form of recreation we enjoy in the human network, networks are improving our experience.

How do you play on the Internet?

Refer to Lab Activity for this chapter

1.1.1.8   Lab - Researching Network Collaboration Tools
In this lab, you will complete the following objectives:

- Part 1: Use Collaboration Tools
- Part 2: Share Documents with Google Drive
- Part 3: Explore Conferencing and Web Meetings
- Part 4: Create Wiki Pages

Refer to Online Course for Illustration

1.1.2   Providing Resources in a Network

1.1.2.1   Networks of Many Sizes

Networks come in all sizes. They can range from simple networks consisting of two computers to networks connecting millions of devices.

Simple networks installed in homes enable sharing of resources, such as printers, documents, pictures and music between a few local computers.

Home office networks and small office networks are often set up by individuals that work from a home or remote office and need to connect to a corporate network or other centralized resources. Additionally, many self-employed entrepreneurs use home office and small office networks to advertise and sell products, order supplies and communicate with customers. Communication over a network is usually more efficient and less expensive than traditional forms of communication, such as regular mail or long distance phone calls.

In businesses and large organizations, networks can be used on an even broader scale to allow employees to provide consolidation, storage, and access to information on network servers. Networks also allow for rapid communication such as email, instant messaging, and collaboration among employees. In addition to internal organizational benefits, many organizations use their networks to provide products and services to customers through their connection to the Internet.

The Internet is the largest network in existence. In fact, the term Internet means a 'network of networks'. The Internet is literally a collection of interconnected private and public networks, such as the ones described above. Businesses, small office networks, and even home networks usually provide a shared connection to the Internet.

It is incredible how quickly the Internet has become an integral part of our daily routines.

Refer to
Online Course
for Illustration

1.1.2.2   Clients and Servers

All computers connected to a network that participate directly in network communication are classified as hosts or end devices. Hosts can send and receive messages on the network. In modern networks, end devices can act as a client, a server, or both. The software installed on the computer determines which role the computer plays.

Servers are hosts that have software installed that enable them to provide information, like email or web pages, to other hosts on the network. Each service requires separate server software. For example, a host requires web server software in order to provide web services to the network.

Clients are computer hosts that have software installed that enable them to request and display the information obtained from the server. An example of client software is a web browser, like Internet Explorer.

Refer to
Online Course
for Illustration

1.1.2.3   Clients and Servers (Cont.)

A computer with server software can provide services simultaneously to one or many clients.

Additionally, a single computer can run multiple types of server software. In a home or small business, it may be necessary for one computer to act as a file server, a web server, and an email server.

A single computer can also run multiple types of client software. There must be client software for every service required. With multiple clients installed, a host can connect to multiple servers at the same time. For example, a user can check email and view a web page while instant messaging and listening to Internet radio.

1.1.2.4   Peer-to-Peer

Client and server software usually runs on separate computers, but it is also possible for one computer to carry out both roles at the same time. In small businesses and homes, many computers function as the servers and clients on the network. This type of network is called a peer-to-peer network.

The simplest peer-to-peer network consists of two directly connected computers using a wired or wireless connection.

Multiple PCs can also be connected to create a larger peer-to-peer network but this requires a network device, such as a hub, to interconnect the computers.

The main disadvantage of a peer-to-peer environment is that the performance of a host can be slowed down if it is acting as both a client and a server at the same time.

In larger businesses, due to the potential for high amounts of network traffic, it is often necessary to have dedicated servers to support the number of service requests.

Refer to
Online Course
for Illustration

1.2   LANs, WANs, and the Internet

1.2.1   Components of a Network

1.2.1.1   Components of the Network

The path that a message takes from source to destination can be as simple as a single cable connecting one computer to another or as complex as a network that literally spans the globe. This network infrastructure is the platform that supports the network. It provides the stable and reliable channel over which our communications can occur.

The network infrastructure contains three categories of network components:

- Devices

- Media

- Services

Click each button in the figure to highlight the corresponding network components.

Devices and media are the physical elements, or hardware, of the network. Hardware is often the visible components of the network platform such as a laptop, PC, switch, router, wireless access point, or the cabling used to connect the devices. Occasionally, some components may not be so visible. In the case of wireless media, messages are transmitted through the air using invisible radio frequency or infrared waves.

Network components are used to provide services and processes. These are the communication programs, called software, that run on the networked devices. A network service provides information in response to a request. Services include many of the common network applications people use every day, like email hosting services and web hosting services. Processes provide the functionality that directs and moves the messages through the network. Processes are less obvious to us but are critical to the operation of networks.

Refer to
Online Course
for Illustration

1.2.1.2   End Devices

The network devices that people are most familiar with are called end devices, or hosts. These devices form the interface between users and the underlying communication network.

Some examples of end devices are:

- Computers (work stations, laptops, file servers, web servers)

- Network printers

- VoIP phones

- TelePresence endpoint

- Security cameras

- Mobile handheld devices (such as smartphones, tablets, PDAs, and wireless debit/credit card readers and barcode scanners)

A host device is either the source or destination of a message transmitted over the network, as shown in the animation. In order to distinguish one host from another, each host on a network is identified by an address. When a host initiates communication, it uses the address of the destination host to specify where the message should be sent.

Refer to **Online Course** for Illustration

1.2.1.3   Intermediary Network Devices

Intermediary devices interconnect end devices. These devices provide connectivity and work behind the scenes to ensure that data flows across the network, as shown in the animation. Intermediary devices connect the individual hosts to the network and can connect multiple individual networks to form an internetwork.

Examples of intermediary network devices are:

- Network Access (switches and wireless access points)

- Internetworking (routers)

- Security (firewalls)

The management of data as it flows through the network is also a role of the intermediary devices. These devices use the destination host address, in conjunction with information about the network interconnections, to determine the path that messages should take through the network.

Processes running on the intermediary network devices perform these functions:

- Regenerate and retransmit data signals

- Maintain information about what pathways exist through the network and internetwork

- Notify other devices of errors and communication failures

- Direct data along alternate pathways when there is a link failure

- Classify and direct messages according to Quality of Service (QoS) priorities

- Permit or deny the flow of data, based on security settings

Refer to **Online Course** for Illustration

1.2.1.4   Network Media

Communication across a network is carried on a medium. The medium provides the channel over which the message travels from source to destination.

Modern networks primarily use three types of media to interconnect devices and to provide the pathway over which data can be transmitted. As shown in the figure, these media are:

- Metallic wires within cables

- Glass or plastic fibers (fiber optic cable)

- Wireless transmission

The signal encoding that must occur for the message to be transmitted is different for each media type. On metallic wires, the data is encoded into electrical impulses that match specific patterns. Fiber optic transmissions rely on pulses of light, within either infrared or visible light ranges. In wireless transmission, patterns of electromagnetic waves depict the various bit values.

Different types of network media have different features and benefits. Not all network media has the same characteristics and is appropriate for the same purpose. The criteria for choosing network media are:

- The distance the media can successfully carry a signal
- The environment in which the media is to be installed
- The amount of data and the speed at which it must be transmitted
- The cost of the media and installation

Refer to
Online Course
for Illustration

1.2.1.5   Network Representations

When conveying complex information such as displaying all the devices and medium in a large internetwork, it is helpful to use visual representations. A diagram provides an easy way to understand the way the devices in a large network are connected. Such a diagram uses symbols to represent the different devices and connections that make up a network. This type of "picture" of a network is known as a topology diagram.

Like any other language, the language of networking uses a common set of symbols to represent the different end devices, network devices, and media, as shown in the figure. The ability to recognize the logical representations of the physical networking components is critical to being able to visualize the organization and operation of a network. Throughout this course and labs, you will learn both how these devices operate and how to perform basic configuration tasks on these devices.

In addition to these representations, specialized terminology is used when discussing how each of these devices and media connect to each other. Important terms to remember are:

- **Network Interface Card** - A NIC, or LAN adapter, provides the physical connection to the network at the PC or other host device. The media connecting the PC to the networking device plugs directly into the NIC.
- **Physical Port** - A connector or outlet on a networking device where the media is connected to a host or other networking device.
- **Interface** - Specialized ports on an internetworking device that connect to individual networks. Because routers are used to interconnect networks, the ports on a router are referred to network interfaces.

Refer to
Online Course
for Illustration

1.2.1.6   Topology Diagrams

Topology diagrams are mandatory for anyone working with a network. It provides a visual map of how the network is connected.

There are two types of topology diagrams including:

- **Physical topology diagrams** - Identify the physical location of intermediary devices, configured ports, and cable installation.
- **Logical topology diagrams** - Identify devices, ports, and IP addressing scheme.

Refer to
Interactive Graphic
in online course.

1.2.1.7   Activity - Network Component Representations and Functions

Refer to
Online Course
for Illustration

1.2.2   LANs and WANs

1.2.2.1   Types of Networks

Network infrastructures can vary greatly in terms of:

- Size of the area covered
- Number of users connected
- Number and types of services available

The figure illustrates the two most common types of network infrastructures:

- **Local Area Network (LAN)** - A network infrastructure that provides access to users and end devices in a small geographical area.
- **Wide Area Network (WAN)** - A network infrastructure that provides access to other networks over a wide geographical area.

Other types of networks include:

- **Metropolitan Area Network (MAN)** - A network infrastructure that spans a physical area larger than a LAN but smaller than a WAN (e.g., a city). MANs are typically operated by a single entity such as a large organization.
- **Wireless LAN (WLAN)** - Similar to a LAN but wirelessly interconnects users and end points in a small geographical area.
- **Storage Area Network (SAN)** - A network infrastructure designed to support file servers and provide data storage, retrieval, and replication. It involves high-end servers, multiple disk arrays (called blocks), and Fibre Channel interconnection technology.

Refer to
Online Course
for Illustration

1.2.2.2   Local Area Networks

Local Area Networks (LANs) are a network infrastructure that spans a small geographical area. Specific features of LANs include:

- LANs interconnect end devices in a limited area such as a home, school, office building, or campus.
- A LAN is usually administered by a single organization or individual. The administrative control that governs the security and access control policies are enforced on the network level.
- LANs provide high speed bandwidth to internal end devices and intermediary devices.

Refer to
Online Course
for Illustration

1.2.2.3   Wide Area Networks

Wide Area Networks (WANs) are a network infrastructure that spans a wide geographical area. WANs are typically managed by service providers (SP) or Internet Service Providers (ISP).

Specific features of WANs include:

- WANs interconnect LANs over wide geographical areas such as between cities, states, provinces, countries, or continents.

- WANs are usually administered by multiple service providers.

- WANs typically provide slower speed links between LANs.

Refer to
Online Course
for Illustration

1.2.3   The Internet

1.2.3.1   The Internet

Although there are benefits to using a LAN or WAN, most individuals need to communicate with a resource on another network, outside of the local network within the home, campus, or organization. This is done using the Internet.

As shown in the figure, the Internet is a worldwide collection of interconnected networks (internetworks or internet for short), cooperating with each other to exchange information using common standards. Through telephone wires, fiber optic cables, wireless transmissions, and satellite links, Internet users can exchange information in a variety of forms.

The Internet is a conglomerate of networks and is not owned by any individual or group. Ensuring effective communication across this diverse infrastructure requires the application of consistent and commonly recognized technologies and standards as well as the cooperation of many network administration agencies. There are organizations that have been developed for the purpose of helping to maintain structure and standardization of Internet protocols and processes. These organizations include the Internet Engineering Task Force (IETF), Internet Corporation for Assigned Names and Numbers (ICANN), and the Internet Architecture Board (IAB), plus many others.

Note   The term internet (with a lower case "i") is used to describe multiple networks interconnected. When referring to the global system of interconnected computer networks or the World Wide Web, the term Internet (with a capital "I") is used.

Refer to
Online Course
for Illustration

1.2.3.2   Intranet and Extranet

There are two other terms which are similar to the term Internet:

- Intranet

- Extranet

Intranet is a term often used to refer to a private connection of LANs and WANs that belongs to an organization, and is designed to be accessible only by the organization's members, employees, or others with authorization. Intranets are basically an internet which is usually only accessible from within the organization.

Organizations may publish web pages on an intranet about internal events, health and safety policies, staff newsletters, and staff phone directories. For example, schools may have intranets that include information on class schedules, online curriculum, and discussion forums. Intranets usually help eliminate paperwork and speed up workflows. The intranet may be accessible to staff working outside of the organization by using secure connections to the internal network.

An organization may use an extranet to provide secure and safe access to individuals who work for a different organizations, but require company data. Examples of extranets include:

- A company providing access to outside suppliers/contractors.

- A hospital providing a booking system to doctors so they can make appointments for their patients.

- A local office of education providing budget and personnel information to the schools in its district.

Refer to
Lab Activity
for this chapter

1.2.3.3   Lab - Researching Converged Network Services

In this lab, you will complete the following objectives:

- Part 1: Survey Your Understanding of Convergence

- Part 2: Research ISPs Offering Converged Services

- Part 3: Research Local ISPs Offering Converged Services

- Part 4: Select Best Local ISP Converged Service

- Part 5: Research Local Company or Public Institution Using Convergence Technologies

Refer to
Online Course
for Illustration

1.2.4   Connecting to the Internet

1.2.4.1   Internet Access Technologies

There are many different ways to connect users and organizations to the Internet.

Home users, teleworkers (remote workers), and small offices typically require a connection to an Internet Service Provider (ISP) to access the Internet. Connection options vary greatly between ISP and geographical location. However, popular choices include broadband cable, broadband digital subscriber line (DSL), wireless WANs, and mobile services.

Organizations typically require access to other corporate sites and the Internet. Fast connections are required to support business services including IP phones, video conferencing, and data center storage.

Business-class interconnections are usually provided by service providers (SP). Popular business-class services include business DSL, leased lines, and Metro Ethernet.

1.2.4.2   Connecting Remote Users to the Internet

The figure illustrates common connection options for small office and home office users, which include:

- **Cable** - Typically offered by cable television service providers, the Internet data signal is carried on the same coaxial cable that delivers cable television. It provides a high bandwidth, always on, connection to the Internet. A special cable modem separates the Internet data signal from the other signals carried on the cable and provides an Ethernet connection to a host computer or LAN.

- **DSL** - Provides a high bandwidth, always on, connection to the Internet. It requires a special high-speed modem that separates the DSL signal from the telephone signal and provides an Ethernet connection to a host computer or LAN. DSL runs over a telephone line, with the line split into three channels. One channel is used for voice telephone calls. This channel allows an individual to receive phone calls without disconnecting from the Internet. A second channel is a faster download channel, used to receive information from the Internet. The third channel is used for sending or uploading information. This channel is usually slightly slower than the download channel. The quality and speed of the DSL connection depends mainly on the quality of the phone line and the distance from your phone company's central office. The farther you are from the central office, the slower the connection.

- **Cellular** - Cellular Internet access uses a cell phone network to connect. Wherever you can get a cellular signal, you can get cellular Internet access. Performance will be limited by the capabilities of the phone and the cell tower to which it is connected. The availability of cellular Internet access is a real benefit in those areas that would otherwise have no Internet connectivity at all, or for those constantly on the go.

- **Satellite** - Satellite service is a good option for homes or offices that do not have access to DSL or cable. Satellite dishes require a clear line of sight to the satellite and so might be difficult in heavily wooded areas or places with other overhead obstructions. Speeds will vary depending on the contract, though they are generally good. Equipment and installation costs can be high (although check the provider for special deals), with a moderate monthly fee thereafter. The availability of satellite Internet access is a real benefit in those areas that would otherwise have no Internet connectivity at all.

- **Dial-up Telephone** - An inexpensive option that uses any phone line and a modem. To connect to the ISP, a user calls the ISP access phone number. The low bandwidth provided by a dial-up modem connection is usually not sufficient for large data transfer, although it is useful for mobile access while traveling. A modem dial-up connection should only be considered when higher speed connection options are not available.

Many homes and small offices are more commonly being connected directly with fibre optic cables. This enables an Internet service provider to provide higher bandwidth speeds and support more services such as Internet, phone, and TV.

The choice of connection varies depending on geographical location and service provider availability.

What are your options for connecting to the Internet?

1.2.4.3   Connecting Businesses to the Internet

Refer to
Online Course
for Illustration

Corporate connection options differ from home user options. Businesses may require higher bandwidth, dedicated bandwidth, and managed services. Connection options available differ depending on the number of service providers located nearby.

The figure illustrates common connection options for organizations, which include:

- **Dedicated Leased Line** - This is a dedicated connection from the service provider to the customer premise. Leased lines are actually reserved circuits that connect geographically separated offices for private voice and/or data networking. The circuits are typically rented at a monthly or yearly rate which tends to make it expensive. In North America, common leased line circuits include T1 (1.54 Mb/s) and T3 (44.7 Mb/s) while in other parts of the world they are available in E1 (2 Mb/s) and E3 (34 Mb/s).

- **Metro Ethernet** - Metro Ethernet is typically available from a provider to the customer premise over a dedicated copper or fiber connection providing bandwidth speeds of 10 Mb/s to 10 Gb/s. Ethernet over Copper (EoC) is more economical than fiber optic Ethernet service in many cases, quite widely available, and reaches speeds of up to 40 Mbps. However, Ethernet over Copper is limited by distance. Fiber optic Ethernet service delivers the fastest connections available at an economical price per megabit. Unfortunately, there are still many areas where this service is unavailable.

- **DSL** - Business DSL is available in various formats. A popular choice is Symmetric Digital Subscriber Lines (SDSL) which is similar to Asymmetric Digital Subscriber Line (ADSL), but provides the same upload and download speeds. ADSL is designed to deliver bandwidth at different rates downstream than upstream. For example, a customer getting Internet access may have downstream rates that range from 1.5 to 9 Mbps, whereas upstream bandwidth ranges are from 16 to 640 kbps. ADSL transmissions work at distances up to 18,000 feet (5,488 meters) over a single copper twisted pair.

- **Satellite** - Satellite service can provide a connection when a wired solution is not available. Satellite dishes require a clear line of sight to the satellite. Equipment and installation costs can be high, with a moderate monthly fee thereafter. Connections tend to be slower and less reliable than its terrestrial competition, which makes it less attractive than other alternatives.

The choice of connection varies depending on geographical location and service provider availability.

Refer to **Packet Tracer Activity** for this chapter

1.2.4.4   Packet Tracer - Network Representation

Packet Tracer is a fun, take-home, flexible software program which will help you with your Cisco Certified Network Associate (CCNA) studies. Packet Tracer allows you to experiment with network behavior, build network models, and ask "what if" questions. In this activity, you will explore a relatively complex network that highlights a few of Packet Tracer's features. While doing so, you will learn how to access Help and the tutorials. You will also learn how to switch between various modes and workspaces. Finally, you will explore how Packet Tracer serves as a modeling tool for network representations.

Refer to **Online Course** for Illustration

1.3   The Network as a Platform

1.3.1   Converged Networks

1.3.1.1   The Converging Network

Modern networks are constantly evolving to meet user demands. Early data networks were limited to exchanging character-based information between connected computer systems. Traditional telephone, radio, and television networks were maintained separately from data networks. In the past, every one of these services required a dedicated network, with different communication channels and different technologies to carry a particular communication signal. Each service had its own set of rules and standards to ensure successful communication.

Consider a school built forty years ago. Back then, classrooms were cabled for the data network, telephone network, and video network for televisions. These separate networks were disparate; meaning that they could not communicate with each other, as shown in Figure 1.

Advances in technology are enabling us to consolidate these different kinds of networks onto one platform referred to as the "converged network". Unlike dedicated networks, converged networks are capable of delivering voice, video streams, text, and graphics between many different types of devices over the same communication channel and network structure, as shown in Figure 2. Previously separate and distinct communication forms have converged onto a common platform. This platform provides access to a wide range of alternative and new communication methods that enable people to interact directly with each other almost instantaneously.

On a converged network there are still many points of contact and many specialized devices such as, personal computers, phones, TVs, and tablet computers, but there is one common network infrastructure. This network infrastructure uses the same set of rules, agreements, and implementation standards.

Refer to
Online Course
for Illustration

1.3.1.2   Planning for the Future

The convergence of the different types of communications networks onto one platform represents the first phase in building the intelligent information network. We are currently in this phase of network evolution. The next phase will be to consolidate not only the different types of messages onto a single network, but to also consolidate the applications that generate, transmit, and secure the messages onto integrated network devices.

Not only will voice and video be transmitted over the same network, the devices that perform the telephone switching and video broadcasting will be the same devices that route the messages through the network. The resulting communications platform will provide high quality application functionality at a reduced cost.

The pace at which the development of exciting new converged network applications is occurring can be attributed to the rapid growth and expansion of the Internet. With only about 10 billion of the 1.5 trillion things currently connected globally, there is vast potential to connect the unconnected via the IoE. This expansion has created a wider audience for whatever message, product, or service can be delivered.

The underlying mechanics and processes that drive this explosive growth have resulted in a network architecture that is both capable of supporting changes and able to grow. As the supporting technology platform for living, learning, working, and playing in the human network, the network architecture of the Internet must adapt to constantly changing requirements for a high quality of service and security.

Refer to
Lab Activity
for this chapter

1.3.1.3   Lab - Mapping the Internet

In this lab, you will complete the following objectives:

■ Part 1: Test Network Connectivity Using Ping

■ Part 2: Trace a Route to a Remote Server Using Windows Tracert

■ Part 3: Trace a Route to a Remote Server Using Web-Based and Software Tools

■ Part 4: Compare Traceroute Results

Refer to
Online Course
for Illustration

1.3.2   Reliable Network

1.3.2.1   The Supporting Network Architecture

Networks must support a wide range of applications and services, as well as operate over many different types of cables and devices, which make up the physical infrastructure. The term network architecture, in this context, refers to the technologies that support the infrastructure and the programmed services and rules, or protocols, that move messages across the network.

As networks evolve, we are discovering that there are four basic characteristics that the underlying architectures need to address in order to meet user expectations:

■ Fault Tolerance (Figure 1)

■ Scalability (Figure 2)

■ Quality of Service (QoS) (Figure 3)

■ Security (Figure 4)

1.3.2.2   Fault Tolerance in Circuit Switched Networks

Fault Tolerance

The expectation is that the Internet is always available to the millions of users who rely on it. This requires a network architecture that is built to be fault tolerant. A fault tolerant network is one that limits the impact of a failure, so that the fewest number of devices are affected by it. It is also built in a way that allows quick recovery when such a failure occurs. These networks depend on multiple paths between the source and destination of a message. If one path fails, the messages can be instantly sent over a different link. Having multiple paths to a destination is known as redundancy.

Circuit-Switched Connection-Oriented Networks

To understand the need for redundancy, we can look at how early telephone systems worked. When a person made a call using a traditional telephone set, the call first went through a setup process. This process identified the telephone switching locations between the person making the call (the source) and the phone set receiving the call (the destination). A temporary path, or circuit, was created for the duration of the telephone call. If any link or device in the circuit failed, the call was dropped. To reconnect, a new call had to be made, with a new circuit. This connection process is referred to as a circuit-switched process and is illustrated in the figure.

Many circuit-switched networks give priority to existing circuit connections at the expense of new circuit requests. After a circuit is established, even if no communication is occurring between the persons on either end of the call, the circuit remains connected and resources used until one of the parties disconnects the call. Because there are only so many circuits that can be created, it is possible to get a message that all circuits are busy and a call cannot be placed. The cost to create many alternate paths with enough capacity to support a large number of simultaneous circuits, and the technologies necessary to dynamically recreate dropped circuits in the event of a failure, is why circuit switched technology was not optimal for the Internet.

Refer to **Online Course** for Illustration

1.3.2.3   Fault Tolerance in Packet-Switched Networks

Packet-Switched Networks

In the search for a network that was more fault tolerant, the early Internet designers researched packet switched networks. The premise for this type of network is that a single message can be broken into multiple message blocks, with each message block containing addressing information to indicate the origination point and final destination. Using this embedded information, these message blocks, called packets, can be sent through the network along various paths, and can be reassembled into the original message when reaching their destination, as illustrated in the figure.

The devices within the network itself are typically unaware of the content of the individual packets. Only visible is the address of the final destination. These addresses are often referred to as IP addresses, represented in a dotted decimal format such as 10.10.10.10. Each packet is sent independently from one location to another. At each location, a routing decision is made as to which path to use to forward the packet towards its final destination. This would be like writing a long message to a friend using ten postcards. Each postcard has the destination address of the recipient. As the postcards are forwarded through the postal system, the destination address is used to determine the next path that postcard should take. Eventually, they will be delivered to the address on the postcards.

If a previously used path is no longer available, the routing function can dynamically choose the next best available path. Because the messages are sent in pieces, rather than as a single complete message, the few packets that may be lost can be retransmitted to the destination along a different path. In many cases, the destination device is unaware that any failure or rerouting occurred. Using our postcard analogy, if one of the postcards is lost along the way, only that postcard needs to be mailed again.

The need for a single, reserved circuit from end-to-end does not exist in a packet switched network. Any piece of a message can be sent through the network using any available path. Additionally, packets containing pieces of messages from different sources can travel the network at the same time. By providing a method to dynamically use redundant paths, without intervention by the user, the Internet has become a fault tolerant method of communication. In our mail analogy, as our postcard travels through the postal system they will share transportation with other postcards, letters and packages. For example, one of the postcards may be placed on an airplane, along with lots of other packages and letters that are being transported toward their final destination.

Although packet-switched connectionless networks are the primary infrastructure for today's Internet, there are some benefits to a connection-oriented system like the circuit-switched telephone system. Because resources at the various switching locations are dedicated to providing a finite number of circuits, the quality and consistency of messages transmitted across a connection-oriented network can be guaranteed. Another benefit is that the provider of the service can charge the users of the network for the period of time that the connection is active. The ability to charge users for active connections through the network is a fundamental premise of the telecommunication service industry.

Refer to
Online Course
for Illustration

1.3.2.4   Scalable Networks

Scalability

Thousands of new users and service providers connect to the Internet each week. In order for the Internet to support this rapid amount of growth, it must be scalable. A scalable network can expand quickly to support new users and applications without impacting the performance of the service being delivered to existing users. The figures show the structure of the Internet.

The fact that the Internet is able to expand at the rate that it is, without seriously impacting the performance experienced by individual users, is a function of the design of the protocols and underlying technologies on which it is built. The Internet has a hierarchical layered structure for addressing, for naming, and for connectivity services. As a result, network traffic that is destined for local or regional services does not need to traverse to a central point for distribution. Common services can be duplicated in different regions, thereby keeping traffic off the higher level backbone networks.

Scalability also refers to the ability to accept new products and applications. Although there is no single organization that regulates the Internet, the many individual networks that provide Internet connectivity cooperate to follow accepted standards and protocols. The adherence to standards enables the manufacturers of hardware and software to concentrate on product development and improvements in the areas of performance and capacity, knowing that the new products can integrate with and enhance the existing infrastructure.

The current Internet architecture, while highly scalable, may not always be able to keep up with the pace of user demand. New protocols and addressing structures are under development to meet the increasing rate at which Internet applications and services are being added.

Refer to
Online Course
for Illustration

1.3.2.5   Providing QoS

Quality of Service

Quality of Service (QoS) is also an ever increasing requirement of networks today. New applications available to users over internetworks, such as voice and live video transmissions, as shown in Figure 1, create higher expectations for the quality of the delivered services. Have you ever tried to watch a video with constant breaks and pauses?

Networks must provide predictable, measurable, and at times, guaranteed services. The packet-switched network architecture does not guarantee that all packets that comprise a particular message will arrive on time, in their correct order, or even that they will arrive at all.

Networks also need mechanisms to manage congested network traffic. Network bandwidth is the measure of the data carrying capacity of the network. In other words, how much information can be transmitted within a specific amount of time? Network bandwidth is measured in the number of bits that can be transmitted in a single second, or bits per second (bps). When simultaneous communications are attempted across the network, the demand for network bandwidth can exceed its availability, creating network congestion. The network simply has more bits to transmit than what the bandwidth of the communication channel can deliver.

In most cases, when the volume of packets is greater than what can be transported across the network, devices queue, or hold, the packets in memory until resources become available to transmit them, as shown in Figure 2. Queuing packets causes delay because new packets cannot be transmitted until previous packets have been processed. If the number of packets to be queued continues to increase, the memory queues fill up and packets are dropped.

Achieving the required QoS by managing the delay and packet loss parameters on a network becomes the secret to a successful end-to-end application quality solution. One way this can be accomplished is through classification. To create QoS classifications of data, we use a combination of communication characteristics and the relative importance assigned to the application, as shown in Figure 3. We then treat all data within the same classification according to the same rules. For example, communication that is time-sensitive, such as voice transmissions, would be classified differently from communication that can tolerate delay, such as file transfers.

Examples of priority decisions for an organization might include:

■ **Time-sensitive communication** - increase priority for services like telephony or video distribution

■ **Non time-sensitive communication** - decrease priority for web page retrieval or email

■ **High importance to organization** - increase priority for production control or business transaction data

■ **Undesirable communication** - decrease priority or block unwanted activity, like peer-to-peer file sharing or live entertainment

Refer to **Online Course** for Illustration

1.3.2.6   Providing Network Security

Security

The Internet has evolved from a tightly controlled internetwork of educational and government organizations to a widely accessible means for transmission of business and personal communications. As a result, the security requirements of the network have changed. The network infrastructure, services, and the data contained on network attached devices are crucial personal and business assets. Compromising the integrity of these assets could have serious consequences, such as:

■ Network outages that prevent communications and transactions from occurring, with consequent loss of business

■ Intellectual property (research ideas, patents, or designs) that is stolen and used by a competitor

■ Personal or private information that is compromised or made public without the users consent

■ Misdirection and loss of personal or business funds

■ Loss of important data that takes a significant labor to replace, or is irreplaceable

There are two types of network security concerns that must be addressed: network infrastructure security and information security.

Securing a network infrastructure includes the physical securing of devices that provide network connectivity, and preventing unauthorized access to the management software that resides on them.

Information security refers to protecting the information contained within the packets being transmitted over the network and the information stored on network attached devices. Security measures taken in a network should:

- Prevent unauthorized disclosure
- Prevent theft of information (Figure 1)
- Prevent unauthorized modification of information
- Prevent Denial of Service (DoS)

In order to achieve the goals of network security, there are three primary requirements, as shown in Figure 2:

- **Ensuring confidentiality** - Data confidentiality means that only the intended and authorized recipients - individuals, processes, or devices – can access and read data. This is accomplished by having a strong system for user authentication, enforcing passwords that are difficult to guess, and requiring users to change them frequently. Encrypting data, so that only the intended recipient can read it, is also part of confidentiality.

- **Maintaining communication integrity** - Data integrity means having the assurance that the information has not been altered in transmission, from origin to destination. Data integrity can be compromised when information has been corrupted - willfully or accidentally. Data integrity is made possible by requiring validation of the sender as well as using mechanisms to validate that the packet has not changed during transmission.

- **Ensuring availability** - Availability means having the assurance of timely and reliable access to data services for authorized users. Network firewall devices, along with desktop and server antivirus software can ensure system reliability and the robustness to detect, repel, and cope with such attacks. Building fully redundant network infrastructures, with few single points of failure, can reduce the impact of these threats.

Refer to
Interactive Graphic
in online course.

1.3.2.7   Activity - Reliable Networks

Refer to
Online Course
for Illustration

1.4   The Changing Network Environment

1.4.1   Network Trends

1.4.1.1   New Trends

When you look at how the Internet has changed so many of the things people do daily, it is hard to believe that it has only been around for most people for about 20 years. It has truly transformed the way individuals and organizations communicate. For example, before the Internet became so widely available, organizations and small businesses largely relied on print marketing to make consumers aware of their products. It was difficult for businesses to determine which households were potential customers, so businesses relied on mass print marketing programs. These programs were expensive and varied in effectiveness. Compare that to how consumers are reached today. Most businesses have an Internet presence where consumers can learn about their products, read reviews from other customers, and order products directly from the web site. Social networking sites partner with businesses to promote products and services. Bloggers partner with businesses to highlight and endorse products and services. Most of this product placement is targeted to the potential consumer, rather than to the masses. Figure 1 shows several predictions for the Internet in the near future.

As new technologies and end user devices come to market, businesses and consumers must continue to adjust to this ever-changing environment. The role of the network is transforming to enable the connections of people, devices, and information. There are several new networking trends that will effect organizations and consumers. Some of the top trends include:

- Any device, to any content, any way

- Online collaboration

- Video

- Cloud computing

These trends are interconnected and will continue to build off of one another in the coming years. The next couple of topics will cover these trends in more detail.

But keep in mind, new trends are being dreamed up and engineered every day. How do you think the Internet will change in the next 10 years? 20 years? Figure 2 is a video that shows some of Cisco's thoughts on future developments.

Refer to
Online Course
for Illustration

1.4.1.2   BYOD

Bring Your Own Device (BYOD)

The concept of any device, to any content, in anyway is a major global trend that requires significant changes to the way devices are used. This trend is known as Bring Your Own Device (BYOD).

BYOD is about end users having the freedom to use personal tools to access information and communicate across a business or campus network. With the growth of consumer devices, and the related drop in cost, employees and students can be expected to have some of the most advanced computing and networking tools for personal use. These personal tools include laptops, netbooks, tablets, smartphones, and e-readers. These can be devices purchased by the company or school, purchased by the individual, or both.

BYOD means any device, with any ownership, used anywhere. For example, in the past, a student who needed to access the campus network or the Internet had to use one of the school's computers. These devices were typically limited and seen as tools only for work done in the classroom or in the library. Extended connectivity through mobile and remote access to the campus network gives students tremendous flexibility and more learning opportunities for the student.

BYOD is an influential trend that has or will touch every IT organization.

Refer to
Online Course
for Illustration

1.4.1.3   Online Collaboration

Online Collaboration

Individuals want to connect to the network, not only for access to data applications, but also to collaborate with one another. Collaboration is defined as "the act of working with another or others on a joint project."

For businesses, collaboration is a critical and strategic priority. To remain competitive, organizations must answer three primary collaboration questions:

- How can they get everyone on the same page?

- With decreased budgets and personnel, how can they balance resources to be in more places at once?

- How can they maintain face-to-face relationships with a growing network of colleagues, customers, partners, and peers in an environment that is more dependent on 24-hour connectivity?

Collaboration is also a priority in education. Students need to collaborate to assist each other in learning, to develop team skills used in the work force, and to work together on team-based projects.

One way to answer these questions and meet these demands in today's environment is through online collaboration tools. In traditional workspaces, and with BYOD environments alike, individuals are taking advantage of voice, video, and conferencing services in collaboration efforts.

The ability to collaborate online is changing business processes. New and expanding collaboration tools allow individuals to quickly and easily collaborate, regardless of physical location. Organizations have much more flexibility in the way they are organized. Individuals are no longer restricted to physical locations. Expert knowledge is easier to access than ever before. Expansions in collaboration allow organizations to improve their information gathering, innovation, and productivity. The figure lists some of the benefits of online collaboration.

Collaboration tools give employees, students, teachers, customers, and partners a way to instantly connect, interact, and conduct business, through whatever communications channels they prefer, and achieve their objectives.

Refer to
Online Course
for Illustration

1.4.1.4   Video Communication

Video Communication

Another trend in networking that is critical in the communication and collaboration effort is video. Video is being used for communications, collaboration, and entertainment. Video calls are becoming more popular, facilitating communications as part of the human network. Video calls can be made to and from anywhere with an Internet connection, including from home or at work.

Video calls and video conferencing is proving particularly powerful for sales processes and for doing business. Video is a useful tool for conducting business at a distance, both locally and globally. Today, businesses are using video to transform the way they do business. Video helps businesses create a competitive advantage, lower costs and reduce the impact on the environment by reducing the need travel. Figure 1 shows the trend of video in communication.

Both consumers and businesses are driving this change. Video is becoming a key requirement for effective collaboration as organizations extend across geographic and cultural boundaries. Video users now demand the ability to view any content, on any device, anywhere.

Businesses are also recognizing the role of video to enhance the human network. The growth of media, and the new uses to which it is being put, is driving the need to integrate audio and video into many forms of communication. The audio conference will coexist with the video conference. Collaboration tools designed to link distributed employees will integrate desktop video to bring teams closer together.

There are many drivers and benefits for including a strategy for using video. Each organization is unique. The exact mix, and nature of the drivers for adopting video, will vary from organization to organization, and by business function. Marketing, for example, may focus on globalization, and fast-changing consumer tastes; while the Chief Information Officer's (CIO) focus may be on cost savings by reducing travel costs of employees needing to meet face-to-face. Figure 2 lists some of the drivers for organizations to develop and implement a video solution strategy.

Figure 3 is a video that gives a closer look at how TelePresence using video can be incorporated into everyday life and business.

Another trend in video is video-on-demand and streaming live video. Delivering video over the network lets us see movies and television programs when we want and where we want.

Refer to
Online Course
for Illustration

1.4.1.5   Cloud Computing

Cloud Computing

Cloud computing is the use of computing resources (hardware and software) that are delivered as a service over a network. A company uses the hardware and software in the cloud and a service fee is charged.

Local computers no longer have to do all the "heavy lifting" when it comes to running network applications. The network of computers that make up the cloud handles them instead. The hardware and software requirements of the user are decreased. The user's computer must interface with the cloud using software, which may be a web browser, and the cloud's network takes care of the rest.

Cloud computing is another global trend changing the way we access and store data. Cloud computing encompasses any subscription-based or pay-per-use service, in real time over the Internet. Cloud computing allows us to store personal files, even backup our entire hard disk drive on servers over the Internet. Applications such as word processing and photo editing can be accessed using the cloud.

For businesses, cloud computing extends IT's capabilities without requiring investment in new infrastructure, training new personnel, or licensing new software. These services are available on demand and delivered economically to any device anywhere in the world without compromising security or function.

The term "cloud computing" really refers to web-based computing. Online banking, online retail stores, and online music downloading are all examples of cloud computing. Cloud applications are usually delivered to the user through a web browser. Users do not need to have any software installed on their end device. This allows many different kinds of devices to connect to the cloud.

Cloud computing offers the following potential benefits:

- **Organizational flexibility** - Users can access the information anytime and anyplace using a web browser.

- **Agility and rapid deployment** - IT department can focus on delivering the tools to mine, analyze, and share the information and knowledge from databases, files, and people.

- **Reduced cost of infrastructure** - Technology is moved from on-site to a cloud provider, eliminating the cost of hardware and applications.

- **Refocus of IT resources** - Cost savings of hardware and applications can be applied elsewhere.

- **Creation of new business models** - Applications and resources are easily accessible, so companies can react quickly to customer needs. This helps them set strategies to promote innovation while potentially entering new markets.

There are four primary types of clouds, as shown in Figure 2. Click each cloud to learn more.

Refer to
Online Course
for Illustration

1.4.1.6 Data Centers

Cloud computing is possible because of data centers. A data center is a facility used to house computer systems and associated components including:

- Redundant data communications connections

- High-speed virtual servers (sometimes referred to as server farms or server clusters)

- Redundant storage systems (typically uses SAN technology)

- Redundant or backup power supplies

- Environmental controls (e.g., air conditioning, fire suppression)

- Security devices

A data center can occupy one room of a building, one or more floors, or an entire building. Modern data centers make use of cloud computing and virtualization to efficiently handle large data transactions. Virtualization is the creation of a virtual version of something, such as a hardware platform, operating system (OS), storage device, or network resources. While a physical computer is an actual discrete device, a virtual machine consists of a set of files and programs running on an actual physical system. Unlike multitasking, which involves running several programs on the same OS; virtualization runs several different OSs in parallel on a single CPU. This drastically reduces administrative and cost overheads.

Data centers are typically very expensive to build and maintain. For this reason only large organizations use privately built data centers to house their data and provide services to users. For example, a large hospital may own a separate data center where patient records are maintained electronically. Smaller organizations, that cannot afford to maintain their own private data center, can reduce the overall cost of ownership by leasing server and storage services from a larger data center organization in the cloud.

The figure is a video about the growing use of cloud computing and data center services.

1.4.2   Networking Technologies for the Home

1.4.2.1   Technology Trends in the Home

Networking trends are not only affecting the way we communicate at work and at school, they are also changing just about every aspect of the home.

The newest home trends include 'smart home technology'. Smart home technology is technology that is integrated into every-day appliances allowing them to interconnect with other devices, making them more 'smart' or automated. For example, imagine being able to prepare a dish and place it in the oven for cooking prior to leaving the house for the day. Imagine if the oven was 'aware' of the dish it was cooking and was connected to your 'calendar of events' so that it could determine what time you should be available to eat, and adjust start times and length of cooking accordingly. It could even adjust cooking times and temperatures based on changes in schedule. Additionally, a smartphone or tablet connection allows the user the ability to connect to the oven directly, to make any desired adjustments. When the dish is "available", the oven sends an alert message to a specified end user device that the dish is done and warming.

This scenario is not long off. In fact, smart home technology is currently being developed for all rooms within a house. Smart home technology will become more of a reality as home networking and high-speed Internet technology becomes more widespread in homes. New home networking technologies are being developed daily to meet these types of growing technology needs.

Refer to
Online Course
for Illustration

1.4.2.2   Powerline Networking

Powerline networking is an emerging trend for home networking that uses existing electrical wiring to connect devices, as shown in the figure. The concept of "no new wires" means the ability to connect a device to the network wherever there is an electrical outlet. This saves the cost of installing data cables and without any additional cost to the electrical bill. Using the same wiring that delivers electricity, powerline networking sends information by sending data on certain frequencies similar to the same technology used for DSL.

Using a HomePlug standard powerline adapter, devices can connect to the LAN wherever there is an electrical outlet. Powerline networking is especially useful when wireless access points cannot be used or cannot reach all the devices in the home. Powerline networking is not designed to be a substitute for dedicated cabling for data networks. However, it is an alternative when data network cables or wireless communications are not a viable option.

Refer to
Online Course
for Illustration

1.4.2.3   Wireless Broadband

Connecting to the Internet is vital in smart home technology. DSL and cable are common technologies used to connect homes and small businesses to the Internet. However, wireless may be another option in many areas.

Wireless Internet Service Provider (WISP)

Wireless Internet Service Provider (WISP) is an ISP that connects subscribers to a designated access point or hot spot using similar wireless technologies found in home wireless local area networks (WLANs). WISPs are more commonly found in rural environments where DSL or cable services are not available.

Although a separate transmission tower may be installed for the antenna, it is common that the antenna is attached to an existing elevated structure such as a water tower or a radio tower. A small dish or antenna is installed on the subscriber's roof in range of the WISP transmitter. The subscriber's access unit is connected to the wired network inside the home. From the perspective of the home user the setup isn't much different than DSL or cable service. The main difference is the connection from the home to the ISP is wireless instead of a physical cable.

Wireless Broadband Service

Another wireless solution for the home and small businesses is wireless broadband. This uses the same cellular technology used to access the Internet with a smart phone or tablet. An antenna is installed outside the house providing either wireless or wired connectivity for devices in the home. In many areas, home wireless broadband is competing directly with DSL and cable services.

Refer to
Online Course
for Illustration

1.4.3   Network Security

1.4.3.1   Security threats

Network security is an integral part of computer networking, regardless of whether the network is limited to a home environment with a single connection to the Internet, or as large as a corporation with thousands of users. The network security implemented must take into account the environment, as well as the tools and requirements of the network. It must be able to secure data, while still allowing for the quality of service that is expected of the network.

Securing a network involves protocols, technologies, devices, tools, and techniques to secure data and mitigate threats. Many external network security threats today are spread over the Internet. The most common external threats to networks include:

- **Viruses, worms, and Trojan horses** - malicious software and arbitrary code running on a user device

- **Spyware and adware** - software installed on a user device that secretly collects information about the user

- **Zero-day attacks, also called zero-hour attacks** - an attack that occurs on the first day that a vulnerability becomes known

- **Hacker attacks** - an attack by a knowledgeable person to user devices or network resources

- **Denial of service attacks** - attacks designed to slow or crash applications and processes on a network device

- **Data interception and theft** - an attack to capture private information from an organization's network

- **Identity theft** - an attack to steal the login credentials of a user in order to access private data

It is equally important to consider internal threats. There have been many studies that show that the most common data breaches happen because of internal users of the network. This can be attributed to lost or stolen devices, accidental misuse by employees, and in the business environment, even malicious employees. With the evolving BYOD strategies, corporate data is much more vulnerable. Therefore, when developing a security policy, it is important to address both external and internal security threats.

Refer to
Online Course
for Illustration

1.4.3.2   Security Solutions

No single solution can protect the network from the variety of threats that exist. For this reason, security should be implemented in multiple layers, using more than one security solution. If one security component fails to identify and protect the network, others still stand.

A home network security implementation is usually rather basic. It is generally implemented on the connecting host devices, as well as at the point of connection to the Internet, and can even rely on contracted services from the ISP.

In contrast the network security implementation for a corporate network usually consists of many components built into the network to monitor and filter traffic. Ideally, all components work together, which minimizes maintenance and improves security.

Network security components for a home or small office network should include, at a minimum:

- **Antivirus and antispyware** - to protect user devices from malicious software

- **Firewall filtering** - to block unauthorized access to the network. This may include a host-based firewall system that is implemented to prevent unauthorized access to the host device, or a basic filtering service on the home router to prevent unauthorized access from the outside world into the network.

In addition to the above, larger networks and corporate networks often have other security requirements:

- **Dedicated firewall systems** - to provide more advanced firewall capability that can filter large amounts of traffic with more granularity

- **Access control lists (ACL)** - to further filter access and traffic forwarding

- **Intrusion prevention systems (IPS)** - to identify fast-spreading threats, such as zero-day or zero-hour attacks

- **Virtual private networks (VPN)** - to provide secure access to remote workers

Network security requirements must take into account the network environment, as well as the various applications, and computing requirements. Both home environments and businesses must be able to secure their data, while still allowing for the quality of service that is expected of each technology. Additionally, the security solution implemented must be adaptable to the growing and changing trends of the network.

The study of network security threats and mitigation techniques starts with a clear understanding of the underlying switching and routing infrastructure used to organize network services.

Refer to
Interactive Graphic
in online course.

1.4.3.3 Activity - Network Security Terminology

Refer to
Online Course
for Illustration

1.4.4 Network Architectures

1.4.4.1 Cisco Network Architectures

The role of the network has changed from a data-only network, to a system that enables the connections of people, devices, and information in a media rich, converged network environment. In order for networks to function efficiently and grow in this type of environment, the network must be built upon a standard network architecture.

The network architecture refers to the devices, connections, and products that are integrated to support the necessary technologies and applications. A well-planned network technology architecture helps ensure the connection of any device across any combination of networks. While ensuring connectivity, it also increases cost efficiency by integrating network security and management, and improves business processes. At the foundation of all network architectures, and in fact, at the foundation of the Internet itself, are routers and switches. Routers and switches transport data, voice, and video communications, as well as allow for wireless access, and provide for security.

Building networks that support our needs of today and the needs and trends of the future starts with a clear understanding of the underlying switching and routing infrastructure. After a basic routing and switching network infrastructure is built, individuals, small businesses, and organizations can grow their network over time, adding features and functionality in an integrated solution.

Refer to
Online Course
for Illustration

1.4.4.2 CCNA

As the use of these integrated, expanding networks increase, so does the need for training for individuals who implement and manage network solutions. This training must begin with the routing and switching foundation. Achieving Cisco Certified Network Associate (CCNA) certification is the first step in helping an individual prepare for a career in networking.

CCNA certification validates an individual's ability to install, configure, operate, and troubleshoot medium-size route and switched networks, including implementation and verification of connections to remote sites in a WAN. CCNA curriculum also includes basic mitigation of security threats, introduction to wireless networking concepts and terminology, and performance-based skills. This CCNA curriculum includes the use of various protocols, such as: IP, Open Shortest Path First (OSPF), Serial Line Interface Protocol, Frame Relay, VLANs, Ethernet, access control lists (ACLs) and others.

This course helps set the stage for networking concepts and basic routing and switching configurations and is a start on your path for CCNA certification.

Refer to
Lab Activity
for this chapter

1.4.4.3 Lab - Researching IT and Networking Job Opportunities

In this lab, you will complete the following objectives:

- Part 1: Research Job Opportunities
- Part 2: Reflect on Research

1.5   Summary

Refer to
Lab Activity
for this chapter

1.5.1.1   Class Activity - Draw Your Concept of the Internet Now

Draw Your Concept of the Internet Now

In this activity, you will use the knowledge you have acquired throughout Chapter 1, and the modeling activity document that you prepared at the beginning of this chapter. You may also refer to the other activities completed in this chapter, including Packet Tracer activities.

Draw a map of the Internet as you see it now. Use the icons presented in the chapter for media, end devices, and intermediary devices.

In your revised drawing, you may wish to include some of the following:

- WANs
- LANs
- Cloud computing
- Internet Service Providers (tiers)

Save your drawing in hard-copy format. If it is an electronic document, save it to a server location provided by your instructor. Be prepared to share and explain your revised work in class.

Refer to
Online Course
for Illustration

1.5.1.2   Summary

Networks and the Internet have changed the way we communicate, learn, work, and even play.

Networks come in all sizes. They can range from simple networks consisting of two computers, to networks connecting millions of devices.

The Internet is the largest network in existence. In fact, the term Internet means a 'network of networks'. The Internet provides the services that enable us to connect and communicate with our families, friends, work, and interests.

The network infrastructure is the platform that supports the network. It provides the stable and reliable channel over which communication can occur. It is made up of network components including end devices, intermediate device, and network media.

Networks must be reliable. This means the network must be fault tolerant, scalable, provide quality of service, and ensure security of the information and resources on the network. Network security is an integral part of computer networking, regardless of whether the network is limited to a home environment with a single connection to the Internet, or as large as a corporation with thousands of users. No single solution can protect the network from the variety of threats that exist. For this reason, security should be implemented in multiple layers, using more than one security solution.

The network infrastructure can vary greatly in terms of size, number of users, and number and types of services that are supported on it. The network infrastructure must grow and adjust to support the way the network is used. The routing and switching platform is the foundation of any network infrastructure.

This chapter focused on networking as a primary platform for supporting communication. The next chapter will introduce you to the Cisco Internet Operating System (IOS) used to enable routing and switching in a Cisco network environment.

Go to the online
course to take the
quiz and exam.

Chapter 1 Quiz

This quiz is designed to provide an additional opportunity to practice the skills and knowledge presented in the chapter and to prepare for the chapter exam. You will be allowed multiple attempts and the grade does not appear in the gradebook.

Chapter 1 Exam

The chapter exam assesses your knowledge of the chapter content.

Your Chapter Notes

Configuring a Network Operating System

2.0 Configuring a Network Operating System

2.0.1 Introduction

2.0.1.1 Introduction to Cisco IOS

Home networks typically interconnect a wide variety of end devices including PCs, laptops, tablets, smartphones, smart TVs, Digital Living Network Alliance (DLNA) compliant network media players, such as the Xbox 360 or PlayStation 3, and more.

All of these end devices are usually connected to a home router. Home routers are actually four devices in one:

- **Router** - Forwards data packets to and receives data packets from the Internet
- **Switch** - Connects end devices using network cables
- **Wireless access point** - Consists of a radio transmitter capable of connecting end devices wirelessly
- **Firewall appliance** - Secures outgoing traffic and restricts incoming traffic

In larger, business networks with significantly more devices and traffic, these devices are often incorporated as independent, stand-alone devices, providing dedicated service. End-devices, such as PCs and laptops, are connected to network switches using wired connections. To send packets beyond the local network, network switches connect to network routers. Other infrastructure devices on a network include wireless access points and dedicated security devices, such as firewalls.

Each device is very different in hardware, use, and capability. But in all cases, it is the operating system that enables the hardware to function.

Operating systems are used on virtually all end user and network devices connected to the Internet. End user devices include devices such as smart phones, tablets, PCs, and laptops. Network devices, or intermediary devices, are devices used to transport data across the network and include switches, routers, wireless access points, and firewalls. The operating system on a network device is known as a network operating system.

The Cisco Internetwork Operating System (IOS) is a generic term for the collection of network operating systems used on Cisco networking devices. Cisco IOS is used for most Cisco devices regardless of the type or size of the device.

This chapter will reference a basic network topology, consisting of two switches and two PCs, to demonstrate the use of Cisco IOS.

Refer to
Lab Activity
for this chapter

2.0.1.2   Class Activity - It Is Just an Operating System

It Is Just an Operating System!

In this activity, imagine that you are employed as an engineer for a car manufacturing company. The company is currently working on a new car model. This model will have selected functions which can be controlled by the driver giving specific voice commands.

Design a set of commands used by this voice-activated control system, and to identify how they are going to be executed. The functions of the car that can be controlled by voice commands are:

- Lights
- Wipers
- Radio
- Telephone set
- Air conditioning
- Ignition

Refer to
Online Course
for Illustration

2.1   IOS Bootcamp

2.1.1   Cisco IOS

2.1.1.1   Operating Systems

All end devices and network devices connected to the Internet require an operating system (OS) to help them perform their function.

When a computer is powered on, it loads the OS, normally from a disk drive, into RAM. The portion of the OS code that interacts directly with the computer hardware is known as the kernel. The portion that interfaces with the applications and user is known as the shell. The user can interact with the shell using either the command-line interface (CLI) or graphical user interface (GUI).

When using the CLI, the user interacts directly with the system in a text-based environment by entering commands on the keyboard at a command prompt. The system executes the command, often providing textual output. The GUI interface allows the user to interact with the system in an environment that uses graphical images, multimedia, and text. Actions are performed by interacting with the images on screen. GUI is more user friendly and requires less knowledge of the command structure to utilize the system. For this reason, many individuals rely on the GUI environments. Many operating systems offer both GUI and CLI.

Click on the hardware, kernel, and shell portions of the figure for more information.

Most end device operating systems are accessed using a GUI, including MS Windows, MAC OS X, Linux, Apple iOS, Android, and more.

The operating system on home routers is usually called firmware. The most common method for configuring a home router is using a web browser to access an easy to use GUI.

Most home routers enable the update of the firmware as new features or security vulnerabilities are discovered.

Infrastructure network devices use a network operating system. The network operating system used on Cisco devices is called the Cisco Internetwork Operating System (IOS). Cisco IOS is a generic term for the collection of network operating systems used on Cisco networking devices. Cisco IOS is used for most Cisco devices regardless of the type or size of the device. The most common method of accessing these devices is using a CLI.

This chapter will focus on a small business network switch topology. The topology consists of two switches and two PCs and will be used to demonstrate the use of Cisco IOS using the CLI.

Refer to
Online Course
for Illustration

2.1.1.2   Purpose of OS

Network operating systems are in many ways similar to the operating systems of PCs. An operating system performs a number of technical functions "behind the scenes" that enable a user to:

- Use a mouse
- View output on a monitor
- Enter text commands
- Select options within a dialog box window

The "behind the scenes" functions for switches and routers are very similar. The IOS on a switch or router provides the network technician with an interface. The technician can enter commands to configure, or program, the device to perform various networking functions. The IOS operational details vary on internetworking devices, depending on the purpose of the device and the features supported.

Cisco IOS is a term that encompasses a number of different operating systems that run on various networking devices. There are many distinct variations of Cisco IOS:

- IOS for switches, routers, and other Cisco networking devices
- IOS numbered versions for a given Cisco networking device
- IOS feature sets providing distinct packages of features and services

Just as a PC may be running Microsoft Windows 8 and a MacBook may be running OS X, a Cisco networking device runs a particular version of the Cisco IOS. The version of IOS is dependent on the type of device being used and the required features. While all devices come with a default IOS and feature set, it is possible to upgrade the IOS version or feature set, in order to obtain additional capabilities.

In this course, you will focus primarily on Cisco IOS Release 15.x. Figure 1 displays a list of IOS software releases for a Cisco Catalyst 2960 Switch. Figure 2 displays a list of IOS software releases for a Cisco 2911 Integrated Services Router (ISR).

Refer to
Online Course
for Illustration

2.1.1.3   Location of the Cisco IOS

The IOS file itself is several megabytes in size and is stored in a semi-permanent memory area called flash. The figure shows a compact flash card. Flash memory provides non-volatile storage. This means that the contents of the memory are not lost when the device loses power. Although the contents of flash are not lost during a loss of power, they can be changed or overwritten if needed. This allows the IOS to be upgraded to a newer version or to have new features added without replacing hardware. Additionally, flash can be used to store multiple versions of IOS software at the same time.

In many Cisco devices, the IOS is copied from flash into random access memory (RAM) when the device is powered on. The IOS then runs from RAM when the device is operating. RAM has many functions including storing data that is used by the device to support network operations. Running the IOS in RAM increases performance of the device, however, RAM is considered volatile memory because data is lost during a power cycle. A power cycle is when a device is purposely or accidently powered off and then powered back on.

The quantity of flash memory and RAM memory required for a given IOS varies dramatically. For the purposes of network maintenance and planning, it is important to determine the flash and RAM requirements for each device, including the maximum flash and RAM configurations. It is possible that the requirements of the newest versions of IOS could demand more RAM and flash than can be installed on some devices.

2.1.1.4   IOS Functions

Refer to **Online Course** for Illustration

Cisco IOS routers and switches perform functions that network professionals depend upon to make their networks operate as expected. Major functions performed or enabled by Cisco routers and switches include:

■ Providing network security

■ IP addressing of virtual and physical interfaces

■ Enabling interface-specific configurations to optimize connectivity of the respective media

■ Routing

■ Enabling quality of service (QoS) technologies

■ Supporting network management technologies

Each feature or service has an associated collection of configuration commands that allow a network technician to implement it.

The services provided by the Cisco IOS are generally accessed using a CLI.

2.1.1.5   Video Demonstration - CCO Accounts and IOS Image Exploration

Refer to **Online Course** for Illustration

This video introduces Cisco Connection Online (CCO). CCO has a wealth of information available regarding Cisco products and services.

Refer to
Online Course
for Illustration

2.1.2   Accessing a Cisco IOS Device

2.1.2.1   Console Access Method

There are several ways to access the CLI environment. The most common methods are:

- Console
- Telnet or SSH
- AUX port

Console

The console port is a management port that provides out-of-band access to Cisco device. Out-of-band access refers to access via a dedicated management channel that is used for device maintenance purposes only. The advantage of using a console port is that the device is accessible even if no networking services have been configured, such as when performing an initial configuration of the networking device. When performing an initial configuration, a computer running terminal emulation software is connected to the console port of the device using a special cable. Configuration commands for setting up the switch or router can be entered on the connected computer.

The console port can also be used when the networking services have failed and remote access of the Cisco IOS device is not possible. If this occurs, a connection to the console can enable a computer to determine the status of the device. By default, the console conveys the device startup, debugging, and error messages. After the network technician is connected to the device, the network technician can perform any configuration commands necessary using the console session.

For many IOS devices, console access does not require any form of security, by default. However, the console should be configured with passwords to prevent unauthorized device access. In the event that a password is lost, there is a special set of procedures for bypassing the password and accessing the device. The device should also be located in a locked room or equipment rack to prevent unauthorized physical access.

Refer to
Online Course
for Illustration

2.1.2.2   Telnet, SSH, and AUX Access Methods

Telnet

Telnet is a method for remotely establishing a CLI session of a device, through a virtual interface, over a network. Unlike the console connection, Telnet sessions require active networking services on the device. The network device must have at least one active interface configured with an Internet address, such as an IPv4 address. Cisco IOS devices include a Telnet server process that allows users to enter configuration commands from a Telnet client. In addition to supporting the Telnet server process, the Cisco IOS device also contains a Telnet client. This allows a network administrator to telnet from the Cisco device CLI to any other device that supports a Telnet server process.

SSH

The Secure Shell (SSH) protocol provides a remote login similar to Telnet, except that it uses more secure network services. SSH provides stronger password authentication than Telnet and uses encryption when transporting session data. This keeps the user ID, password, and the details of the management session private. As a best practice, use SSH instead of Telnet whenever possible.

Most versions of Cisco IOS include an SSH server. In some devices, this service is enabled by default. Other devices require the SSH server to be enabled manually. IOS devices also include an SSH client that can be used to establish SSH sessions with other devices.

AUX

An older way to establish a CLI session remotely is via a telephone dialup connection using a modem connected to the auxiliary (AUX) port of a router, which is highlighted in the figure. Similar to the console connection, the AUX method is also an out-of-band connection and does not require any networking services to be configured or available on the device. In the event that network services have failed, it may be possible for a remote administrator to access the switch or router over a telephone line.

The AUX port can also be used locally, like the console port, with a direct connection to a computer running a terminal emulation program. However, the console port is preferred over the AUX port for troubleshooting because it displays startup, debugging, and error messages by default.

Note   Cisco Catalyst switches do not support an auxiliary connection.

Refer to **Online Course** for Illustration

2.1.2.3   Terminal Emulation Programs

There are a number of excellent terminal emulation programs available for connecting to a networking device either by a serial connection over a console port or by a Telnet/SSH connection. Some of these include:

- PuTTY (Figure 1)
- Tera Term (Figure 2)
- SecureCRT (Figure 3)
- HyperTerminal
- OS X Terminal

These programs allow you to enhance your productivity by adjusting window sizes, changing font sizes, and changing color schemes.

Refer to **Interactive Graphic** in online course.

2.1.2.4   Activity – Accessing Devices

Refer to **Online Course** for Illustration

2.1.3   Navigating the IOS

2.1.3.1   Cisco IOS Modes of Operation

After a network technician is connected to a device, it is possible to configure it. The network technician must navigate through various modes of the IOS. The Cisco IOS modes are quite similar for switches and routers. The CLI uses a hierarchical structure for the modes.

In hierarchical order from most basic to most specialized, the major modes are:

- User executive (User EXEC) mode

- Privileged executive (Privileged EXEC) mode

- Global configuration mode

- Other specific configuration modes, such as interface configuration mode

Each mode has a distinctive prompt and is used to accomplish particular tasks with a specific set of commands that are available only to that mode. For example, global configuration mode allows a technician to configure settings on the device that affects the device as a whole, such as configuring a name for the device. However, a different mode is required if the network technician wants to configure security settings on a specific port on a switch, for example. In this case, the network technician must enter interface configuration mode for that specific port. All configurations that are entered in interface configuration mode apply only to that port.

The hierarchical structure can be configured to provide security. Different authentication can be required for each hierarchical mode. This controls the level of access that network personnel can be granted.

The figure shows the IOS mode structure with typical prompts and features.

Refer to
Online Course
for Illustration

2.1.3.2   Primary Modes

The two primary modes of operation are user EXEC mode and privileged EXEC mode. As a security feature, the Cisco IOS software separates the EXEC sessions into two levels of access. As shown in the figure, the privileged EXEC mode has a higher level of authority in what it allows the user to do with the device.

User EXEC Mode

The user EXEC mode has limited capabilities but is useful for some basic operations. The user EXEC mode is at the most basic level of the modal hierarchical structure. This mode is the first mode encountered upon entrance into the CLI of an IOS device.

The user EXEC mode allows only a limited number of basic monitoring commands. This is often referred to as view-only mode. The user EXEC level does not allow the execution of any commands that might change the configuration of the device.

By default, there is no authentication required to access the user EXEC mode from the console. However, it is a good practice to ensure that authentication is configured during the initial configuration.

The user EXEC mode is identified by the CLI prompt that ends with the > symbol. This is an example that shows the > symbol in the prompt:

```
Switch>
```

Privileged EXEC Mode

The execution of configuration and management commands requires that the network administrator use the privileged EXEC mode or a more specific mode in the hierarchy. This means that a user must enter user EXEC mode first, and from there, access privileged EXEC mode.

The privileged EXEC mode can be identified by the prompt ending with the # symbol.

```
Switch#
```

By default, privileged EXEC mode does not require authentication. It is a good practice to ensure that authentication is configured.

Global configuration mode and all other more specific configuration modes can only be reached from the privileged EXEC mode. In a later section of this chapter, we will examine device configuration and some of the configuration modes.

Refer to
Online Course
for Illustration

2.1.3.3 Global Configuration Mode and Submodes

Global configuration mode and interface configuration modes can only be reached from the privileged EXEC mode.

Global Configuration Mode

The primary configuration mode is called global configuration or global config. From global configuration mode, CLI configuration changes are made that affect the operation of the device as a whole. The global configuration mode is accessed before accessing specific configuration modes.

The following CLI command is used to take the device from privileged EXEC mode to the global configuration mode and to allow entry of configuration commands from a terminal:

```
Switch# configure terminal
```

After the command is executed, the prompt changes to show that the switch is in global configuration mode.

```
Switch(config)#
```

Specific Configuration Modes

From the global configuration mode, the user can enter different sub-configuration modes. Each of these modes allows the configuration of a particular part or function of the IOS device. The list below shows a few of them:

- **Interface mode** - to configure one of the network interfaces (Fa0/0, S0/0/0)
- **Line mode** - to configure one of the physical or virtual lines (console, AUX, VTY)

Figure 1 shows the prompts for some of these modes. To exit a specific configuration mode and return to global configuration mode, enter **exit** at a prompt. To leave configuration mode completely and return to privileged EXEC mode, enter **end** or use the key sequence **Ctrl-Z**.

Command Prompts

When using the CLI, the mode is identified by the command-line prompt that is unique to that mode. By default, every prompt begins with the device name. Following the name, the remainder of the prompt indicates the mode. For example, the default prompt for the global configuration mode on a switch would be:

```
Switch(config)#
```

As commands are used and modes are changed, the prompt changes to reflect the current context as shown in Figure 2.

Refer to
Online Course
for Illustration

2.1.3.4   Navigating between IOS Modes

Moving Between the User EXEC and Privileged EXEC Modes

The `enable` and `disable` commands are used to change the CLI between the user EXEC mode and the privileged EXEC mode, respectively.

In order to access the privileged EXEC mode, use the `enable` command. The privileged EXEC mode is sometimes called the enable mode.

The syntax for entering the `enable` command is:

```
Switch> enable
```

This command is executed without the need for an argument or keyword. After the Enter key is pressed, the prompt changes to:

```
Switch#
```

The # at the end of the prompt indicates that the switch is now in privileged EXEC mode.

If password authentication is configured for the privileged EXEC mode, the IOS prompts for the password.

For example:

```
Switch> enable
Password:
Switch#
```

The `disable` command is used to return from the privileged EXEC to the user EXEC mode.

For example:

```
Switch# disable
Switch>
```

As the figure shows, the commands for accessing the privileged EXEC mode and for returning to the user EXEC mode on a Cisco router are identical to those used on a Cisco switch.

Refer to
Online Course
for Illustration

2.1.3.5   Navigating between IOS Modes (Cont.)

Moving from and to Global Configuration Mode and Submodes

To quit from the global configuration mode and return to the privileged EXEC mode, enter the `exit` command.

Note that entering the `exit` command in privileged EXEC mode causes the console session to be ended. That is, upon entering `exit` in privileged EXEC mode, you will be presented with the screen that you see when you first initiate a console session. At this screen you have to press the Enter key to enter user EXEC mode.

To move from any submode of the global configuration mode to the mode one step above it in the hierarchy of modes, enter the `exit` command. Figure 1 illustrates moving from user EXEC mode to privileged EXEC mode, then entering global configuration mode, interface configuration mode, back to global configuration mode and back again to privileged EXEC mode using the `exit` command.

To move from any submode of the privileged EXEC mode to the privileged EXEC mode, enter the `end` command or enter the key combination **Ctrl+Z**. Figure 2 illustrates moving from VLAN configuration mode all the way back to privileged EXEC mode using the **end** command.

To move from any submode of the global configuration mode to another "immediate" submode of the global configuration mode, simply enter the corresponding command that is normally entered from global configuration mode. Figure 3 illustrates moving from the line configuration mode, `Switch(config-line)#`, to the interface configuration mode, `Switch(config-if)#`, without having to exit line configuration mode.

Refer to
Online Course
for Illustration

2.1.3.6   Video Demonstration - Navigating the IOS

This video demonstrates navigation through the different CLI command modes of both a router and a switch using Cisco IOS.

2.1.4   The Command Structure

2.1.4.1   IOS Command Structure

Basic IOS Command Structure

A Cisco IOS device supports many commands. Each IOS command has a specific format or syntax and can only be executed at the appropriate mode. The general syntax for a command is the command followed by any appropriate keywords and arguments. Some commands include a subset of keywords and arguments that provide additional functionality. Commands are used to execute an action, and the keywords are used to identify where or how to execute the command.

As shown in Figure 1, the command is the initial word or words entered in the command line following the prompt. The commands are not case-sensitive. Following the command are one or more keywords and arguments. After entering each complete command, including any keywords and arguments, press the Enter key to submit the command to the command interpreter.

The keywords describe specific parameters to the command interpreter. For example, the **show** command is used to display information about the device. This command has various keywords that must be used to define what particular output should be displayed. For example:

```
Switch# show running-config
```

The command **show** is followed by the keyword **running-config**. The keyword specifies that the running configuration is to be displayed as the output.

IOS Command Conventions

A command might require one or more arguments. Unlike a keyword, an argument is generally not a predefined word. An argument is a value or variable defined by the user. To determine the keywords and arguments required for a command, refer to the command syntax. The syntax provides the pattern or format that must be used when entering a command.

For instance the syntax for using the **description** command is:

```
Switch(config-if)# description string
```

As shown in Figure 2, boldface text indicates commands and keywords that are typed as shown and italic text indicates an argument for which you supply the value. For the **description** command, the argument is a string value. The string value can be any text string of up to 80 characters.

Therefore, when applying a description to an interface with the **description** command, enter a line such as this:

```
Switch(config-if)# description MainHQ Office Switch
```

The command is **description** and the user defined argument is **MainHQ Office Switch**.

The following examples demonstrate some conventions used to document and use IOS commands.

For the **ping** command:

Syntax:

```
Switch> ping IP-address
```

Example with values:

```
Switch> ping 10.10.10.5
```

The command is **ping** and the user defined argument is the **10.10.10.5**.

Similarly, the syntax for entering the **traceroute** command is:

Syntax:

```
Switch> traceroute IP-address
```

Example with values:

```
Switch> traceroute 192.168.254.254
```

The command is **traceroute** and the user defined argument is the **192.168.254.254**.

Refer to
Online Course
for Illustration

2.1.4.2   Cisco IOS Command Reference

The Cisco IOS Command Reference is a collection of online documentation which describes in detail the IOS commands used on Cisco devices. The Command Reference is the ultimate source of information for a particular IOS command, similar to how a dictionary is the ultimate source for information about a particular word.

The Command Reference is a fundamental resource that network engineers use to check various characteristics of a given IOS command. Some of the more common characteristics are:

- **Syntax** - the most detailed version of the syntax for a command that can be found
- **Default** - the manner in which the command is implemented on a device with a default configuration
- **Mode** - the configuration mode on the device where the command is entered
- **History** - descriptions of how the command is implemented relative to the IOS version
- **Usage Guidelines** - guidelines describing specifically how to implement the command
- **Examples** - useful examples that illustrate common scenarios that use the command

To navigate to the Command Reference and find a particular command follow the steps below:

Step 1.   Go to www.cisco.com.

Step 2.   Click **Support**.

Step 3.   Click **Networking Software** (IOS & NX-OS).

Step 4.   Click **15.2M&T** (for example).

Step 5.   Click **Reference Guides**.

Step 6.   Click **CommandReferences**.

Step 7.   Click the particular technology that encompasses the command you are referencing.

Step 8.   Click the link on the left that alphabetically matches the command you are referencing.

Step 9.   Click the link for the command.

For example, the `description` command is found under the *Cisco IOS Interface and Hardware Component Command Reference*, under the link for the alphabetic range *D through E*.

Note   Complete PDF versions of the command references for a particular technology can be downloaded from links on the page that you reach after completing Step 7 above.

Refer to
Online Course
for Illustration

2.1.4.3 Context-Sensitive Help

The IOS has several forms of help available:

- Context-Sensitive Help

- Command Syntax Check

- Hot Keys and Shortcuts

Context-Sensitive Help

The context-sensitive help provides a list of commands and the arguments associated with those commands within the context of the current mode. To access context-sensitive help, enter a question mark, ?, at any prompt. There is an immediate response without the need to use the Enter key.

One use of context-sensitive help is to get a list of available commands. This can be used when you are unsure of the name for a command or you want to see if the IOS supports a particular command in a particular mode.

For example, to list the commands available at the user EXEC level, enter a question mark, ?, at the Switch> prompt.

Another use of context-sensitive help is to display a list of commands or keywords that start with a specific character or characters. After entering a character sequence, if a question mark is immediately entered, without a space, the IOS will display a list of commands or keywords for this context that start with the characters that were entered.

For example, enter `sh?` to get a list of commands that begins with the character sequence `sh`.

A final type of context-sensitive help is used to determine which options, keywords, or arguments are matched with a specific command. When entering a command, enter a space followed by a `?` to determine what can or should be entered next.

As shown in the figure, after typing the command `clock set 19:50:00`, we can enter the `?` to determine the additional options or keywords available for this command.

Refer to
Online Course
for Illustration

2.1.4.4   Command Syntax Check
Command Syntax Check

When a command is submitted by pressing the Enter key, the command line interpreter parses the command from left to right to determine what action is being requested. The IOS generally only provides negative feedback, as shown in Figure 1. If the interpreter understands the command, the requested action is executed and the CLI returns to the appropriate prompt. However, if the interpreter cannot understand the command being entered, it will provide feedback describing what is wrong with the command.

Figure 2 shows three different types of error messages:

■ Ambiguous command

■ Incomplete command

■ Incorrect command

The `clock set` command is an ideal IOS command for experimenting with the various command syntax check help messages as shown in Figure 1. Figure 2 provides help for the three types of error messages.

2.1.4.5   Hot Keys and Shortcuts
Hot Keys and Shortcuts

The IOS CLI provides hot keys and shortcuts that make configuring, monitoring, and troubleshooting easier.

The figure shows most of the shortcuts. The following are worthy of special note:

■ **Down Arrow** - Allows the user to scroll forward through former commands

■ **Up Arrow** - Allows the user to scroll backward through former commands

■ **Tab** - Completes the remainder of a partially typed command or keyword

■ **Ctrl-A** - Moves to the beginning of the line

■ **Ctrl-E** - Moves to the end of the line

■ **Ctrl-R** - Redisplays a line

■ **Ctrl-Z** - Exits the configuration mode and returns to user EXEC

■ **Ctrl-C** - Exits the configuration mode or aborts the current command

■ **Ctrl-Shift-6** - Allows the user to interrupt an IOS process such as ping or traceroute

Examining some of these in more detail:

Tab

Tab complete is used to complete the remainder of abbreviated commands and parameters if the abbreviation contains enough letters to be different from any other currently available commands or parameters. When enough of the command or keyword has been entered to appear unique, press the **Tab** key and the CLI will display the rest of the command or keyword.

This is a good technique to use when you are learning because it allows you to see the full word used for the command or keyword.

Ctrl-R

Redisplay the line will refresh the line just typed. Use **Ctrl-R** to redisplay the line. For example, you may find that the IOS is returning a message to the CLI just as you are typing a line. You can use **Ctrl-R** to refresh the line and avoid having to retype it.

In this example, a message regarding a failed interface is returned in the middle of a command.

```
Switch# show mac-
16w4d: %LINK-5-CHANGED: Interface FastEthernet0/10, changed state to down
16w4d: %LINEPROTO-5-UPDOWN: Line protocol on Interface FastEthernet0/10, changed
state to down
```

To redisplay to line that you were typing use **Ctrl-R**:

```
Switch# show mac
```

Ctrl-Z

Exit configuration mode will leave any configuration mode and return to privileged EXEC mode. Because the IOS has a hierarchical mode structure, you may find yourself several levels down. Rather than exit each mode individually, use **Ctrl-Z** to return directly to the privileged EXEC prompt at the top level.

Up and Down Arrows

Previous command keys will recall the history of commands entered. The Cisco IOS software buffers several past commands and characters so that entries can be recalled. The buffer is useful for re-entering commands without retyping.

Key sequences are available to scroll through these buffered commands. Use the **Up Arrow** key (**Ctrl-P**) to display the previously entered commands. Each time this key is pressed, the next successively older command will be displayed. Use the **Down Arrow** key (**Ctrl-N**) to scroll forward through the history to display the more recent commands.

Ctrl-Shift-6

The escape sequence will interrupt any running process. When an IOS process is initiated from the CLI, such as a ping or traceroute, the command runs until it is complete or is interrupted. While the process is running, the CLI is unresponsive. To interrupt the output and interact with the CLI, press **Ctrl-Shift-6**.

Ctrl-C

This interrupts the entry of a command and exits the configuration mode. This is useful after entering a command that needs to be cancelled.

Abbreviated commands or keywords

Commands and keywords can be abbreviated to the minimum number of characters that identify a unique selection. For example, the `configure` command can be abbreviated to `conf` because `configure` is the only command that begins with `conf`. An abbreviation of `con` will not work because more than one command begins with `con`.

Keywords can also be abbreviated.

As another example, `show interfaces` can be abbreviated like this:

```
Switch# show interfaces
Switch# show int
```

You can abbreviate both the command and the keywords, for example:

```
Switch# sh int
```

2.1.4.6   IOS Examination Commands

In order to verify and troubleshoot network operation, we must examine the operation of the devices. The basic examination command is the `show` command.

There are many different variations of this command. As you develop more skill with the IOS, you will learn to use and interpret the output of the `show` commands. Use the `show ?` command to get a list of available commands in a given context, or mode.

A typical `show` command can provide information about the configuration, operation, and status of parts of a Cisco switch or router. The figure highlights some of the common IOS commands.

In this course, we focus on mostly basic `show` commands.

A very commonly used `show` command is `show interfaces`. This command displays statistics for all interfaces on the device. To view the statistics for a specific interface, enter the `show interfaces` command followed by the specific interface type and slot/port number. For example:

```
Switch# show interfaces fastethernet 0/1
```

Some other `show` commands frequently used by network technicians include:

`show startup-config` - Displays the saved configuration located in NVRAM.

`show running-config` - Displays the contents of the currently running configuration file.

The More Prompt

When a command returns more output than can be displayed on a single screen, the `--More--` prompt appears at the bottom of the screen. When a `--More--` prompt appears, press the **Space bar** to view the next portion of output. To display only the next line, press the **Enter** key. If any other key is pressed, the output is cancelled and you are returned to the prompt.

Refer to
Online Course
for Illustration

2.1.4.7   The show version Command

One of the most commonly used commands on a switch or router is:

```
Switch# show version
```

This command displays information about the currently loaded IOS version, along with hardware and device information. If you are logged into a router or switch remotely, the **show version** command is an excellent means of quickly finding useful summary information about the particular device to which you are connected. Some of the information points shown from this command are:

- **Software version** - IOS software version (stored in flash)

- **Bootstrap version** - Bootstrap version (stored in Boot ROM)

- **System up-time** - Time since last reboot

- **System restart info** - Method of restart (e.g., power cycle, crash)

- **Software image name** - IOS filename stored in flash

- **Router type and processor type** - Model number and processor type

- **Memory type and allocation (shared/main)** - Main Processor RAM and Shared Packet I/O buffering

- **Software features** - Supported protocols/feature sets

- **Hardware interfaces** - Interfaces available on the device

- **Configuration register** - Sets bootup specifications, console speed setting, and related parameters

Figure 1 displays the output for a Cisco 1941 ISR, while Figure 2 displays the output for a Cisco 2960 Catalyst switch.

Refer to **Packet Tracer Activity** for this chapter

2.1.4.8   Packet Tracer - Navigating the IOS

In this activity, you will practice skills necessary for navigating the Cisco IOS, including different user access modes, various configuration modes, and common commands you use on a regular basis. You also practice accessing the context-sensitive help by configuring the **clock** command.

Refer to **Lab Activity** for this chapter

2.1.4.9   Lab - Establishing a Console Session with Tera Term

In this lab, you will complete the following objectives:

- Part 1: Access a Cisco Switch through the Serial Console Port

- Part 2: Display and Configure Basic Device Settings

- Part 3: (Optional) Access a Cisco Router Using a Mini-USB Console Cable

2.2   Getting Basic

2.2.1   Hostnames

2.2.1.1   Why the Switch

As discussed, Cisco switches and Cisco routers have many similarities. They support a similar modal operating system support similar command structures, and support many of the same commands. In addition, both devices have identical initial configuration steps when implementing them in a network.

However, a Cisco IOS switch is one of the simplest devices that can be configured on a network. This is because there are no configurations that are required prior to the device functioning. At its most basic, a switch can be plugged in with no configuration, but it will still switch data between connected devices.

A switch is also one of the fundamental devices used in the creation of a small network. By connecting two PCs to a switch, those PCs will instantly have connectivity with one another.

For these reasons, the remainder of this chapter will focus on the creation of a small, two PC network connected via a switch configured with initial settings. Initial settings include setting a name for the switch, limiting access to the device configuration, configuring banner messages, and saving the configuration.

> Refer to
> **Online Course**
> for Illustration

2.2.1.2   Device Names

When configuring a networking device, one of the first steps is configuring a unique device name, or hostname. Hostnames appear in CLI prompts, can be used in various authentication processes between devices, and should be used on topology diagrams.

Hostnames are configured on the active networking device. If the device name is not explicitly configured, a factory-assigned default device name is used by Cisco IOS. The default name for a Cisco IOS switch is "Switch."

Imagine if an internetwork had several switches that were all named with the default name "Switch" (as shown in the figure). This could create considerable confusion during network configuration and maintenance. When accessing a remote device using SSH, it is important to have confirmation that you are connected to the proper device. If all devices were left with their default names, it would be difficult to identify that the proper device is connected.

By choosing names wisely, it is easier to remember, discuss, document, and identify network devices. To name devices in a consistent and useful way requires the establishment of a naming convention that spans the company or, at least, the location. It is a good practice to create the naming convention at the same time as the addressing scheme to allow for continuity within an organization.

Some guidelines for naming conventions are that names should:

- Start with a letter

- Contain no spaces

- End with a letter or digit

- Use only letters, digits, and dashes

- Be less than 64 characters in length

The hostnames used in the device IOS preserve capitalization and lowercase characters. Therefore, it allows you to capitalize a name as you ordinarily would. This contrasts with most Internet naming schemes, where uppercase and lowercase characters are treated identically.

Refer to
Online Course
for Illustration

2.2.1.3   Hostnames

Hostnames allow devices to be identified by network administrators over a network or the Internet.

Applying Names Example

Let's use an example of three switches connected together in a network, spanning three different floors.

To create a naming convention for switches, take into consideration the location and the purpose of the devices.

For example, in the figure we have named the three switches as Sw-Floor-1, Sw-Floor-2, and Sw-Floor-3.

In the network documentation, we would include these names, and the reasons for choosing them, to ensure continuity in our naming convention as devices are added.

Once the naming convention has been identified, the next step is to apply the names to the devices using the CLI.

Refer to
Online Course
for Illustration

2.2.1.4   Configuring Hostnames

Configure IOS Hostname

From the privileged EXEC mode, access the global configuration mode by entering the `configure terminal` command:

```
Switch# configure terminal
```

After the command is executed, the prompt will change to:

```
Switch(config)#
```

As shown in the figure, in the global configuration mode, enter the hostname:

```
Switch(config)# hostname Sw-Floor-1
```

After the command is executed, the prompt will change to:

```
Sw-Floor-1 (config)#
```

Notice that the hostname appears in the prompt. To exit global configuration mode, use the `exit` command.

Always make sure that your documentation is updated each time a device is added or modified. Identify devices in the documentation by their location, purpose, and address.

Note   To undo the effects of a command, preface the command with the **no** keyword.

For example, to remove the name of a device, use:

```
Sw-Floor-1 (config)# no hostname
Switch(config)#
```

Notice that the **no hostname** command caused the switch to revert to the default hostname of "Switch."

In the figure, practice entering a hostname on a switch.

2.2.2 Limiting Access to Device Configurations

2.2.2.1 Securing Device Access

Physically limiting access to network devices by placing them in closets and locked racks is good practice; however, passwords are the primary defense against unauthorized access to network devices. Every device, even home routers, should have locally configured passwords to limit access. Later, we will introduce how to strengthen security by requiring a username along with a password. For now, we will present basic security precautions using only passwords.

As discussed previously, the IOS uses hierarchical modes to help with device security. As part of this security enforcement, the IOS can accept several passwords to allow different access privileges to the device.

The passwords introduced here are:

- **Enable password** - Limits access to the privileged EXEC mode
- **Enable secret** - Encrypted, limits access to the privileged EXEC mode
- **Console password** - Limits device access using the console connection
- **VTY password** - Limits device access over Telnet

As good practice, use different authentication passwords for each of these levels of access. Although logging in with multiple and different passwords is inconvenient, it is a necessary precaution to properly protect the network infrastructure from unauthorized access.

Additionally, use strong passwords that are not easily guessed. The use of weak or easily guessed passwords continues to be a security issue in many facets of the business world.

Consider these key points when choosing passwords:

- Use passwords that are more than 8 characters in length.
- Use a combination of upper and lowercase letters, numbers, special characters, and/or numeric sequences in passwords.
- Avoid using the same password for all devices.
- Avoid using common words such as password or administrator, because these are easily guessed.

Note   In most of the labs in this course, we will be using simple passwords such as **cisco** or **class**. These passwords are considered weak and easily guessable and should be avoided in a work environment. We only use these passwords for convenience in a classroom setting or to illustrate configuration examples.

Refer to
Online Course
for Illustration

2.2.2.2   Securing Privileged EXEC Access

To secure privileged EXEC access, use the **enable secret** password command. An older, less secure variation of this command is the **enable password** password command. Although either of these commands can be used to establish authentication before access to privileged EXEC (enable) mode is permitted, it is recommended to use the **enable secret** command. The **enable secret** command provides greater security because the password is encrypted.

Example command to set passwords:

```
Switch(config)# enable secret class
```

The example in the figure illustrates how a password is not requested when first using the **enable** command. Next the **enable secret class** command is configured and now privileged EXEC access is secured. Notice that for security reasons, the password is not displayed when it is being entered.

Refer to
Online Course
for Illustration

2.2.2.3   Securing User EXEC Access

The console port of network devices must be secured, at a bare minimum, by requiring the user to supply a strong password. This reduces the chance of unauthorized personnel physically plugging a cable into the device and gaining device access.

The following commands are used in global configuration mode to set a password for the console line:

```
Switch(config)# line console 0
Switch(config-line)# password cisco
Switch(config-line)# login
```

From global configuration mode, the command **line console 0** is used to enter line configuration mode for the console. The zero is used to represent the first (and in most cases only) console interface.

The second command, **password cisco** specifies a password for the console line.

The **login** command configures the switch to require authentication upon login. When login is enabled and a password set, the console user will be prompted to enter a password before gaining access to the CLI.

VTY Password

The vty lines allow access to a Cisco device via Telnet. By default, many Cisco switches support up to 16 vty lines that are numbered 0 to 15. The number of vty lines supported on a Cisco router varies with the type of router and the IOS version. However, five is the most common number of vty lines configured. These lines are numbered 0 to 4 by default, though additional lines can be configured. A password needs to be set for all available vty lines. The same password can be set for all connections. However, it is often desirable that a unique password be set for one line to provide a fall-back for administrative entry to the device if the other connections are in use.

Example commands used to set a password on vty lines:

```
Switch(config)# line vty 0 15
Switch(config-line)# password cisco
Switch(config-line)# login
```

By default, the IOS includes the `login` command on the VTY lines. This prevents Telnet access to the device without authentication. If, by mistake, the `no login` command is set, which removes the requirement for authentication, unauthorized persons could connect across the network to the line using Telnet. This would be a major security risk.

The figure illustrates the securing of the user EXEC access on the console and Telnet lines.

Refer to
Online Course
for Illustration

2.2.2.4   Encrypting Password Display

Another useful command prevents passwords from showing up as plain text when viewing the configuration files. This is the `service password-encryption` command.

This command causes the encryption of passwords to occur when a password is configured. The `service password-encryption` command applies weak encryption to all unencrypted passwords. This encryption applies only to passwords in the configuration file, not to passwords as they are sent over media. The purpose of this command is to keep unauthorized individuals from viewing passwords in the configuration file.

If you execute the `show running-config` or `show startup-config` command prior to the `service password-encryption` command being executed, the unencrypted passwords are visible in the configuration output. The service password-encryption can then be executed and the encryption will be applied to the passwords. Once the encryption has been applied, removing the encryption service does not reverse the encryption.

In the figure, practice entering the command to configure password encryption.

Refer to
Online Course
for Illustration

2.2.2.5   Banner Messages

Although requiring passwords is one way to keep unauthorized personnel out of a network, it is vital to provide a method for declaring that only authorized personnel should attempt to gain entry into the device. To do this, add a banner to the device output.

Banners can be an important part of the legal process in the event that someone is prosecuted for breaking into a device. Some legal systems do not allow prosecution, or even the monitoring of users, unless a notification is visible.

The exact content or wording of a banner depends on the local laws and corporate policies. Here are some examples of information to include in a banner:

- "Use of the device is specifically for authorized personnel."
- "Activity may be monitored."
- "Legal action will be pursued for any unauthorized use."

Because banners can be seen by anyone who attempts to log in, the message must be worded very carefully. Any wording that implies that a login is "welcome" or "invited" is not appropriate. If a person disrupts the network after gaining unauthorized entry, proving liability will be difficult if there is the appearance of an invitation.

The creation of banners is a simple process; however, banners should be used appropriately. When a banner is utilized it should never welcome someone to the device. It should detail that only authorized personnel are allowed to access the device. Further, the banner can include scheduled system shutdowns and other information that affects all network users.

The IOS provides multiple types of banners. One common banner is the message of the day (MOTD). It is often used for legal notification because it is displayed to all connected terminals.

Configure MOTD using the `banner motd` command from global configuration mode.

The `banner motd` command requires the use of delimiters to identify the content of the banner message. The `banner motd` command is followed by a space and a delimiting character. Then, one or more lines of text are entered to represent the banner message. A second occurrence of the delimiting character denotes the end of the message. The delimiting character can be any character as long as it does not occur in the message. For this reason, symbols such as the "#" are often used.

The syntax to configure a MOTD, from global configuration mode is:

```
Switch(config)# banner motd # message #
```

Once the command is executed, the banner will be displayed on all subsequent attempts to access the device until the banner is removed.

The example in the figure illustrates a banner configured with the delimiting "#" symbol. Notice how the banner is now displayed when accessing the switch.

Refer to
Online Course
for Illustration

2.2.3   Saving Configurations

2.2.3.1   Configuration Files

The running configuration file reflects the current configuration applied to a Cisco IOS device. It contains the commands used to determine how the device operates on the network, as shown in Figure 1. Modifying a running configuration affects the operation of a Cisco device immediately.

The running configuration file is stored in the working memory of the device, or random access memory (RAM). This means that the running configuration file is temporarily active while the Cisco device is running (powered on). However, if power to the device is lost or if the device is restarted, all configuration changes will be lost unless they have been saved.

After making changes to a running configuration file, consider these distinct options:

- Return the device to its original configuration.
- Remove all configurations from the device.
- Make the changed configuration the new startup configuration.

The startup configuration file reflects the configuration that will be used by the device upon reboot. The startup configuration file is stored in NVRAM. When a network device has been configured and the running configuration has been modified, it is important to save those changes to the startup configuration file. Doing so prevents changes from being lost due to power failure or a deliberate restart.

Before committing to the changes, use the appropriate **show** commands to verify the device's operation. As shown in the figure, the **show running-config** command can be used to see a running configuration file. When the changes are verified to be correct, use the **copy running-config startup-config** command at the privileged EXEC mode prompt. The command to save the running configuration to startup configuration file is:

```
Switch# copy running-config startup-config
```

After being executed, the running configuration file updates the startup configuration file.

If the changes made to the running configuration do not have the desired effect, it may become necessary to restore the device to its previous configuration. Assuming that we have not overwritten the startup configuration with the changes, we can replace the running configuration with the startup configuration. This is best done by restarting the device using the **reload** command at the privileged EXEC mode prompt.

When initiating a reload, the IOS will detect that the running config has changes that were not saved to startup configuration. A prompt will appear to ask whether to save the changes made. To discard the changes, enter **n** or **no**.

An additional prompt will appear to confirm the reload. To confirm, press Enter. Pressing any other key will abort the process.

For example:

```
Switch# reload
System configuration has been modified. Save? [yes/no]: n
Proceed with reload? [confirm]
*Apr 13 01:34:15.758: %SYS-5-RELOAD: Reload requested by console. Reload Reason:
Reload Command.
System Bootstrap, Version 12.3(8r)T8, RELEASE SOFTWARE (fc1)
Technical Support: http://www.cisco.com/techsupport
Copyright (c) 2004 by cisco Systems, Inc.
PLD version 0x10
GIO ASIC version 0x127
c1841 processor with 131072 Kbytes of main memory
Main memory is configured to 64 bit mode with parity disabled
```

If undesired changes are saved to the startup configuration, it may be necessary to clear all the configurations. This requires erasing the startup configuration and restarting the device.

The startup configuration is removed by using the **erase startup-config** command.

To erase the startup configuration file use **erase NVRAM:startup-config** or **erase startup-config** at the privileged EXEC mode prompt:

```
Switch# erase startup-config
```

After the command is issued, the switch will prompt you for confirmation:

```
Erasing the nvram filesystem will remove all configuration files! Continue? [con-
firm]
```

Confirm is the default response. To confirm and erase the startup configuration file, press Enter. Pressing any other key will abort the process.

Caution   Exercise caution when using the **erase** command. This command can be used to erase any file in the device. Improper use of the command can erase the IOS itself or another critical file.

On a switch you must also issue the `delete vlan.dat` command in addition to the `erase startup-config` command in order to return the device to its default "out-of-the-box" configuration (comparable to a factory reset):

```
Switch# delete vlan.dat
Delete filename [vlan.dat]?
Delete flash:vlan.dat? [confirm]
Switch# erase startup-config
Erasing the nvram filesystem will remove all configuration files! Continue? [confirm]
[OK]
Erase of nvram: complete
Switch#
```

After removing the startup configuration from NVRAM (and deleting the vlan.dat file in the case of a switch), reload the device to remove the current running configuration file from RAM. The device will then load the default startup configuration that was originally shipped with the device into the running configuration.

In Figure 2, practice entering commands to save the running configuration from RAM to NVRAM.

Refer to
Online Course
for Illustration

2.2.3.2   Capturing Text

Backup Configurations with Text Capture

In addition to saving running configurations to the startup configuration, configuration files can also be saved and archived to a text document. This sequence of steps ensures that a working copy of the configuration files is available for editing or reuse later.

In Figure 1, configuration files can be saved and archived to a text document using Tera Term.

The steps are:

- On the File menu, click **Log**.
- Choose the location. Tera Term will begin capturing text.
- After capture has been started, execute the `show running-config` or `show start-up-config` command at the privileged EXEC prompt. Text displayed in the terminal window will be placed into the chosen file.
- When the capture is complete, select **Close** in the Tera Term: Log window.
- View the output to verify that it was not corrupted.

Similarly, Figure 2 shows how files can be saved and archived in a text document using HyperTerminal.

Restoring Text Configurations

A configuration file can be copied from storage to a device. When copied into the terminal, the IOS executes each line of the configuration text as a command. The file will probably require editing before copying. It is advisable to change the encrypted passwords to plain text and remove the parameter, either the number 5 or 7, which specifies that the password is encrypted. Non-command text such as "--More--" and IOS messages must be removed. This process is discussed in the lab.

Further, at the CLI, the device must be set at the global configuration mode to receive the commands from the text file being copied.

When using Tera Term, the steps are:

- Edit text to remove non-commands and save.
- On the **File** menu, click **Send** file.
- Locate the file to be copied into the device and click **Open**.
- Tera Term will paste the file into the device.

The text in the file will be applied as commands in the CLI and become the running configuration on the device. This is a convenient method for manually configuring a device.

Refer to **Packet Tracer Activity** for this chapter

2.2.3.3   Packet Tracer - Configuring Initial Switch Settings

In this activity, you will perform basic switch configurations. You will secure access to the command-line interface (CLI) and console ports using encrypted and plain text passwords. You will also learn how to configure messages for users logging into the switch. These banners are also used to warn unauthorized users that access is prohibited.

Refer to **Online Course** for Illustration

2.3   Address Schemes

2.3.1   Ports and Addresses

2.3.1.1   IP Addressing of Devices

The use of IP addresses, whether IPv4 or IPv6, is the primary means of enabling devices to locate one another and establish end-to-end communication on the Internet. In fact, in any internetwork, IP addresses are essential for devices to communicate from source to destination and back.

Each end device on a network must be configured with IP addresses. Some examples of end devices are:

- Computers (work stations, laptops, file servers, web servers)
- Network printers
- VoIP phones
- Security cameras
- Smart phones
- Mobile handheld devices (such as wireless barcode scanners)

The structure of an IPv4 address is called dotted decimal notation and is represented with four decimal numbers between 0 and 255. IPv4 addresses are numbers assigned to individual devices connected to a network. They are logical in nature, in that they provide information about the location of the device.

With the IP address, a subnet mask is also necessary. A subnet mask is a special type of IPv4 address that, coupled with the IP address, determines which particular subnet of a larger network the device is a member.

IP addresses can be assigned to both physical ports and virtual interfaces on devices. A virtual interface means that there is no physical hardware on the device associated with it.

Refer to
Online Course
for Illustration

2.3.1.2   Interfaces and Ports

Network communications depend on end user device interfaces, networking device interfaces, and the cables that connect them.

Each physical interface has specifications, or standards, that define it; a cable connecting to the interface must be designed to match the physical standards of the interface. Types of network media include twisted-pair copper cables, fiber-optic cables, coaxial cables, or wireless. Different types of network media have different features and benefits. Not all network media has the same characteristics and is appropriate for the same purpose. Some of the differences between various types of media include:

- Distance the media can successfully carry a signal
- Environment in which the media is to be installed
- Amount of data and the speed at which it must be transmitted
- Cost of the media and installation

Not only does each link on the Internet require a specific network media type, but each link also requires a particular network technology. Ethernet is the most common local area network (LAN) technology used today. Ethernet ports are found on end user devices, switch devices, and other networking devices that can physically connect to the network using a cable. For a cable to connect devices using an Ethernet port, the cable must have the correct connector, an RJ-45.

Cisco IOS switches have physical ports for devices to connect to, but also have one or more switch virtual interfaces (SVIs). These are virtual interfaces, because there is no physical hardware on the device associated with it; an SVI is created in software. The virtual interface provides a means to remotely manage a switch over a network using IPv4. Each switch comes with one SVI appearing in the default configuration "out-of-the-box." The default SVI is interface VLAN1.

Refer to
Online Course
for Illustration

2.3.2   Addressing Devices

2.3.2.1   Configuring a Switch Virtual Interface

To access the switch remotely, an IP address and a subnet mask must be configured on the SVI:

- **IP address -** Together with subnet mask, uniquely identifies end device on the internetwork
- **Subnet mask -** Determines which part of a larger network is used by an IP address

For now the focus is IPv4; later you will explore IPv6.

You will learn the meaning behind all of these IP addresses soon, but for now the point is to quickly configure the switch to support remote access. The figure displays the command to enable IP connectivity to S1, using IP address 192.168.10.2:

- **interface vlan 1** - Used to navigate to the interface configuration mode from the global configuration mode

- **ip address 192.168.10.2 255.255.255.0** - Configures the IP address and subnet mask for the switch (this is just one of many possible combinations for an IP address and subnet mask)

- **no shutdown** - Administratively enables the interface to an active state

After these commands are configured, the switch has all the IP elements ready for communication over the network.

Note   The switch will still need to have one or more physical ports configured, as well as the VTY lines, to complete the configuration which enables remote management of the switch.

Practice configuring a switch virtual interface by entering commands in the figure.

Refer to **Online Course** for Illustration

2.3.2.2   Manual IP Address Configuration for End Devices

In order for an end device to communicate over the network, it must be configured with the correct IP address information. Much like a switch SVI, the end device must be configured with an IP address and subnet mask. This information is configured on the PC settings.

All of these settings must be configured on an end device in order for it to properly connect to the network. This information is configured under the PC network settings. In addition to IP address and subnet mask information, it is also possible to configure default gateway and DNS server information, as shown in the figure.

The default gateway address is the IP address of the router interface used for network traffic to exit the local network. The default gateway is an IP address that is often assigned by the network administrator and is used when traffic must be routed to another network.

The DNS server address is the IP address of the Domain Name System (DNS) server, which is used to translate IP addresses to web addresses, such as www.cisco.com. All devices on the Internet are assigned and reached via an IP address. However, it is easier for people to remember names over numbers. Therefore, websites are given names for simplicity. The DNS server is used to maintain the mapping between the IP addresses and names of various devices.

Refer to **Online Course** for Illustration

2.3.2.3   Automatic IP Address Configuration for End Devices

IP address information can be entered into the PC manually, or using Dynamic Host Configuration Protocol (DHCP). DHCP allows end devices to have IP information automatically configured.

DHCP is a technology that is used in almost every business network. The best way to understand why DHCP is so popular is by considering all the extra work that would have to take place without it.

DHCP enables automatic IPv4 address configuration for every end device in a network with DHCP enabled. Imagine the amount of time that would be consumed if every time you connected to the network you had to manually enter the IP address, the subnet mask, the default gateway, and the DNS server. Multiply that by every user and every one of their devices on the network and you see the problem.

DHCP is an example of technology at its best. One of the primary purposes of any technology is to make it easier to perform the tasks they want to do or need to do. With DHCP, the end user walks into the area served by a given network, plugs in an Ethernet cable or enables a wireless connection, and they are immediately allocated the necessary IPv4 information required to fully communicate over the network.

As shown in Figure 1, to configure DHCP on a Windows PC, you only need to select "Obtain an IP address automatically" and "Obtain DNS server address automatically". Your PC will be assigned information from an IP address pool and associated IP information set up on the DHCP server.

It is possible to display the IP configuration settings on a Windows PC by using the `ipconfig` command at the command prompt. The output will show the IP address, subnet mask, and gateway that the PC received from the DHCP server.

Practice displaying the IP address of a Windows PC by entering commands in Figure 2.

Refer to
Online Course
for Illustration

2.3.2.4   IP Address Conflicts

If a static (manual) IP address is defined for a network device, for example, a printer, and then a DHCP server is installed, duplicate IP address conflicts may occur between the network device and a PC obtaining automatic IP addressing information from the DHCP server. The conflict also may occur if you manually define a static IP address to a network device during a network failure involving the DHCP server; after the network failure resolves and the DHCP server becomes accessible over the network, the conflict arises.

To resolve such an IP addressing conflict convert the network device with the static IP address to a DHCP client; or on the DHCP server, exclude the static IP address of the end device from the DHCP scope.

The second solution requires that you have administrative privileges on the DHCP server and that you are familiar with configuring DHCP on a server.

You may also encounter IP addressing conflicts when manually configuring IP on an end device in a network that only uses static IP addresses. In this case you must determine which IP addresses are available on the particular IP subnet and configure accordingly. This case illustrates why it is so important for a network administrator to maintain detailed documentation, including IP address assignments, for end devices.

Note   Usually static IP addresses are used with servers and printers in a small- to medium-sized business network, while employee devices use DHCP-allocated IP address information.

Refer to **Packet Tracer Activity** for this chapter

2.3.2.5   Packet Tracer - Implementing Basic Connectivity

In this activity, you will first perform basic switch configurations. Then you will implement basic connectivity by configuring IP addressing on switches and PCs. When the IP addressing configuration is complete, you will use various `show` commands to verify configurations and use the `ping` command to verify basic connectivity between devices.

Refer to
Online Course
for Illustration

2.3.3 Verifying Connectivity

2.3.3.1 Test the Loopback Address on an End Device

Testing the Loopback

The figure shows the first step in the testing sequence. The `ping` command is used to verify the internal IP configuration on a local host. This test is accomplished by using the `ping` command on a reserved address called the loopback (127.0.0.1). The loopback address, 127.0.0.1, is defined by the TCP/IP protocol as a reserved address that routes packets back to the host.

Ping commands are entered into a command line on the local host using the syntax:

```
C:\> ping 127.0.0.1
```

The reply from this command would look something like this:

```
Reply from 127.0.0.1: bytes=32 time<1ms TTL=128
Reply from 127.0.0.1: bytes=32 time<1ms TTL=128
Reply from 127.0.0.1: bytes=32 time<1ms TTL=128
Reply from 127.0.0.1: bytes=32 time<1ms TTL=128
Ping statistics for 127.0.0.1:
Packets: Sent = 4, Received = 4, Lost = 0 (0% loss),
Approximate round trip times in milli-seconds:
Minimum = 0ms, Maximum = 0ms, Average = 0ms
```

The result indicates that four test packets of 32 bytes each were sent and returned from host 127.0.0.1 in a time of less than 1 ms. This successful ping request verifies that the network interface card, drivers, and the TCP/IP implementation are all functioning correctly.

Practice testing a loopback address by entering commands in Figure 2.

Refer to
Online Course
for Illustration

2.3.3.2 Testing the Interface Assignment

In the same way that you use commands and utilities to verify a host configuration, you use commands to verify the interfaces of intermediary devices. The IOS provides commands to verify the operation of router and switch interfaces.

Verifying the Switch Interfaces

Examining S1 and S2, you use the `show ip interface brief` command to verify the condition of the switch interfaces, as shown in the figure. The IP address assigned to VLAN 1 interface on S1 is 192.168.10.2. The IP address assigned to VLAN 1 interface on S2 is 192.168.10.3. The physical interfaces F0/1 and F0/2 on S1 are operational, as are the physical interfaces F0/1 and F0/2 on S2.

Practice verification of a VLAN interface by entering commands in the figure.

Refer to
Online Course
for Illustration

2.3.3.3 Testing End-to-End Connectivity

Testing PC-to-Switch Connectivity

The `ping` command can be used on a PC, just as on a Cisco IOS device. The figure shows that a ping from PC1 to the IP address of the S1 VLAN 1 interface, 192.168.10.2, should be successful.

Testing End-to-End Connectivity

The IP address of PC1 is 192.168.10.10, with subnet mask 255.255.255.0, and default gateway 192.168.10.1.

The IP address of PC2 is 192.168.10.11, with subnet mask 255.255.255.0, and default gateway 192.168.10.1.

A ping from PC1 to PC2 should also be successful. A successful ping from PC1 to PC2 verifies end-to-end connectivity in the network!

Refer to
Lab Activity
for this chapter

2.3.3.4   Lab - Building a Simple Network

In this lab, you will complete the following objectives:

- Part 1: Set Up the Network Topology (Ethernet only)
- Part 2: Configure PC Hosts
- Part 3: Configure and Verify Basic Switch Settings

Refer to
Lab Activity
for this chapter

2.3.3.5   Lab - Configuring a Switch Management Address

In this lab, you will complete the following objectives:

- Part 1: Configure a Basic Network Device
- Part 2: Verify and Test Network Connectivity

2.4   Summary

Refer to
Lab Activity
for this chapter

2.4.1.1   Class Activity - Tutor Me

Tutor me

Students will work in pairs. Packet Tracer is required for this activity.

Assume that a new colleague has asked you for an orientation to the Cisco IOS CLI. This colleague has never worked with Cisco devices before.

You explain the basic CLI commands and structure, because you want your colleague to understand that the CLI is a simple, yet powerful, command language that can be easily understood and navigated.

Use Packet Tracer and one of the activities available in this chapter as a simple network model (for example, Lab Activity 2.3.3.5 LAB – Configuring a Switch Management Address).

Focus on these areas:

- While the commands are technical, do they resemble any statements from plain English?

- How is the set of commands organized into subgroups or modes? How does an administrator know which mode he or she is currently using?

- What are the individual commands to configure the basic settings of a Cisco device? How would you explain this command in simple terms? Use parallels to real life whenever appropriate.

Suggest how to group different commands together according to their modes so that a minimum number of moves between modes will be needed.

Refer to **Packet Tracer Activity** for this chapter

2.4.1.2   Packet Tracer - Skills Integration Challenge

As a recently hired LAN technician, your network manager has asked you to demonstrate your ability to configure a small LAN. Your tasks include configuring initial settings on two switches using the Cisco IOS and configuring IP address parameters on host devices to provide end-to-end connectivity. You are to use two switches and two hosts/PCs on a cabled and powered network.

Refer to **Online Course** for Illustration

2.4.1.3   Summary

Cisco IOS is a term that encompasses a number of different operating systems, which runs on various networking devices. The technician can enter commands to configure, or program, the device to perform various networking functions. Cisco IOS routers and switches perform functions that network professionals depend upon to make their networks operate as expected.

The services provided by the Cisco IOS are generally accessed using a command-line interface (CLI), which is accessed by either the console port, the AUX port, or through telnet or SSH. Once connected to the CLI, network technicians can make configuration changes to Cisco IOS devices. The Cisco IOS is designed as a modal operating system, which means a network technician must navigate through various hierarchical modes of the IOS. Each mode supports different IOS commands.

The Cisco IOS Command Reference is a collection of online documents that describe in detail the IOS commands used on Cisco devices, such as Cisco IOS routers and switches.

Cisco IOS routers and switches support a similar modal operating system, support similar command structures, and support many of the same commands. In addition, both devices have identical initial configuration steps when implementing them in a network.

This chapter introduced the Cisco IOS. It detailed the various modes of the Cisco IOS and examined the basic command structure that is used to configure it. It also walked through the initial settings of a Cisco IOS switch device, include setting a name, limiting access to the device configuration, configuring banner messages, and saving the configuration.

The next chapter explores how packets are moved across the network infrastructure and introduce you to the rules of packet communication.

Go to the online course to take the quiz and exam.

Chapter 2 Quiz

This quiz is designed to provide an additional opportunity to practice the skills and knowledge presented in the chapter and to prepare for the chapter exam. You will be allowed multiple attempts and the grade does not appear in the gradebook.

Chapter 2 Exam

The chapter exam assesses your knowledge of the chapter content.

Your Chapter Notes

Network Protocols and Communications

3.0   Network Protocols and Communications

3.0.1.1   Introduction

More and more, it is networks that connect us. People communicate online from everywhere. Conversations in classrooms spill into instant message chat sessions, and online debates continue at school. New services are being developed daily to take advantage of the network.

Rather than developing unique and separate systems for the delivery of each new service, the network industry as a whole has adopted a developmental framework that allows designers to understand current network platforms, and maintain them. At the same time, this framework is used to facilitate the development of new technologies to support future communications needs and technology enhancements.

Central to this developmental framework, is the use of generally-accepted models that describe network rules and functions.

Within this chapter, you will learn about these models, as well as the standards that make networks work, and how communication occurs over a network.

Refer to **Lab Activity** for this chapter

3.0.1.2   Class Activity - Designing a Communications System

Let's just talk about this...

You have just purchased a new automobile for your personal use. After driving the car for a week or so, you find that it is not working correctly.

After discussing the problem with several of your peers, you decide to take it to an automotive repair facility that they highly recommend. It is the only repair facility located in close proximity to you.

When you arrive at the repair facility, you find that all of the mechanics speak another language. You are having difficulty explaining the automobile's performance problems, but the repairs really need to be done. You are not sure you can drive it back home to research other options.

You must find a way to work with the repair facility to ensure that your automobile is fixed correctly.

How will you communicate with the mechanics in this firm? Design a communications model to ensure that the car is properly repaired.

Refer to
Online Course
for Illustration

3.1   Rules of Communication

3.1.1   The Rules

3.1.1.1   What is Communication?

A network can be as complex as devices connected across the Internet, or as simple as two computers directly connected to one another with a single cable, and anything in-between. Networks can vary in size, shape, and function. However, simply having the physical connection between end devices is not enough to enable communication. For communication to occur, devices must know "how" to communicate.

People exchange ideas using many different communication methods. However, regardless of the method chosen, all communication methods have three elements in common. The first of these elements is the message source, or sender. Message sources are people, or electronic devices, that need to send a message to other individuals or devices. The second element of communication is the destination, or receiver, of the message. The destination receives the message and interprets it. A third element, called a channel, consists of the media that provides the pathway over which the message travels from source to destination.

Communication begins with a message, or information, that must be sent from a source to a destination. The sending of this message, whether by face-to-face communication or over a network, is governed by rules called protocols. These protocols are specific to the type of communication method occurring. In our day-to-day personal communication, the rules we use to communicate over one medium, like a telephone call, are not necessarily the same as the protocols for using another medium, such as sending a letter.

For example, consider two people communicating face-to-face, as shown in Figure 1. Prior to communicating, they must agree on how to communicate. If the communication is using voice, they must first agree on the language. Next, when they have a message to share, they must be able to format that message in a way that is understandable. For example, if someone uses the English language, but poor sentence structure, the message can easily be misunderstood. Each of these tasks describes protocols put in place to accomplish communication. This is true of computer communication, as shown in Figure 2.

Think of how many different rules or protocols govern all the different methods of communication that exist in the world today.

Refer to
Online Course
for Illustration

3.1.1.2   Establishing the Rules

Establishing the Rules

Before communicating with one another, individuals must use established rules or agreements to govern the conversation. For example, consider Figure1, protocols are necessary for effective communication. The protocols used are specific to the characteristics of the communication method, including the characteristics of the source, destination and channel. These rules, or protocols, must be followed in order for the message to be successfully delivered and understood. There are many protocols available that govern successful human communication. Once there is an agreed upon method of communicating (face-to-face, telephone, letter, photography), the protocols put in place must account for the following requirements:

- An identified sender and receiver
- Common language and grammar
- Speed and timing of delivery
- Confirmation or acknowledgement requirements

The protocols that are used in network communications share many of the fundamental traits as those protocols used to govern successful human conversations, see Figure 2. In addition to identifying the source and destination, computer and network protocols define the details of how a message is transmitted across a network to answer the above requirements. While there are many protocols that must interact, common computer protocols include:

- Message encoding
- Message formatting and encapsulation
- Message size
- Message timing
- Message delivery options

Each of these will be discussed in more detail next.

Refer to
Online Course
for Illustration

3.1.1.3   Message Encoding

Message Encoding

One of the first steps to sending a message is encoding it. Encoding is the process of converting information into another, acceptable form, for transmission. Decoding reverses this process in order to interpret the information.

Imagine a person planning a holiday trip with a friend, and calling the friend to discuss the details of where they want to go, as shown in Figure 1. To communicate the message, the sender must first convert, or encode, their thoughts and perceptions about the location into words. The words are spoken into the telephone using the sounds and inflections of spoken language that convey the message. On the other end of the telephone line, the person listening to the description, receives and decodes the sounds in order to visualize the image of the sunset described by the sender.

Encoding also occurs in computer communication, as shown in Figure 2. Encoding between hosts must be in an appropriate form for the medium. Messages sent across the network are first converted into bits by the sending host. Each bit is encoded into a pattern of sounds, light waves, or electrical impulses depending on the network media over which the bits are transmitted. The destination host receives and decodes the signals in order to interpret the message.

Refer to
Online Course
for Illustration

3.1.1.4   Message Formatting and Encapsulation

Message Formatting and Encapsulation

When a message is sent from source to destination, it must use a specific format or structure. Message formats depend on the type of message and the channel that is used to deliver the message.

Letter writing is one of the most common forms of written human communication. For centuries, the agreed format for personal letters has not changed. In many cultures, a personal letter contains the following elements:

- An identifier of the recipient
- A salutation or greeting
- The message content
- A closing phrase
- An identifier of the sender

In addition to having the correct format, most personal letters must also be enclosed, or encapsulated, in an envelope for delivery, as shown in Figure 1. The envelope has the address of the sender and receiver on it, each located at the proper place on the envelope. If the destination address and formatting are not correct, the letter is not delivered. The process of placing one message format (the letter) inside another message format (the envelope) is called encapsulation. De-encapsulation occurs when the process is reversed by the recipient and the letter is removed from the envelope.

A letter writer uses an accepted format to ensure that the letter is delivered and understood by the recipient. In the same way, a message that is sent over a computer network follows specific format rules for it to be delivered and processed. Just as a letter is encapsulated in an envelope for delivery, so too are computer messages encapsulated. Each computer message is encapsulated in a specific format, called a frame, before it is sent over the network. A frame acts like an envelope; it provides the address of the intended destination and the address of the source host, as shown in Figure 2.

The format and contents of a frame are determined by the type of message being sent and the channel over which it is communicated. Messages that are not correctly formatted are not successfully delivered to or processed by the destination host.

3.1.1.5   Message Size

Message Size

Another rule of communication is size. When people communicate with each other, the messages that they send are usually broken into smaller parts or sentences. These sentences are limited in size to what the receiving person can process at one time, as shown in Figure 1. An individual conversation may be made up of many smaller sentences to ensure that each part of the message is received and understood. Imagine what it would be like to read this course if it all appeared as one long sentence; it would not be easy to read and comprehend.

Likewise, when a long message is sent from one host to another over a network, it is necessary to break the message into smaller pieces, as shown in Figure 2. The rules that govern the size of the pieces, or frames, communicated across the network are very strict. They can also be different, depending on the channel used. Frames that are too long or too short are not delivered.

The size restrictions of frames require the source host to break a long message into individual pieces that meet both the minimum and maximum size requirements. This is known as segmenting. Each segment is encapsulated in a separate frame with the address information, and is sent over the network. At the receiving host, the messages are de-encapsulated and put back together to be processed and interpreted.

Refer to **Online Course** for Illustration

3.1.1.6 Message Timing

Message Timing

Another factor that affects how well a message is received and understood is timing. People use timing to determine when to speak, how fast or slow to talk, and how long to wait for a response. These are the rules of engagement.

Access Method

Access method determines when someone is able to send a message. These timing rules are based on the environment. For example, you may be able to speak whenever you have something to say. In this environment, a person must wait until no one else is talking before speaking. If two people talk at the same time, a collision of information occurs and it is necessary for the two to back off and start again, as shown in Figure 1. Likewise, it is necessary for computers to define an access method. Hosts on a network need an access method to know when to begin sending messages and how to respond when errors occur.

Flow Control

Timing also affects how much information can be sent and the speed that it can be delivered. If one person speaks too quickly, it is difficult for the other person to hear and understand the message, as shown in Figure 2. The receiving person must ask the sender to slow down. In network communication, a sending host can transmit messages at a faster rate than the destination host can receive and process. Source and destination hosts use flow control to negotiate correct timing for successful communication.

Response Timeout

If a person asks a question and does not hear a response within an acceptable amount of time, the person assumes that no answer is coming and reacts accordingly, as show in Figure 3. The person may repeat the question, or may go on with the conversation. Hosts on the network also have rules that specify how long to wait for responses and what action to take if a response timeout occurs.

Refer to **Online Course** for Illustration

3.1.1.7 Message Delivery Options

Message Delivery Options

A message may need to be best delivered in different ways, as shown in Figure 1. Sometimes, a person wants to communicate information to a single individual. At other times, the person may need to send information to a group of people at the same time, or even to all people in the same area. A conversation between two people is an example of a one-to-one delivery. When a group of recipients need to receive the same message simultaneously, a one-to-many or one-to-all message delivery is necessary.

There are also times when the sender of a message needs to be sure that the message is delivered successfully to the destination. In these cases, it is necessary for the recipient to return an acknowledgement to the sender. If no acknowledgement is required, the delivery option is referred to as unacknowledged.

Hosts on a network use similar delivery options to communicate, as shown in Figure 2.

A one-to-one delivery option is referred to as a unicast, meaning that there is only a single destination for the message.

When a host needs to send messages using a one-to-many delivery option, it is referred to as a multicast. Multicasting is the delivery of the same message to a group of host destinations simultaneously.

If all hosts on the network need to receive the message at the same time, a broadcast is used. Broadcasting represents a one-to-all message delivery option. Additionally, hosts have requirements for acknowledged versus unacknowledged messages.

Refer to **Online Course** for Illustration

3.2 Network Protocols and Standards

3.2.1 Protocols

3.2.1.1 Protocols: Rules that Govern Communications

Just like in human communication, the various network and computer protocols must be able to interact and work together for network communication to be successful. A group of inter-related protocols necessary to perform a communication function is called a protocol suite. Protocol suites are implemented by hosts and networking devices in software, hardware or both.

One of the best ways to visualize how the protocols within a suite interact is to view the interaction as a stack. A protocol stack shows how the individual protocols within a suite are implemented. The protocols are viewed in terms of layers, with each higher level service depending on the functionality defined by the protocols shown in the lower levels. The lower layers of the stack are concerned with moving data over the network and providing services to the upper layers, which are focused on the content of the message being sent. As the figure shows, we can use layers to describe the activity occurring in our face-to-face communication example. At the bottom layer, the physical layer, we have two people, each with a voice that can say words out loud. At the second layer, the rules layer, we have an agreement to speak in a common language. At the top layer, the content layer, there are words that are actually spoken. This is the content of the communication.

Were we to witness this conversation, we would not actually see layers floating in space. The use of layers is a model that provides a way to conveniently break a complex task into parts and describe how they work.

Refer to **Online Course** for Illustration

3.2.1.2 Network Protocols

At the human level, some communication rules are formal and others are simply understood based on custom and practice. For devices to successfully communicate, a network protocol suite must describe precise requirements and interactions. Networking protocols define a common format and set of rules for exchanging messages between devices. Some common networking protocols are IP, HTTP, and DHCP.

The figures illustrate networking protocols that describe the following processes:

- How the message is formatted or structured, as shown in Figure 1

- The process by which networking devices share information about pathways with other networks, as shown in Figure 2

- How and when error and system messages are passed between devices, as shown in Figure 3

- The setup and termination of data transfer sessions, as shown in Figure 4

For example, IP defines how a packet of data is delivered within a network or to a remote network. The information in the IPv4 protocol is transmitted in a specific format so that the receiver can interpret it correctly. This is not much different than the protocol used to address an envelope when mailing a letter. The information must adhere to a certain format or the letter cannot be delivered to the destination by the post office.

Refer to
Online Course
for Illustration

3.2.1.3   Interaction of Protocols

An example of using the protocol suite in network communications is the interaction between a web server and a web client. This interaction uses a number of protocols and standards in the process of exchanging information between them. The different protocols work together to ensure that the messages are received and understood by both parties. Examples of these protocols are:

- **Application Protocol** - Hypertext Transfer Protocol (HTTP) is a protocol that governs the way a web server and a web client interact. HTTP defines the content and formatting of the requests and responses that are exchanged between the client and server. Both the client and the web server software implement HTTP as part of the application. HTTP relies on other protocols to govern how the messages are transported between the client and server.

- **Transport Protocol** - Transmission Control Protocol (TCP) is the transport protocol that manages the individual conversations between web servers and web clients. TCP divides the HTTP messages into smaller pieces, called segments. These segments are sent between the web server and client processes running at the destination host. TCP is also responsible for controlling the size and rate at which messages are exchanged between the server and the client.

- **Internet Protocol** - IP is responsible for taking the formatted segments from TCP, encapsulating them into packets, assigning them the appropriate addresses, and delivering them across the best path to the destination host.

- **Network Access Protocols** - Network access protocols describe two primary functions, communication over a data link and the physical transmission of data on the network media. Data-link management protocols take the packets from IP and format them to be transmitted over the media. The standards and protocols for the physical media govern how the signals are sent and how they are interpreted by the receiving clients. An example of a network access protocol is Ethernet.

Refer to **Online Course** for Illustration

3.2.2 Protocol Suites

3.2.2.1 Protocol Suites and Industry Standards

As stated previously, a protocol suite is a set of protocols that work together to provide comprehensive network communication services. A protocol suite may be specified by a standards organization or developed by a vendor.

The protocols IP, HTTP, and DHCP are all part of the Internet protocol suite known as Transmission Control Protocol/IP (TCP/IP). The TCP/IP protocol suite is an open standard, meaning these protocols are freely available to the public, and any vendor is able to implement these protocols on their hardware or in their software.

A standards-based protocol is a process or protocol that has been endorsed by the networking industry and ratified, or approved, by a standards organization. The use of standards in developing and implementing protocols ensures that products from different manufacturers can interoperate successfully. If a protocol is not rigidly observed by a particular manufacturer, their equipment or software may not be able to successfully communicate with products made by other manufacturers.

In data communications, for example, if one end of a conversation is using a protocol to govern one-way communication and the other end is assuming a protocol describing two-way communication, in all probability, no data will be exchanged.

Some protocols are proprietary. Proprietary, in this context, means that one company or vendor controls the definition of the protocol and how it functions. Some proprietary protocols can be used by different organizations with permission from the owner. Others can only be implemented on equipment manufactured by the proprietary vendor. Examples of proprietary protocols are AppleTalk and Novell Netware.

Several companies may even work together to create a proprietary protocol. It is not uncommon for a vendor (or group of vendors) to develop a proprietary protocol to meet the needs of its customers and later assist in making that proprietary protocol an open standard. For example, Ethernet was a protocol originally developed by Bob Metcalfe at the XEROX Palo Alto Research Center (PARC) in the 1970s. In 1979, Bob Metcalfe formed his own company, 3COM, and worked with Digital Equipment Corporation (DEC), Intel, and Xerox to promote the "DIX" standard for Ethernet. In 1985, the Institute of Electrical and Electronics Engineers (IEEE) published the IEEE 802.3 standard that was almost identical to Ethernet. Today, 802.3 is the common standard used on local-area networks (LANs). Another example, most recently, Cisco opened the EIGRP routing protocol as an informational RFC to meet the needs of customers who desire to use the protocol in a multivendor network.

Refer to **Online Course** for Illustration

3.2.2.2 Creation of the Internet and Development of TCP/IP

The IP suite is a suite of protocols required for transmitting and receiving information using the Internet. It is commonly known as TCP/IP because the first two networking protocols defined for this standard were TCP and IP. The open standards-based TCP/IP has replaced other vendor proprietary protocol suites, such as Apple's AppleTalk and Novell's Internetwork Packet Exchange/Sequenced Packet Exchange (IPX/SPX).

The first packet switching network and predecessor to today's Internet was the Advanced Research Projects Agency Network (ARPANET), which came to life in 1969 by connecting mainframe computers at four locations. ARPANET was funded by the U.S. Department of Defense for use by universities and research laboratories. Bolt, Beranek and Newman (BBN) was the contractor that did much of the initial development of the ARPANET, including creating the first router known as an Interface Message Processor (IMP).

In 1973, Robert Kahn and Vinton Cerf began work on TCP to develop the next generation of the ARPANET. TCP was designed to replace ARPANET's current Network Control Program (NCP). In 1978, TCP was divided into two protocols: TCP and IP. Later, other protocols were added to the TCP/IP suite of protocols including Telnet, FTP, DNS, and many others.

Click through the timeline in the figure to see details about the development of other network protocols and applications.

Refer to
Online Course
for Illustration

3.2.2.3   TCP/IP Protocol Suite and Communication Process

Today, the suite includes dozens of protocols, as shown in Figure 1. Click each protocol to view its description. They are organized in layers using the TCP/IP protocol model. TCP/IP protocols are included in the internet layer to the application layer when referencing the TCP/IP model. The lower layer protocols in the data link or network access layer are responsible for delivering the IP packet over the physical medium. These lower layer protocols are developed by standards organizations, such as IEEE.

The TCP/IP protocol suite is implemented as a TCP/IP stack on both the sending and receiving hosts to provide end-to-end delivery of applications over a network. The 802.3 or Ethernet protocols are used to transmit the IP packet over the physical medium used by the LAN.

Figures 2 and 3 demonstrate the complete communication process using an example of a web server transmitting data to a client.

Click the Play button to view the animated demonstrations:

1. The web server's Hypertext Markup Language (HTML) page is the data to be sent.

2. The application protocol HTTP header is added to the front of the HTML data. The header contains various information, including the HTTP version the server is using and a status code indicating it has information for the web client.

3. The HTTP application layer protocol delivers the HTML-formatted web page data to the transport layer. The TCP transport layer protocol is used to manage the individual conversation between the web server and web client.

4. Next, the IP information is added to the front of the TCP information. IP assigns the appropriate source and destination IP addresses. This information is known as an IP packet.

5. The Ethernet protocol adds information to both ends of the IP packet, known as a data link frame. This frame is delivered to the nearest router along the path towards the web client. This router removes the Ethernet information, analyzes the IP packet, determines the best path for the packet, inserts the packet into a new frame, and sends it to the next neighboring router towards the destination. Each router removes and adds new data link information before forwarding the packet.

6. This data is now transported through the internetwork, which consists of media and intermediary devices.

7. The client receives the data link frames that contain the data and each protocol header is processed and then removed in the opposite order that it was added. The Ethernet information is processed and removed, followed by the IP protocol information, then the TCP information, and finally the HTTP information.

8. The web page information is then passed on to the client's web browser software.

Refer to
Interactive Graphic
in online course.

3.2.2.4   Activity – Mapping the Protocols of the TCP/IP Suite

Refer to
Online Course
for Illustration

3.2.3   Standards Organizations

3.2.3.1   Open Standards

Open standards encourage competition and innovation. They also guarantee that no single company's product can monopolize the market, or have an unfair advantage over its competition. A good example of this is when purchasing a wireless router for the home. There are many different choices available from a variety of vendors, all of which incorporate standard protocols such as IPv4, DHCP, 802.3 (Ethernet), and 802.11 (Wireless LAN). These open standards also allow a client running Apple's OS X operating system to download a web page from a web server running the Linux operating system. This is because both operating systems implement the open standard protocols, such as those in the TCP/IP suite.

Standards organizations are important in maintaining an open Internet with freely accessible specifications and protocols that can be implemented by any vendor. A standards organization may draft a set of rules entirely on its own or in other cases may select a proprietary protocol as the basis for the standard. If a proprietary protocol is used, it usually involves the vendor who created the protocol.

Standards organizations are usually vendor-neutral, non-profit organizations established to develop and promote the concept of open standards.

Standards organizations include:

- The Internet Society (ISOC)
- The Internet Architecture Board (IAB)
- The Internet Engineering Task Force (IETF)
- The Institute of Electrical and Electronics Engineers (IEEE)
- The International Organization for Standardization (ISO)

Each of these organizations will be discussed in more detail in the next couple of pages.

In the figure, click each logo to view standards information.

Refer to
Online Course
for Illustration

3.2.3.2   ISOC, IAB, and IETF

The Internet Society (ISOC) is responsible for promoting open development, evolution, and Internet use throughout the world. ISOC facilitates the open development of standards and protocols for the technical infrastructure of the Internet, including the oversight of the Internet Architecture Board (IAB).

The Internet Architecture Board (IAB) is responsible for the overall management and development of Internet standards. The IAB provides oversight of the architecture for protocols and procedures used by the Internet. The IAB consists of 13 members, including the chair of the Internet Engineering Task Force (IETF). IAB members serve as individuals and not representatives of any company, agency, or other organization.

The IETF's mission is to develop, update, and maintain Internet and TCP/IP technologies. One of the key responsibilities of the IETF is to produce Request for Comments (RFC) documents, which are a memorandum describing protocols, processes, and technologies for the Internet. The IETF consists of working groups (WGs), the primary mechanism for developing IETF specifications and guidelines. WGs are short term, and after the objectives of the group are met, the WG is terminated. The Internet Engineering Steering Group (IESG) is responsible for the technical management of the IETF and the Internet standards process.

The Internet Research Task Force (IRTF) is focused on long-term research related to Internet and TCP/IP protocols, applications, architecture, and technologies. While the IETF focuses on shorter-term issues of creating standards, the IRTF consists of research groups for long-term development efforts. Some of the current research groups include Anti-Spam Research Group (ASRG), Crypto Forum Research Group (CFRG), Peer-to-Peer Research Group (P2PRG), and Router Research Group (RRG).

3.2.3.3 IEEE

Refer to **Online Course** for Illustration

The Institute of Electrical and Electronics Engineers (IEEE, pronounced "I-triple-E") is a professional organization for those in the electrical engineering and electronics fields who are dedicated to advancing technological innovation and creating standards. As of 2012, IEEE consists of 38 societies, publishes 130 journals, and sponsors more than 1,300 conferences each year worldwide. The IEEE has over 1,300 standards and projects currently under development.

IEEE has more than 400,000 members in more than 160 countries. More than 107,000 of those members are student members. IEEE provides educational and career enhancement opportunities to promote the skills and knowledge with the electronics industry.

IEEE is one of the leading standard producing organizations in the world. It creates and maintains standards affecting a wide range of industries including power and energy, healthcare, telecommunications, and networking. The IEEE 802 family of standards deals with local area networks and metropolitan area networks, including both wired and wireless. As shown in the figure, each IEEE standard consists of a WG responsible for creating and improving the standards.

The IEEE 802.3 and IEEE 802.11 standards are significant IEEE standards in computer networking. The IEEE 802.3 standard defines Media Access Control (MAC) for wired Ethernet. This technology is usually for LANs, but also has wide-area network (WAN) applications. The 802.11 standard defines a set of standards for implementing wireless local-area networks (WLANs). This standard defines the Open Systems Interconnection (OSI) physical and data link MAC for wireless communications.

3.2.3.4 ISO

Refer to **Online Course** for Illustration

ISO, the International Organization for Standardization, is the world's largest developer of international standards for a wide variety of products and services. ISO is not an acronym for the organization's name; rather the ISO term is based on the Greek word "isos", meaning equal. The International Organization for Standardization chose the ISO term to affirm its position as being equal to all countries.

In networking, ISO is best known for its Open Systems Interconnection (OSI) reference model. ISO published the OSI reference model in 1984 to develop a layered framework for networking protocols. The original objective of this project was not only to create a reference model but also to serve as a foundation for a suite of protocols to be used for the Internet. This was known as the OSI protocol suite. However, due to the rising popularity of the TCP/IP suite, developed by Robert Kahn, Vinton Cerf, and others, the OSI protocol suite was not chosen as the protocol suite for the Internet. Instead, the TCP/IP protocol suite was selected. The OSI protocol suite was implemented on telecommunications equipment and can still be found in legacy telecommunication networks.

You may be familiar with some of the products that use ISO standards. The ISO file extension is used on many CD images to signify that it uses the ISO 9660 standard for its file system. ISO is also responsible for creating standards for routing protocols.

3.2.3.5   Other Standards Organizations

Refer to **Online Course** for Illustration

Networking standards involve several other standards organizations. Some of the more common ones are:

- **EIA** - The Electronic Industries Alliance (EIA), previously known as the Electronics Industries Association, is an international standards and trade organization for electronics organizations. The EIA is best known for its standards related to electrical wiring, connectors, and the 19-inch racks used to mount networking equipment.

- **TIA** - The Telecommunications Industry Association (TIA) is responsible for developing communication standards in a variety of areas including radio equipment, cellular towers, Voice over IP (VoIP) devices, satellite communications, and more. Many of their standards are produced in collaboration with the EIA.

- **ITU-T** - The International Telecommunications Union-Telecommunication Standardization Sector (ITU-T) is one of the largest and oldest communication standard organizations. The ITU-T defines standards for video compression, Internet Protocol Television (IPTV), and broadband communications, such as a digital subscriber line (DSL). For example, when dialing another country, ITU country codes are used to make the connection.

- **ICANN** - The Internet Corporation for Assigned Names and Numbers (ICANN) is a non-profit organization based in the United States that coordinates IP address allocation, the management of domain names used by DNS, and the protocol identifiers or port numbers used by TCP and UDP protocols. ICANN creates policies and has overall responsibility for these assignments.

- **IANA** - The Internet Assigned Numbers Authority (IANA) is a department of ICANN responsible for overseeing and managing IP address allocation, domain name management, and protocol identifiers for ICANN.

Familiarization with the organizations that develop standards used in networking will help you have a better understanding of how these standards create an open, vendor-neutral Internet, and allow you to learn about new standards as they develop.

Refer to
Lab Activity
for this chapter

3.2.3.6   Lab - Researching Networking Standards

In this lab, you will complete the following objectives:

- Part 1: Research Networking Standards Organizations
- Part 2: Reflect on Internet and Computer Networking Experiences

Refer to
Interactive Graphic
in online course.

3.2.3.7   Activity - Standards Body Scavenger Hunt

Refer to
Online Course
for Illustration

3.2.4   Reference Models

3.2.4.1   The Benefits of Using a Layered Model

A layered model, such as the TCP/IP model, is often used to help visualize the interaction between various protocols. A layered model depicts the operation of the protocols occurring within each layer, as well as the interaction of protocols with the layers above and below each layer.

There are benefits to using a layered model to describe network protocols and operations. Using a layered model:

- Assists in protocol design, because protocols that operate at a specific layer have defined information that they act upon and a defined interface to the layers above and below.

- Fosters competition because products from different vendors can work together.

- Prevents technology or capability changes in one layer from affecting other layers above and below.

- Provides a common language to describe networking functions and capabilities.

There are two basic types of networking models:

- **Protocol model** - This model closely matches the structure of a particular protocol suite. The hierarchical set of related protocols in a suite typically represents all the functionality required to interface the human network with the data network. The TCP/IP model is a protocol model, because it describes the functions that occur at each layer of protocols within the TCP/IP suite.

- **Reference model** - This model provides consistency within all types of network protocols and services by describing what has to be done at a particular layer, but not prescribing how it should be accomplished. A reference model is not intended to be an implementation specification or to provide a sufficient level of detail to define precisely the services of the network architecture. The primary purpose of a reference model is to aid in clearer understanding of the functions and processes involved.

The OSI model is the most widely known internetwork reference model. It is used for data network design, operation specifications, and troubleshooting.

As shown in the figure, the TCP/IP and OSI models are the primary models used when discussing network functionality. Designers of network protocols, services, or devices can create their own models to represent their products. Ultimately, designers are required to communicate to the industry by relating their product or service to either the OSI model or the TCP/IP model, or to both.

Refer to **Online Course** for Illustration

3.2.4.2   The OSI Reference Model

Initially the OSI model was designed by the ISO to provide a framework on which to build a suite of open systems protocols. The vision was that this set of protocols would be used to develop an international network that would not be dependent on proprietary systems.

Ultimately, the speed at which the TCP/IP-based Internet was adopted, and the rate at which it expanded, caused the development and acceptance of the OSI protocol suite to lag behind. Although a few of the developed protocols using the OSI specifications are widely used today, the seven-layer OSI model has made major contributions to the development of other protocols and products for all types of new networks.

The OSI model provides an extensive list of functions and services that can occur at each layer. It also describes the interaction of each layer with the layers directly above and below it. Although the content of this course is structured around the OSI reference model, the focus of discussion is the protocols identified in the TCP/IP protocol model. Click each layer name to view the details.

Note   Whereas the TCP/IP model layers are referred to only by name, the seven OSI model layers are more often referred to by number rather than by name. For instance, the physical layer is referred to as Layer 1 of the OSI model.

3.2.4.3   The TCP/IP Protocol Model

The TCP/IP protocol model for internetwork communications was created in the early 1970s and is sometimes referred to as the Internet model. As shown in the figure, it defines four categories of functions that must occur for communications to be successful. The architecture of the TCP/IP protocol suite follows the structure of this model. Because of this, the Internet model is commonly referred to as the TCP/IP model.

Most protocol models describe a vendor-specific protocol stack. However, because the TCP/IP model is an open standard, one company does not control the definition of the model. The definitions of the standard and the TCP/IP protocols are discussed in a public forum and defined in a publicly available set of RFCs. The RFCs contain both the formal specification of data communications protocols and resources that describe the use of the protocols.

The RFCs also contain technical and organizational documents about the Internet, including the technical specifications and policy documents produced by the IETF.

Refer to **Online Course** for Illustration

3.2.4.4   Comparing the OSI Model with the TCP/IP Model

The protocols that make up the TCP/IP protocol suite can be described in terms of the OSI reference model. In the OSI model, the network access layer and the application layer of the TCP/IP model are further divided to describe discrete functions that must occur at these layers.

At the network access layer, the TCP/IP protocol suite does not specify which protocols to use when transmitting over a physical medium; it only describes the handoff from the internet layer to the physical network protocols. OSI Layers 1 and 2 discuss the necessary procedures to access the media and the physical means to send data over a network.

As shown in the figure, the critical parallels between the two network models occur at the OSI Layers 3 and 4. OSI Layer 3, the network layer, is almost universally used to describe the range of processes that occur in all data networks to address and route messages through an internetwork. IP is the TCP/IP suite protocol that includes the functionality described at OSI Layer 3.

Layer 4, the transport layer of the OSI model, describes general services and functions that provide ordered and reliable delivery of data between source and destination hosts. These functions include acknowledgement, error recovery, and sequencing. At this layer, the TCP/IP protocols TCP and User Datagram Protocol (UDP) provide the necessary functionality.

The TCP/IP application layer includes a number of protocols that provide specific functionality to a variety of end user applications. The OSI model Layers 5, 6, and 7 are used as references for application software developers and vendors to produce products that operate on networks.

Refer to Interactive Graphic in online course.

3.2.4.5   Activity – Identify Layers and Functions

Refer to Packet Tracer Activity for this chapter

3.2.4.6   Packet Tracer - Investigating the TCP/IP and OSI Models in Action

This simulation activity is intended to provide a foundation for understanding the TCP/IP protocol suite and the relationship to the OSI model. Simulation mode allows you to view the data contents being sent across the network at each layer.

As data moves through the network, it is broken down into smaller pieces and identified so that the pieces can be put back together when they arrive at the destination. Each piece is assigned a specific name (protocol data unit [PDU]) and associated with a specific layer of the TCP/IP and OSI models. Packet Tracer simulation mode enables you to view each of the layers and the associated PDU. The following steps lead the user through the process of requesting a web page from a web server by using the web browser application available on a client PC.

Even though much of the information displayed will be discussed in more detail later, this is an opportunity to explore the functionality of Packet Tracer and be able to visualize the encapsulation process.

Refer to Lab Activity for this chapter

3.2.4.7   Lab - Researching RFCs

In this lab, you will complete the following objectives:

■ Part 1: RFC Editor

■ Part 2: Publishing RFCs

Refer to
Online Course
for Illustration

3.3   Moving Data in the Network

3.3.1   Data Encapsulation

3.3.1.1   Communicating the Messages

In theory, a single communication, such as a music video or an email message, could be sent across a network from a source to a destination as one massive, uninterrupted stream of bits. If messages were actually transmitted in this manner, it would mean that no other device would be able to send or receive messages on the same network while this data transfer was in progress. These large streams of data would result in significant delays. Further, if a link in the interconnected network infrastructure failed during the transmission, the complete message would be lost and have to be retransmitted in full.

A better approach is to divide the data into smaller, more manageable pieces to send over the network. This division of the data stream into smaller pieces is called segmentation. Segmenting messages has two primary benefits:

- By sending smaller individual pieces from source to destination, many different conversations can be interleaved on the network. The process used to interleave the pieces of separate conversations together on the network is called multiplexing. Click each button in Figure 1, and then click the Play button to view the animations of segmentation and multiplexing.

- Segmentation can increase the reliability of network communications. The separate pieces of each message need not travel the same pathway across the network from source to destination. If a particular path becomes congested with data traffic or fails, individual pieces of the message can still be directed to the destination using alternate pathways. If part of the message fails to make it to the destination, only the missing parts need to be retransmitted.

The downside to using segmentation and multiplexing to transmit messages across a network is the level of complexity that is added to the process. Imagine if you had to send a 100-page letter, but each envelope would only hold one page. The process of addressing, labeling, sending, receiving, and opening the entire 100 envelopes would be time-consuming for both the sender and the recipient.

In network communications, each segment of the message must go through a similar process to ensure that it gets to the correct destination and can be reassembled into the content of the original message, as shown in Figure 2.

Various types of devices throughout the network participate in ensuring that the pieces of the message arrive reliably at their destination.

Refer to
Online Course
for Illustration

3.3.1.2   Protocol Data Units (PDUs)

As application data is passed down the protocol stack on its way to be transmitted across the network media, various protocols add information to it at each level. This is commonly known as the encapsulation process.

The form that a piece of data takes at any layer is called a protocol data unit (PDU). During encapsulation, each succeeding layer encapsulates the PDU that it receives from the layer above in accordance with the protocol being used. At each stage of the process, a PDU has a different name to reflect its new functions. Although there is no universal naming convention for PDUs, in this course, the PDUs are named according to the protocols of the TCP/IP suite, as shown in the figure:

- **Data** - The general term for the PDU used at the application layer

- **Segment** - Transport layer PDU

- **Packet** - Internet layer PDU

- **Frame** - Network access layer PDU

- **Bits** - A PDU used when physically transmitting data over the medium

Refer to
Online Course
for Illustration

3.3.1.3   Encapsulation

Data encapsulation is the process that adds additional protocol header information to the data before transmission. In most forms of data communications, the original data is encapsulated or wrapped in several protocols before being transmitted.

When sending messages on a network, the protocol stack on a host operates from top to bottom. In the web server example, we can use the TCP/IP model to illustrate the process of sending an HTML web page to a client.

The application layer protocol, HTTP, begins the process by delivering the HTML formatted web page data to the transport layer. There the application data is broken into TCP segments. Each TCP segment is given a label, called a header, containing information about which process running on the destination computer should receive the message. It also contains the information that enables the destination process to reassemble the data back to its original format.

The transport layer encapsulates the web page HTML data within the segment and sends it to the internet layer, where the IP protocol is implemented. Here the entire TCP segment is encapsulated within an IP packet, which adds another label, called the IP header. The IP header contains source and destination host IP addresses, as well as information necessary to deliver the packet to its corresponding destination process.

Next, the IP packet is sent to the network access layer where it is encapsulated within a frame header and trailer. Each frame header contains a source and destination physical address. The physical address uniquely identifies the devices on the local network. The trailer contains error checking information. Finally the bits are encoded onto the media by the server network interface card (NIC). Click the Play button in the figure to see the encapsulation process.

Refer to
Online Course
for Illustration

3.3.1.4   De-encapsulation

This process is reversed at the receiving host, and is known as de-encapsulation. De-encapsulation is the process used by a receiving device to remove one or more of the protocol headers. The data is de-encapsulated as it moves up the stack toward the end-user application. Click the Play button in the figure to see the de-encapsulation process.

Refer to
Interactive Graphic
in online course.

3.3.1.5   Activity – Identify the PDU Layer

Refer to
Online Course
for Illustration

3.3.2   Accessing Local Resources

3.3.2.1   Network Addresses and Data Link addresses

OSI model describes the processes of encoding, formatting, segmenting, and encapsulating data for transmission over the network. The network layer and data link layer are responsible for delivering the data from the source device or sender, to the destination device or receiver. Protocols at both layers contain source and destination addresses, but their addresses have different purposes.

Network Address

The network layer, or Layer 3, logical address contains information required to deliver the IP packet from the source device to the destination device. A Layer 3 IP address has two parts, the network prefix and the host part. The network prefix is used by routers to forward the packet to the proper network. The host part is used by the last router in the path to deliver the packet to the destination device.

An IP packet contains two IP addresses:

- **Source IP address** - The IP address of the sending device.

- **Destination IP address** - The IP address of the receiving device. The destination IP address is used by routers to forward a packet to its destination.

Data Link Address

The data link, or Layer 2, physical address has a different role. The purpose of the data link address is to deliver the data link frame from one network interface to another network interface on the same network. Before an IP packet can be sent over a wired or wireless network it must be encapsulated in a data link frame so it can be transmitted over the physical medium, the actual network. Ethernet LANs and wireless LANs are two examples of networks that have different physical media each with its own type of data link protocol.

The IP packet is encapsulated into a data link frame to be delivered to the destination network. The source and destination data link addresses are added, as shown in the figure:

- **Source data link address** - The physical address of the device that is sending the packet. Initially this is the NIC that is the source of the IP packet.

- **Destination data link address** - The physical address of the network interface of either the next hop router or the network interface of the destination device.

Refer to
Online Course
for Illustration

3.3.2.2   Communicating with a Device on the Same Network

To understand how communication is successful in the network, it is important to understand the roles of both the network layer addresses and the data link addresses when a device is communicating with another device on the same network. In this example we have a client computer, PC1, communicating with a file server, FTP server, on the same IP network.

Network Addresses

The network layer addresses, or IP addresses, indicate the network and host address of the source and destination. The network portion of the address will be the same; only the host or device portion of the address will be different.

- **Source IP address** - The IP address of the sending device, the client computer PC1: 192.168.1.110.

- **Destination IP address** - The IP address of the receiving device, FTP server: 192.168.1.9.

Data Link Addresses

When the sender and receiver of the IP packet are on the same network, the data link frame is sent directly to the receiving device. On an Ethernet network, the data link addresses are known as Ethernet MAC addresses. MAC addresses are 48-bit addresses that are physically embedded on the Ethernet NIC. A MAC address is also known as the physical address or burned-in address (BIA).

- **Source MAC address** - This is the data link address, or the Ethernet MAC address, of the device that sends the IP packet, PC1. The MAC address of the Ethernet NIC of PC1 is AA-AA-AA-AA-AA-AA.

- **Destination MAC address** - When the receiving device is on the same network as the sending device, this is the data link address of the receiving device. In this example, the destination MAC address is the MAC address of the FTP server: CC-CC-CC-CC-CC-CC.

The source and destination addresses are added to the Ethernet frame. The frame with the encapsulated IP packet can now be transmitted from PC1 directly to the FTP server.

Refer to **Online Course** for Illustration

3.3.2.3   MAC and IP Addresses

It should now be clear that to send data to another host on the same LAN the source host must know both the physical and logical addresses of the destination host. Once this is known, it can create a frame and send it out on the network media. The source host can learn the destination IP address in a number of ways. For example, it may learn the IP address through the use of the Domain Name System (DNS), or it may know the destination IP address because the address is entered in the application manually, such as when a user specifies the IP address of a destination FTP server. But how does a host determine the Ethernet MAC address of another device?

Most network applications rely on the logical IP address of the destination to identify the location of the communicating hosts. The data link MAC address is required to deliver the encapsulated IP packet inside the Ethernet frame across the network to the destination.

The sending host uses a protocol called Address Resolution Protocol (ARP) to discover the MAC address of any host on the same local network. The sending host sends an ARP Request message to the entire LAN. The ARP Request is a broadcast message. The ARP Request contains the IP address of the destination device. Every device on the LAN examines the ARP Request to see if it contains its own IP address. Only the device with the IP address contained in the ARP Request responds with an ARP Reply. The ARP Reply includes the MAC address associated with the IP address in the ARP Request.

Refer to
Online Course
for Illustration

3.3.3   Accessing Remote Resources

3.3.3.1   Default Gateway

The method that a host uses to send messages to a destination on a remote network differs from the way a host sends messages to a destination on the same local network. When a host needs to send a message to another host located on the same network, it will forward the message directly. A host will use ARP to discover the MAC address of the destination host. It includes the destination IP address within the packet header and encapsulates the packet into a frame containing the MAC address of the destination and forwards it.

When a host needs to send a message to a remote network, it must use the router, also known as the default gateway. The default gateway is the IP address of an interface on a router on the same network as the sending host.

It is important that the address of the default gateway be configured on each host on the local network. If no default gateway address is configured in the host TCP/IP settings, or if the wrong default gateway is specified, messages addressed to hosts on remote networks cannot be delivered.

In the figure, the hosts on the LAN are using R1 as the default gateway with its 192.168.1.1 address configured in their TCP/IP settings. If the destination of a PDU is on a different IP network, the hosts send the PDUs to the default gateway on the router for further transmission.

Refer to
Online Course
for Illustration

3.3.3.2   Communicating with a Device on a Remote Network

But what are the roles of the network layer address and the data link layer address when a device is communicating with a device on a remote network? In this example we have a client computer, PC1, communicating with a server, named Web Server, on a different IP network.

Network Addresses

IP addresses indicate the network and device addresses of the source and destination. When the sender of the packet is on a different network from the receiver, the source and destination IP addresses will represent hosts on different networks. This will be indicated by the network portion of the IP address of the destination host.

- **Source IP address** - The IP address of the sending device, the client computer PC1: 192.168.1.110.

- **Destination IP address** - The IP address of the receiving device, the server, Web Server: 172.16.1.99.

Data Link Addresses

When the sender and receiver of the IP packet are on different networks, the Ethernet data link frame cannot be sent directly to the destination host because the host is not directly reachable in the network of the sender. The Ethernet frame must be sent to another device known as the router or default gateway. In our example, the default gateway is R1. R1 has an interface and an IP address that is on the same network as PC1. This allows PC1 to reach the router directly.

- **Source MAC address** - The Ethernet MAC address of the sending device, PC1. The MAC address of the Ethernet interface of PC1 is AA-AA-AA-AA-AA-AA.

Destination MAC address - When the receiving device is on a different network from the sending device, this is the Ethernet MAC address of the default gateway or router. In this example, the destination MAC address is the MAC address of the R1 Ethernet interface that is attached to the PC1 network, which is 11-11-11-11-11-11.

The Ethernet frame with the encapsulated IP packet can now be transmitted to R1. R1 forwards the packet to the destination, Web Server. This may mean that R1 forwards the packet to another router or directly to Web Server if the destination is on a network connected to R1.

How does the sending device determine the MAC address of the router?

Each device knows the IP address of the router through the default gateway address configured in its TCP/IP settings. The default gateway address is the address of the router interface connected to the same local network as the source device. All devices on the local network use the default gateway address to send messages to the router. After the host knows the default gateway IP address, it can use ARP to determine the MAC address of that default gateway. The MAC address of the default gateway is then placed in the frame.

Refer to **Packet Tracer Activity** for this chapter

3.3.3.3   Packet Tracer - Explore a Network

This simulation activity is intended to help you understand the flow of traffic and the contents of data packets as they traverse a complex network. Communications will be examined at three different locations simulating typical business and home networks.

Refer to **Lab Activity** for this chapter

3.3.3.4   Lab - Using Wireshark to View Network Traffic

In this lab, you will complete the following objectives:

- Part 1: Download and Install Wireshark
- Part 2: Capture and Analyze Local ICMP Data in Wireshark
- Part 3: Capture and Analyze Remote ICMP Data in Wireshark

Refer to **Online Course** for Illustration

3.4   Summary

Refer to **Lab Activity** for this chapter

3.4.1.1   Class Activity - Guaranteed to Work!

Guaranteed to work!

You have just completed the Chapter 3 content regarding network protocols and standards.

Assuming you resolved the beginning of this chapter's modeling activity, how would you compare the following steps taken to design a communications system to the networking models used for communications?

- Establishing a language to communicate
- Dividing the message into small steps, delivered a little at a time, to facilitate understanding of the problem

- Checking to see if the data has been delivered fully and correctly
- Timing needed to ensure quality data communication and delivery

Refer to
Online Course
for Illustration

3.4.1.2 Summary

Data networks are systems of end devices, intermediary devices, and the media connecting the devices. For communication to occur, these devices must know how to communicate.

These devices must comply with communication rules and protocols. TCP/IP is an example of a protocol suite. Most protocols are created by a standards organization such as the IETF or IEEE. The Institute of Electrical and Electronics Engineers is a professional organization for those in the electrical engineering and electronics fields. ISO, the International Organization for Standardization, is the world's largest developer of international standards for a wide variety of products and services.

The most widely-used networking models are the OSI and TCP/IP models. Associating the protocols that set the rules of data communications with the different layers of these models is useful in determining which devices and services are applied at specific points as data passes across LANs and WANs.

Data that passes down the stack of the OSI model is segmented into pieces and encapsulated with addresses and other labels. The process is reversed as the pieces are de-encapsulated and passed up the destination protocol stack. The OSI model describes the processes of encoding, formatting, segmenting, and encapsulating data for transmission over the network.

The TCP/IP protocol suite is an open standard protocol that has been endorsed by the networking industry and ratified, or approved, by a standards organization. The Internet Protocol Suite is a suite of protocols required for transmitting and receiving information using the Internet.

Protocol Data Units (PDUs) are named according to the protocols of the TCP/IP suite: data, segment, packet, frame, and bits.

Applying models allows individuals, companies, and trade associations to analyze current networks and plan the networks of the future.

Go to the online course to take the quiz and exam.

Chapter 3 Quiz

This quiz is designed to provide an additional opportunity to practice the skills and knowledge presented in the chapter and to prepare for the chapter exam. You will be allowed multiple attempts and the grade does not appear in the gradebook.

Chapter 3 Exam

The chapter exam assesses your knowledge of the chapter content.

Your Chapter Notes

CHAPTER 4

Network Access

4.0 Network Access

4.0.1.1 Introduction

To support our communication, the OSI model divides the functions of a data network into layers. Each layer works with the layers above and below in order to transmit data. Two layers within the OSI model are so closely tied, that according to the TCP/IP model, they are in essence one layer. Those two layers are the data link layer and the physical layer.

On the sending device, it is the role of the data link layer to prepare data for transmission and control how that data accesses the physical media. However, the physical layer controls how the data is transmitted onto the physical media by encoding the binary digits that represent data into signals.

On the receiving end, the physical layer receives signals across the connecting media. After decoding the signal back into data, the physical layer passes the data to the data link layer for acceptance and processing.

This chapter begins with the general functions of the physical layer and the standards and protocols that manage the transmission of data across local media. It also introduces the functions of the data link layer and the protocols associated with it.

Refer to
Lab Activity
for this chapter

4.0.1.2 Class Activity – Managing the Medium

Managing the Medium

You and your colleague are attending a networking conference. There are many lectures and presentations held during this event, and because they overlap, each of you can only choose a limited set of sessions to attend.

Therefore, you decide to split, each of you attending a separate set of presentations, and after the event ends, you share the slides and the knowledge each of you gained during the event.

Try to answer the following questions:

- How would you personally organize a conference where multiple sessions are held at the same time? Would you put all of them into a single conference room or would you use multiple rooms? What would be the reason?

- Assume that the conference room is properly fitted with audiovisual equipment to display large-size video and amplify voice. If a person wanted to attend a specific session, does the seating arrangement make a difference, or is it sufficient to visit the proper conference room?

- Would it be considered positive or harmful if the speech from one conference room somehow leaked into another?

- If questions or inquiries arise during a presentation, should attendees simply shout out their question, or should there be some form of process for handling questions, such as documenting them and handing them over to a facilitator? What would happen without this process?

- If an interesting topic elicits a larger discussion where many attendees have questions or comments, can this result in the session running out of its time without going through the entire intended content? Why is that so?

- Imagine that the session is a panel, i.e. a more free discussion of attendees with panelists and optionally with themselves. If a person wants to address another person within the same room, can he/she do it directly? What would be necessary to do if a panelist wanted to invite another person to join who is not presently in the room?

- What was accomplished by the isolation of multiple sessions into separate conference rooms if, after the event, people can meet and share the information?

> Refer to
> **Online Course**
> for Illustration

4.1   Physical Layer Protocols

4.1.1   Getting It Connected

4.1.1.1   Connecting to the Network

Whether connecting to a local printer in the home or to a web site in another country, before any network communications can occur, a physical connection to a local network must be established first. A physical connection can be a wired connection using a cable or a wireless connection using radio waves.

The type of physical connection used is totally dependent upon the setup of the network. For example, in many corporate offices, employees have desktop or laptop computers that are physically connected, via cable, to a shared switch. This type of setup is a wired network, in which data is transmitted across a physical cable.

In addition to wired connections, some businesses may also offer wireless connections for laptops, tablets, and smartphones. With wireless devices, data is transmitted using radio waves. The use of wireless connectivity is becoming more common as individuals, and businesses alike, discover the advantages of offering wireless services. In order to offer wireless capability, a network must incorporate a wireless access point (WAP) for devices to connect to.

Switch devices and wireless access points are often two separate dedicated devices within a network implementation. However, there are also devices that offer both wired and wireless connectivity. In many homes, for example, individuals are implementing home integrated service routers (ISRs), as shown in Figure 1. ISRs offer a switching component with multiple ports, allowing multiple devices to be connected to the local area network (LAN) using cables, as shown in Figure 2. Additionally, many ISRs also include a WAP, which allows wireless devices to connect as well.

Refer to
Online Course
for Illustration

4.1.1.2   Network Interface Cards

Network Interface Cards (NICs) connect a device to the network. Ethernet NICs are used for a wired connection whereas WLAN (Wireless Local Area Network) NICs are used for wireless. An end-user device may include one or both types of NICs. A network printer, for example, may only have an Ethernet NIC, and therefore, must connect to the network using an Ethernet cable. Other devices, such as tablets and smartphones, might only contain a WLAN NIC and must use a wireless connection.

Not all physical connections are equal, in terms of the performance level, when connecting to a network.

For example, a wireless device will experience degradation in performance based on its distance to a wireless access point. The further the device is from the access point the weaker the wireless signal it receives. This can mean less bandwidth or no wireless connection at all. The figure shows that a wireless range extender can be used to regenerate the wireless signal to other parts of the house that are too far from the wireless access point. Alternatively, a wired connection will not degrade in performance, however, is extremely limited in movement and generally requires static positioning.

All wireless devices must share access to the airwaves connecting to the wireless access point. This means slower network performance may occur as more wireless devices access the network simultaneously. A wired device does not need to share its access to the network with other devices. Each wired device has a separate communications channel over its own Ethernet cable. This is important when considering some applications, like online gaming, streaming video, and video conferencing, which require more dedicated bandwidth than other applications.

Over the next couple of topics you will learn more about the physical layer connections that occur and how those connections affect the transportation of data.

4.1.2   Purpose of the Physical Layer

Refer to
Lab Activity
for this chapter

4.1.2.1   The Physical Layer

The OSI physical layer provides the means to transport the bits that make up a data link layer frame across the network media. This layer accepts a complete frame from the data link layer and encodes it as a series of signals that are transmitted onto the local media. The encoded bits that comprise a frame are received by either an end device or an intermediate device.

The process that data undergoes from a source node to a destination node is:

- The user data is segmented by the transport layer, placed into packets by the network layer, and further encapsulated as frames by the data link layer.
- The physical layer encodes the frames and creates the electrical, optical, or radio wave signals that represent the bits in each frame.
- These signals are then sent on the media one at a time.
- The destination node physical layer retrieves these individual signals from the media, restores them to their bit representations, and passes the bits up to the data link layer as a complete frame.

Refer to
Online Course
for Illustration

4.1.2.2 Physical Layer Media

There are three basic forms of network media. The physical layer produces the representation and groupings of bits for each type of media as:

- **Copper cable:** The signals are patterns of electrical pulses.

- **Fiber-optic cable:** The signals are patterns of light.

- **Wireless:** The signals are patterns of microwave transmissions.

The figure displays signaling examples for copper, fiber-optic, and wireless.

To enable physical layer interoperability, all aspects of these functions are governed by standard organizations.

Refer to
Online Course
for Illustration

4.1.2.3 Physical Layer Standards

The protocols and operations of the upper OSI layers are performed in software designed by software engineers and computer scientists. For example, the services and protocols in the TCP/IP suite are defined by the Internet Engineering Task Force (IETF) in RFCs as shown in Figure 1.

The physical layer consists of electronic circuitry, media, and connectors developed by engineers. Therefore, it is appropriate that the standards governing this hardware are defined by the relevant electrical and communications engineering organizations.

There are many different international and national organizations, regulatory government organizations, and private companies involved in establishing and maintaining physical layer standards. For instance, the physical layer hardware, media, encoding, and signaling standards are defined and governed by the:

- International Organization for Standardization (ISO)

- Telecommunications Industry Association/Electronic Industries Association (TIA/EIA)

- International Telecommunication Union (ITU)

- American National Standards Institute (ANSI)

- Institute of Electrical and Electronics Engineers (IEEE)

- National telecommunications regulatory authorities including the Federal Communication Commission (FCC) in the USA and the European Telecommunications Standards Institute (ESTI)

In addition to these, there are often regional cabling standards groups such as CSA (Canadian Standards Association), CENELEC (European Committee for Electrotechnical Standardization), and JSA/JSI (Japanese Standards Association), developing local specifications.

Figure 2 lists the major contributors and some of their relevant physical layer standards.

Refer to
Lab Activity
for this chapter

4.1.2.4 Lab - Identifying Network Devices and Cabling

In this lab, you will complete the following objectives:

- Part 1: Identify Network Devices

- Part 2: Identify Network Media

Refer to
Online Course
for Illustration

4.1.3   Fundamental Principles of Layer 1

4.1.3.1   Physical Layer Fundamental Principles

The physical layer standards address three functional areas:

Physical Components

The physical components are the electronic hardware devices, media, and other connectors that transmit and carry the signals to represent the bits. Hardware components such as network adapters (NICs), interfaces and connectors, cable materials, and cable designs are all specified in standards associated with the physical layer. The various ports and interfaces on a Cisco 1941 router are also examples of physical components with specific connectors and pinouts resulting from standards.

Encoding

Encoding or line encoding is a method of converting a stream of data bits into a predefined "code". Codes are groupings of bits used to provide a predictable pattern that can be recognized by both the sender and the received. In the case of networking, encoding is a pattern of voltage or current used to represent bits; the 0s and 1s.

In addition to creating codes for data, encoding methods at the physical layer may also provide codes for control purposes such as identifying the beginning and end of a frame.

Common network encoding methods include:

- **Manchester encoding:** A 0 is represented by a high to low voltage transition and a 1 is represented as a low to high voltage transition. This type of encoding is used in older versions of Ethernet, RFID and Near Field Communication.

- **Non-Return to Zero (NRZ):** This is a common means of encoding data that has two states termed "zero" and "one" and no neutral or rest position. A 0 may be represented by one voltage level on the media and a 1 might be represented by a different voltage on the media.

Note   Faster data rates require more complex encoding, such as 4B/5B, however, explanation of these methods is beyond the scope of this course.

Signaling

The physical layer must generate the electrical, optical, or wireless signals that represent the "1" and "0" on the media. The method of representing the bits is called the signaling method. The physical layer standards must define what type of signal represents a "1" and what type of signal represents a "0". This can be as simple as a change in the level of an electrical signal or optical pulse. For example, a long pulse might represent a 1, whereas a short pulse represents a 0.

This is similar to how Morse code is used for communication. Morse code is another signaling method that uses a series of on-off tones, lights, or clicks to send text over telephone wires or between ships at sea.

Signals can be transmitted in one of two ways:

- **Asynchronous:** Data signals are transmitted without an associated clock signal. The time spacing between data characters or blocks may be of arbitrary duration, meaning the spacing is not standardized. Therefore, frames require start and stop indicator flags.

- **Synchronous:** Data signals are sent along with a clock signal which occurs at evenly spaced time durations referred to as the bit time.

There are many ways to transmit signals. A common method to send data is using modulation techniques. Modulation is the process by which the characteristic of one wave (the signal) modifies another wave (the carrier). The following modulation techniques have been widely used in transmitting data on a medium:

- **Frequency modulation (FM):** A method of transmission in which the carrier frequency varies in accordance with the signal.

- **Amplitude modulation (AM):** A transmission technique in which the amplitude of the carrier varies in accordance with the signal.

- **Pulse-coded modulation (PCM):** A technique in which an analog signal, such as a voice, is converted into a digital signal by sampling the signal's amplitude and expressing the different amplitudes as a binary number. The sampling rate must be at least twice the highest frequency in the signal.

The nature of the actual signals representing the bits on the media will depend on the signaling method in use. Some methods may use one attribute of signal to represent a single 0 and use another attribute of signal to represent a single 1.

Figure 2 illustrates the how AM and FM techniques are used to send a signal.

Refer to
Online Course
for Illustration

4.1.3.2   Bandwidth

Different physical media support the transfer of bits at different speeds. Data transfer is usually discussed in terms of bandwidth and throughput.

Bandwidth is the capacity of a medium to carry data. Digital bandwidth measures the amount of data that can flow from one place to another in a given amount of time. Bandwidth is typically measured in kilobits per second (kb/s) or megabits per second (Mb/s).

The practical bandwidth of a network is determined by a combination of factors:

- The properties of the physical media
- The technologies chosen for signaling and detecting network signals

Physical media properties, current technologies, and the laws of physics all play a role in determining available bandwidth.

The table shows the commonly used units of measure for bandwidth.

4.1.3.3   Throughput

Throughput is the measure of the transfer of bits across the media over a given period of time.

Due to a number of factors, throughput usually does not match the specified bandwidth in physical layer implementations. Many factors influence throughput including:

- The amount of traffic
- The type of traffic
- The latency created by the number of network devices encountered between source and destination

Latency refers to the amount of time, to include delays, for data to travel from one given point to another.

In an internetwork or network with multiple segments, throughput cannot be faster than the slowest link of the path from source to destination. Even if all or most of the segments have high bandwidth, it will only take one segment in the path with low throughput to create a bottleneck to the throughput of the entire network.

There are many online speed tests that can reveal the throughput of an Internet connection. The figure provides sample results from a speed test.

Note   There is a third measurement to measure the transfer of usable data that is known as goodput. Goodput is the measure of usable data transferred over a given period of time. Goodput is throughput minus traffic overhead for establishing sessions, acknowledgements, and encapsulation.

Refer to
Online Course
for Illustration

4.1.3.4   Types of Physical Media

The physical layer produces the representation and groupings of bits as voltages, radio frequencies, or light pulses. Various standards organizations have contributed to the definition of the physical, electrical, and mechanical properties of the media available for different data communications. These specifications guarantee that cables and connectors will function as anticipated with different data link layer implementations.

As an example, standards for copper media are defined for the:

- Type of copper cabling used
- Bandwidth of the communication
- Type of connectors used
- Pinout and color codes of connections to the media
- Maximum distance of the media

The figure shows different types of interfaces and ports available on a 1941 router.

Refer to
Interactive Graphic
in online course.

4.1.3.5   Activity - Physical Layer Terminology

Refer to
Online Course
for Illustration

4.2   Network Media

4.2.1   Copper Cabling

4.2.1.1   Characteristics of Copper Media

Networks use copper media because it is inexpensive, easy to install, and has low resistance to electrical current. However, copper media is limited by distance and signal interference.

Data is transmitted on copper cables as electrical pulses. A detector in the network interface of a destination device must receive a signal that can be successfully decoded to match the signal sent. However, the longer the signal travels, the more it deteriorates in a phenomenon referred to as signal attenuation. For this reason, all copper media must follow strict distance limitations as specified by the guiding standards.

The timing and voltage values of the electrical pulses are also susceptible to interference from two sources:

- **Electromagnetic interference (EMI) or radio frequency interference (RFI)** - EMI and RFI signals can distort and corrupt the data signals being carried by copper media. Potential sources of EMI and RFI include radio waves and electromagnetic devices such as fluorescent lights or electric motors as shown in the figure.

- **Crosstalk -** Crosstalk is a disturbance caused by the electric or magnetic fields of a signal on one wire to the signal in an adjacent wire. In telephone circuits, crosstalk can result in hearing part of another voice conversation from an adjacent circuit. Specifically, when electrical current flows through a wire, it creates a small, circular magnetic field around the wire which can be picked up by an adjacent wire.

Play the animation in the figure to see how data transmission can be affected by interference.

To counter the negative effects of EMI and RFI, some types of copper cables are wrapped in metallic shielding and require proper grounding connections.

To counter the negative effects of crosstalk, some types of copper cables have opposing circuit wire pairs twisted together which effectively cancels the crosstalk.

The susceptibility of copper cables to electronic noise can also be limited by:

- Selecting the cable type or category most suited to a given networking environment.

- Designing a cable infrastructure to avoid known and potential sources of interference in the building structure.

- Using cabling techniques that include the proper handling and termination of the cables.

Refer to
Online Course
for Illustration

4.2.1.2   Copper Media

There are three main types of copper media used in networking:

- Unshielded Twisted-Pair (UTP)
- Shielded Twisted-Pair (STP)
- Coaxial

These cables are used to interconnect nodes on a LAN and infrastructure devices such as switches, routers, and wireless access points. Each type of connection and the accompanying devices have cabling requirements stipulated by physical layer standards.

Different physical layer standards specify the use of different connectors. These standards specify the mechanical dimensions of the connectors and the acceptable electrical properties of each type. Networking media use modular jacks and plugs to provide easy connection and disconnection. Also, a single type of physical connector may be used for multiple types of connections. For example, the RJ-45 connector is widely used in LANs with one type of media and in some WANs with another media type.

Refer to
Online Course
for Illustration

4.2.1.3   Unshielded Twisted-Pair Cable

Unshielded twisted-pair (UTP) cabling is the most common networking media. UTP cabling, terminated with RJ-45 connectors, is used for interconnecting network hosts with intermediate networking devices, such as switches and routers.

In LANs, UTP cable consists of four pairs of color-coded wires that have been twisted together and then encased in a flexible plastic sheath which protects from minor physical damage. The twisting of wires helps protect against signal interference from other wires.

As seen in the figure, the color codes identify the individual pairs and wires in the pairs and aid in cable termination.

Refer to
Online Course
for Illustration

4.2.1.4   Shielded Twisted-Pair (STP) Cable

Shielded twisted-pair (STP) provides better noise protection than UTP cabling. However, compared to UTP cable, STP cable is significantly more expensive and difficult to install. Like UTP cable, STP uses an RJ-45 connector.

STP cable combines the techniques of shielding to counter EMI and RFI and wire twisting to counter crosstalk. To gain the full benefit of the shielding, STP cables are terminated with special shielded STP data connectors. If the cable is improperly grounded, the shield may act like an antenna and pick up unwanted signals.

Different types of STP cables with different characteristics are available. However, there are two common variations of STP:

- STP cable shields the entire bundle of wires with foil eliminating virtually all interference (more common).
- STP cable shields the entire bundle of wires as well as the individual wire pairs with foil eliminating all interference.

The STP cable shown uses four pairs of wires, each wrapped in a foil shield, which are then wrapped in an overall metallic braid or foil.

For many years, STP was the cabling structure specified for use in Token Ring network installations. With the decline of Token Ring the demand for shielded twisted-pair cabling also waned. However, the new 10 GB standard for Ethernet has a provision for the use of STP cabling which is providing a renewed interest in shielded twisted-pair cabling.

Refer to **Online Course** for Illustration

4.2.1.5   Coaxial Cable

Coaxial cable, or coax for short, gets its name from the fact that there are two conductors that share the same axis. As shown in the figure, coaxial cable consists of:

■ A copper conductor used to transmit the electronic signals.

■ The copper conductor is surrounded by a layer of flexible plastic insulation.

■ The insulating material is surrounded in a woven copper braid, or metallic foil, that acts as the second wire in the circuit and as a shield for the inner conductor. This second layer, or shield, also reduces the amount of outside electromagnetic interference.

■ The entire cable is covered with a cable jacket to protect it from minor physical damage.

Note   There are different types of connectors used with coax cable.

Coaxial cable was traditionally used in cable television capable of transmitting in one direction. It was also used extensively in early Ethernet installations.

Although UTP cable has essentially replaced coaxial cable in modern Ethernet installations, the coaxial cable design has been adapted for use in:

■ **Wireless installations:** Coaxial cables attach antennas to wireless devices. The coaxial cable carries radio frequency (RF) energy between the antennas and the radio equipment.

■ **Cable Internet installations:** Cable service providers are currently converting their one-way systems to two-way systems to provide Internet connectivity to their customers. To provide these services, portions of the coaxial cable and supporting amplification elements are replaced with fiber-optic cable. However, the final connection to the customer's location and the wiring inside the customer's premises is still coax cable. This combined use of fiber and coax is referred to as hybrid fiber coax (HFC).

Refer to **Online Course** for Illustration

4.2.1.6   Copper Media Safety

All three types of copper media are susceptible to fire and electrical hazards.

Fire hazards exist since cable insulation and sheaths may be flammable or produce toxic fumes when heated or burned. Building authorities or organizations may stipulate related safety standards for cabling and hardware installations.

Electrical hazards are a potential problem since the copper wires could conduct electricity in undesirable ways. This could subject personnel and equipment to a range of electrical hazards. For example, a defective network device could conduct currents to the chassis of other network devices. Additionally, network cabling could present undesirable voltage levels when used to connect devices that have power sources with different ground potentials.

Such situations are possible when copper cabling is used to connect networks in different buildings or on different floors of buildings that use different power facilities. Finally, copper cabling may conduct voltages caused by lightning strikes to network devices.

The result of undesirable voltages and currents can include damage to network devices and connected computers, or injury to personnel. It is important that copper cabling be installed appropriately, and according to the relevant specifications and building codes, in order to avoid potentially dangerous and damaging situations.

The figure displays proper cabling practices to avoid potential fire and electrical hazards.

Refer to
Interactive Graphic
in online course.

4.2.1.7   Activity - Copper Media Characteristics

Refer to
Online Course
for Illustration

4.2.2   UTP Cabling

4.2.2.1   Properties of UTP Cabling

When used as a networking medium, unshielded twisted-pair (UTP) cabling consists of four pairs of color-coded wires that have been twisted together and then encased in a flexible plastic sheath. Network UTP cable has four pairs of either 22- or 24-gauge copper wire. A UTP cable has an external diameter of approximately 0.43 cm (0.17 inches), and its small size can be advantageous during installation.

UTP cable does not use shielding to counter the effects of EMI and RFI. Instead, cable designers have discovered that they can limit the negative effect of crosstalk by:

- **Cancellation:** Designers now pair wires in a circuit. When two wires in an electrical circuit are placed close together, their magnetic fields are the exact opposite of each other. Therefore, the two magnetic fields cancel each other out and also cancel out any outside EMI and RFI signals.

- **Varying the number of twists per wire pair:** To further enhance the cancellation effect of paired circuit wires designers vary the number of twists of each wire pair in a cable. UTP cable must follow precise specifications governing how many twists or braids are permitted per meter (3.28 feet) of cable. Notice in the figure that the orange/ orange white pairs are twisted less than the blue/white blue pair. Each colored pair is twisted a different number of times.

UTP cable relies solely on the cancellation effect produced by the twisted wire pairs to limit signal degradation and effectively provide self-shielding for wire pairs within the network media.

Refer to
Online Course
for Illustration

4.2.2.2   UTP Cabling Standards

UTP cabling conforms to the standards established jointly by the TIA/EIA. Specifically, TIA/EIA-568A stipulates the commercial cabling standards for LAN installations and is the standard most commonly used in LAN cabling environments. Some of the elements defined are:

- Cable types

- Cable lengths

- Connectors

- Cable termination
- Methods of testing cable

The electrical characteristics of copper cabling are defined by the Institute of Electrical and Electronics Engineers (IEEE). IEEE rates UTP cabling according to its performance. Cables are placed into categories according to their ability to carry higher bandwidth rates. For example, Category 5 (Cat5) cable is used commonly in 100BASE-TX FastEthernet installations. Other categories include Enhanced Category 5 (Cat5e) cable, Category 6 (Cat6), and Category 6a.

Cables in higher categories are designed and constructed to support higher data rates. As new gigabit speed Ethernet technologies are being developed and adopted, Cat5e is now the minimally acceptable cable type, with Cat6 being the recommended type for new building installations.

The figure highlights the various categories of UTP cabling.

Note   Some manufacturers are making cables exceeding the TIA/EIA Category 6a specifications and refer to these as Category 7.

Refer to **Online Course** for Illustration

4.2.2.3   UTP Connectors

UTP cable is usually terminated with an ISO 8877 specified RJ-45 connector. This connector is used for a range of physical layer specifications, one of which is Ethernet. The TIA/EIA 568 standard describes the wire color codes to pin assignments (pinouts) for Ethernet cables.

The video in Figure 1 displays a UTP cable terminated with an RJ-45 connector.

As shown in Figure 2, the RJ-45 connector is the male component, crimped at the end of the cable. The socket is the female component in a network device, wall, cubicle partition outlet, or patch panel.

Each time copper cabling is terminated there is the possibility of signal loss and the introduction of noise to the communication circuit. When terminated improperly, each cable is a potential source of physical layer performance degradation. It is essential that all copper media terminations be of high quality to ensure optimum performance with current and future network technologies.

Figure 3 displays an example of a badly terminated UTP cable and a well terminated UTP cable.

Refer to **Online Course** for Illustration

4.2.2.4   Types of UTP Cable

Different situations may require UTP cables to be wired according to different wiring conventions. This means that the individual wires in the cable have to be connected in different orders to different sets of pins in the RJ-45 connectors.

The following are main cable types that are obtained by using specific wiring conventions:

- **Ethernet Straight-through:** The most common type of networking cable. It is commonly used to interconnect a host to a switch and a switch to a router.

- **Ethernet Crossover:** An uncommon cable used to interconnect similar devices together. For example to connect a switch to a switch, a host to a host, or a router to a router.

- **Rollover:** A Cisco proprietary cable used to connect to a router or switch console port.

Using a crossover or straight-through cable incorrectly between devices may not damage the devices, but connectivity and communication between the devices will not take place. This is a common error in the lab and checking that the device connections are correct should be the first troubleshooting action if connectivity is not achieved.

The figure shows the UTP cable type, related standards, and typical application of these cables. It also identifies the individual wire pairs for the TIA 568A and TIA 568B standards.

Refer to
Online Course
for Illustration

4.2.2.5   Testing UTP Cables

After installation, a UTP cable tester should be used to test for the following parameters:

- Wire map

- Cable length

- Signal loss due to attenuation

- Crosstalk

It is recommended to thoroughly check that all UTP installation requirements are met.

Refer to
Interactive Graphic
in online course.

4.2.2.6   Activity - Cable Pinouts

Refer to
Lab Activity
for this chapter

4.2.2.7   Lab - Building an Ethernet Crossover Cable

In this lab, you will complete the following objectives:

- Part 1: Analyze Ethernet Cabling Standards and Pinouts

- Part 2: Build an Ethernet Crossover Cable

- Part 3: Test an Ethernet Crossover Cable

Refer to
Online Course
for Illustration

4.2.3   Fiber Optic Cabling

4.2.3.1   Properties of Fiber Optic Cabling

Optical fiber cable has become very popular for interconnecting infrastructure network devices. It permits the transmission of data over longer distances and at higher bandwidths (data rates) than any other networking media.

Optical fiber is a flexible but extremely thin transparent strand of very pure glass (silica) not much bigger than a human hair. Bits are encoded on the fiber as light impulses. The fiber-optic cable acts as a waveguide, or "light pipe," to transmit light between the two ends with minimal loss of signal.

As an analogy, consider an empty paper towel roll with the inside coated like a mirror that is a thousand meters in length and a small laser pointer is used to send Morse code signals at the speed of light. Essentially that is how a fiber-optic cable operates, except that it is smaller in diameter and uses sophisticated light emitting and receiving technologies.

Unlike copper wires, fiber-optic cable can transmit signals with less attenuation and is completely immune to EMI and RFI.

Fiber-optic cabling is now being used in four types of industry:

- **Enterprise Networks:** Fiber is used for backbone cabling applications and interconnecting infrastructure devices.

- **FTTH and Access Networks:** Fiber-to-the-home (FTTH) is used to provide always-on broadband services to homes and small businesses. FTTH supports affordable high-speed Internet access, as well as telecommuting, telemedicine, and video on demand.

- **Long-Haul Networks:** Service providers use long-haul terrestrial optical fiber networks to connect countries and cities. Networks typically range from a few dozen to a few thousand kilometers and use up to 10 Gb/s-based systems.

- **Submarine Networks:** Special fiber cables are used to provide reliable high-speed, high-capacity solutions capable of or surviving in harsh undersea environments up to transoceanic distances.

Our focus is the use of fiber within the enterprise.

Refer to **Online Course** for Illustration

4.2.3.2   Fiber Media Cable Design

Although an optical fiber is very thin, it is composed of two kinds of glass and a protective outer shield. Specifically, these are the:

- **Core:** Consists of pure glass and is the part of the fiber where light is carried.

- **Cladding:** The glass that surrounds the core and acts as a mirror. The light pulses propagate down the core while the cladding reflects the light pulses. This keeps the light pulses contained in the fiber core in a phenomenon known as total internal reflection.

- **Jacket:** Typically a PVC jacket that protects the core and cladding. It may also include strengthening materials and a buffer (coating) whose purpose is to protect the glass from scratches and moisture.

Although susceptible to sharp bends, the properties of the core and cladding have been altered at the molecular level to make it very strong. Optical fiber is proof tested through a rigorous manufacturing process for strength at a minimum of 100,000 pounds per square inch. Optical fiber is durable enough to withstand handling during installation and deployment in harsh environmental conditions in networks all around the world.

Refer to **Online Course** for Illustration

4.2.3.3   Types of Fiber Media

Light pulses representing the transmitted data as bits on the media are generated by either:

- Lasers
- Light emitting diodes (LEDs)

Electronic semi-conductor devices called photodiodes detect the light pulses and convert them to voltages that can then be reconstructed into data frames.

Note The laser light transmitted over fiber-optic cabling can damage the human eye. Care must be taken to avoid looking into the end of an active optical fiber.

Fiber-optic cables can be broadly classified into two types:

- **Single-mode fiber (SMF):** Consists of a very small core and uses expensive laser technology to send a single ray of light. Popular in long-distance situations spanning hundreds of kilometers such as required in long haul telephony and cable TV applications.

- **Multimode fiber (MMF):** Consists of a larger core and uses LED emitters to send light pulses. Specifically, light from an LED enters the multimode fiber at different angles. Popular in LANs because they can be powered by low cost LEDs. It provides bandwidth up to 10 Gb/s over link lengths of up to 550 meters.

Figures 1 and 2 highlight the characteristics of multimode and single-mode fiber. One of the highlighted differences between multimode and single-mode fiber is the amount of dispersion. Dispersion refers to the spreading out of a light pulse over time. The more dispersion there is, the greater the loss in signal strength.

Refer to
Online Course
for Illustration

4.2.3.4   Network Fiber Connectors

An optical fiber connector terminates the end of an optical fiber. A variety of optical fiber connectors are available. The main differences among the types of connectors are dimensions and methods of mechanical coupling. Generally, organizations standardize on one kind of connector, depending on the equipment that they commonly use, or they standardize per type of fiber (one for MMF, one for SMF). Taking into account all the generations of connectors, about 70 connector types are in use today.

As shown in Figure 1, the three most popular network fiber-optic connectors include:

- **Straight-Tip (ST):** An older bayonet style connector widely used with multimode fiber.

- **Subscriber Connector (SC):** Sometimes referred to as square connector or standard connector. It is a widely adopted LAN and WAN connector that uses a push-pull mechanism to ensure positive insertion. This connector type is used with multimode and single-mode fiber.

- **Lucent Connector (LC):** Sometimes called a little or local connector, is quickly growing in popularity due to its smaller size. It is used with single-mode fiber and also supports multimode fiber.

Note Other fiber connectors such as the Ferrule Connector (FC) and Sub Miniature A (SMA) are not popular in LAN and WAN deployments. Obsolete connectors include bi-conic (obsolete) and D4 connectors. These connectors are beyond the scope of this chapter.

Because light can only travel in one direction over optical fiber, two fibers are required to support full duplex operation. Therefore, fiber-optic patch cables bundle together two optical fiber cables and terminate them with a pair of standard single fiber connectors. Some fiber connectors accept both the transmitting and receiving fibers in a single connector know as a duplex connector also shown in Figure 1.

Fiber patch cords are required for interconnecting infrastructure devices. For example, Figure 2 displays various common patch cords:

- SC-SC multimode patch cord

- LC-LC single-mode patch cord

- ST-LC multimode patch cord

- SC-ST single-mode patch cord

Fiber cables should be protected with a small plastic cap when not in use.

Also notice the use of color to distinguish between single-mode and multimode patch cords. The reason is because of the TIA-598 standard which recommends the use of a yellow jacket for single-mode fiber cables, and orange (or aqua) for multimode fiber cables.

Refer to
Online Course
for Illustration

4.2.3.5   Testing Fiber Cables

Terminating and splicing fiber-optic cabling requires special training and equipment. Incorrect termination of fiber-optic media will result in diminished signaling distances or complete transmission failure.

Three common types of fiber-optic termination and splicing errors are:

- **Misalignment:** The fiber-optic media are not precisely aligned to one another when joined.

- **End gap:** The media does not completely touch at the splice or connection.

- **End finish:** The media ends are not well polished or dirt is present at the termination.

A quick and easy field test can be performed by shining a bright flashlight into one end of the fiber while observing the other end of the fiber. If light is visible, then the fiber is capable of passing light. Although this does not ensure the performance of the fiber, it is a quick and inexpensive way to find a broken fiber.

It is recommended that an optical tester such as shown in the figure be used to test fiber-optic cables. An Optical Time Domain Reflectometer (OTDR) can be used to test each fiber-optic cable segment. This device injects a test pulse of light into the cable and measures back scatter and reflection of light detected as a function of time. The OTDR will calculate the approximate distance at which these faults are detected along the length of the cable.

Refer to
Online Course
for Illustration

4.2.3.6   Fiber versus Copper

There are many advantages to using fiber-optic cable compared to copper cables.

Given that the fibers used in fiber-optic media are not electrical conductors, the media is immune to electromagnetic interference and will not conduct unwanted electrical currents due to grounding issues. Because optical fibers are thin and have relatively low signal loss, they can be operated at much greater lengths than copper media, without the need for signal regeneration. Some optical fiber physical layer specifications allow lengths that can reach multiple kilometers.

Optical fiber media implementation issues include:

- More expensive (usually) than copper media over the same distance (but for a higher capacity)

- Different skills and equipment required to terminate and splice the cable infrastructure

- More careful handling than copper media

At present, in most enterprise environments, optical fiber is primarily used as backbone cabling for high-traffic point-to-point connections between data distribution facilities and for the interconnection of buildings in multi-building campuses. Because optical fiber does not conduct electricity and has low signal loss, it is well suited for these uses.

The figure highlights some of these differences.

4.2.3.7   Activity - Fiber Optics Terminology

4.2.4   Wireless Media

Refer to
Online Course
for Illustration

4.2.4.1   Properties of Wireless Media

Wireless media carry electromagnetic signals that represent the binary digits of data communications using radio or microwave frequencies.

As a networking medium, wireless is not restricted to conductors or pathways, as are copper and fiber media. Wireless media provides the greatest mobility options of all media. As well, the number of wireless enabled devices is continuously increasing. For these reasons, wireless has become the medium of choice for home networks. As network bandwidth options increase, wireless is quickly gaining in popularity in enterprise networks.

The figure highlights various wireless related symbols.

However, wireless does have some areas of concern including:

- **Coverage area:** Wireless data communication technologies work well in open environments. However, certain construction materials used in buildings and structures, and the local terrain, will limit the effective coverage.

- **Interference:** Wireless is susceptible to interference and can be disrupted by such common devices as household cordless phones, some types of fluorescent lights, microwave ovens, and other wireless communications.

- **Security:** Wireless communication coverage requires no access to a physical strand of media. Therefore, devices and users who are not authorized for access to the network can gain access to the transmission. Consequently, network security is a major component of wireless network administration.

Although wireless is increasing in popularity for desktop connectivity, copper and fiber are the most popular physical layer media for network deployments.

Refer to
Online Course
for Illustration

4.2.4.2   Types of Wireless Media

The IEEE and telecommunications industry standards for wireless data communications cover both the data link and physical layers.

Four common data communications standards that apply to wireless media are:

- **Standard IEEE 802.11:** Wireless LAN (WLAN) technology, commonly referred to as Wi-Fi, uses a contention or non-deterministic system with a Carrier Sense Multiple Access/Collision Avoidance (CSMA/CA) media access process.

- **Standard IEEE 802.15:** Wireless Personal Area Network (WPAN) standard, commonly known as "Bluetooth", uses a device pairing process to communicate over distances from 1 to 100 meters.

- **Standard IEEE 802.16:** Commonly known as Worldwide Interoperability for Microwave Access (WiMAX), uses a point-to-multipoint topology to provide wireless broadband access.

The figure highlights some of the differences between wireless media.

Note   Other wireless technologies such as cellular and satellite communications can also provide data network connectivity. However, these wireless technologies are out of scope for this chapter.

In each of the above examples, physical layer specifications are applied to areas that include:

- Data to radio signal encoding
- Frequency and power of transmission
- Signal reception and decoding requirements
- Antenna design and construction

Note   Wi-Fi is a trademark of the Wi-Fi Alliance. Wi-Fi is used with certified products that belong to WLAN devices that are based on the IEEE 802.11 standards.

Refer to
Online Course
for Illustration

4.2.4.3   Wireless LAN

A common wireless data implementation is enabling devices to wirelessly connect via a LAN. In general, a wireless LAN requires the following network devices:

- **Wireless Access Point (AP):** Concentrates the wireless signals from users and connects, usually through a copper cable, to the existing copper-based network infrastructure, such as Ethernet. Home and small business wireless routers integrate the functions of a router, switch, and access point into one device as shown in the figure.

- **Wireless NIC adapters:** Provides wireless communication capability to each network host.

As the technology has developed, a number of WLAN Ethernet-based standards have emerged. Care needs to be taken in purchasing wireless devices to ensure compatibility and interoperability.

The benefits of wireless data communications technologies are evident, especially the savings on costly premises wiring and the convenience of host mobility. However, network administrators need to develop and apply stringent security policies and processes to protect wireless LANs from unauthorized access and damage.

Refer to
Online Course
for Illustration

4.2.4.4   802.11 Wi-Fi Standards

Various 802.11 standards have evolved over the years. Standards include:

- **IEEE 802.11a:** Operates in the 5 GHz frequency band and offers speeds of up to 54 Mb/s. Because this standard operates at higher frequencies, it has a smaller coverage area and is less effective at penetrating building structures. Devices operating under this standard are not interoperable with the 802.11b and 802.11g standards described below.

- **IEEE 802.11b:** Operates in the 2.4 GHz frequency band and offers speeds of up to 11 Mb/s. Devices implementing this standard have a longer range and are better able to penetrate building structures than devices based on 802.11a.

- **IEEE 802.11g:** Operates in the 2.4 GHz frequency band and offers speeds of up to 54 Mbps. Devices implementing this standard therefore operate at the same radio frequency and range as 802.11b but with the bandwidth of 802.11a.

- **IEEE 802.11n:** Operates in the 2.4 GHz or 5 GHz frequency bands. The typical expected data rates are 100 Mb/s to 600 Mb/s with a distance range of up to 70 meters. It is backward compatible with 802.11a/b/g devices.

- **IEEE 802.11ac:** Can simultaneously operate in the 2.4 GHz and 5.5 GHz frequency bands providing data rates up to 450 Mb/s and 1.3 Gb/s (1300 Mb/s.) It is backward compatible with 802.11a/b/g/n devices.

- **IEEE 802.11ad:** Also known as "WiGig". It uses a tri-band Wi-Fi solution using 2.4 GHz, 5 GHz, and 60 GHz and offers theoretical speeds of up to 7 Gb/s.

The figure highlights some of these differences.

Refer to **Packet Tracer Activity** for this chapter

4.2.4.5   Packet Tracer - Connecting a Wired and Wireless LAN

When working in Packet Tracer (a lab environment or a corporate setting), you should know how to select the appropriate cable and how to properly connect devices. This activity will examine device configurations in Packet Tracer, selecting the proper cable based on the configuration, and connecting the devices. This activity will also explore the physical view of the network in Packet Tracer.

Refer to
Lab Activity
for this chapter

4.2.4.6   Lab - Viewing Wired and Wireless NIC Information

In this lab, you will complete the following objectives:

- Part 1: Identify and Work with PC NICs

- Part 2: Identify and Use the System Tray Network Icons

Refer to
Online Course
for Illustration

4.3   Data Link Layer Protocols

4.3.1   Purpose of the Data Link Layer

4.3.1.1   The Data Link Layer

The TCP/IP network access layer is the equivalent of the OSI:

■ Data link (Layer 2)

■ Physical (Layer 1)

As shown in the figure, the data link layer is responsible for the exchange of frames between nodes over a physical network media. It allows the upper layers to access the media and controls how data is placed and received on the media.

Note   The Layer 2 notation for network devices connected to a common medium is called a node.

Specifically the data link layer performs these two basic services:

■ It accepts Layer 3 packets and packages them into data units called frames.

■ It controls media access control and performs error detection.

The data link layer effectively separates the media transitions that occur as the packet is forwarded from the communication processes of the higher layers. The data link layer receives packets from and directs packets to an upper layer protocol, in this case IPv4 or IPv6. This upper layer protocol does not need to be aware of which media the communication will use.

Note   In this chapter, media and medium do not refer to digital content and multimedia such as audio, animation, television, and video. Media refers to the material that actually carries the data signals, such as copper cable and optical fiber.

Refer to
Online Course
for Illustration

4.3.1.2   Data Link Sublayers

The data link layer is actually divided into two sublayers:

■ **Logical Link Control (LLC):** This upper sublayer defines the software processes that provide services to the network layer protocols. It places information in the frame that identifies which network layer protocol is being used for the frame. This information allows multiple Layer 3 protocols, such as IPv4 and IPv6, to utilize the same network interface and media.

■ **Media Access Control (MAC):** This lower sublayer defines the media access processes performed by the hardware. It provides data link layer addressing and delimiting of data according to the physical signaling requirements of the medium and the type of data link layer protocol in use.

Separating the data link layer into sublayers allows for one type of frame defined by the upper layer to access different types of media defined by the lower layer. Such is the case in many LAN technologies, including Ethernet.

The figure illustrates how the data link layer is separated into the LLC and MAC sublayers. The LLC communicates with the network layer while the MAC sublayer allows various network access technologies. For instance, the MAC sublayer communicates with Ethernet LAN technology to send and receive frames over copper or fiber-optic cable. The MAC sublayer also communicates with wireless technologies such as Wi-Fi and Bluetooth to send and receive frames wirelessly.

4.3.1.3   Media Access Control

Refer to Online Course for Illustration

Layer 2 protocols specify the encapsulation of a packet into a frame and the techniques for getting the encapsulated packet on and off each medium. The technique used for getting the frame on and off media is called the media access control method.

As packets travel from source host to destination host, they typically traverse over different physical networks. These physical networks can consist of different types of physical media such as copper wires, optical fibers, and wireless consisting of electromagnetic signals, radio and microwave frequencies, and satellite links.

The packets do not have a way to directly access these different media. It is the role of the OSI data link layer to prepare network layer packets for transmission and to control access to the physical media. The media access control methods described by the data link layer protocols define the processes by which network devices can access the network media and transmit frames in diverse network environments.

Without the data link layer, network layer protocols such as IP, would have to make provisions for connecting to every type of media that could exist along a delivery path. Moreover, IP would have to adapt every time a new network technology or medium was developed. This process would hamper protocol and network media innovation and development. This is a key reason for using a layered approach to networking.

The animation in the figure provides an example of a PC in Paris connecting to a laptop in Japan. Although the two hosts are communicating using IP exclusively, it is likely that numerous data link layer protocols are being used to transport the IP packets over various types of LANs and WANs. Each transition at a router may require a different data link layer protocol for transport on a new medium.

4.3.1.4   Providing Access to Media

Refer to Online Course for Illustration

Different media access control methods may be required during the course of a single communication. Each network environment that packets encounter as they travel from a local host to a remote host can have different characteristics. For example, an Ethernet LAN consists of many hosts contending to access the network medium on an ad hoc basis. Serial links consist of a direct connection between only two devices over which data flows sequentially as bits in an orderly way.

Router interfaces encapsulate the packet into the appropriate frame, and a suitable media access control method is used to access each link. In any given exchange of network layer packets, there may be numerous data link layer and media transitions. At each hop along the path, a router:

- Accepts a frame from a medium

- De-encapsulates the frame

- Re-encapsulates the packet into a new frame

- Forwards the new frame appropriate to the medium of that segment of the physical network

The router in the figure has an Ethernet interface to connect to the LAN and a serial interface to connect to the WAN. As the router processes frames, it will use data link layer services to receive the frame from one medium, de-encapsulate it to the Layer 3 PDU, re-encapsulate the PDU into a new frame, and place the frame on the medium of the next link of the network.

Refer to
Online Course
for Illustration

4.3.2   Layer 2 Frame Structure

4.3.2.1   Formatting Data for Transmission

The data link layer prepares a packet for transport across the local media by encapsulating it with a header and a trailer to create a frame. The description of a frame is a key element of each data link layer protocol.

Data link layer protocols require control information to enable the protocols to function. Control information typically answers:

- Which nodes are in communication with each other?

- When does communication between individual nodes begin and when does it end?

- Which errors occurred while the nodes communicated?

- Which nodes will communicate next?

Unlike the other PDUs that have been discussed in this course, the data link layer frame includes:

- **Header:** Contains control information, such as addressing, and is located at the beginning of the PDU.

- **Data:** Contains the IP header, transport layer header, and application data.

- **Trailer:** Contains control information for error detection added to the end of the PDU.

These frame elements are shown in the figure, and will be discussed in greater detail.

Refer to
Online Course
for Illustration

4.3.2.2   Creating a Frame

When data travels on the media, it is converted into a stream of bits, or 1s and 0s. If a node is receiving long streams of bits, how does it determine where a frame starts and stops or which bits represent the address?

Framing breaks the stream into decipherable groupings, with control information inserted in the header and trailer as values in different fields. This format gives the physical signals a structure that can be received by nodes and decoded into packets at the destination.

As shown in the figure, generic frame field types include:

- **Frame start and stop indicator flags:** Used by the MAC sublayer to identify the beginning and end limits of the frame.

- **Addressing:** Used by the MAC sublayer to identify the source and destination nodes.

- **Type:** Used by the LLC to identify the Layer 3 protocol.

- **Control:** Identifies special flow control services.

- **Data:** Contains the frame payload (i.e., packet header, segment header, and the data).

- **Error Detection:** Included after the data to form the trailer, these frame fields are used for error detection.

Not all protocols include all of these fields. The standards for a specific data link protocol define the actual frame format.

Note   Examples of frame formats will be discussed at the end of this chapter.

Refer to
Interactive Graphic
in online course.

4.3.2.3   Activity - Generic Frame Fields

Refer to
Online Course
for Illustration

4.3.3   Layer 2 Standards

4.3.3.1   Data Link Layer Standards

Unlike the protocols of the upper layers of the TCP/IP suite, data link layer protocols are generally not defined by Request for Comments (RFCs). Although the Internet Engineering Task Force (IETF) maintains the functional protocols and services for the TCP/IP protocol suite in the upper layers, the IETF does not define the functions and operation of that model's network access layer.

Specifically the data link layer services and specifications are defined by multiple standards based on a variety of technologies and media to which the protocols are applied. Some of these standards integrate both Layer 2 and Layer 1 services.

The functional protocols and services at the data link layer are described by:

- Engineering organizations which set public and open standards and protocols.

- Communications companies which set and use proprietary protocols to take advantage of new advances in technology or market opportunities.

Engineering organizations that define open standards and protocols that apply to the data link layer include:

- Institute of Electrical and Electronics Engineers (IEEE)

- International Telecommunication Union (ITU)

- International Organization for Standardization (ISO)
- American National Standards Institute (ANSI)

The table in the figure highlights various standard organizations and some of their more important data link layer protocols.

4.3.3.2   Activity - Data Link Layer Standards Organizations

Refer to
Online Course
for Illustration

4.4   Media Access Control

4.4.1   Topologies

4.4.1.1   Controlling Access to the Media

Regulating the placement of data frames onto the media is controlled by the media access control sublayer.

Media access control is the equivalent of traffic rules that regulate the entrance of motor vehicles onto a roadway. The absence of any media access control would be the equivalent of vehicles ignoring all other traffic and entering the road without regard to the other vehicles. However, not all roads and entrances are the same. Traffic can enter the road by merging, by waiting for its turn at a stop sign, or by obeying signal lights. A driver follows a different set of rules for each type of entrance.

In the same way, there are different ways to regulate placing frames onto the media. The protocols at the data link layer define the rules for access to different media. Some media access control methods use highly-controlled processes to ensure that frames are safely placed on the media. These methods are defined by sophisticated protocols, which require mechanisms that introduce overhead onto the network.

Among the different implementations of the data link layer protocols, there are different methods of controlling access to the media. These media access control techniques define if and how the nodes share the media.

The actual media access control method used depends on:

- **Topology:** How the connection between the nodes appears to the data link layer.

- **Media sharing:** How the nodes share the media. The media sharing can be point-to-point such as in WAN connections or shared such as in LAN networks.

Refer to
Online Course
for Illustration

4.4.1.2   Physical and Logical Topologies

The topology of a network is the arrangement or relationship of the network devices and the interconnections between them. LAN and WAN topologies can be viewed in two ways:

- **Physical topology:** Refers to the physical connections and identifies how end devices and infrastructure devices such as routers, switches, and wireless access points are interconnected. Physical topologies are usually point-to-point or star. See Figure 1.

- **Logical topology:** Refers to the way a network transfers frames from one node to the next. This arrangement consists of virtual connections between the nodes of a network. These logical signal paths are defined by data link layer protocols. The logical topology of point-to-point links is relatively simple while shared media offers deterministic and a non-deterministic media access control methods. See Figure 2.

The data link layer "sees" the logical topology of a network when controlling data access to the media. It is the logical topology that influences the type of network framing and media access control used.

Refer to **Online Course** for Illustration

4.4.2   WAN Topologies

4.4.2.1   Common Physical WAN Topologies

WANs are commonly interconnected using the following physical topologies:

- **Point-to-Point:** This is the simplest topology which consists of a permanent link between two endpoints. For this reason, this is a very popular WAN topology.

- **Hub and Spoke:** A WAN version of the star topology in which a central site interconnects branch sites using point-to-point links.

- **Mesh:** This topology provides high availability, but requires that every end system be interconnected to every other system. Therefore the administrative and physical costs can be significant. Each link is essentially a point-to-point link to the other node. Variations of this topology include a partial mesh where some but not all of end devices are interconnected.

The three common physical WAN topologies are illustrated in the figure.

Refer to **Online Course** for Illustration

4.4.2.2   Physical Point-to-Point Topology

Physical point-to-point topologies directly connect two nodes as shown in the figure.

In this arrangement, two nodes do not have to share the media with other hosts. Additionally, a node does not have to make any determination about whether an incoming frame is destined for it or another node. Therefore, the logical data link protocols can be very simple as all frames on the media can only travel to or from the two nodes. The frames are placed on the media by the node at one end and taken off the media by the node at the other end of the point-to-point circuit.

Data link layer protocols could provide more sophisticated media access control processes for logical point-to-point topologies, but this would only add unnecessary protocol overhead.

Refer to **Online Course** for Illustration

4.4.2.3   Logical Point-to-Point Topology

The end nodes communicating in a point-to-point network can be physically connected via a number of intermediate devices. However, the use of physical devices in the network does not affect the logical topology.

As shown in Figure 1, the source and destination node may be indirectly connected to each other over some geographical distance. In some cases, the logical connection between nodes forms what is called a virtual circuit. A virtual circuit is a logical connection created within a network between two network devices. The two nodes on either end of the virtual circuit exchange the frames with each other. This occurs even if the frames are directed through intermediary devices. Virtual circuits are important logical communication constructs used by some Layer 2 technologies.

The media access method used by the data link protocol is determined by the logical point-to-point topology, not the physical topology. This means that the logical point-to-point connection between two nodes may not necessarily be between two physical nodes at each end of a single physical link.

Figure 2 shows the physical devices in-between the two routers.

Refer to
Online Course
for Illustration

4.4.2.4   Half and Full Duplex

Figure 1 shows a point-to-point topology. In point-to-point networks, data can flow in one of two ways:

- **Half-duplex communication:** Both devices can both transmit and receive on the media but cannot do so simultaneously. Ethernet has established arbitration rules for resolving conflicts arising from instances when more than one station attempts to transmit at the same time. Figure 2 shows half-duplex communication.

- **Full-duplex communication:** Both devices can transmit and receive on the media at the same time. The data link layer assumes that the media is available for transmission for both nodes at any time. Therefore, there is no media arbitration necessary in the data link layer. Figure 3 shows full-duplex communication.

Refer to
Online Course
for Illustration

4.4.3   LAN Topologies

4.4.3.1   Physical LAN Topologies

Physical topology defines how the end systems are physically interconnected. In shared media LANs, end devices can be interconnected using the following physical topologies:

- **Star:** End devices are connected to a central intermediate device. Early star topologies interconnected end devices using hubs. However, star topologies now use switches. The star topology is the most common physical LAN topology primarily because it is easy to install, very scalable (easy to add and remove end devices), and easy to troubleshoot.

- **Extended star or hybrid:** This is a combination of the other topologies such as star networks interconnected to each other using a bus topology.

- **Bus:** All end systems are chained to each other and terminated in some form on each end. Infrastructure devices such as switches are not required to interconnect the end devices. Bus topologies were used in legacy Ethernet networks because it was inexpensive to use and easy to set up.

■ **Ring:** End systems are connected to their respective neighbor forming a ring. Unlike the bus topology, the ring does not need to be terminated. Ring topologies were used in legacy Fiber Distributed Data Interface (FDDI) networks. Specifically, FDDI networks employ a second ring for fault tolerance or performance enhancements.

The figure illustrates how end devices are interconnected on LANs.

Refer to
Online Course
for Illustration

4.4.3.2   Logical Topology for Shared Media

Logical topology of a network is closely related to the mechanism used to manage network access. Access methods provide the procedures to manage network access so that all stations have access. When several entities share the same media, some mechanism must be in place to control access. Access methods are applied to networks to regulate this media access.

Some network topologies share a common medium with multiple nodes. At any one time, there may be a number of devices attempting to send and receive data using the network media. There are rules that govern how these devices share the media.

There are two basic media access control methods for shared media:

■ **Contention-based access:** All nodes compete for the use of the medium but have a plan if there are collisions. Figure 1 shows contention-based access.

■ **Controlled access:** Each node has its own time to use the medium. Figure 2 shows controlled access.

The data link layer protocol specifies the media access control method that will provide the appropriate balance between frame control, frame protection, and network overhead.

Refer to
Online Course
for Illustration

4.4.3.3   Contention-Based Access

When using a non-deterministic contention-based method, a network device can attempt to access the medium whenever it has data to send. To prevent complete chaos on the media, these methods use a Carrier Sense Multiple Access (CSMA) process to first detect if the media is carrying a signal.

If a carrier signal on the media from another node is detected, it means that another device is transmitting. When the device attempting to transmit sees that the media is busy, it will wait and try again after a short time period. If no carrier signal is detected, the device transmits its data. Ethernet and wireless networks use contention-based media access control.

It is possible that the CSMA process will fail and two devices will transmit at the same time creating a data collision. If this occurs, the data sent by both devices will be corrupted and will need to be resent.

Contention-based media access control methods do not have the overhead of controlled access methods. A mechanism for tracking whose turn it is to access the media is not required. However, the contention-based systems do not scale well under heavy media use. As use and the number of nodes increases, the probability of successful media access without a collision decreases. Additionally, the recovery mechanisms required to correct errors due to these collisions further diminishes the throughput.

CSMA is usually implemented in conjunction with a method for resolving the media contention. The two commonly used methods are:

- **Carrier sense multiple access with collision detection (CSMA/CD):** The end device monitors the media for the presence of a data signal. If a data signal is absent and therefore the media is free, the device transmits the data. If signals are then detected that show another device was transmitting at the same time, all devices stop sending and try again later. Traditional forms of Ethernet use this method.

- **Carrier sense multiple access with collision avoidance (CSMA/CA):** The end device examines the media for the presence of a data signal. If the media is free, the device sends a notification across the media of its intent to use it. Once it receives a clearance to transmit, the device then sends the data. This method is used by 802.11 wireless networking technologies.

The figure illustrates the following:

- How contention-based access methods operates
- Characteristics of contention-based access methods
- Examples of contention-based access methods

Refer to
Online Course
for Illustration

4.4.3.4   Multi-Access Topology

A logical multi-access topology enables a number of nodes to communicate by using the same shared media. Data from only one node can be placed on the medium at any one time. Every node sees all the frames that are on the medium, but only the node to which the frame is addressed processes the contents of the frame.

Having many nodes share access to the medium requires a data link media access control method to regulate the transmission of data and thereby reduce collisions between different signals.

Play the animation to see how nodes access the media in a multi-access topology.

Refer to
Online Course
for Illustration

4.4.3.5   Controlled Access

When using the controlled access method, network devices take turns, in sequence, to access the medium. If an end device does not need to access the medium, then the opportunity passes to the next end device. This process is facilitated by use of a token. An end device acquires the token and places a frame on the media, no other device can do so until the frame has arrived and been processed at the destination, releasing the token.

Note   This method is also known as scheduled access or deterministic.

Although controlled access is well-ordered and provides predictable throughput, deterministic methods can be inefficient because a device has to wait for its turn before it can use the medium.

Controlled access examples include:

■ Token Ring (IEEE 802.5)

■ Fiber Distributed Data Interface (FDDI) which is based on the IEEE 802.4 token bus protocol.

Note   Both of these media access control methods are considered obsolete.

The figure illustrates the following:

■ How controlled access methods operate

■ Characteristics of controlled access methods

■ Examples of controlled access methods

Refer to
Online Course
for Illustration

4.4.3.6   Ring Topology

In a logical ring topology, each node in turn receives a frame. If the frame is not addressed to the node, the node passes the frame to the next node. This allows a ring to use a controlled media access control technique called token passing.

Nodes in a logical ring topology remove the frame from the ring, examine the address, and send it on if it is not addressed for that node. In a ring, all nodes around the ring (between the source and destination node) examine the frame.

There are multiple media access control techniques that could be used with a logical ring, depending on the level of control required. For example, only one frame at a time is usually carried by the media. If there is no data being transmitted, a signal (known as a token) may be placed on the media and a node can only place a data frame on the media when it has the token.

Remember that the data link layer "sees" a logical ring topology. The actual physical cabling topology could be another topology.

Play the animation to see how nodes access the media in a logical ring topology.

Refer to
Interactive Graphic
in online ccurse.

4.4.3.7   Activity - Logical and Physical Topologies

4.4.4   Data Link Frame

Refer to
Online Course
for Illustration

4.4.4.1   The Frame

Although there are many different data link layer protocols that describe data link layer frames, each frame type has three basic parts:

■ Header

■ Data

■ Trailer

All data link layer protocols encapsulate the Layer 3 PDU within the data field of the frame. However, the structure of the frame and the fields contained in the header and trailer vary according to the protocol.

The data link layer protocol describes the features required for the transport of packets across different media. These features of the protocol are integrated into the encapsulation of the frame. When the frame arrives at its destination and the data link protocol takes the frame off the media, the framing information is read and discarded.

There is no one frame structure that meets the needs of all data transportation across all types of media. Depending on the environment, the amount of control information needed in the frame varies to match the media access control requirements of the media and logical topology.

As shown in Figure 1, a fragile environment requires more control. However, a protected environment, as shown in Figure 2, requires fewer controls.

Refer to
Online Course
for Illustration

4.4.4.2   The Header

The frame header contains the control information specified by the data link layer protocol for the specific logical topology and media used.

Frame control information is unique to each type of protocol. It is used by the Layer 2 protocol to provide features demanded by the communication environment.

The figure displays the Ethernet frame header fields:

- **Start Frame field:** Indicates the beginning of the frame.

- **Source and Destination Address fields:** Indicates the source and destination nodes on the media.

- **Type field:** Indicates the upper layer service contained in the frame.

Different data link layer protocols may use different fields from those mentioned. For example other Layer 2 protocol header frame fields could include:

- **Priority/Quality of Service field:** Indicates a particular type of communication service for processing.

- **Logical connection control field:** Used to establish a logical connection between nodes.

- **Physical link control field:** Used to establish the media link.

- **Flow control field:** Used to start and stop traffic over the media.

- **Congestion control field:** Indicates congestion in the media.

Because the purposes and functions of data link layer protocols are related to the specific topologies and media, each protocol has to be examined to gain a detailed understanding of its frame structure. As protocols are discussed in this course, more information about the frame structure will be explained.

Refer to
Online Course
for Illustration

4.4.4.3   Layer 2 Address

The data link layer provides addressing that is used in transporting a frame across a shared local media. Device addresses at this layer are referred to as physical addresses. Data link layer addressing is contained within the frame header and specifies the frame destination node on the local network. The frame header may also contain the source address of the frame.

Unlike Layer 3 logical addresses, which are hierarchical, physical addresses do not indicate on what network the device is located. Rather, the physical address is a unique device specific address. If the device is moved to another network or subnet, it will still function with the same Layer 2 physical address.

An address that is device-specific and non-hierarchical cannot be used to locate a device across large networks or the Internet. This would be like trying to find a single house within the entire world, with nothing more than a house number and street name. The physical address, however, can be used to locate a device within a limited area. For this reason, the data link layer address is only used for local delivery. Addresses at this layer have no meaning beyond the local network. Compare this to Layer 3, where addresses in the packet header are carried from source host to destination host regardless of the number of network hops along the route.

If the data must pass onto another network segment, an intermediate device, such as a router, is necessary. The router must accept the frame based on the physical address and de-encapsulate the frame in order to examine the hierarchical address, or IP address. Using the IP address, the router is able to determine the network location of the destination device and the best path to reach it. Once it knows where to forward the packet, the router then creates a new frame for the packet, and the new frame is sent onto the next segment toward its final destination.

The figure highlights Layer 2 address requirements in multi-access and point-to-point topologies.

Refer to
Online Course
for Illustration

4.4.4.4   The Trailer

Data link layer protocols add a trailer to the end of each frame. The trailer is used to determine if the frame arrived without error. This process is called error detection and is accomplished by placing a logical or mathematical summary of the bits that comprise the frame in the trailer. Error detection is added at the data link layer because the signals on the media could be subject to interference, distortion, or loss that would substantially change the bit values that those signals represent.

A transmitting node creates a logical summary of the contents of the frame. This is known as the cyclic redundancy check (CRC) value. This value is placed in the Frame Check Sequence (FCS) field of the frame to represent the contents of the frame.

Click the FCS and Stop Frame fields in the figure for more information.

When the frame arrives at the destination node, the receiving node calculates its own logical summary, or CRC, of the frame. The receiving node compares the two CRC values. If the two values are the same, the frame is considered to have arrived as transmitted. If the CRC value in the FCS differs from the CRC calculated at the receiving node, the frame is discarded.

Therefore, the FCS field is used to determine if errors occurred in the transmission and reception of the frame. The error detection mechanism provided by the use of the FCS field discovers most errors caused on the media.

There is always the small possibility that a frame with a good CRC result is actually corrupt. Errors in bits may cancel each other out when the CRC is calculated. Upper layer protocols would then be required to detect and correct this data loss.

4.4.4.5   LAN and WAN Frames

Refer to **Online Course** for Illustration

In a TCP/IP network, all OSI Layer 2 protocols work with the IP at OSI Layer 3. However, the actual Layer 2 protocol used depends on the logical topology of the network and the implementation of the physical layer. Given the wide range of physical media used across the range of topologies in networking, there are a correspondingly high number of Layer 2 protocols in use.

Each protocol performs media access control for specified Layer 2 logical topologies. This means that a number of different network devices can act as nodes that operate at the data link layer when implementing these protocols. These devices include the network adapter or network interface cards (NICs) on computers as well as the interfaces on routers and Layer 2 switches.

The Layer 2 protocol used for a particular network topology is determined by the technology used to implement that topology. The technology is, in turn, determined by the size of the network - in terms of the number of hosts and the geographic scope - and the services to be provided over the network.

A LAN typically uses a high bandwidth technology that is capable of supporting large numbers of hosts. A LAN's relatively small geographic area (a single building or a multi-building campus) and its high density of users make this technology cost effective.

However, using a high bandwidth technology is usually not cost-effective for WANs that cover large geographic areas (cities or multiple cities, for example). The cost of the long distance physical links and the technology used to carry the signals over those distances typically results in lower bandwidth capacity.

Difference in bandwidth normally results in the use of different protocols for LANs and WANs.

Common data link layer protocols include:

- Ethernet
- Point-to-Point Protocol (PPP)
- 802.11 Wireless

Other protocols covered in the CCNA curriculum are High-Level Data Link Control (HDLC) and Frame Relay.

Click Play to see examples of Layer 2 protocols.

Refer to
Online Course
for Illustration

4.4.4.6   Ethernet Frame

Ethernet

Ethernet is the dominant LAN technology. It is a family of networking technologies that are defined in the IEEE 802.2 and 802.3 standards.

Ethernet standards define both the Layer 2 protocols and the Layer 1 technologies. Ethernet is the most widely used LAN technology and supports data bandwidths of 10 Mbps, 100 Mbps, 1 Gbps (1,000 Mbps), or 10 Gbps (10,000 Mbps).

The basic frame format and the IEEE sublayers of OSI Layers 1 and 2 remain consistent across all forms of Ethernet. However, the methods for detecting and placing data on the media vary with different implementations.

Ethernet provides unacknowledged connectionless service over a shared media using CSMA/CD as the media access methods. Shared media requires that the Ethernet frame header use a data link layer address to identify the source and destination nodes. As with most LAN protocols, this address is referred to as the MAC address of the node. An Ethernet MAC address is 48 bits and is generally represented in hexadecimal format.

The figure shows the many fields of the Ethernet frame. At the data link layer, the frame structure is nearly identical for all speeds of Ethernet. However, at the physical layer, different versions of Ethernet place the bits onto the media differently. Ethernet is discussed in more detail in the next chapter.

4.4.4.7   PPP Frame

Point-to-Point Protocol

Another data link layer protocol is the Point-to-Point Protocol (PPP). PPP is a protocol used to deliver frames between two nodes. Unlike many data link layer protocols that are defined by electrical engineering organizations, the PPP standard is defined by RFCs. PPP was developed as a WAN protocol and remains the protocol of choice to implement many serial WANs. PPP can be used on various physical media, including twisted pair, fiber-optic lines, and satellite transmission, as well as for virtual connections.

PPP uses a layered architecture. To accommodate the different types of media, PPP establishes logical connections, called sessions, between two nodes. The PPP session hides the underlying physical media from the upper PPP protocol. These sessions also provide PPP with a method for encapsulating multiple protocols over a point-to-point link. Each protocol encapsulated over the link establishes its own PPP session.

PPP also allows the two nodes to negotiate options within the PPP session. This includes authentication, compression, and multilink (the use of multiple physical connections).

Refer to the figure for the basic fields in a PPP frame.

4.4.4.8   802.11 Wireless Frame

802.11 Wireless

The IEEE 802.11 standard uses the same 802.2 LLC and 48-bit addressing scheme as other 802 LANs. However, there are many differences at the MAC sublayer and physical layer. In a wireless environment, the environment requires special considerations. There is no definable physical connectivity; therefore, external factors may interfere with data transfer and it is difficult to control access. To meet these challenges, wireless standards have additional controls.

The IEEE 802.11 standard is commonly referred to as Wi-Fi. It is a contention-based system using a CSMA/CA media access process. CSMA/CA specifies a random backoff procedure for all nodes that are waiting to transmit. The most likely opportunity for medium contention is just after the medium becomes available. Making the nodes back off for a random period greatly reduces the likelihood of a collision.

802.11 networks also use data link acknowledgements to confirm that a frame is received successfully. If the sending station does not detect the acknowledgement frame, either because the original data frame or the acknowledgment was not received intact, the frame is retransmitted. This explicit acknowledgement overcomes interference and other radio-related problems.

Other services supported by 802.11 are authentication, association (connectivity to a wireless device), and privacy (encryption).

As shown in the figure, an 802.11 frame contains these fields:

- **Protocol Version field:** Version of 802.11 frame in use
- **Type and Subtype fields:** Identifies one of three functions and sub functions of the frame: control, data, and management
- **To DS field:** Set to 1 in data frames destined for the distribution system (devices in the wireless structure)
- **From DS field:** Set to 1 in data frames exiting the distribution system
- **More Fragments field:** Set to 1 for frames that have another fragment
- **Retry field:** Set to 1 if the frame is a retransmission of an earlier frame
- **Power Management field:** Set to 1 to indicate that a node will be in power-save mode
- **More Data field:** Set to 1 to indicate to a node in power-save mode that more frames are buffered for that node
- **Wired Equivalent Privacy (WEP) field:** Set to 1 if the frame contains WEP encrypted information for security
- **Order field:** Set to 1 in a data type frame that uses Strictly Ordered service class (does not need reordering)
- **Duration/ID field:** Depending on the type of frame, represents either the time, in microseconds, required to transmit the frame or an association identity (AID) for the station that transmitted the frame
- **Destination Address (DA) field:** MAC address of the final destination node in the network
- **Source Address (SA) field:** MAC address of the node that initiated the frame
- **Receiver Address (RA) field:** MAC address that identifies the wireless device that is the immediate recipient of the frame
- **Fragment Number field:** Indicates the number for each fragment of a frame
- **Sequence Number field:** Indicates the sequence number assigned to the frame; retransmitted frames are identified by duplicate sequence numbers

- **Transmitter Address (TA) field:** MAC address that identifies the wireless device that transmitted the frame

- **Frame Body field:** Contains the information being transported; for data frames, typically an IP packet

- **FCS field:** Contains a 32-bit cyclic redundancy check (CRC) of the frame

Refer to
Interactive Graphic
in online course.

4.4.4.9   Activity - Frame Fields

Refer to
Online Course
for Illustration

4.5   Summary

Refer to
Lab Activity
for this chapter

4.5.1.1   Class Activity - Linked In!

Linked In!

Note   This activity is best completed in groups of 2-3 students.

Your small business is moving to a new location! Your building is brand new, and you have been tasked to come up with a physical model so that network port installation can begin.

Use the blueprint provided for this activity (your Instructor will provide you with a copy from the Instructor Planning Guide) – the area indicated by Number 1 is the reception area – the area numbered RR is the restroom area.

All rooms are within Category 6, UTP specifications (100 meters), so you have no worries about hard-wiring the building to code. Each room in the diagram must have at least one network connection available for users/intermediary devices.

With your teammate(s), indicate on the drawing:

- The location of your network main distribution facility, while keeping security in mind.

- The number of intermediary devices that you would use and where you would place them.

- The type of cabling that would be used (UTP, STP, wireless, fiber optics, etc.) and where would the ports be placed.

- The types of end devices that would be used (wired, wireless, laptops, desktops, tablets, etc.).

Do not go "overboard" on your design – just use the content from the chapter to be able to justify your decisions to the class.

Refer to
Online Course
for Illustration

4.5.1.2   Summary

The TCP/IP network access layer is the equivalent of the OSI data link layer (Layer 2) and the physical layer (Layer 1).

The OSI physical layer provides the means to transport the bits that make up a data link layer frame across the network media. The physical components are the electronic hardware devices, media, and other connectors that transmit and carry the signals to represent the bits. Hardware components such as network adapters (NICs), interfaces and connectors, cable materials, and cable designs are all specified in standards associated with the physical layer. The physical layer standards address three functional areas: physical components, frame encoding technique, and signaling method.

Using the proper media is an important part of network communications. Without the proper physical connection, either wired or wireless, communications between any two devices will not occur.

Wired communication consists of copper media and fiber cable.

- There are three main types of copper media used in networking: unshielded-twisted pair (UTP), shielded-twisted pair (STP), and coaxial cable. UTP cabling is the most common copper networking media.

- Optical fiber cable has become very popular for interconnecting infrastructure network devices. It permits the transmission of data over longer distances and at higher bandwidths (data rates) than any other networking media. Unlike copper wires, fiber-optic cable can transmit signals with less attenuation and is completely immune to EMI and RFI.

Wireless media carry electromagnetic signals that represent the binary digits of data communications using radio or microwave frequencies.

The number of wireless enabled devices continues to increase. For these reasons, wireless has become the medium of choice for home networks and is quickly gaining in popularity in enterprise networks.

The data link layer is responsible for the exchange of frames between nodes over a physical network media. It allows the upper layers to access the media and controls how data is placed and received on the media.

Among the different implementations of the data link layer protocols, there are different methods of controlling access to the media. These media access control techniques define if and how the nodes share the media. The actual media access control method used depends on the topology and media sharing. LAN and WAN topologies can be physical or logical. It is the logical topology that influences the type of network framing and media access control used. WANs are commonly interconnected using the point-to-point, hub and spoke, or mesh physical topologies. In shared media LANs, end devices can be interconnected using the star, bus, ring, or extended star (hybrid) physical topologies.

All data link layer protocols encapsulate the Layer 3 PDU within the data field of the frame. However, the structure of the frame and the fields contained in the header and trailer vary according to the protocol.

Go to the online course to take the quiz and exam.

Chapter 4 Quiz

This quiz is designed to provide an additional opportunity to practice the skills and knowledge presented in the chapter and to prepare for the chapter exam. You will be allowed multiple attempts and the grade does not appear in the gradebook.

Chapter 4 Exam

The chapter exam assesses your knowledge of the chapter content.

Your Chapter Notes

Ethernet

5.0 Ethernet

5.0.1.1 Introduction

The OSI physical layer provides the means to transport the bits that make up a data link layer frame across the network media.

Ethernet is now the predominant LAN technology in the world. Ethernet operates in the data link layer and the physical layer. The Ethernet protocol standards define many aspects of network communication including frame format, frame size, timing, and encoding. When messages are sent between hosts on an Ethernet network, the hosts format the messages into the frame layout that is specified by the standards. Frames are also referred to as Protocol Data Units (PDUs).

Because Ethernet is comprised of standards at these lower layers, it may best be understood in reference to the OSI model. The OSI model separates the data link layer functionalities of addressing, framing, and accessing the media from the physical layer standards of the media. Ethernet standards define both the Layer 2 protocols and the Layer 1 technologies. Although Ethernet specifications support different media, bandwidths, and other Layer 1 and 2 variations, the basic frame format and address scheme is the same for all varieties of Ethernet.

This chapter examines the characteristics and operation of Ethernet as it has evolved from a shared media, contention-based data communications technology to today's high bandwidth, full-duplex technology.

Refer to
Lab Activity
for this chapter

5.0.1.2 Class Activity – Join My Social Circle!

Join My Social Circle!

Much of our network communication takes the form of messaging (text or instant), video contact, social media postings, etc.

For this activity, choose one of the communication networks you use most:

- Text (or instant) messaging
- Audio/video conferencing
- Emailing
- Gaming

Now that you have selected a network communication type, record your answers to the following questions:

- Is there a procedure you must follow to register others and yourself so that you form a communications group?

- How do you initiate contact with the person/people with whom you wish to communicate?

- How do you limit your conversations so they are received by only those with whom you wish to communicate?

Be prepared to discuss your recorded answers in class.

Refer to
Online Course
for Illustration

5.1   Ethernet Protocol

5.1.1   Ethernet Operation

5.1.1.1   LLC and MAC Sublayers

Ethernet is the most widely used LAN technology used today.

Ethernet operates in the data link layer and the physical layer. It is a family of networking technologies that are defined in the IEEE 802.2 and 802.3 standards. Ethernet supports data bandwidths of:

- 10 Mb/s

- 100 Mb/s

- 1000 Mb/s (1 Gb/s)

- 10,000 Mb/s (10 Gb/s)

- 40,000 Mb/s (40 Gb/s)

- 100,000 Mb/s (100 Gb/s)

As shown in Figure 1, Ethernet standards define both the Layer 2 protocols and the Layer 1 technologies. For the Layer 2 protocols, as with all 802 IEEE standards, Ethernet relies on the two separate sublayers of the data link layer to operate, the Logical Link Control (LLC) and the MAC sublayers.

LLC sublayer

The Ethernet LLC sublayer handles the communication between the upper layers and the lower layers. This is typically between the networking software and the device hardware. The LLC sublayer takes the network protocol data, which is typically an IPv4 packet, and adds control information to help deliver the packet to the destination node. The LLC is used to communicate with the upper layers of the application, and transition the packet to the lower layers for delivery.

LLC is implemented in software, and its implementation is independent of the hardware. In a computer, the LLC can be considered the driver software for the NIC. The NIC driver is a program that interacts directly with the hardware on the NIC to pass the data between the MAC sublayer and the physical media.

MAC sublayer

MAC constitutes the lower sublayer of the data link layer. MAC is implemented by hardware, typically in the computer NIC. The specifics are specified in the IEEE 802.3 standards. Figure 2 lists common IEEE Ethernet standards.

Refer to
Online Course
for Illustration

5.1.1.2   MAC Sublayer

As shown in the figure, the Ethernet MAC sublayer has two primary responsibilities:

- Data encapsulation
- Media access control

Data encapsulation

The data encapsulation process includes frame assembly before transmission, and frame disassembly upon reception of a frame. In forming the frame, the MAC layer adds a header and trailer to the network layer PDU.

Data encapsulation provides three primary functions:

- **Frame delimiting:** The framing process provides important delimiters that are used to identify a group of bits that make up a frame. This process provides synchronization between the transmitting and receiving nodes.

- **Addressing:** The encapsulation process also provides for data link layer addressing. Each Ethernet header added in the frame contains the physical address (MAC address) that enables a frame to be delivered to a destination node.

- **Error detection:** Each Ethernet frame contains a trailer with a cyclic redundancy check (CRC) of the frame contents. After reception of a frame, the receiving node creates a CRC to compare to the one in the frame. If these two CRC calculations match, the frame can be trusted to have been received without error.

The use of frames aids in the transmission of bits as they are placed on the media and in the grouping of bits at the receiving node.

Media Access Control

The second responsibility of the MAC sublayer is media access control. Media access control is responsible for the placement of frames on the media and the removal of frames from the media. As its name implies, it controls access to the media. This sublayer communicates directly with the physical layer.

The underlying logical topology of Ethernet is a multi-access bus; therefore, all nodes (devices) on a single network segment share the medium. Ethernet is a contention-based method of networking. Recall that a contention-based method, or non-deterministic method, means that any device can try to transmit data across the shared medium whenever it has data to send. However, much like if two people try to talk simultaneously, if multiple devices on a single medium attempt to forward data simultaneously, the data will collide resulting in corrupted, unusable data. For this reason, Ethernet provides a method for controlling how the nodes share access through the use a Carrier Sense Multiple Access (CSMA) technology.

Refer to
Online Course
for Illustration

5.1.1.3　Media Access Control

The CSMA process is used to first detect if the media is carrying a signal. If a carrier signal on the media from another node is detected, it means that another device is transmitting. When the device attempting to transmit sees that the media is busy, it will wait and try again after a short time period. If no carrier signal is detected, the device transmits its data. It is possible that the CSMA process will fail and two devices will transmit at the same time. This is called a data collision. If this occurs, the data sent by both devices will be corrupted and will need to be resent.

Contention-based media access control methods do not require mechanisms for tracking whose turn it is to access the media; therefore, they do not have the overhead of controlled access methods. However, the contention-based systems do not scale well under heavy media use. As use and the number of nodes increases, the probability of successful media access without a collision decreases. Additionally, the recovery mechanisms required to correct errors due to these collisions further diminishes the throughput.

As shown in the figure, CSMA is usually implemented in conjunction with a method for resolving media contention. The two commonly used methods are:

CSMA/Collision Detection

In CSMA/Collision Detection (CSMA/CD), the device monitors the media for the presence of a data signal. If a data signal is absent, indicating that the media is free, the device transmits the data. If signals are then detected that show another device was transmitting at the same time, all devices stop sending and try again later. Traditional forms of Ethernet were developed to use this method.

The widespread incorporation of switched technologies in modern networks has largely displaced the original need for CSMA/CD in local-area networks. Almost all wired connections between devices in a LAN today are full-duplex connections - a device is able to send and receive simultaneously. This means, that while Ethernet networks are designed with CSMA/CD technology, with today's intermediate devices, collisions do not occur and the processes utilized by CSMA/CD are really unnecessary.

However, wireless connections in a LAN environment still have to take collisions into account. Wireless LAN devices utilize the CSMA/Collision Avoidance (CSMA/CA) media access method.

CSMA/Collision Avoidance

In CSMA/CA, the device examines the media for the presence of a data signal. If the media is free, the device sends a notification across the media of its intent to use it. The device then sends the data. This method is used by 802.11 wireless networking technologies.

Refer to
Online Course
for Illustration

5.1.1.4　MAC Address: Ethernet Identity

As previously stated, the underlying logical topology of Ethernet is a multi-access bus. Every network device is connected to the same, shared media, and all the nodes receive all frames transmitted. The issue is if all devices are receiving every frame, how can each individual device identify if it is the intended receiver without the overhead of having to process and de-encapsulate the frame to get to the IP address? The issue becomes even more problematic in large, high traffic volume networks where lots of frames are forwarded.

To prevent the excessive overhead involved in the processing of every frame, a unique identifier called a MAC address was created to identify the actual source and destination nodes within an Ethernet network. Regardless of which variety of Ethernet is used, MAC addressing provided a method for device identification at the lower level of the OSI model. As you may recall, MAC addressing is added as part of a Layer 2 PDU. An Ethernet MAC address is a 48-bit binary value expressed as 12 hexadecimal digits (4 bits per hexadecimal digit).

MAC Address Structure

MAC addresses must be globally unique. The MAC address value is a direct result of IEEE-enforced rules for vendors to ensure globally unique addresses for each Ethernet device. The rules established by IEEE require any vendor that sells Ethernet devices to register with IEEE. The IEEE assigns the vendor a 3-byte (24-bit) code, called the Organizationally Unique Identifier (OUI).

IEEE requires a vendor to follow two simple rules, as shown in the figure:

- All MAC addresses assigned to a NIC or other Ethernet device must use that vendor's assigned OUI as the first 3 bytes.

All MAC addresses with the same OUI must be assigned a unique value (vendor code or serial number) in the last 3 bytes.

Refer to
Online Course
for Illustration

5.1.1.5   Frame Processing

The MAC address is often referred to as a burned-in address (BIA) because, historically, this address is burned into ROM (Read-Only Memory) on the NIC. This means that the address is encoded into the ROM chip permanently - it cannot be changed by software.

Note   On modern PC operating systems and NICs, it is possible to change the MAC address in software. This is useful when attempting to gain access to a network that filters based on BIA - consequently, filtering, or controlling, traffic based on the MAC address is no longer as secure.

MAC addresses are assigned to workstations, servers, printers, switches, and routers - any device that must originate and/or receive data on the network. All devices connected to an Ethernet LAN have MAC-addressed interfaces. Different hardware and software manufacturers might represent the MAC address in different hexadecimal formats. The address formats might be similar to:

- 00-05-9A-3C-78-00

- 00:05:9A:3C:78:00

- 0005.9A3C.7800

When the computer starts up, the first thing the NIC does is copies the MAC address from ROM into RAM. When a device is forwarding a message to an Ethernet network, it attaches header information to the packet. The header information contains the source and destination MAC address. The source device sends the data through the network.

Each NIC in the network views the information, at the MAC sublayer, to see if the destination MAC address in the frame matches the device's physical MAC address stored in RAM. If there is no match, the device discards the frame. When the frame reaches the destination where the MAC of the NIC matches the destination MAC of the frame, the NIC passes the frame up the OSI layers, where the de-encapsulation process takes place.

Refer to
Interactive Graphic
in online course.

5.1.1.6   Activity - MAC and LLC Sublayers

Refer to
Online Course
for Illustration

5.1.2   Ethernet Frame Attributes

5.1.2.1   Ethernet Encapsulation

Since the creation of Ethernet in 1973, standards have evolved for specifying faster and more flexible versions of the technology. This ability for Ethernet to improve over time is one of the main reasons that it has become so popular. Early versions of Ethernet were relatively slow at 10 Mbps. The latest versions of Ethernet operate at 10 Gigabits per second and faster. Figure 1 highlights changes in the various versions of Ethernet.

At the data link layer, the frame structure is nearly identical for all speeds of Ethernet. The Ethernet frame structure adds headers and trailers around the Layer 3 PDU to encapsulate the message being sent.

Both the Ethernet header and trailer have several sections of information that are used by the Ethernet protocol. Each section of the frame is called a field. As shown in Figure 2, there are two styles of Ethernet framing:

■ IEEE 802.3 Ethernet standard which has been updated several times to include new technologies

■ The DIX Ethernet standard which is now referred to Ethernet II

The differences between framing styles are minimal. The most significant difference between the two standards is the addition of a Start Frame Delimiter (SFD) and the change of the Type field to a Length field in the 802.3.

Ethernet II is the Ethernet frame format used in TCP/IP networks.

Refer to
Online Course
for Illustration

5.1.2.2   Ethernet Frame Size

Both the Ethernet II and IEEE 802.3 standards define the minimum frame size as 64 bytes and the maximum as 1518 bytes. This includes all bytes from the Destination MAC Address field through the Frame Check Sequence (FCS) field. The Preamble and Start Frame Delimiter fields are not included when describing the size of a frame.

Any frame less than 64 bytes in length is considered a "collision fragment" or "runt frame" and is automatically discarded by receiving stations.

The IEEE 802.3ac standard, released in 1998, extended the maximum allowable frame size to 1522 bytes. The frame size was increased to accommodate a technology called Virtual Local Area Network (VLAN). VLANs are created within a switched network and will be presented in a later course. Also, many quality of service (QoS) technologies leverage the User Priority field to implement various levels of service, such as priority service for voice traffic. The figure displays the fields contained in the 802.1Q VLAN tag.

If the size of a transmitted frame is less than the minimum or greater than the maximum, the receiving device drops the frame. Dropped frames are likely to be the result of collisions or other unwanted signals and are therefore considered invalid.

At the data link layer the frame structure is nearly identical. At the physical layer different versions of Ethernet vary in their method for detecting and placing data on the media.

Refer to
Online Course
for Illustration

5.1.2.3   Introduction to the Ethernet Frame

The primary fields in the Ethernet frame are:

- **Preamble and Start Frame Delimiter Fields:** The Preamble (7 bytes) and Start Frame Delimiter (SFD), also called the Start of Frame (1 byte), fields are used for synchronization between the sending and receiving devices. These first eight bytes of the frame are used to get the attention of the receiving nodes. Essentially, the first few bytes tell the receivers to get ready to receive a new frame.

- **Destination MAC Address Field:** This 6-byte field is the identifier for the intended recipient. As you will recall, this address is used by Layer 2 to assist devices in determining if a frame is addressed to them. The address in the frame is compared to the MAC address in the device. If there is a match, the device accepts the frame.

- **Source MAC Address Field:** This 6-byte field identifies the frame's originating NIC or interface.

- **Length Field:** For any IEEE 802.3 standard earlier than 1997 the Length field defines the exact length of the frame's data field. This is used later as part of the FCS to ensure that the message was received properly. Otherwise the purpose of the field is to describe which higher-layer protocol is present. If the two-octet value is equal to or greater than 0x0600 hexadecimal or 1536 decimal, then the contents of the Data field are decoded according to the EtherType protocol indicated. Whereas if the value is equal to or less than 0x05DC hexadecimal or 1500 decimal then the Length field is being used to indicate the use of the IEEE 802.3 frame format. This is how Ethernet II and 802.3 frames are differentiated.

- **Data Field:** This field (46 - 1500 bytes) contains the encapsulated data from a higher layer, which is a generic Layer 3 PDU, or more commonly, an IPv4 packet. All frames must be at least 64 bytes long. If a small packet is encapsulated, additional bits called a pad are used to increase the size of the frame to this minimum size.

- **Frame Check Sequence Field:** The Frame Check Sequence (FCS) field (4 bytes) is used to detect errors in a frame. It uses a cyclic redundancy check (CRC). The sending device includes the results of a CRC in the FCS field of the frame. The receiving device receives the frame and generates a CRC to look for errors. If the calculations match, no error occurred. Calculations that do not match are an indication that the data has changed; therefore, the frame is dropped. A change in the data could be the result of a disruption of the electrical signals that represent the bits.

Refer to
Interactive Graphic
in online course.

5.1.2.4   Activity - Ethernet Frame Fields

Refer to
Online Course
for Illustration

5.1.3   Ethernet MAC

5.1.3.1   MAC Addresses and Hexadecimal

The use of the MAC address is one of the most important aspects of the Ethernet LAN technology. MAC addresses use hexadecimal numbering.

Hexadecimal is a word that is used both as a noun and as an adjective. When used by itself (as a noun) it means the hexadecimal number system. Hexadecimal provides a convenient way to represent binary values. Just as decimal is a base ten number system and binary is a base two number system, hexadecimal is a base sixteen system.

The base sixteen number system uses the numbers 0 to 9 and the letters A to F. Figure 1 shows the equivalent decimal and hexadecimal values for binary 0000 to 1111. It is easier for us to express a value as a single hexadecimal digit than as four binary bits.

Given that 8 bits (a byte) is a common binary grouping, binary 00000000 to 11111111 can be represented in hexadecimal as the range 00 to FF. Leading zeroes are always displayed to complete the 8-bit representation. For example, the binary value 0000 1010 is shown in hexadecimal as 0A.

Note   It is important to distinguish hexadecimal values from decimal values regarding the characters 0 to 9, as shown in Figure 1.

Representing Hexadecimal Values

Hexadecimal is usually represented in text by the value preceded by 0x (for example 0x73) or a subscript 16. Less commonly, it may be followed by an H, for example 73H. However, because subscript text is not recognized in command line or programming environments, the technical representation of hexadecimal is preceded with "0x" (zero X). Therefore, the examples above would be shown as 0x0A and 0x73 respectively.

Hexadecimal is used to represent Ethernet MAC addresses and IP Version 6 addresses.

Hexadecimal Conversions

Number conversions between decimal and hexadecimal values are straightforward, but quickly dividing or multiplying by 16 is not always convenient. If such conversions are required, it is usually easier to convert the decimal or hexadecimal value to binary, and then to convert the binary value to either decimal or hexadecimal as appropriate.

With practice, it is possible to recognize the binary bit patterns that match the decimal and hexadecimal values. Figure 2 shows these patterns for selected 8-bit values.

Refer to
Online Course
for Illustration

5.1.3.2   MAC Address Representations

On a Windows host, the `ipconfig /all` command can be used to identify the MAC address of an Ethernet adapter. In Figure 1, notice the display indicates the Physical Address (MAC) of the computer to be 00-18-DE-C7-F3-FB. If you have access, you may wish to try this on your own computer.

Depending on the device and the operating system, you will see various representations of MAC addresses, as displayed in Figure 2. Cisco routers and switches use the form XXXX. XXXX.XXXX where X is a hexadecimal character.

Refer to
Online Course
for Illustration

5.1.3.3   Unicast MAC Address

In Ethernet, different MAC addresses are used for Layer 2 unicast, broadcast, and multi-cast communications.

A unicast MAC address is the unique address used when a frame is sent from a single transmitting device to a single destination device.

In the example shown in the figure, a host with IP address 192.168.1.5 (source) requests a web page from the server at IP address 192.168.1.200. For a unicast packet to be sent and received, a destination IP address must be in the IP packet header. A corresponding desti-nation MAC address must also be present in the Ethernet frame header. The IP address and MAC address combine to deliver data to one specific destination host.

Refer to
Online Course
for Illustration

5.1.3.4   Broadcast MAC Address

A broadcast packet contains a destination IP address that has all ones (1s) in the host por-tion. This numbering in the address means that all hosts on that local network (broadcast domain) will receive and process the packet. Many network protocols, such as DHCP and Address Resolution Protocol (ARP), use broadcasts. How ARP uses broadcasts to map Layer 2 to Layer 3 addresses is discussed later in this chapter.

As shown in the figure, a broadcast IP address for a network needs a corresponding broad-cast MAC address in the Ethernet frame. On Ethernet networks, the broadcast MAC address is 48 ones displayed as hexadecimal FF-FF-FF-FF-FF-FF.

Refer to
Online Course
for Illustration

5.1.3.5   Multicast MAC Address

Multicast addresses allow a source device to send a packet to a group of devices. Devices that belong to a multicast group are assigned a multicast group IP address. The range of IPv4 multicast addresses is 224.0.0.0 to 239.255.255.255. Because multicast addresses rep-resent a group of addresses (sometimes called a host group), they can only be used as the destination of a packet. The source will always have a unicast address.

Multicast addresses would be used in remote gaming, where many players are connected remotely but playing the same game. Another use of multicast addresses is in distance learning through video conferencing, where many students are connected to the same class.

As with the unicast and broadcast addresses, the multicast IP address requires a corre-sponding multicast MAC address to actually deliver frames on a local network. The multi-cast MAC address is a special value that begins with 01-00-5E in hexadecimal. The remain-ing portion of the multicast MAC address is created by converting the lower 23 bits of the IP multicast group address into 6 hexadecimal characters.

An example, as shown in the animation, is the multicast hexadecimal address 01-00-5E-00-00-C8.

Refer to
Lab Activity
for this chapter

5.1.3.6   Lab - Viewing Network Device MAC Addresses

In this lab, you will complete the following objectives:

- Part 1: Set Up the Topology and Initialize Devices
- Part 2: Configure Devices and Verify Connectivity
- Part 3: Display, Describe, and Analyze Ethernet MAC Addresses

Refer to
Online Course
for Illustration

5.1.4   MAC and IP

5.1.4.1   MAC and IP

There are two primary addresses assigned to a host device:

- Physical address (the MAC address)
- Logical address (the IP address)

Both the MAC address and IP address work together to identify a device on the network. The process of using the MAC address and the IP address to find a computer is similar to the process of using a name and address of an individual to send a letter.

A person's name usually does not change. A person's address on the other hand, relates to where they live and can change.

Similar to the name of a person, the MAC address on a host does not change; it is physically assigned to the host NIC and is known as the physical address. The physical address remains the same regardless of where the host is placed.

The IP address is similar to the address of a person. This address is based on where the host is actually located. Using this address, it is possible for a frame to determine the location of where a frame should be sent. The IP address, or network address, is known as a logical address because it is assigned logically. It is assigned to each host by a network administrator based on the local network that the host is connected to. The figure demonstrates the hierarchical nature of locating an individual based on a "logical" address. Click each grouping to view how the address filters down.

Both the physical MAC and logical IP addresses are required for a computer to communicate on a hierarchical network, just like both the name and address of a person are required to send a letter.

Refer to
Online Course
for Illustration

5.1.4.2   End-to-End Connectivity, MAC, and IP

A source device will send a packet based on an IP address. One of the most common ways a source device determines the IP address of a destination device is through Domain Name Service (DNS), in which an IP address is associated to a domain name. For example, www.cisco.com is equal to 209.165.200.225. This IP address will get the packet to the network location of the destination device. It is this IP address that routers will use to determine the best path to reach a destination. So, in short, IP addressing determines the end-to-end behavior of an IP packet.

However, along each link in a path, an IP packet is encapsulated in a frame specific to the particular data link technology associated with that link, such as Ethernet. End devices on an Ethernet network do not accept and process frames based on IP addresses, rather, a frame is accepted and processed based on MAC addresses.

On Ethernet networks, MAC addresses are used to identify, at a lower level, the source and destination hosts. When a host on an Ethernet network communicates, it sends frames containing its own MAC address as the source and the MAC address of the intended recipient as the destination. All hosts that receive the frame will read the destination MAC address. If the destination MAC address matches the MAC address configured on the host NIC, only then will the host process the message.

Figure 1 shows how a data packet, containing IP address information, is encapsulated with data link layer framing containing the MAC address information.

Figure 2 shows how frames are encapsulated based on the technology of the actual link.

How are the IP addresses of the IP packets in a data flow associated with the MAC addresses on each link along the path to the destination? This is done through a process called Address Resolution Protocol (ARP).

Refer to
Lab Activity
for this chapter

5.1.4.3   Lab - Using Wireshark to Examine Ethernet Frames

In this lab, you will complete the following objectives:

- Part 1: Examine the Header Fields in an Ethernet II Frame

- Part 2: Use Wireshark to Capture and Analyze Ethernet Frames

Refer to **Packet Tracer Activity** for this chapter

5.1.4.4   Packet Tracer - Identify MAC and IP Addresses

This activity is optimized for viewing PDUs. The devices are already configured. You will gather PDU information in simulation mode and answer a series of questions about the data you collect.

Refer to
Online Course
for Illustration

5.2   Address Resolution Protocol

5.2.1   ARP

5.2.1.1   Introduction to ARP

Recall that each node on an IP network has both a MAC address and an IP address. In order to send data, the node must use both of these addresses. The node must use its own MAC and IP addresses in the source fields and must provide both a MAC address and an IP address for the destination. While the IP address of the destination will be provided by a higher OSI layer, the sending node needs a way to find the MAC address of the destination for a given Ethernet link. This is the purpose of ARP.

ARP relies on certain types of Ethernet broadcast messages and Ethernet unicast messages, called ARP requests and ARP replies.

The ARP protocol provides two basic functions:

- Resolving IPv4 addresses to MAC addresses

- Maintaining a table of mappings

Refer to
Online Course
for Illustration

5.2.1.2   ARP Functions

Resolving IPv4 Addresses to MAC Addresses

For a frame to be placed on the LAN media, it must have a destination MAC address. When a packet is sent to the data link layer to be encapsulated into a frame, the node refers to a table in its memory to find the data link layer address that is mapped to the destination IPv4 address. This table is called the ARP table or the ARP cache. The ARP table is stored in the RAM of the device.

Each entry, or row, of the ARP table binds an IP address with a MAC address. We call the relationship between the two values a map - it simply means that you can locate an IP address in the table and discover the corresponding MAC address. The ARP table temporarily saves (caches) the mapping for the devices on the local LAN.

To begin the process, a transmitting node attempts to locate the MAC address mapped to an IPv4 destination. If this map is found in the table, the node uses the MAC address as the destination MAC in the frame that encapsulates the IPv4 packet. The frame is then encoded onto the networking media.

Maintaining the ARP Table

The ARP table is maintained dynamically. There are two ways that a device can gather MAC addresses. One way is to monitor the traffic that occurs on the local network segment. As a node receives frames from the media, it can record the source IP and MAC address as a mapping in the ARP table. As frames are transmitted on the network, the device populates the ARP table with address pairs.

Another way a device can get an address pair is to send an ARP request as shown in the figure. An ARP request is a Layer 2 broadcast to all devices on the Ethernet LAN. The ARP request contains the IP address of the destination host and the broadcast MAC address, FFFF.FFFF.FFFF. Since this is a broadcast, all nodes on the Ethernet LAN will receive it and look at the contents. The node with the IP address that matches the IP address in the ARP request will reply. The reply will be a unicast frame that includes the MAC address that corresponds to the IP address in the request. This response is then used to make a new entry in the ARP table of the sending node.

Entries in the ARP table are time stamped in much the same way that MAC table entries are time stamped in switches. If a device does not receive a frame from a particular device by the time the time stamp expires, the entry for this device is removed from the ARP table.

Additionally, static map entries can be entered in an ARP table, but this is rarely done. Static ARP table entries do not expire over time and must be manually removed.

Refer to
Online Course
for Illustration

5.2.1.3   ARP Operation

Creating the Frame

What does a node do when it needs to create a frame and the ARP cache does not contain a map of an IP address to a destination MAC address? It generates an ARP request!

When ARP receives a request to map an IPv4 address to a MAC address, it looks for the cached map in its ARP table. If an entry is not found, the encapsulation of the IPv4 packet fails and the Layer 2 processes notify ARP that it needs a map. The ARP processes then send out an ARP request packet to discover the MAC address of the destination device on the local network. If a device receiving the request has the destination IP address, it responds with an ARP reply. A map is created in the ARP table. Packets for that IPv4 address can now be encapsulated in frames.

If no device responds to the ARP request, the packet is dropped because a frame cannot be created. This encapsulation failure is reported to the upper layers of the device. If the device is an intermediary device, like a router, the upper layers may choose to respond to the source host with an error in an ICMPv4 packet.

See Figures 1-5 to view the process used to get the MAC address of the node on the local physical network.

Refer to
Online Course
for Illustration

5.2.1.4   ARP Role in Remote Communication

All frames must be delivered to a node on the local network segment. If the destination IPv4 host is on the local network, the frame will use the MAC address of this device as the destination MAC address.

If the destination IPv4 host is not on the local network, the source node needs to deliver the frame to the router interface that is the gateway or next hop used to reach that destination. The source node will use the MAC address of the gateway as the destination address for frames containing an IPv4 packet addressed to hosts on other networks.

The gateway address of the router interface is stored in the IPv4 configuration of the hosts. When a host creates a packet for a destination, it compares the destination IP address and its own IP address to determine if the two IP addresses are located on the same Layer 3 network. If the receiving host is not on the same network, the source uses the ARP process to determine a MAC address for the router interface serving as the gateway.

In the event that the gateway entry is not in the table, the normal ARP process will send an ARP request to retrieve the MAC address associated with the IP address of the router interface.

See Figures 1-5 to view the process used to get the MAC address of the gateway.

Refer to
Online Course
for Illustration

5.2.1.5   Removing Entries from an ARP Table

For each device, an ARP cache timer removes ARP entries that have not been used for a specified period of time. The times differ depending on the device and its operating system. For example, some Windows operating systems store ARP cache entries for 2 minutes. If the entry is used again during that time, the ARP timer for that entry is extended to 10 minutes.

Commands may also be used to manually remove all or some of the entries in the ARP table. After an entry has been removed, the process for sending an ARP request and receiving an ARP reply must occur again to enter the map in the ARP table.

Each device has an operating system-specific command to delete the contents of the ARP cache. These commands do not invoke the execution of ARP in any way. They merely remove the entries of the ARP table. ARP service is integrated within the IPv4 protocol and implemented by the device. Its operation is transparent to both upper layer applications and users.

As shown in the figure, it is sometimes necessary to remove an ARP table entry.

Refer to
Online Course
for Illustration

5.2.1.6   ARP Tables on Networking Devices

On a Cisco router, the `show ip arp` command is used to display the ARP table, as shown in Figure 1.

On a Windows 7 PC, the `arp –a` command is used to display the ARP table, as shown in Figure 2.

Refer to **Packet Tracer Activity** for this chapter

5.2.1.7   Packet Tracer - Examine the ARP Table

This activity is optimized for viewing PDUs. The devices are already configured. You will gather PDU information in simulation mode and answer a series of questions about the data you collect.

Refer to **Lab Activity** for this chapter

5.2.1.8   Lab - Observing ARP with the Windows CLI, IOS CLI, and Wireshark

In this lab, you will complete the following objectives:

■ Part 1: Build and Configure the Network

■ Part 2: Use the Windows ARP Command

■ Part 3: Use the IOS Show ARP Command

■ Part 4: Use Wireshark to Examine ARP Exchanges

Refer to
Online Course
for Illustration

5.2.2   ARP Issues

5.2.2.1   How ARP Can Create Problems

The figure shows two potential issues with ARP.

Overhead on the Media

As a broadcast frame, an ARP request is received and processed by every device on the local network. On a typical business network, these broadcasts would probably have minimal impact on network performance. However, if a large number of devices were to be powered up and all start accessing network services at the same time, there could be some reduction in performance for a short period of time. For example, if all students in a lab logged into classroom computers and attempted to access the Internet at the same time, there could be delays. However, after the devices send out the initial ARP broadcasts and have learned the necessary MAC addresses, any impact on the network will be minimized.

Security

In some cases, the use of ARP can lead to a potential security risk. ARP spoofing, or ARP poisoning, is a technique used by an attacker to inject the wrong MAC address association into a network by issuing fake ARP requests. An attacker forges the MAC address of a device and then frames can be sent to the wrong destination.

Manually configuring static ARP associations is one way to prevent ARP spoofing. Authorized MAC addresses can be configured on some network devices to restrict network access to only those devices listed.

Refer to
Online Course
for Illustration

5.2.2.2   Mitigating ARP Problems

Broadcast and security issues related to ARP can be mitigated with modern switches. Cisco switches support several security technologies specifically designed to mitigate Ethernet issues related to broadcasts, in general, and ARP, in particular.

Switches provide segmentation of a LAN, dividing the LAN into independent collision domains. Each port on a switch represents a separate collision domain and provides the full media bandwidth to the node or nodes connected on that port. While switches do not by default prevent broadcasts from propagating to connected devices, they do isolate unicast Ethernet communications so that they are only "heard" by the source and destination devices. So if there are a large number of ARP requests, each ARP reply will only be between two devices.

With regard to mitigating various types of broadcast attacks, to which Ethernet networks are prone, network engineers implement Cisco switch security technologies such as specialized access lists and port security.

Refer to
Online Course
for Illustration

5.3   LAN Switches

5.3.1   Switching

5.3.1.1   Switch Port Fundamentals

Recall that the logical topology of an Ethernet network is a multi-access bus in which devices all share access to the same medium. This logical topology determines how hosts on the network view and process frames sent and received on the network. However, the physical topology of most Ethernet networks today is that of a star or extended star. This means that on most Ethernet networks, end devices are typically connected, in a point-to-point basis, to a Layer 2 LAN switch.

A Layer 2 LAN switch performs switching and filtering based only on the OSI data link layer (Layer 2) MAC address. A switch is completely transparent to network protocols and user applications. A Layer 2 switch builds a MAC address table that it uses to make forwarding decisions. Layer 2 switches depend on routers to pass data between independent IP subnetworks.

Refer to
Online Course
for Illustration

5.3.1.2   Switch MAC Address Table

Switches use MAC addresses to direct network communications through their switch fabric to the appropriate port toward the destination node. The switch fabric is the integrated circuits and the accompanying machine programming that allows the data paths through the switch to be controlled. For a switch to know which port to use to transmit a unicast frame, it must first learn which nodes exist on each of its ports.

A switch determines how to handle incoming data frames by using its MAC address table. A switch builds its MAC address table by recording the MAC addresses of the nodes connected to each of its ports. Once a MAC address for a specific node on a specific port is recorded in the address table, the switch then knows to send traffic destined for that specific node out the port mapped to that node for subsequent transmissions.

When an incoming data frame is received by a switch and the destination MAC address is not in the table, the switch forwards the frame out all ports, except for the port on which it was received. When the destination node responds, the switch records the node's MAC address in the address table from the frame's source address field. In networks with multiple interconnected switches, the MAC address tables record multiple MAC addresses for the ports connecting the switches which reflect the node's beyond. Typically, switch ports used to interconnect two switches have multiple MAC addresses recorded in the MAC address table.

To see how this works, view each of the steps in Figures 1-6.

The following describes this process:

Step 1.   The switch receives a broadcast frame from PC1 on Port 1.

Step 2.   The switch enters the source MAC address and the switch port that received the frame into the address table.

Step 3.   Because the destination address is a broadcast, the switch floods the frame to all ports, except the port on which it received the frame.

Step 4.   The destination device replies to the broadcast with a unicast frame addressed to PC1.

Step 5.   The switch enters the source MAC address of PC2 and the port number of the switch port that received the frame into the address table. The destination address of the frame and its associated port is found in the MAC address table.

Step 6.   The switch can now forward frames between source and destination devices without flooding, because it has entries in the address table that identify the associated ports.

Note   The MAC address table is sometimes referred to as a content addressable memory (CAM) table. While the term CAM table is fairly common, for the purposes of this course, we will refer to it as a MAC address table.

Refer to
Online Course
for Illustration

5.3.1.3   Duplex Settings

Though transparent to network protocols and user applications, switches can operate in different modes that can have both positive and negative effects when forwarding Ethernet frames on a network. One of the most basic settings of a switch is the duplex setting of each individual port connected to each host device. A port on a switch must be configured to match the duplex settings of the media type. There are two types of duplex settings used for communications on an Ethernet network: half duplex and full duplex.

Half Duplex

Half-duplex communication relies on unidirectional data flow where sending and receiving data are not performed at the same time. This is similar to how walkie-talkies or two-way radios function in that only one person can talk at any one time. If someone talks while someone else is already speaking, a collision occurs. As a result, half-duplex communication implements CSMA/CD to help reduce the potential for collisions and detect them when they do happen. Half-duplex communications have performance issues due to the constant waiting, because data can only flow in one direction at a time. Half-duplex connections are typically seen in older hardware, such as hubs. Nodes that are attached to hubs that share their connection to a switch port must operate in half-duplex mode because the end computers must be able to detect collisions. Nodes can operate in a half-duplex mode if the NIC card cannot be configured for full duplex operations. In this case the port on the switch defaults to a half-duplex mode as well. Because of these limitations, full-duplex communication has replaced half duplex in more current hardware.

Full Duplex

In full-duplex communication, data flow is bidirectional, so data can be sent and received at the same time. The bidirectional support enhances performance by reducing the wait time between transmissions. Most Ethernet, Fast Ethernet, and Gigabit Ethernet NICs sold today offer full-duplex capability. In full-duplex mode, the collision detect circuit is disabled. Frames sent by the two connected end nodes cannot collide because the end nodes use two separate circuits in the network cable. Each full-duplex connection uses only one port. Full-duplex connections require a switch that supports full duplex or a direct connection between two nodes that each support full duplex. Nodes that are directly attached to a dedicated switch port with NICs that support full duplex should be connected to switch ports that are configured to operate in full-duplex mode.

The figure shows the two duplex settings available on modern network equipment.

A Cisco Catalyst switch supports three duplex settings:

- The full option sets full-duplex mode.

- The half option sets half-duplex mode.

- The auto option sets autonegotiation of duplex mode. With autonegotiation enabled, the two ports communicate to decide the best mode of operation.

For Fast Ethernet and 10/100/1000 ports, the default is auto. For 100BASE-FX ports, the default is full. The 10/100/1000 ports operate in either half- or full-duplex mode when they are set to 10 or 100 Mb/s, but when set to 1,000 Mb/s, they operate only in full-duplex mode.

5.3.1.4   Auto-MDIX

Refer to
Online Course
for Illustration

In addition to having the correct duplex setting, it is also necessary to have the correct cable type defined for each port. Connections between specific devices, such as switch-to-switch, switch-to-router, switch-to-host, and router-to-host device, once required the use of a specific cable types (crossover or straight-through). Instead, most switch devices now support the `mdix auto` interface configuration command in the CLI to enable the automatic medium-dependent interface crossover (auto-MDIX) feature.

When the auto-MDIX feature is enabled, the switch detects the required cable type for copper Ethernet connections and configures the interfaces accordingly. Therefore, you can use either a crossover or a straight-through cable for connections to a copper 10/100/1000 port on the switch, regardless of the type of device on the other end of the connection.

The auto-MDIX feature is enabled by default on switches running Cisco IOS Release 12.2(18)SE or later. For releases between Cisco IOS Release 12.1(14)EA1 and 12.2(18)SE, the auto-MDIX feature is disabled by default.

Refer to
Online Course
for Illustration

5.3.1.5   Frame Forwarding Methods on Cisco Switches

In the past, switches used one of the following forwarding methods for switching data between network ports:

- Store-and-forward switching
- Cut-through switching

Figure 1 highlights differences between these two methods.

In store-and-forward switching, when the switch receives the frame, it stores the data in buffers until the complete frame has been received. During the storage process, the switch analyzes the frame for information about its destination. In this process, the switch also performs an error check using the Cyclic Redundancy Check (CRC) trailer portion of the Ethernet frame.

CRC uses a mathematical formula, based on the number of bits (1s) in the frame, to determine whether the received frame has an error. After confirming the integrity of the frame, the frame is forwarded out the appropriate port toward its destination. When an error is detected in a frame, the switch discards the frame. Discarding frames with errors reduces the amount of bandwidth consumed by corrupt data. Store-and-forward switching is required for Quality of Service (QoS) analysis on converged networks where frame classification for traffic prioritization is necessary. For example, voice over IP data streams need to have priority over web-browsing traffic.

In Figure 2, play the animation for a demonstration of the store-and-forward process. Store-and-forward is the sole forwarding method used on current models of Cisco Catalyst switches.

Refer to
Online Course
for Illustration

5.3.1.6   Cut-Through Switching

In cut-through switching, the switch acts upon the data as soon as it is received, even if the transmission is not complete. The switch buffers just enough of the frame to read the destination MAC address so that it can determine to which port to forward the data. The destination MAC address is located in the first 6 bytes of the frame following the preamble. The switch looks up the destination MAC address in its switching table, determines the outgoing interface port, and forwards the frame onto its destination through the designated switch port. The switch does not perform any error checking on the frame. Because the switch does not have to wait for the entire frame to be completely buffered, and because the switch does not perform any error checking, cut-through switching is faster than store-and-forward switching. However, because the switch does not perform any error checking, it forwards corrupt frames throughout the network. The corrupt frames consume bandwidth while they are being forwarded. The destination NIC eventually discards the corrupt frames.

Play the animation for a demonstration of the cut-through switching process.

There are two variants of cut-through switching:

- **Fast-forward switching:** Fast-forward switching offers the lowest level of latency. Fast-forward switching immediately forwards a packet after reading the destination address. Because fast-forward switching starts forwarding before the entire packet has been received, there may be times when packets are relayed with errors. This occurs infrequently, and the destination network adapter discards the faulty packet upon receipt.

In fast-forward mode, latency is measured from the first bit received to the first bit transmitted. Fast-forward switching is the typical cut-through method of switching.

- **Fragment-free switching:** In fragment-free switching, the switch stores the first 64 bytes of the frame before forwarding. Fragment-free switching can be viewed as a compromise between store-and-forward switching and fast-forward switching. The reason fragment-free switching stores only the first 64 bytes of the frame is that most network errors and collisions occur during the first 64 bytes. Fragment-free switching tries to enhance fast-forward switching by performing a small error check on the first 64 bytes of the frame to ensure that a collision has not occurred before forwarding the frame. Fragment-free switching is a compromise between the high latency and high integrity of store-and-forward switching, and the low latency and reduced integrity of fast-forward switching.

The figure shows an example of cut-through switching.

Some switches are configured to perform cut-through switching on a per-port basis until a user-defined error threshold is reached and then they automatically change to store-and-forward. When the error rate falls below the threshold, the port automatically changes back to cut-through switching.

Refer to
Interactive Graphic
in online course.

5.3.1.7   Activity - Frame Forwarding Methods

Refer to
Online Course
for Illustration

5.3.1.8   Memory Buffering on Switches

As discussed, a switch analyzes some or all of a packet before it forwards it to the destination host. An Ethernet switch may use a buffering technique to store frames before forwarding them. Buffering may also be used when the destination port is busy due to congestion and the switch stores the frame until it can be transmitted.

As shown in the figure, there are two methods of memory buffering: port-based and shared memory.

Port-based Memory Buffering

In port-based memory buffering, frames are stored in queues that are linked to specific incoming and outgoing ports. A frame is transmitted to the outgoing port only when all the frames ahead of it in the queue have been successfully transmitted. It is possible for a single frame to delay the transmission of all the frames in memory because of a busy destination port. This delay occurs even if the other frames could be transmitted to open destination ports.

Shared Memory Buffering

Shared memory buffering deposits all frames into a common memory buffer that all the ports on the switch share. The amount of buffer memory required by a port is dynamically allocated. The frames in the buffer are linked dynamically to the destination port. This allows the packet to be received on one port and then transmitted on another port, without moving it to a different queue.

The switch keeps a map of frame to port links showing where a packet needs to be transmitted. The map link is cleared after the frame has been successfully transmitted. The number of frames stored in the buffer is restricted by the size of the entire memory buffer and not limited to a single port buffer. This permits larger frames to be transmitted with fewer dropped frames. This is especially important to asymmetric switching. Asymmetric switching allows for different data rates on different ports. This allows more bandwidth to be dedicated to certain ports, such as a port connected to a server.

Refer to
Interactive Graphic
in online course.

5.3.1.9   Activity - Switch It!

Refer to
Lab Activity
for this chapter

5.3.1.10   Lab - Viewing the Switch MAC Address Table

In this lab, you will complete the following objectives:

- Part 1: Build and Configure the Network
- Part 2: Examine the Switch MAC Address Table

Refer to
Online Course
for Illustration

5.3.2   Fixed or Modular

5.3.2.1   Fixed versus Modular Configuration

When selecting a switch, it is important to understand the key features of the switch options available. This means that it is necessary to decide on features such as whether Power over Ethernet (PoE) is necessary, and the preferred "forwarding rate".

As shown in Figure 1, PoE allows a switch to deliver power to a device, such as IP phones and some wireless access points, over the existing Ethernet cabling. This allows more flexibility for installation.

The forwarding rate defines the processing capabilities of a switch by rating how much data the switch can process per second. Switch product lines are classified by forwarding rates. Entry-layer switches have lower forwarding rates than enterprise-layer switches. Other considerations include whether the device is stackable or non-stackable as well as the thickness of the switch (expressed in number of rack units), and port density, or the number of ports available on a single switch. The port density of a device can vary depending on whether the device is a fixed configuration device or a modular device.

These options are sometimes referred to as switch form factors.

Fixed Configuration Switches

Fixed configuration switches are just as you might expect, fixed in their configuration. What that means is that you cannot add features or options to the switch beyond those that originally came with the switch. The particular model you purchase determines the features and options available. For example, if you purchase a 24-port gigabit fixed switch, you cannot add additional ports when you need them. There are typically different configuration choices that vary in how many and what types of ports are included.

Modular Switches

Modular switches offer more flexibility in their configuration. Modular switches typically come with different sized chassis that allow for the installation of different numbers of modular line cards. The line cards actually contain the ports. The line card fits into the switch chassis like expansion cards fit into a PC. The larger the chassis, the more modules it can support. As you can see in the figure, there can be many different chassis sizes to choose from. If you bought a modular switch with a 24-port line card, you could easily add an additional 24 port line card, to bring the total number of ports up to 48.

Figure 2 displays examples of fixed configuration, modular, and stackable configuration switches.

Refer to
Online Course
for Illustration

5.3.2.2   Module Options for Cisco Switch Slots

The Cisco switch product lines are widely deployed globally, in large part due to the flexibility they provide for add-on options. Not only does the Cisco IOS have the richest set of features available relative to any other network operating system, but the IOS is tailor fit to each Cisco networking device, switches in particular.

To illustrate the options available, which are literally too voluminous to list here, we focus on the Catalyst 3560 switches. The Catalyst 3560 switches have Switch Form-Factor Pluggable (SFP) ports that support a number of SFP transceiver modules. Here is a list of the SFP modules supported on one or more types of 3560 switches:

Fast Ethernet SFP Modules –

- 100BASE-FX (multimode fiber-optic (MMF)) for 2 kilometers (km)
- 100BASE-LX10 (single-mode fiber-optic (SMF)) for 2km
- 100BASE-BX10 (SMF) for 10 km
- 100BASE-EX (SMF) for 40 km
- 100BASE-ZX (SMF) for 80 km

Gigabit Ethernet SFP Modules –

- 1000BASE-SX 50/62.5 µm (MMF) up to 550/220 m
- 1000BASE-LX/LH (SMF/MMF) up to 10/0.550 k
- 1000BASE-ZX (SMF) up to 70 km
- 1000BASE-BX10-D&1000BASE-BX10-U (SMF) up to 10 km
- 1000BASE-T (copper wire transceiver)

10 Gigabit Ethernet SFP Modules –

- 10G-SR (MMF) up 400 m
- 10G-SR-X (MMF) up to 400 m (supporting extended temperature range)
- 10G-LRM (MMF) up to 220 m
- FET-10G (MMF) up to 100 m (for Nexus fabric uplinks)
- 10G-LR (SMF) up to 10 km
- 10G-LR-X (SMF) up to 10 km (supporting extended temperature range)
- 10G-ER (SMF) up to 40 km
- 10G-ZR (SMF) up to 80 km
- Twinax (copper wire transceiver) up to 10 m
- Active Optical up to 10 m (for intra/inter-rack connections)

40 Gigabit Ethernet and 100 Gigabit Ethernet modules are supported on high-end Cisco devices, such as the Catalyst 6500, the CRS router, the ASR 9000 series router, and the Nexus 7000 series switch.

Refer to **Online Course** for Illustration

5.3.3 Layer 3 Switching

5.3.3.1 Layer 2 versus Layer 3 Switching

In addition to determining the various switch form factors, it may also be necessary to choose between a Layer 2 LAN switch and a Layer 3 switch.

Recall that a Layer 2 LAN switch performs switching and filtering based only on the OSI data link layer (Layer 2) MAC address and depends upon routers to pass data between independent IP subnetworks (see Figure 1).

As shown in Figure 2, a Layer 3 switch, such as the Catalyst 3560, functions similarly to a Layer 2 switch, such as the Catalyst 2960, but instead of using only the Layer 2 MAC address information for forwarding decisions, a Layer 3 switch can also use IP address information. Instead of only learning which MAC addresses are associated with each of its ports, a Layer 3 switch can also learn which IP addresses are associated with its interfaces. This allows the Layer 3 switch to direct traffic throughout the network based on IP address information as well.

Layer 3 switches are also capable of performing Layer 3 routing functions, reducing the need for dedicated routers on a LAN. Because Layer 3 switches have specialized switching hardware, they can typically route data as quickly as they can switch.

Refer to **Online Course** for Illustration

5.3.3.2 Cisco Express Forwarding

Cisco devices which support Layer 3 switching utilize Cisco Express Forwarding (CEF). This forwarding method is quite complex, but fortunately, like any good technology, is carried out in large part "behind the scenes". Normally very little CEF configuration is required on a Cisco device.

Basically, CEF decouples the usual strict interdependence between Layer 2 and Layer 3 decision making. What makes forwarding IP packets slow is the constant referencing back-and-forth between Layer 2 and Layer 3 constructs within a networking device. So, to the extent that Layer 2 and Layer 3 data structures can be decoupled, forwarding is accelerated.

The two main components of CEF operation are the:

- Forwarding Information Base (FIB)
- Adjacency tables

The FIB is conceptually similar to a routing table. A router uses the routing table to determine best path to a destination network based on the network portion of the destination IP address. With CEF, information previously stored in the route cache is, instead, stored in several data structures for CEF switching. The data structures provide optimized lookup for efficient packet forwarding. A networking device uses the FIB lookup table to make destination-based switching decisions without having to access the route cache.

The FIB is updated when changes occur in the network and contains all routes known at the time.

Adjacency tables maintain Layer 2 next-hop addresses for all FIB entries.

The separation of the reachability information (in the FIB table) and the forwarding information (in the adjacency table), provides a number of benefits:

- The adjacency table can be built separately from the FIB table, allowing both to be built without any packets being process switched.

- The MAC header rewrite used to forward a packet is not stored in cache entries, so changes in a MAC header rewrite string do not require invalidation of cache entries.

CEF is enabled by default on most Cisco devices that perform Layer 3 switching.

Refer to
Online Course
for Illustration

5.3.3.3   Types of Layer 3 Interfaces

Cisco networking devices support a number of distinct types of Layer 3 interfaces. A Layer 3 interface is one that supports forwarding IP packets toward a final destination based on the IP address.

The major types of Layer 3 interfaces are:

- **Switch Virtual Interface (SVI)** - Logical interface on a switch associated with a virtual local area network (VLAN).

- **Routed Port** - Physical port on a Layer 3 switch configured to act as a router port.

- **Layer 3 EtherChannel** - Logical interface on a Cisco device associated with a bundle of routed ports.

As shown previously, an SVI for the default VLAN (VLAN1) must be enabled to provide IP host connectivity to the switch and permit remote switch administration. SVIs must also be configured to allow routing between VLANs. As stated, SVIs are logical interfaces configured for specific VLANs; to route between two or more VLANs, each VLAN must have a separate SVI enabled.

Routed ports enable (Layer 3) Cisco switches to effectively serve as routers. Each port on such a switch can be configured as a port on an independent IP network.

Layer 3 EtherChannels are used to bundle Layer 3 Ethernet links between Cisco devices in order to aggregate bandwidth, typically on uplinks.

Note   In addition to SVIs and L3 EtherChannels, other logical interfaces on Cisco devices include loopback interfaces and tunnel interfaces.

Refer to
Online Course
for Illustration

5.3.3.4   Configuring a Routed Port on a Layer 3 Switch

A switch port can be configured to be a Layer 3 routed port and behave like a regular router interface. Specifically, a routed port:

- Is not associated with a particular VLAN.

- Can be configured with a Layer 3 routing protocol.

- Is a Layer 3 interface only and does not support Layer 2 protocol.

Configure routed ports by putting the interface into Layer 3 mode with the `no switch-port` interface configuration command. Then assign an IP address to the port. That's it!

You will learn more about the functions of routing in the next chapter.

Refer to **Packet Tracer Activity** for this chapter

5.3.3.5 Packet Tracer - Configure Layer 3 Switches

The Network Administrator is replacing the current router and switch with a new Layer 3 switch. As the Network Technician, it is your job to configure the switch and place it into service. You will be working after hours to minimize disruption to the business.

Refer to **Online Course** for Illustration

5.4 Summary

Refer to **Lab Activity** for this chapter

5.4.1.1 Class Activity - MAC and Choose...

MAC and Choose...

Note This activity can be completed individually, in small groups, or in a full-classroom learning environment.

Please view the video located at the following link:http://www.netevents.tv/video/bob-metcalfe-the-history-of-ethernet

Topics discussed include not only where we have come from in Ethernet development, but where we are going with Ethernet technology (a futuristic approach).

After viewing the video and comparing its contents to Chapter 5, go to the web and search for information about Ethernet. Use a constructivist approach:

- What did Ethernet look like when it was first developed?
- How has Ethernet stayed the same over the past 25 years or so, and what changes are being made to make it more useful/applicable to today's data transmission methods?

Collect three pictures of old, current, and future Ethernet physical media and devices (focus on switches) – share these pictures with the class and discuss:

- How have Ethernet physical media and intermediary devices changed?
- How have Ethernet physical media and intermediary devices stayed the same?
- How will Ethernet change in the future?

Refer to **Online Course** for Illustration

5.4.1.2 Summary

Ethernet is the most widely used LAN technology today. It is a family of networking technologies that are defined in the IEEE 802.2 and 802.3 standards. Ethernet standards define both the Layer 2 protocols and the Layer 1 technologies. For the Layer 2 protocols, as with all 802 IEEE standards, Ethernet relies on the two separate sublayers of the data link layer to operate, the Logical Link Control (LLC) and the MAC sublayers.

At the data link layer, the frame structure is nearly identical for all speeds of Ethernet. The Ethernet frame structure adds headers and trailers around the Layer 3 PDU to encapsulate the message being sent.

There are two styles of Ethernet framing: IEEE 802.3 Ethernet standard and the DIX Ethernet standard which is now referred to Ethernet II. The most significant difference between the two standards is the addition of a Start Frame Delimiter (SFD) and the change of the Type field to a Length field in the 802.3. Ethernet II is the Ethernet frame format used in TCP/IP networks. As an implementation of the IEEE 802.2/3 standards, the Ethernet frame provides MAC addressing and error checking.

The Layer 2 addressing provided by Ethernet supports unicast, multicast, and broadcast communications. Ethernet uses the Address Resolution Protocol to determine the MAC addresses of destinations and map them against known network layer addresses.

Each node on an IP network has both a MAC address and an IP address. The node must use its own MAC and IP addresses in the source fields and must provide both a MAC address and an IP address for the destination. While the IP address of the destination will be provided by a higher OSI layer, the sending node must find the MAC address of the destination for a given Ethernet link. This is the purpose of ARP.

ARP relies on certain types of Ethernet broadcast messages and Ethernet unicast messages, called ARP requests and ARP replies. The ARP protocol resolves IPv4 addresses to MAC addresses and maintains a table of mappings.

On most Ethernet networks, end devices are typically connected, in a point-to-point basis, to a Layer 2 LAN switch. A Layer 2 LAN switch performs switching and filtering based only on the OSI data link layer (Layer 2) MAC address. A Layer 2 switch builds a MAC address table that it uses to make forwarding decisions. Layer 2 switches depend on routers to pass data between independent IP subnetworks.

Layer 3 switches are also capable of performing Layer 3 routing functions, reducing the need for dedicated routers on a LAN. Because Layer 3 switches have specialized switching hardware, they can typically route data as quickly as they can switch.

Go to the online course to take the quiz and exam.

Chapter 5 Quiz

This quiz is designed to provide an additional opportunity to practice the skills and knowledge presented in the chapter and to prepare for the chapter exam. You will be allowed multiple attempts and the grade does not appear in the gradebook.

Chapter 5 Exam

The chapter exam assesses your knowledge of the chapter content.

Your Chapter Notes

Network Layer

6.0 Network Layer

6.0.1.1 Introduction

Network applications and services on one end device can communicate with applications and services running on another end device. How is this data communicated across the network in an efficient way?

The protocols of the OSI model network layer specify addressing and processes that enable transport layer data to be packaged and transported. The network layer encapsulation enables data to be passed to a destination within a network (or on another network) with minimum overhead.

This chapter focuses on the role of the network layer. It examines how it divides networks into groups of hosts to manage the flow of data packets within a network. It also covers how communication between networks is facilitated. This communication between networks is called routing.

Refer to **Lab Activity** for this chapter

6.0.1.2 Class Activity – The Road Less Traveled...

The road less traveled...or is it?

During the upcoming weekend, you decide to visit a schoolmate who is currently at home sick. You know his street address but you have never been to his town before. Instead of looking up the address on the map, you decide to take it easy and to simply ask town residents for directions after you arrive by train. The citizens you ask for directions are very helpful. However, they all have an interesting habit. Instead of explaining the entire route to your destination, they all tell you, "Take this road and as soon as you arrive at the nearest crossroad, ask somebody there again."

Somewhat bemused at this apparent oddity, you follow these instructions and finally arrive, crossroad by crossroad, and road by road, at your friend's house.

Answer the following questions:

- Would it have made a significant difference if you were told about the whole route or a larger part of the route instead of just being directed to the nearest crossroad?

- Would it have been more helpful to ask about the specific street address or just about the street name? What would happen if the person you asked for directions did not know where the destination street was or directed you through an incorrect road?

- Assume that on your way back home, you again choose to ask residents for directions. Would it be guaranteed that you would be directed via the same route you took to get to your friend's home? Explain your answer.

- Is it necessary to explain where you depart from when asking directions to an intended destination?

Refer to
Online Course
for Illustration

6.1   Network Layer Protocols

6.1.1   Network Layer in Communication

6.1.1.1   The Network Layer

The network layer, or OSI Layer 3, provides services to allow end devices to exchange data across the network. To accomplish this end-to-end transport, the network layer uses four basic processes:

- **Addressing end devices** - In the same way that a phone has a unique telephone number, end devices must be configured with a unique IP address for identification on the network. An end device with a configured IP address is referred to as a host.

- **Encapsulation** - The network layer receives a protocol data unit (PDU) from the transport layer. In a process called encapsulation, the network layer adds IP header information, such as the IP address of the source (sending) and destination (receiving) hosts. After header information is added to the PDU, the PDU is called a packet.

- **Routing** - The network layer provides services to direct packets to a destination host on another network. To travel to other networks, the packet must be processed by a router. The role of the router is to select paths for and direct packets toward the destination host in a process known as routing. A packet may cross many intermediary devices before reaching the destination host. Each route the packet takes to reach the destination host is called a hop.

- **De-encapsulation** - When the packet arrives at the network layer of the destination host, the host checks the IP header of the packet. If the destination IP address within the header matches its own IP address, the IP header is removed from the packet. This process of removing headers from lower layers is known as de-encapsulation. After the packet is de-encapsulated by the network layer, the resulting Layer 4 PDU is passed up to the appropriate service at the transport layer.

Unlike the transport layer (OSI Layer 4), which manages the data transport between the processes running on each host, network layer protocols specify the packet structure and processing used to carry the data from one host to another host. Operating without regard to the data carried in each packet allows the network layer to carry packets for multiple types of communications between multiple hosts.

The animation in the figure demonstrates the exchange of data.

Refer to
Online Course
for Illustration

6.1.1.2   Network Layer Protocols

There are several network layer protocols in existence; however, only the following two are commonly implemented as show in the figure:

- Internet Protocol version 4 (IPv4)

- Internet Protocol version 6 (IPv6)

Other legacy network layer protocols that are not widely used include:

- Novell Internetwork Packet Exchange (IPX)

- AppleTalk

- Connectionless Network Service (CLNS/DECNet)

Discussion of these legacy protocols will be minimal.

Refer to
Online Course
for Illustration

6.1.2   Characteristics of the IP protocol

6.1.2.1   Characteristics of IP

IP is the network layer service implemented by the TCP/IP protocol suite.

IP was designed as a protocol with low overhead. It provides only the functions that are necessary to deliver a packet from a source to a destination over an interconnected system of networks. The protocol was not designed to track and manage the flow of packets. These functions, if required, are performed by other protocols in other layers.

The basic characteristics of IP are:

- **Connectionless** - No connection with the destination is established before sending data packets.

- **Best Effort (unreliable)** - Packet delivery is not guaranteed.

- **Media Independent** - Operation is independent of the medium carrying the data.

Refer to
Online Course
for Illustration

6.1.2.2   IP – Connectionless

The role of the network layer is to transport packets between hosts while placing as little burden on the network as possible. The network layer is not concerned with, or even aware of, the type of communication contained inside of a packet. IP is connectionless, meaning that no dedicated end-to-end connection is created before data is sent. Connectionless communication is conceptually similar to sending a letter to someone without notifying the recipient in advance.

As shown in Figure 1, the postal service uses the information on a letter to deliver the letter to a recipient. The address on the envelope does not provide information as to whether the receiver is present, whether the letter arrives, or whether the receiver can read the letter. In fact, the postal service is unaware of the information contained within the contents of the packet that it is delivering and, therefore cannot provide any error correction mechanisms.

Connectionless data communications work on the same principle.

IP is connectionless and, therefore, requires no initial exchange of control information to establish an end-to-end connection before packets are forwarded. IP also does not require additional fields in the protocol data unit (PDU) header to maintain an established connection. This process greatly reduces the overhead of IP. However, with no pre-established end-to-end connection, senders are unaware whether destination devices are present and functional when sending packets, nor are they aware if the destination receives the packet, or if they are able to access and read the packet. Figure 2 shows an example of connectionless communication.

Refer to **Online Course** for Illustration

6.1.2.3   IP – Best Effort Delivery

IP is often referred to as an unreliable or best-effort delivery protocol. This does not mean that IP works properly sometimes and does not function well at other times, nor does it mean that it is a poor data communications protocol. Unreliable simply means that IP does not have the capability to manage and recover from undelivered or corrupt packets. This is because while IP packets are sent with information about the location of delivery, it contains no information that can be processed to inform the sender whether delivery was successful. There is no synchronization data included in the packet header for tracking the order of packet delivery. There are also no acknowledgments of packet delivery with IP, and there is no error control data to track whether packets were delivered without corruption. Packets may arrive at the destination corrupted, out of sequence, or not at all. Based on the information provided in the IP header, there is no capability for packet retransmissions if errors such as these occur.

If out-of-order or missing packets create problems for the application using the data, then upper layer services, such as TCP, must resolve these issues. This allows IP to function very efficiently. If reliability overhead were included in IP, then communications that do not require connections or reliability would be burdened with the bandwidth consumption and delay produced by this overhead. In the TCP/IP suite, the transport layer can use either TCP or UDP based on the need for reliability in communication. Leaving the reliability decision to the transport layer makes IP more adaptable and accommodating for different types of communication.

The figure shows an example of IP communications. Connection-oriented protocols, such as TCP, require that control data be exchanged to establish the connection. To maintain information about the connection, TCP also requires additional fields in the PDU header.

Refer to **Online Course** for Illustration

6.1.2.4   IP – Media Independent

The network layer is also not burdened with the characteristics of the media on which packets are transported. IP operates independently of the media that carry the data at lower layers of the protocol stack. As shown in the figure, any individual IP packet can be communicated electrically over cable, as optical signals over fiber, or wirelessly as radio signals.

It is the responsibility of the OSI data link layer to take an IP packet and prepare it for transmission over the communications medium. This means that the transport of IP packets is not limited to any particular medium.

There is, however, one major characteristic of the media that the network layer considers: the maximum size of the PDU that each medium can transport. This characteristic is referred to as the maximum transmission unit (MTU). Part of the control communication between the data link layer and the network layer is the establishment of a maximum size for the packet. The data link layer passes the MTU value up to the network layer. The network layer then determines how large packets should be.

In some cases, an intermediate device, usually a router, must split up a packet when forwarding it from one medium to a medium with a smaller MTU. This process is called fragmenting the packet or fragmentation.

Refer to
Online Course
for Illustration

6.1.2.5   Encapsulating IP

IP encapsulates, or packages, the transport layer segment by adding an IP header. This header is used to deliver the packet to the destination host. The IP header remains in place from the time the packet leaves the network layer of the source host until it arrives at the network layer of the destination host.

Figure 1 shows the process for creating the transport layer PDU. Figure 2 shows the subsequent process for creating the network layer PDU.

The process of encapsulating data layer by layer enables the services at the different layers to develop and scale without affecting other layers. This means that transport layer segments can be readily packaged by IPv4 or IPv6 or by any new protocol that might be developed in the future.

Routers can implement these different network layer protocols to operate concurrently over a network to and from the same or different hosts. The routing performed by these intermediate device only considers the contents of the packet header that encapsulates the segment. In all cases, the data portion of the packet, that is, the encapsulated transport layer PDU, remains unchanged during the network layer processes.

Refer to
Interactive Graphic
in online course.

6.1.2.6   Activity - IP Characteristics

Refer to
Online Course
for Illustration

6.1.3   IPv4 Packet

6.1.3.1   IPv4 Packet Header

IPv4 has been in use since 1983 when it was deployed on the Advanced Research Projects Agency Network (ARPANET), which was the precursor to the Internet. The Internet is largely based on IPv4, which is still the most widely-used network layer protocol.

An IPv4 packet has two parts:

- **IP Header** - Identifies the packet characteristics.

- **Payload** - Contains the Layer 4 segment information and the actual data.

As shown in the figure, an IPv4 packet header consists of fields containing important information about the packet. These fields contain binary numbers which are examined by the Layer 3 process. The binary values of each field identify various settings of the IP packet.

Significant fields in the IPv4 header include:

- **Version** - Contains a 4-bit binary value identifying the IP packet version. For IPv4 packets, this field is always set to 0100.

- **Differentiated Services (DS)** - Formerly called the Type of Service (ToS) field, the DS field is an 8-bit field used to determine the priority of each packet. The first 6 bits identify the Differentiated Services Code Point (DSCP) value that is used by a quality of service (QoS) mechanism. The last 2 bits identify the explicit congestion notification (ECN) value that can be used to prevent dropped packets during times of network congestion.

- **Time-to-Live (TTL)** - Contains an 8-bit binary value that is used to limit the lifetime of a packet. It is specified in seconds but is commonly referred to as hop count. The packet sender sets the initial time-to-live (TTL) value and is decreased by one each time the packet is processed by a router, or hop. If the TTL field decrements to zero, the router discards the packet and sends an Internet Control Message Protocol (ICMP) Time Exceeded message to the source IP address. The **traceroute** command uses this field to identify the routers used between the source and destination.

- **Protocol** - This 8-bit binary value indicates the data payload type that the packet is carrying, which enables the network layer to pass the data to the appropriate upper-layer protocol. Common values include ICMP (0x01), TCP (0x06), and UDP (0x11).

- **Source IP Address** - Contains a 32-bit binary value that represents the source IP address of the packet.

- **Destination IP Address** - Contains a 32-bit binary value that represents the destination IP address of the packet.

The two most commonly referenced fields are the source and destination IP addresses. These fields identify where the packet is from and where it is going. Typically these addresses do not change while travelling from the source to the destination.

6.1.3.2   IPv4 Header Fields

Refer to
Online Course
for Illustration

The remaining fields are used to identify and validate the packet, or to reorder a fragmented packet.

The fields used to identify and validate the packet include:

- **Internet Header Length (IHL)** - Contains a 4-bit binary value identifying the number of 32-bit words in the header. The IHL value varies due to the Options and Padding fields. The minimum value for this field is 5 (i.e., 5×32 = 160 bits = 20 bytes) and the maximum value is 15 (i.e., 15×32 = 480 bits = 60 bytes).

- **Total Length** - Sometimes referred to as the Packet Length, this 16-bit field defines the entire packet (fragment) size, including header and data, in bytes. The minimum length packet is 20 bytes (20-byte header + 0 bytes data) and the maximum is 65,535 bytes.

- **Header Checksum** - The 16-bit field is used for error checking of the IP header. The checksum of the header is recalculated and compared to the value in the checksum field. If the values do not match, the packet is discarded.

A router may have to fragment a packet when forwarding it from one medium to another medium that has a smaller MTU. When this happens, fragmentation occurs and the IPv4 packet uses the following fields to keep track of the fragments:

- **Identification** - This 16-bit field uniquely identifies the fragment of an original IP packet.

■ **Flags** - This 3-bit field identifies how the packet is fragmented. It is used with the Fragment Offset and Identification fields to help reconstruct the fragment into the original packet.

■ **Fragment Offset** - This 13-bit field identifies the order in which to place the packet fragment in the reconstruction of the original unfragmented packet.

Note   The Options and Padding fields are rarely used and beyond the scope of this chapter.

Refer to
Online Course
for Illustration

6.1.3.3   Sample IPv4 Headers

Wireshark is a useful network monitoring tool for anyone working with networks and can be used with most labs in the Cisco Certified Network Associate (CCNA) courses for data analysis and troubleshooting. It can be used to view sample values contained in IP header fields.

The three figures contain sample captures of various IP packets:

■ Figure 1 displays the contents of packet number 2 in this sample capture. Note that the Source is listed as 192.168.1.109 and the Destination is listed as 192.168.1.1. The middle window contains information about the IPv4 header, such as the header length, total length, and any flags that are set.

■ Figure 2 displays the contents of packet number 8 in this sample capture. This is an HTTP packet. Also notice the presence of information beyond the TCP section.

■ Finally, Figure 3 displays the contents of packet number 16 in this sample capture. The sample packet is a ping request from host 192.168.1.109 to host 192.168.1.1. Notice how there is no TCP or UDP information because this is an Internet Control Message Protocol (ICMP) packet.

Refer to
Interactive Graphic
in online course.

6.1.3.4   Activity - IPv4 Header Fields

Refer to
Online Course
for Illustration

6.1.4   IPv6 Packet

6.1.4.1   Limitations of IPv4

Through the years, IPv4 has been updated to address new challenges. However, even with changes, IPv4 still has three major issues:

■ **IP address depletion** - IPv4 has a limited number of unique public IP addresses available. Although there are approximately 4 billion IPv4 addresses, the increasing number of new IP-enabled devices, always-on connections, and the potential growth of less-developed regions have increased the need for more addresses.

■ **Internet routing table expansion** - A routing table is used by routers to make best path determinations. As the number of servers (nodes) connected to the Internet increases, so too does the number of network routes. These IPv4 routes consume a great deal of memory and processor resources on Internet routers.

■ **Lack of end-to-end connectivity** - Network Address Translation (NAT) is a technology commonly implemented within IPv4 networks. NAT provides a way for multiple devices to share a single public IP address. However, because the public IP address is shared, the IP address of an internal network host is hidden. This can be problematic for technologies that require end-to-end connectivity.

Refer to
Online Course
for Illustration

6.1.4.2   Introducing IPv6

In the early 1990s, the Internet Engineering Task Force (IETF) grew concerned about the issues with IPv4 and began to look for a replacement. This activity led to the development of IP version 6 (IPv6). IPv6 overcomes the limitations of IPv4 and is a powerful enhancement with features that better suit current and foreseeable network demands.

Improvements that IPv6 provides include:

■ **Increased address space** - IPv6 addresses are based on 128-bit hierarchical addressing as opposed to IPv4 with 32 bits. This dramatically increases the number of available IP addresses.

■ **Improved packet handling** - The IPv6 header has been simplified with fewer fields. This improves packet handling by intermediate routers and also provides support for extensions and options for increased scalability/longevity.

■ **Eliminates the need for NAT** - With such a large number of public IPv6 addresses, Network Address Translation (NAT) is not needed. Customer sites, from the largest enterprises to single households, can get a public IPv6 network address. This avoids some of the NAT-induced application problems experienced by applications requiring end-to-end connectivity.

■ **Integrated security** - IPv6 natively supports authentication and privacy capabilities. With IPv4, additional features had to be implemented to do this.

The 32-bit IPv4 address space provides approximately 4,294,967,296 unique addresses. Of these, only 3.7 billion addresses are assignable, because the IPv4 addressing system separates the addresses into classes, and reserves addresses for multicasting, testing, and other specific uses.

As shown in the figure, IP version 6 address space provides 340,282,366,920,938,463,463,374,607,431,768,211,456, or 340 undecillion addresses, which is roughly equivalent to every grain of sand on Earth.

Refer to
Online Course
for Illustration

6.1.4.3   Encapsulating IPv6

One of the major design improvements of IPv6 over IPv4 is the simplified IPv6 header.

The IPv4 header consists of 20 octets (up to 60 bytes if the Options field is used) and 12 basic header fields, not including the Options field and Padding field.

The IPv6 header consists of 40 octets (largely due to the length of the source and destination IPv6 addresses) and 8 header fields (3 IPv4 basic header fields and 5 additional header fields).

Figure 1 shows the IPv4 header structure. As shown in the figure, for IPv6, some fields have remained the same, some fields from the IPv4 header are not used, and some fields have changed names and positions.

In addition, a new field has been added to IPv6 that is not used in IPv4. The IPv6 simplified header is shown in Figure 2.

The IPv6 simplified header offers several advantages over IPv4:

- Better routing efficiency for performance and forwarding-rate scalability

- No requirement for processing checksums

- Simplified and more efficient extension header mechanisms (as opposed to the IPv4 Options field)

- A Flow Label field for per-flow processing with no need to open the transport inner packet to identify the various traffic flows

Refer to
Online Course
for Illustration

6.1.4.4   IPv6 Packet Header

The fields in the IPv6 packet header include:

- **Version** - This field contains a 4-bit binary value identifying the IP packet version. For IPv6 packets, this field is always set to 0110.

- **Traffic Class** - This 8-bit field is equivalent to the IPv4 Differentiated Services (DS) field. It also contains a 6-bit Differentiated Services Code Point (DSCP) value used to classify packets and a 2-bit Explicit Congestion Notification (ECN) used for traffic congestion control.

- **Flow Label** - This 20-bit field provides a special service for real-time applications. It can be used to inform routers and switches to maintain the same path for the packet flow so that packets are not reordered.

- **Payload Length** - This 16-bit field is equivalent to the Total Length field in the IPv4 header. It defines the entire packet (fragment) size, including header and optional extensions.

- **Next Header** - This 8-bit field is equivalent to the IPv4 Protocol field. It indicates the data payload type that the packet is carrying, enabling the network layer to pass the data to the appropriate upper-layer protocol. This field is also used if there are optional extension headers added to the IPv6 packet.

- **Hop Limit:** - This 8-bit field replaces the IPv4 TTL field. This value is decremented by one by each router that forwards the packet. When the counter reaches 0 the packet is discarded and an ICMPv6 message is forwarded to the sending host, indicating that the packet did not reach its destination.

- **Source Address** - This 128-bit field identifies the IPv6 address of the receiving host.

- **Destination Address** - This 128-bit field identifies the IPv6 address of the receiving host.

An IPv6 packet may also contain extension headers (EH), which provide optional network layer information. Extension headers are optional and are placed between the IPv6 header and the payload. EHs are used for fragmentation, security, to support mobility, and more.

Refer to
Online Course
for Illustration

6.1.4.5   Sample IPv6 Header

When viewing IPv6 Wireshark captures, notice that the IPv6 header has markedly fewer fields than an IPv4 header. This makes the IPv6 header easier and quicker for the router to process.

The IPv6 address itself looks very different. Because of the larger 128-bit IPv6 addresses, the hexadecimal numbering system is used to simplify the address representation. IPv6 addresses use colons to separate entries into a series of 16-bit hexadecimal blocks.

Figure 1 displays the contents of packet number 46 in this sample capture. The packet contains the initial message of the TCP 3-way handshake between an IPv6 host and an IPv6 server. Notice the values in the expanded IPv6 header section. Also notice how this is a TCP packet and that it does not contain any other information beyond the TCP section.

Figure 2 displays the contents of packet number 49 in this sample capture. The packet contains the initial HyperText Transfer Protocol (HTTP) GET message to the server. Notice how this is an HTTP packet and that it now contains information beyond the TCP section.

Finally, Figure 3 displays the contents of packet number 1 in this sample capture. The sample packet is an ICMPv6 Neighbor Solicitation message. Notice how there is no TCP or UDP information.

Refer to
Interactive Graphic
in online course.

6.1.4.6   Activity - IPv6 Header Fields

Refer to
Online Course
for Illustration

6.2   Routing

6.2.1   How a Host Routes

6.2.1.1   Host Forwarding Decision

Another role of the network layer is to direct packets between hosts. A host can send a packet to:

- **Itself** - This is a special IP address of 127.0.0.1 which is referred to as the loopback interface. This loopback address is automatically assigned to a host when TCP/IP is running. The ability for a host to send a packet to itself using network functionality is useful for testing purposes. Any IP within the network 127.0.0.0/8 refers to the local host.

- **Local host** - This is a host on the same network as the sending host. The hosts share the same network address.

- **Remote host** - This is a host on a remote network. The hosts do not share the same network address.

Whether a packet is destined for a local host or a remote host is determined by the IP address and subnet mask combination of the source (or sending) device compared to the IP address and subnet mask of the destination device.

In a home or business network you may have several wired and wireless devices interconnected together using an intermediate device such as a LAN switch and/or a wireless access point (WAP). This intermediate device provides interconnections between local hosts on the local network. Local hosts can reach each other and share information without the need of any additional devices. If a host is sending a packet to a device that is configured with the same IP network as the host device, the packet is simply forwarded out of the host interface, through the intermediate device, to the destination device directly.

Of course in most situations we want our devices to be able to connect beyond the local network segment: out to other homes, businesses, and the Internet. Devices that are beyond the local network segment are known as remote hosts. When a source device sends a packet to a remote destination device, then the help of routers and routing is needed. Routing is the process of identifying the best path to a destination. The router connected to the local network segment is referred to as the **default gateway**.

Refer to
Online Course
for Illustration

6.2.1.2   Default Gateway

The default gateway is the device that routes traffic from the local network to devices on remote networks. In a home or small business environment, the default gateway is often used to connect the local network to the Internet.

If the host is sending a packet to a device on a different IP network, then the host must forward the packet through the intermediate device to the default gateway. This is because a host device does not maintain routing information, beyond the local network, to reach remote destinations. The default gateway does. The default gateway, which is most often a router, maintains a routing table. A routing table is a data file in RAM that is used to store route information about directly connected network, as well as entries of remote networks the device has learned about. A router uses the information in the routing table to determine the best path to reach those destinations.

So how does a host keep track of whether or not to forward packets to the default gateway? Hosts must maintain their own, local, routing table to ensure that network layer packets are directed to the correct destination network. The local table of the host typically contains:

- **Direct connection** - This is a route to the loopback interface (127.0.0.1).

- **Local network route** - The network which the host is connected to is automatically populated in the host routing table.

- **Local default route** - The default route represents the route that packets must take to reach all remote network addresses. The default route is created when a default gateway address is present on the host. The default gateway address is the IP address of the network interface of the router that is connected to the local network. The default gateway address can be configured on the host manually or learned dynamically.

It is important to note that the default route, and therefore, the default gateway, is only used when a host must forward packets to a remote network. It is not required, nor even needs to be configured, if only sending packets to devices on the local network.

For example, consider a network printer/scanner. If the network printer has an IP address and subnet mask configured, then local hosts can send documents to the printer to be printed. Additionally, the printer can forward documents that have been scanned to any local hosts. As long as the printer is only used locally, a default gateway address is not required. In fact, by not configuring a default gateway address on the printer, you are effectively denying Internet access, which may be a wise security choice. No Internet access means no security risk. While devices, such as printers, may offer the capability to perform automatic updates via the Internet, it is usually easier and more secure to achieve those same updates via a local upload from a secured local host, such as a PC.

Refer to **Online Course** for Illustration

6.2.1.3   IPv4 Host Routing Table

On a Windows host, the `route print` or `netstat -r` command can be used to display the host routing table. Both commands generate the same output. The output may seem overwhelming at first, but is fairly simple to understand.

Entering the `netstat -r` command or the equivalent `route print` command, displays three sections related to the current TCP/IP network connections:

- **Interface List** - Lists the Media Access Control (MAC) address and assigned interface number of every network-capable interface on the host including Ethernet, Wi-Fi, and Bluetooth adapters.

- **IPv4 Route Table** - Lists all known IPv4 routes, including direct connections, local network, and local default routes.

- **IPv6 Route Table** - Lists all known IPv6 routes, including direct connections, local network, and local default routes.

Note   Command output varies, depending on how the host is configured and the interface types it has.

The figure displays the IPv4 Route Table section of the output. Notice the output is divided into five columns which identify:

- **Network Destination** - Lists the reachable networks.

- **Netmask** - Lists a subnet mask that informs the host how to determine the network and the host portions of the IP address.

- **Gateway** - Lists the address used by the local computer to get to a remote network destination. If a destination is directly reachable, it will show as "on-link" in this column.

- **Interface** - Lists the address of the physical interface used to send the packet to the gateway that is used to reach the network destination.

- **Metric** - Lists the cost of each route and is used to determine the best route to a destination.

Refer to **Online Course** for Illustration

6.2.1.4   IPv4 Host Routing Entries

To help simplify the output, the destination networks can be grouped into five sections as identified by the highlighted areas in the figure:

0.0.0.0

The local default route; that is, all packets with destinations that do not match other specified addresses in the routing table are forwarded to the gateway. Therefore, all non-matching destination routes are sent to the gateway with IP address 192.168.10.1 (R1) exiting from the interface with IP address 192.168.10.10. Note that the final destination address specified in the packet does not change; rather, the host simply knows to forward the packet to the gateway for further processing.

127.0.0.0 – 127.255.255.255

These loopback addresses all relate to the direct connection and provide services to the local host.

192.168.10.0 - 192.168.10.255

These addresses all relate to the host and local network. All packets with destination addresses that fall into this category will exit out of the 192.168.10.10 interface.

- **192.168.10.0** - The local network route address; represents all computers on the 192.168.10.x network.

- **192.168.10.10** - The address of the local host.

- **192.168.10.255** - The network broadcast address; sends messages to all hosts on the local network route.

224.0.0.0

These are special multicast class D addresses reserved for use through either the loopback interface (127.0.0.1) or the host IP address (192.168.10.10).

255.255.255.255

The last two addresses represent the limited broadcast IP address values for use through either the loopback interface (127.0.0.1) or the host IP address (192.168.10.10). These addresses can be used to find a DHCP server before the local IP is determined.

Refer to **Online Course** for Illustration

6.2.1.5   Sample IPv4 Host Routing Table

For example, if PC1 wanted to send a packet to 192.168.10.20, it would:

1. Consult the IPv4 Route Table.

2. Match the destination IP address with the 192.168.10.0 Network Destination entry to reveal that the host is on the same network (On-link).

3. PC1 would then send the packet toward the final destination using its local interface (192.168.10.10).

Figure 1 highlights the matched route.

If PC1 wanted to send a packet to a remote host located at 10.10.10.10, it would:

1. Consult the IPv4 Route Table.

2. Find that there is no exact match for the destination IP address.

3. Choose the local default route (0.0.0.0) to reveal that it should forward the packet to the 192.168.10.1 gateway address.

4. PC1 then forwards the packet to the gateway for using its local interface (192.168.10.10). The gateway device then determines the next path for the packet to reach the final destination address of 10.10.10.10.

Figure 2 highlights the matched route.

Refer to
Online Course
for Illustration

6.2.1.6   Sample IPv6 Host Routing Table

The output of the IPv6 Route Table differs in column headings and format due to the longer IPv6 addresses.

The IPv6 Route Table section displays four columns which identify:

- **If** - Lists the interface numbers from the Interface List section of the `netstat -r` command. The interface numbers correspond to the network capable interface on the host, including Ethernet, Wi-Fi, and Bluetooth adapters.

- **Metric** - Lists the cost of each route to a destination. Lower numbers indicate preferred routes.

- **Network Destination** - Lists the reachable networks.

- **Gateway** - Lists the address used by the local host to forward packets to a remote network destination. On-link indicates that the host is currently connected to it.

For example, the figure displays the IPv6 Route section generated by the `netstat -r` command to reveal the following network destinations:

- **::/0** - This is the IPv6 equivalent of the local default route.

- **::1/128** - This is equivalent to the IPv4 loopback address and provides services to the local host.

- **2001::/32** - This is the global unicast network prefix.

- **2001:0:9d38:953c:2c30:3071:e718:a926/128** - This is the global unicast IPv6 address of the local computer.

- **fe80::/64** - This is the local link network route address and represents all computers on the local link IPv6 network.

- **fe80::2c30:3071:e718:a926/128** - This is the link local IPv6 address of the local computer.

- **ff00::/8** - These are special reserved multicast class D addresses equivalent to the IPv4 224.x.x.x addresses.

Note   Interfaces in IPv6 commonly have two IPv6 addresses: a link local address and a global unicast address. Also, notice that there are no broadcast addresses in IPv6. IPv6 addresses will be discussed further in the next chapter.

Refer to
Interactive Graphic
in online course.

6.2.1.7   Activity - Identify Elements of a Host Routing Table Entry

Refer to
Online Course
for Illustration

6.2.2   Router Routing Tables

6.2.2.1   Router Packet Forwarding Decision

When a host sends a packet to another host, it will use its routing table to determine where to send the packet. If the destination host is on a remote network, the packet is forwarded to the address of a gateway device.

What happens when a packet arrives on a router interface? The router looks at its routing table to determine where to forward packets.

The routing table of a router stores information about:

- **Directly-connected routes** - These routes come from the active router interfaces. Routers add a directly connected route when an interface is configured with an IP address and is activated. Each of the router's interfaces is connected to a different network segment. Routers maintain information about the network segments that they are connected to within the routing table.

- **Remote routes** - These routes come from remote networks connected to other routers. Routes to these networks can either be manually configured on the local router by the network administrator or dynamically configured by enabling the local router to exchange routing information with other routers using dynamic routing protocols.

The figure identifies the directly connected networks and remote networks of router R1.

Refer to
Online Course
for Illustration

6.2.2.2   IPv4 Router Routing Table

A host routing table includes only information about directly-connected networks. A host requires a default gateway to send packets to a remote destination. The routing table of a router contains similar information but can also identify specific remote networks.

The routing table of a router is similar to the routing table of a host. They both identify the:

- Destination network

- Metric associated with the destination network

- Gateway to get to the destination network

On a Cisco IOS router, the `show ip route` command can be used to display the routing table of a router. A router also provides additional route information, including how the route was learned, when it was last updated, and which specific interface to use to get to a predefined destination.

When a packet arrives at the router interface, the router examines the packet header to determine the destination network. If the destination network matches a route in the routing table, the router forwards the packet using the information specified in the routing table. If there are two or more possible routes to the same destination, the metric is used to decide which route appears on the routing table.

The figure shows the routing table of R1 in a simple network. Unlike the host routing table, there are no column headings identifying the information contained in a routing table entry. Therefore, it is important to learn the meaning of the different types of information included in each entry.

Refer to
Online Course
for Illustration

6.2.2.3   Directly Connected Routing Table Entries

Two routing table entries are automatically created when an active router interface is configured with an IP address and subnet mask. The figure displays the routing table entries on R1 for the directly connected network 192.168.10.0. These entries were automatically added to the routing table when the GigabitEthernet 0/0 interface was configured and activated. The entries contain the following information:

Route Source

The route source is labeled "A" in the figure. It identifies how the route was learned. Directly connected interfaces have two route source codes.

- **C** - Identifies a directly connected network. Directly connected networks are automatically created when an interface is configured with an IP address and activated.

- **L** - Identifies that this is a link local route. Link local routes are automatically created when an interface is configured with an IP address and activated.

Destination network

The destination network is labeled "B" in the figure. It identifies the address of the remote network.

Outgoing interface

The outgoing interface is labeled "C" in the figure. It identifies the exit interface to use when forwarding packets to the destination network.

Note   Link local routing table entries did not appear in routing tables prior to IOS Release 15.

A router typically has multiple interfaces configured. The routing table stores information about both directly-connected and remote routes. As with directly connected networks, the route source identifies how the route was learned. For example, common codes for remote networks include:

- **S** - Identifies that the route was manually created by an administrator to reach a specific network. This is known as a static route.

- **D** - Identifies that the route was learned dynamically from another router using the Enhanced Interior Gateway Routing Protocol (EIGRP).

- **O** - Identifies that the route was learned dynamically from another router using the Open Shortest Path First (OSPF) routing protocol.

Note   Other codes are beyond the scope of this chapter.

Refer to
Online Course
for Illustration

6.2.2.4   Remote Network Routing Table Entries

The figure displays a routing table entry on R1 for the route to remote network 10.1.1.0. The entry identifies the following information:

- **Route source** - Identifies how the route was learned.

- **Destination network** - Identifies the address of the remote network.

- **Administrative distance** - Identifies the trustworthiness of the route source.

- **Metric** - Identifies the value assigned to reach the remote network. Lower values indicate preferred routes.

- **Next-hop** - Identifies the IP address of the next router to forward the packet.

- **Route timestamp** - Identifies when the route was last heard from.

- **Outgoing interface** - Identifies the exit interface to use to forward a packet toward the final destination.

Refer to
Online Course
for Illustration

6.2.2.5   Next-Hop Address

A next hop is the address of the device that will process the packet next. For a host on a network, the address of the default gateway (router interface) is the next hop for all packets that must be sent to another network. In the routing table of a router, each route to a remote network lists a next hop.

When a packet destined for a remote network arrives at the router, the router matches the destination network to a route in the routing table. If a match is found, the router forwards the packet to the IP address of the next hop router using the interface identified by the route entry.

A next hop router is the gateway to remote networks.

For example, in the figure, a packet arriving at R1 destined for either the 10.1.1.0 or 10.1.2.0 network is forwarded to the next-hop address 209.165.200.226 using the Serial 0/0/0 interface.

Networks directly connected to a router have no next-hop address, because a router can forward packets directly to hosts on these networks using the designated interface.

Packets cannot be forwarded by the router without a route for the destination network in the routing table. If a route representing the destination network is not in the routing table, the packet is dropped (that is, not forwarded).

However, just as a host can use a default gateway to forward a packet to an unknown destination, a router can also be configured to use a default static route to create a Gateway of Last Resort. The Gateway of Last Resort will be covered in more detail in the CCNA Routing course.

Refer to
Online Course
for Illustration

6.2.2.6   Sample Router IPv4 Routing Table

Assume PC1 with IP address 192.168.10.10 wants to send a packet to another host on the same network. PC1 would check the IPv4 route table based on the destination IP address. Then, PC1 would discover that the host is on the same network and simply send it out of its interface (On-link).

Note   R1 is not involved in the transfer of the packet. If PC1 forwards a packet to any network other than its local network, then it must use the services of router R1, and forward the packet to its local default route (192.168.10.1).

The following examples illustrate how a host and a router make packet routing decisions by consulting their respective routing tables:

Example 1: PC1 wants to verify connectivity to its local default gateway at 192.168.10.1 (the router interface):

1. PC1 consults the IPv4 route table based on the destination IP address.

2. PC1 discovers that the host is on the same network and simply sends a ping packet out of its interface (On-link).

3. R1 receives the packet on its Gigabit Ethernet 0/0 (G0/0) interface and looks at the destination IP address.

4. R1 consults its routing table.

5. R1 matches the destination IP address to the **L 192.168.10.1/32** routing table entry and discovers that this route points to its own local interface, as shown in Figure 1.

6. R1 opens the remainder of the IP packet and responds accordingly.

Example 2: PC1 wants to send a packet to PC2 (192.168.11.10):

1. PC1 consults the IPv4 route table and discovers that there is no exact match.

2. PC1 therefore uses the all route network (0.0.0.0) and sends the packet using the local default route (192.168.10.1).

3. R1 receives the packet on its Gigabit Ethernet 0/0 (G0/0) interface and looks at the destination IP address (192.168.11.10).

4. R1 consults its routing table and matches the destination IP address to the **C 192.168.11.0/24** routing table entry, as shown in Figure 2.

5. R1 forwards the packet out of its directly connected Gigabit Ethernet 0/1 interface (G0/1).

6. PC2 receives the packet and consults its host IPv4 routing table.

7. PC2 discovers that the packet is addressed to it, opens the remainder of the packet, and responds accordingly.

Example 3: PC1 wants to send a packet to 209.165.200.226:

1. PC1 consults the IPv4 route table and discover that there is no exact match.

2. PC1 therefore uses the default route (0.0.0.0/0) and sends the packet using the default gateway (192.168.10.1).

3. R1 receives the packet on its Gigabit Ethernet 0/0 (G0/0) interface and looks at the destination IP address (209.165.200.226).

4. R1 consults its routing table and matches the destination IP address to the **C 209.165.200.224/30** routing table entry, as shown in Figure 3.

5. R1 forwards the packet out of its directly connected Serial 0/0/0 interface (S0/0/0).

Example 4: PC1 wants to send a packet to the host with IP address 10.1.1.10:

1. PC1 consults the IPv4 route table and discovers that there is no exact match.

2. PC1 therefore uses the all route network (0.0.0.0) and sends it to its local default route (192.168.10.1).

3. R1 receives the packet on its Gigabit Ethernet 0/0 (G0/0) interface and looks at the destination IP address (10.1.1.10).

4. R1 consults its routing table and matches the destination IP address to the **D 10.1.1.0/24** routing table entry, as shown in Figure 4.

5. R1 discovers it has to send the packet to the next-hop address 209.165.200.226.

6. R1 again consults its routing table and matches the destination IP address to the **C 209.165.200.224/30** routing table entry, as shown in Figure 4.

7. R1 forwards the packet out of its directly connected Serial 0/0/0 interface (S0/0/0).

Refer to
Interactive Graphic
in online course.

6.2.2.7   Activity - Identify Elements of a Router Routing Table Entry

Refer to
Lab Activity
for this chapter

6.2.2.8   Lab - View Host Routing Tables

In this lab, you will complete the following objectives:

■ Part 1: Access the Host Routing Table

■ Part 2: Examine IPv4 Host Routing Table Entries

■ Part 3: Examine IPv6 Host Routing Table Entries

Refer to
Online Course
for Illustration

6.3   Routers

6.3.1   Anatomy of a Router

6.3.1.1   A Router is a Computer

There are many types of infrastructure routers available. In fact, Cisco routers are designed to address the needs of:

■ **Branch** - Teleworkers, small business, and medium-size branch sites. Includes Cisco 800, 1900, 2900, and 3900 Integrated Series Routers (ISR) G2 (2nd generation).

■ **WAN** - Large businesses, organizations, and enterprises. Includes the Cisco Catalyst 6500 Series Switches and the Cisco Aggregation Service Router (ASR) 1000.

■ **Service Provider** - Large service providers. Includes Cisco ASR 1000, Cisco ASR 9000, Cisco XR 12000, Cisco CRS-3 Carrier Routing System, and 7600 Series routers.

The focus of CCNA certification is on the branch family of routers. The figure displays the Cisco 1900, 2900, and 3900 ISR G2 family of routers.

Regardless of their function, size or complexity, all router models are essentially computers. Just like computers, tablets, and smart devices, routers also require:

■ Operating systems (OS)

■ Central processing units (CPU)

- Random-access memory (RAM)

- Read-only memory (ROM)

A router also has special memory that includes Flash and nonvolatile random-access memory (NVRAM).

Refer to
Online Course
for Illustration

6.3.1.2   Router CPU and OS

Like all computers, tablets, and smart devices, Cisco devices require a CPU to execute OS instructions, such as system initialization, routing functions, and switching functions.

The CPU requires an OS to provide routing and switching functions. The Cisco Internetwork Operating System (IOS) is the system software used for most Cisco devices regardless of the size and type of the device. It is used for routers, LAN switches, small wireless access points, large routers with dozens of interfaces, and many other devices.

The highlighted component in the figure is the CPU of a Cisco 1941 router with the heat-sink attached.

Refer to
Online Course
for Illustration

6.3.1.3   Router Memory

A router has access to four types of memory: RAM, ROM, NVRAM, and Flash.

RAM

RAM is used to store various applications and processes including:

- **Cisco IOS** - The IOS is copied into RAM during bootup.

- **Running configuration file** - This is the configuration file that stores the configuration commands that the router IOS is currently using. It is also known as the running-config.

- **IP routing table** - This file stores information about directly-connected and remote networks. It is used to determine the best path to use to forward packets.

- **ARP cache** - This cache contains the IPv4 address to MAC address mappings, similar to the Address Resolution Protocol (ARP) cache on a PC. The ARP cache is used on routers that have LAN interfaces, such as Ethernet interfaces.

- **Packet buffer** - Packets are temporarily stored in a buffer when received on an interface or before they exit an interface.

Like computers, Cisco routers actually use dynamic random-access memory (DRAM). DRAM is a very common kind of RAM that stores the instructions and data needed to be executed by the CPU. Unlike ROM, RAM is volatile memory and requires continual power to maintain its information. It loses all of its content when the router is powered down or restarted.

By default 1941 routers come with 512 MB of DRAM soldered on the main system board (onboard) and one dual in-line memory module (DIMM) slot for memory upgrades of up to an additional 2.0 GB. Cisco 2901, 2911, and 2921 models come with 512 MB of onboard DRAM. Note that first generation ISRs and older Cisco routers do not have onboard RAM.

ROM

Cisco routers use ROM to store:

- **Bootup instructions** - Provides the startup instructions.

- **Basic diagnostic software** - Performs the power-on self-test (POST) of all components.

- **Limited IOS** - Provides a limited backup version of the OS, in case the router cannot load the full featured IOS.

ROM is firmware embedded on an integrated circuit inside the router and does not lose its contents when the router loses power or is restarted.

NVRAM

NVRAM is used by the Cisco IOS as permanent storage for the startup configuration file (startup-config). Like ROM, NVRAM does not lose its contents when power is turned off.

Flash Memory

Flash memory is non-volatile computer memory used as permanent storage for the IOS and other system related files. The IOS is copied from flash into RAM during the bootup process.

Cisco 1941 routers come with two external Compact Flash slots. Each slot can support high-speed storage densities upgradeable to 4GB in density.

The figure summarizes the four types of memory.

6.3.1.4   Inside a Router

Although there are several different types and models of routers, every router has the same general hardware components.

The figure shows the inside of a Cisco 1841 first generation ISR. Click the components to see a brief description of the components.

Note that the figure also includes highlights of other components found in a router, such as the power supply, cooling fan, heat shields, and an advanced integration module (AIM), which are beyond the scope of this chapter.

Note   A networking professional should be familiar with and understand the function of the main internal components of a router, rather than the exact location of those components inside a specific router. Depending on the model, those components are located in different places inside the router.

6.3.1.5   Router Backplane

Refer to **Online Course** for Illustration

A Cisco 1941 router includes the following connections:

- **Console ports** - Two console ports for the initial configuration and command-line interface (CLI) management access using a regular RJ-45 port and a new USB Type-B (mini-B USB) connector.

- **AUX port** - An RJ-45 port for remote management access; this is similar to the Console port.

■ **Two LAN interfaces** - Two Gigabit Ethernet interfaces for LAN access.

■ **Enhanced high-speed WAN interface card (EHWIC) slots** - Two slots that provide modularity and flexibility by enabling the router to support different types of interface modules, including Serial, digital subscriber line (DSL), switch port, and wireless.

The Cisco 1941 ISR also has storage slots to support expanded capabilities. Dual-compact flash memory slots are capable of supporting a 4 GB compact flash card each for increased storage space. Two USB host ports are included for additional storage space and secure token capability.

Compact flash can store the Cisco IOS software image, log files, voice configuration files, HTML files, backup configurations, or any other file needed for the system. By default, only slot 0 is populated with a compact flash card from the factory, and it is the default boot location.

The figure identifies the location of these connections and slots.

<table>
<tr><td>Refer to
Online Course
for Illustration</td></tr>
</table>

6.3.1.6 Connecting to a Router

Cisco devices, routers, and switches typically interconnect many devices. For this reason, these devices have several types of ports and interfaces. These ports and interfaces are used to connect cables to the device.

The connections on a Cisco router can be grouped into two categories:

■ **Management ports** - These are the console and auxiliary ports used to configure, manage, and troubleshoot the router. Unlike LAN and WAN interfaces, management ports are not used for packet forwarding.

■ **Inband Router interfaces** - These are the LAN and WAN interfaces configured with IP addressing to carry user traffic. Ethernet interfaces are the most common LAN connections, while common WAN connections include serial and DSL interfaces.

The figure highlights the ports and interfaces of a Cisco 1941 ISR G2 router.

Like many networking devices, Cisco devices use light emitting diode (LED) indicators to provide status information. An interface LED indicates the activity of the corresponding interface. If an LED is off when the interface is active and the interface is correctly connected, this may be an indication of a problem with that interface. If an interface is extremely busy, its LED is always on.

<table>
<tr><td>Refer to
Online Course
for Illustration</td></tr>
</table>

6.3.1.7 LAN and WAN Interfaces

Similar to a Cisco switch, there are several ways to access the CLI environment on a Cisco router. The most common methods are:

■ **Console** - Uses a low speed serial or USB connection to provide direct connect, out-of-band management access to a Cisco device.

■ **Telnet or SSH** - Two methods for remotely accessing a CLI session across an active network interface.

■ **AUX port** - Used for remote management of the router using a dial-up telephone line and modem.

The console and AUX port are located on the router.

In addition to these ports, routers also have network interfaces to receive and forward IP packets. Routers have multiple interfaces that are used to connect to multiple networks. Typically, the interfaces connect to various types of networks, which mean that different types of media and connectors are required.

Every interface on the router is a member or host on a different IP network. Each interface must be configured with an IP address and subnet mask of a different network. The Cisco IOS does not allow two active interfaces on the same router to belong to the same network.

Router interfaces can be grouped into two categories:

- **Ethernet LAN interfaces** - Used for connecting cables that terminate with LAN devices, such as computers and switches. This interface can also be used to connect routers to each other. Several conventions for naming Ethernet interfaces are popular: the older Ethernet, FastEthernet, and Gigabit Ethernet. The name used depends on the device type and model.

- **Serial WAN interfaces** - Used for connecting routers to external networks, usually over a larger geographical distance. Similar to LAN interfaces, each serial WAN interface has its own IP address and subnet mask, which identifies it as a member of a specific network.

The figure shows the LAN Interfaces and serial interfaces on the router.

Refer to
Interactive Graphic
in online course.

6.3.1.8   Activity - Identify Router Components

Refer to
Lab Activity
for this chapter

6.3.1.9   Lab - Exploring Router Physical Characteristics

In this lab, you will complete the following objectives:

- Part 1: Examine Router External Characteristics

- Part 2: Examine Router Internal Characteristics Using Show Commands

Refer to **Packet
Tracer Activity**
for this chapter

6.3.1.10   Packet Tracer - Exploring Internetworking Devices

In this activity, you will explore the different options available on internetworking devices. You will also be required to determine which options provide the necessary connectivity when connecting multiple devices. Finally, you will add the correct modules and connect the devices.

Refer to
Online Course
for Illustration

6.3.2   Router Boot-up

6.3.2.1   Cisco IOS

The Cisco IOS operational details vary on different internetworking devices, depending on the device's purpose and feature set. However, Cisco IOS for routers provides the following:

- Addressing

- Interfaces

- Routing

- Security

- QoS

- Resources Management

The IOS file itself is several megabytes in size and similar to Cisco IOS switches, is stored in flash memory. Using flash allows the IOS to be upgraded to newer versions or to have new features added. During bootup, the IOS is copied from flash memory into RAM. DRAM is much faster than flash; therefore, copying the IOS into RAM increases the performance of the device.

Refer to
Online Course
for Illustration

6.3.2.2   Bootset Files

As shown in the figure, a router loads the following two files into RAM when it is booted:

- **IOS image file** - The IOS facilitates the basic operation of the device's hardware components. The IOS image file is stored in flash memory.

- **Startup configuration file** - The startup configuration file contains commands that are used to initially configure a router and create the running configuration file stored in in RAM. The startup configuration file is stored in NVRAM. All configuration changes are stored in the running configuration file and are implemented immediately by the IOS.

The running configuration is modified when the network administrator performs device configuration. When changes are made to the running-config file, it should be saved to NVRAM as the startup configuration file, in case the router is restarted or loses power.

Refer to
Online Course
for Illustration

6.3.2.3   Router Bootup Process

There are three major phases to the bootup process that is shown in Figure 1:

1. Perform the POST and load the bootstrap program.

2. Locate and load the Cisco IOS software.

3. Locate and load the startup configuration file or enter setup mode.

1. Performing POST and Load Bootstrap Program (Figure 2)

The Power-On Self Test (POST) is a common process that occurs on almost every computer during bootup. The POST process is used to test the router hardware. When the router is powered on, software on the ROM chip conducts the POST. During this self-test, the router executes diagnostics from ROM on several hardware components, including the CPU, RAM, and NVRAM. After the POST has been completed, the router executes the bootstrap program.

After the POST, the bootstrap program is copied from ROM into RAM. Once in RAM, the CPU executes the instructions in the bootstrap program. The main task of the bootstrap program is to locate the Cisco IOS and load it into RAM.

Note   At this point, if you have a console connection to the router, you begin to see output on the screen.

2. Locating and Loading Cisco IOS (Figure 3)

The IOS is typically stored in flash memory and is copied into RAM for execution by the CPU. During self-decompression of the IOS image file, a string of pounds signs (#) will be displayed.

If the IOS image is not located in flash, then the router may look for it using a TFTP server. If a full IOS image cannot be located, a scaled-down version of the IOS is copied from ROM into RAM. This version of IOS is used to help diagnose any problems and can be used to load a complete version of the IOS into RAM.

3. Locating and Loading the Configuration File (Figure 4)

The bootstrap program then searches for the startup configuration file (also known as startup-config), in NVRAM. This file has the previously saved configuration commands and parameters. If it exists, then it is copied into RAM as the running configuration file, running-config. The running-config file contains interface addresses, starts routing processes, configures router passwords, and defines other characteristics of the router.

If the startup-config file does not exist in NVRAM, the router may search for a Trivial File Transfer Protocol (TFTP) server. If the router detects that it has an active link to another configured router, it sends a broadcast searching for a configuration file across the active link.

If a TFTP server is not found, then the router displays the setup mode prompt. Setup mode is a series of questions prompting the user for basic configuration information. Setup mode is not intended to be used to enter complex router configurations, and it is not commonly used by network administrators.

Note   Setup mode is not used in this course to configure the router. When prompted to enter setup mode, always answer **no**. If you answer yes and enter setup mode, press **Ctrl+C** at any time to terminate the setup process.

Refer to
Online Course
for Illustration

6.3.2.4   Show Version Output

You can use the `show version` command to verify and troubleshoot some of the basic hardware and software components of the router. The command displays information about the version of the Cisco IOS software currently running on the router, the version of the bootstrap program, and information about the hardware configuration, including the amount of system memory.

The output from the `show version` command includes:

- **IOS version** - Version of the Cisco IOS software in RAM and that is being used by the router.

- **ROM Bootstrap Program** - Displays the version of the system bootstrap software, stored in ROM that was initially used to boot up the router.

- **Location of IOS** - Displays where the bootstrap program is located and loaded the Cisco IOS, and the complete filename of the IOS image.

- **CPU and Amount of RAM** - The first part of this line displays the type of CPU on this router. The last part of this line displays the amount of DRAM. Some series of routers, like the Cisco 1941 ISR, use a fraction of DRAM as packet memory. Packet memory is used for buffering packets. To determine the total amount of DRAM on the router, add both numbers.

■ **Interfaces** - Displays the physical interfaces on the router. In this example, the Cisco 1941 ISR has two Gigabit Ethernet interfaces and two low-speed serial interfaces.

■ **Amount of NVRAM and Flash** - This is the amount of NVRAM and the amount of flash memory on the router. NVRAM is used to store the startup-config file and flash is used to permanently store the Cisco IOS.

The last line of the `show version` command displays the current, configured value of the software configuration register in hexadecimal. If there is a second value displayed in parentheses, it denotes the configuration register value that is used during the next reload.

The configuration register has several uses, including password recovery. The factory default setting for the configuration register is 0x2102. This value indicates that the router attempts to load a Cisco IOS software image from flash memory and load the startup configuration file from NVRAM.

Refer to **Online Course** for Illustration

6.3.2.5   Video Demonstration - The Router Boot Process

Refer to **Interactive Graphic** in online course.

6.3.2.6   Activity - The Router Boot Process

Refer to **Online Course** for Illustration

6.4   Configuring a Cisco Router

6.4.1   Configure Initial Settings

6.4.1.1   Router Configuration Steps

Cisco routers and Cisco switches have many similarities. They support a similar modal operating system, support similar command structures, and support many of the same commands. In addition, both devices have identical initial configuration steps when implementing them in a network.

Similar to configuring a switch, the following steps should be completed when configuring initial settings on a router:

1. Assign a device name using the `hostname` global configuration command. (Figure 1)

2. Set passwords. (Figure 2)

    ■ Secure privileged EXEC mode access using the `enable secret` command.

    ■ Secure EXEC mode access using the `login` command on the console port, and the `password` command to set the password.

    ■ Secure virtual access similar to securing EXEC access mode, except on the Virtual Teletype (VTY) port.

    ■ Use the `service password-encryption` global configuration command to prevent passwords from displaying as plain text in the configuration file.

3. Provide legal notification using the `banner motd` (message of the day [MOTD]) global configuration command. (Figure 3)

4. Save the configuration using the `copy run start` command. (Figure 4)

5. Verify the configuration using the `show run` command.

Figure 5 is a syntax checker that allows you to practice these configuration steps.

Refer to **Packet Tracer Activity** for this chapter

6.4.1.2   Packet Tracer - Configure Initial Router Settings

In this activity, you will perform basic router configurations. You will secure access to the CLI and console port using encrypted and plain text passwords. You will also configure messages for users logging into the router. These banners also warn unauthorized users that access is prohibited. Finally, you will verify and save your running configuration.

Refer to **Online Course** for Illustration

6.4.2   Configure Interfaces

6.4.2.1   Configure LAN Interfaces

For routers to be reachable, router interfaces must be configured. Therefore, to enable a specific interface, enter interface configuration mode using the `interface` type-and-number global configuration mode command.

There are many different types of interfaces available on Cisco routers. In this example, the Cisco 1941 router is equipped with two Gigabit Ethernet interfaces and a serial WAN interface card (WIC) consisting of two interfaces; the interfaces are named as follows:

- Gigabit Ethernet 0/0 (G0/0)

- Gigabit Ethernet 0/1 (G0/1)

- Serial 0/0/0 (S0/0/0)

- Serial 0/0/1 (S0/0/1)

To enable a router interface, configure the following:

- **IPv4 address and subnet mask** - Configures the IP address and subnet mask using the `ip address` subnet-mask interface configuration command.

- **Activate the interface** - By default, LAN and WAN interfaces are not activated. The interface must be activated using the `no shutdown` command. This is similar to powering on the interface. The interface must also be connected to another device (a hub, a switch, or another router) for the physical layer to be active.

Although not required, it is good practice to configure a description on each interface to help document the network information. The description text is limited to 240 characters. On production networks, a description can be helpful in troubleshooting by providing information about the type of network that the interface is connected to and if there are any other routers on that network. If the interface connects to an ISP or service carrier, it is helpful to enter the third party connection and contact information.

Figure 1 shows the configuration of the LAN interfaces connected to R1. In Figure 2, practice configuring a LAN interface.

Note   Command abbreviations are used for the configuration of Gigabit Ethernet 0/1.

Refer to
Online Course
for Illustration

6.4.2.2   Verify Interface Configuration

There are several commands that can be used to verify interface configuration. The most useful of these is the `show ip interface brief` command. The output generated displays all interfaces, their IP address, and their current status. The configured and connected interfaces should display a Status of "up" and Protocol of "up". Anything else would indicate a problem with either the configuration or the cabling.

You can verify connectivity from the interface using the `ping` command. Cisco routers send five consecutive pings and measure minimal, average, and maximum round trip times. Exclamation marks verify connectivity.

Figure 1 displays the output of the `show ip interface brief` command, which reveals that the LAN interfaces and the WAN link are all activate and operational. Notice that the `ping` command generated five exclamation marks verifying connectivity to R2.

Other interface verification commands include:

- `show ip route` - Displays the contents of the IPv4 routing table stored in RAM.
- `show interfaces` - Displays statistics for all interfaces on the device.
- `show ip interface` - Displays the IPv4 statistics for all interfaces on a router.

Figure 2 displays the output of the `show ip route` command. Notice the three directly connected network entries and the local link interface entries.

Remember to save the configuration using the `copy running-config startup-config` command.

Refer to
Online Course
for Illustration

6.4.3   Configuring the Default Gateway

6.4.3.1   Default Gateway on a Host

Most routers have, at a minimum, two interfaces. Each interface is configured with a separate IP address in a separate network.

For an end device to communicate over the network, it must be configured with the correct IP address information, including the default gateway address. The default gateway is only used when the host wants to send a packet to a device on another network. The default gateway address is generally the router interface address attached to the local network of the host. While it does not matter what address is actually configured on the router interface, the IP address of the host device and the router interface address must be in the same network.

The figures display a topology of a router with two separate interfaces. Each interface is connected to a separate network. G0/0 is connected to network 192.168.10.0, while G0/1 is connected to network 192.168.11.0. Each host device is configured with the appropriate default gateway address.

In Figure 1, PC1 sends a packet to PC2. In this example, the default gateway is not used; rather, PC1 addresses the packet with the IP address of PC2 and forwards the packet directly to PC2 through the switch.

In Figure 2, PC1 sends a packet to PC3. In this example, PC1 addresses the packet with the IP address of PC3, but then forwards the packet to the router. The router accepts the packet, accesses its route table to determine the appropriate exit interface based on the destination address, and then forwards the packet out of the appropriate interface to reach PC3.

Refer to
Online Course
for Illustration

6.4.3.2   Default Gateway on a Switch

A default gateway is used by all devices that require the use of a router to determine the best path to a remote destination. End devices require default gateway addresses, but so do intermediate devices, such as the Cisco IOS switch.

The IP address information on a switch is only necessary to manage the switch remotely. In other words, to be able to telnet to the switch, the switch must have an IP address to Telnet to. If the switch is only accessed from devices within the local network, only an IP address is required.

Configuring the IP address on a switch is done on the switch virtual interface (SVI):

```
S1(config)# interface vlan1
S1(config-vlan)# ip address 192.168.10.50 255.255.255.0
S1(config-vlan)# no shut
```

However, if the switch must be accessible by devices in a different network, the switch must be configured with a default gateway address, because packets that originate from the switch are handled just like packets that originate from a host device. Therefore, packets that originate from the switch and are destined for a device on the same network are forwarded directly to the appropriate device. Packets that originate from the switch and are destined for a device on a remote network must be forwarded to the default gateway for path determination.

To configure a default gateway on a switch use the following global configuration command:

```
S1(config)# ip default-gateway 192.168.10.1
```

Figure 1 shows an administrator connecting to a switch on a remote network. For the switch to forward response packets to the administrator, the default gateway must be configured.

A common misconception is that the switch uses its configured default gateway address to determine where to forward packets originating from hosts connected to the switch and destined for hosts on a remote network. Actually, the IP address and default gateway information is only used for packets that originate from the switch. Packets originating from hosts connected to the switch must already have default gateway information configured to communicate on remote networks. In Figure 2, practice configuring a default gateway on a switch.

Refer to **Packet Tracer Activity** for this chapter

6.4.3.3   Packet Tracer - Connect a Router to a LAN

In this activity, you will use various **show** commands to display the current state of the router. You will then use the Addressing Table to configure router Ethernet interfaces. Finally, you will use commands to verify and test your configurations.

Refer to **Packet Tracer Activity** for this chapter

6.4.3.4   Packet Tracer - Troubleshooting Default Gateway Issues

For a device to communicate across multiple networks, it must be configured with an IP address, subnet mask, and a default gateway. The default gateway is used when the host wants to send a packet to a device on another network. The default gateway address is generally the router interface address attached to the local network to which the host is connected. In this activity, you will finish documenting the network. You will then verify the network documentation by testing end-to-end connectivity and troubleshooting issues. The troubleshooting method you will use consists of the following steps:

- Verify the network documentation and use tests to isolate problems.
- Determine an appropriate solution for a given problem.
- Implement the solution.
- Test to verify the problem is resolved.
- Document the solution.

Refer to **Lab Activity** for this chapter

6.4.3.5   Lab - Initializing and Reloading a Router and Switch

In this lab, you will complete the following objectives:

- Part 1: Set Up the Topology and Initialize Devices
- Part 2: Configure Devices and Verify Connectivity
- Part 3: Display Device Information

6.5   Summary

Refer to **Lab Activity** for this chapter

6.5.1.1   Class Activity – Can You Read This Map?

Can you read this map?

Note   It is suggested that students work in pairs; however, if preferred, students can complete this activity individually.

Your instructor will provide you with output generated by a router's `show ip route` command. Use Packet Tracer to build a topology model using this routing information.

At a minimum, the following should be used in your topology model:

- 1 Catalyst 2960 switch
- 1 Cisco Series 1941 Router with one HWIC-4ESW switching port modular card and IOS version 15.1 or higher
- 3 PCs (can be servers, generic PCs, laptops, etc.)

Use the note tool in Packet Tracer to indicate the addresses of the router interfaces and possible addresses for the end devices you chose for your model. Label all end devices, ports, and addresses ascertained from the `show ip route` output/routing table information in your Packet Tracer file. Save your work in hard or soft copy to share with the class.

Refer to **Packet Tracer Activity** for this chapter

6.5.1.2   Packet Tracer - Skills Integration Challenge

Your network manager is impressed with your performance in your job as a LAN technician. She would like you to now demonstrate your ability to configure a router connecting two LANs. Your tasks include configuring basic settings on a router and a switch using the Cisco IOS. You will then verify your configurations, as well as configurations on existing devices by testing end-to-end connectivity.

Refer to **Online Course** for Illustration

6.5.1.3   Summary

The network layer, or OSI Layer 3, provides services to allow end devices to exchange data across the network. To accomplish this end-to-end transport, the network layer uses four basic processes: IP addressing for end devices, encapsulation, routing, and de-encapsulation.

The Internet is largely based on IPv4, which is still the most widely-used network layer protocol. An IPv4 packet contains the IP header and the payload. However, IPv4 has a limited number of unique public IP addresses available. This led to the development of IP version 6 (IPv6). The IPv6 simplified header offers several advantages over IPv4, including better routing efficiency, simplified extension headers, and capability for per-flow processing. Plus, IPv6 addresses are based on 128-bit hierarchical addressing as opposed to IPv4 with 32 bits. This dramatically increases the number of available IP addresses.

In addition to hierarchical addressing, the network layer is also responsible for routing.

Hosts require a local routing table to ensure that packets are directed to the correct destination network. The local table of a host typically contains the direct connection, the local network route and the local default route. The local default route is the route to the default gateway.

The default gateway is the IP address of a router interface connected to the local network. When a host needs to forward a packet to a destination address that is not on the same network as the host, the packet is sent to the default gateway for further processing.

When a router, such as the default gateway, receives a packet, it examines the destination IP address to determine the destination network. The routing table of a router stores information about directly-connected routes and remote routes to IP networks. If the router has an entry in its routing table for the destination network, the router forwards the packet. If no routing entry exists, the router may forward the packet to its own default route, if one is configured, or it will drop the packet.

Routing table entries can be configured manually on each router to provide static routing or the routers may communicate route information dynamically between each other using a routing protocol.

In order for routers to be reachable, the router interface must be configured. To enable a specific interface, enter interface configuration mode using the `interface` type-and-number global configuration mode command.

Go to the online course to take the quiz and exam.

Chapter 6 Quiz

This quiz is designed to provide an additional opportunity to practice the skills and knowledge presented in the chapter and to prepare for the chapter exam. You will be allowed multiple attempts and the grade does not appear in the gradebook.

Chapter 6 Exam

The chapter exam assesses your knowledge of the chapter content.

Your Chapter Notes

Transport Layer

7.0 Transportation Layer

7.0.1.1 Introduction

Data networks and the Internet support the human network by supplying reliable communication between people. On a single device, people can use multiple applications and services such as email, the web, and instant messaging to send messages or retrieve information. Applications such as email clients, web browsers, and instant messaging clients allow people to use computers and networks to send messages and find information.

Data from each of these applications is packaged, transported, and delivered to the appropriate application on the destination device. The processes described in the OSI transport layer accept data from the application layer and prepare it for addressing at the network layer. The transport layer **prepares** data for transmission across the network. A source computer communicates with a receiving computer to decide how to break up data into **segments**, how to make sure none of the segments get lost, and how to verify all the segments arrived. When thinking about the transport layer, think of a shipping department preparing a single order of multiple packages for delivery.

In this chapter, we examine the role of the transport layer in encapsulating application data for use by the network layer. The transport layer also encompasses these functions:

- Enables multiple applications such as emailing and social networking to communicate over the network at the same time on a single device

- Ensures that, if required, all the data is received reliably and in order by the correct application

- Employs error handling mechanisms

Learning Objectives

Upon completion of this chapter, you will be able to:

- Explain the need for the transport layer.

- Identify the role of the transport layer as it provides the end-to-end transfer of data between applications.

- Describe the role of two TCP/IP transport layer protocols: TCP and UDP.

- Explain the key functions of the transport layer, including reliability, port addressing, and segmentation.

■ Explain how TCP and UDP each handle key functions.

■ Identify when it is appropriate to use TCP or UDP and provide examples of applications that use each protocol.

Refer to
Lab Activity
for this chapter

7.0.1.2   Class Activity - We Need to Talk - Game

We Need to Talk

Note: This activity works best with medium-sized groups of 6 to 8 students per group.

The instructor will whisper a complex message to the first student in a group. An example of the message might be "Our final exam will be given next Tuesday, February 5th, at 2 p.m. in Room 1151."

That student whispers the message to the next student in the group. Each group follows this process until all members of each group have heard the whispered message. Here are the rules you are to follow:

■ You can whisper the message only once to your neighbor.

■ The message must keep moving from one person to the other with no skipping of participants.

■ The instructor should ask a student to keep time of the full message activity from first participant to last participant stating the messages. The first or last person would mostly likely be the best one to keep this time.

■ The last student will say aloud exactly what he or she heard.

The instructor will then restate the original message so that the group can compare it to the message that was delivered by the last student in the group.

Refer to
Online Course
for Illustration

7.1   Transport Layer Protocols

7.1.1   Transportation of Data

7.1.1.1   Role of the Transport Layer

The transport layer is responsible for establishing a temporary communication session between two applications and delivering data between them. An application generates data that is sent from an application on a source host to an application on a destination host, without regard to the destination host type, the type of media over which the data must travel, the path taken by the data, the congestion on a link, or the size of the network. As shown in the figure, the transport layer is the link between the application layer and the lower layers that are responsible for network transmission.

The transport layer provides a method of delivering data across the network in a way that ensures the data can be properly put back together on the receiving end. The transport layer provides for the segmentation of data, and the controls necessary to reassemble these segments into the various communication streams. In TCP/IP, these segmentation and reassembly processes can be achieved using two very different transport layer protocols: Transmission Control Protocol (TCP) and User Datagram Protocol (UDP).

The primary responsibilities of transport layer protocols are:

- Tracking the individual communication between applications on the source and destination hosts

- Segmenting data for manageability and reassembling segmented data into streams of application data at the destination

- Identifying the proper application for each communication stream

Refer to **Online Course** for Illustration

7.1.1.2   Role of the Transport Layer (Cont.)

Tracking Individual Conversations

At the transport layer, each particular set of data flowing between a source application and a destination application is known as a conversation (Figure 1). A host may have multiple applications that are communicating across the network simultaneously. Each of these applications communicates with one or more applications on one or more remote hosts. It is the responsibility of the transport layer to maintain and track these multiple conversations.

Segmenting Data and Reassembling Segments

Data must be prepared to be sent across the media in manageable pieces. Most networks have a limitation on the amount of data that can be included in a single packet. Transport layer protocols have services that segment the application data into blocks of data that are an appropriate size (Figure 2). This service includes the encapsulation required on each piece of data. A header, used for reassembly, is added to each block of data. This header is used to track the data stream.

At the destination, the transport layer must be able to reconstruct the pieces of data into a complete data stream that is useful to the application layer. The protocols at the transport layer describe how the transport layer header information is used to reassemble the data pieces into streams to be passed to the application layer.

Identifying the Applications

There may be many applications or services running on each host in the network. To pass data streams to the proper applications, the transport layer must identify the target application (Figure 3). To accomplish this, the transport layer assigns each application an identifier. This identifier is called a port number. Each software process that needs to access the network is assigned a port number unique in that host. The transport layer uses ports to identify the application or service.

Refer to **Online Course** for Illustration

7.1.1.3   Conversation Multiplexing

Conversation Multiplexing

Sending some types of data (for example, a streaming video) across a network, as one complete communication stream, could use all of the available bandwidth and prevent other communications from occurring at the same time. It also makes error recovery and retransmission of damaged data difficult.

The figure shows that segmenting the data into smaller chunks enables many different communications, from many different users, to be interleaved (multiplexed) on the same network. Segmentation of the data by transport layer protocols also provides the means to both send and receive data when running multiple applications concurrently on a computer.

Without segmentation, only one application would be able to receive data. For example, a streaming video, the media would be completely consumed by the one communication stream instead of shared. You could not receive emails, chat on instant messenger, or view web pages while also viewing the video.

To identify each segment of data, the transport layer adds to the segment a header containing binary data. This header contains fields of bits. It is the values in these fields that enable different transport layer protocols to perform different functions in managing data communication.

Refer to
Online Course
for Illustration

7.1.1.4   Transport Layer Reliability

The transport layer is also responsible for managing reliability requirements of a conversation. Different applications have different transport reliability requirements.

IP is concerned only with the structure, addressing, and routing of packets. IP does not specify how the delivery or transportation of the packets takes place. Transport protocols specify how to transfer messages between hosts. TCP/IP provides two transport layer protocols, Transmission Control Protocol (TCP) and User Datagram Protocol (UDP), as shown in the figure. IP uses these transport protocols to enable hosts to communicate and transfer data.

TCP is considered a reliable, full-featured transport layer protocol, which ensures that all of the data arrives at the destination. In contrast, UDP is a very simple transport layer protocol that does not provide for any reliability.

7.1.1.5   TCP

As previously stated, TCP is considered a reliable transport protocol, which means that TCP includes processes to ensure reliable delivery between applications through the use of acknowledged delivery. TCP transport is analogous to sending packages that are tracked from source destination. If a FedEx order is broken up into several shipments, a customer can check online to see the order of the delivery.

With TCP, the three basic operations of reliability are:

■ Tracking transmitted data segments

■ Acknowledging received data

■ Retransmitting any unacknowledged data

TCP breaks up a message into small pieces known as segments. The segments are numbered in sequence and passed to the IP process for assembly into packets. TCP keeps track of the number of segments that have been sent to a specific host from a specific application. If the sender does not receive an acknowledgement within a certain period of time, it assumes that the segments were lost and retransmits them. Only the portion of the message that is lost is resent, not the entire message. On the receiving host, TCP is responsible for reassembling the message segments and passing them to the application. The File

Transfer Protocol (FTP) and the Hypertext Transfer Protocol (HTTP) are examples of applications that use TCP to ensure data delivery.

Click the Play button in the figure to see an animation of TCP segments being transmitted from sender to receiver.

These reliability processes place additional overhead on network resources due to the processes of acknowledgement, tracking, and retransmission. To support these reliability processes, more control data is exchanged between the sending and receiving hosts. This control information is contained in a TCP header.

Refer to **Online Course** for Illustration

7.1.1.6   UDP

While the TCP reliability functions provide more robust communication between applications, they also incur additional overhead and possible delays in transmission. There is a trade-off between the value of reliability and the burden it places on network resources. Imposing overhead to ensure reliability for some applications could reduce the usefulness of the application and can even be detrimental to the application. In such cases, UDP is a better transport protocol.

UDP provides just the basic functions for delivering data segments between the appropriate applications, with very little overhead and data checking. UDP is known as a best-effort delivery protocol. In the context of networking, best-effort delivery is referred to as unreliable, because there is no acknowledgement that the data is received at the destination. With UDP, there are no transport layer processes that inform the sender if successful delivery has occurred.

UDP is similar to placing a regular, non-registered, letter in the mail. The sender of the letter is not aware of whether a receiver is available to receive the letter, nor is the post office responsible for tracking the letter or informing the sender if the letter does not arrive at the final destination.

Click the Play button in the figure to see an animation of UDP segments being transmitted from sender to receiver.

Refer to **Online Course** for Illustration

7.1.1.7   The Right Transport Layer Protocol for the Right Application

Both TCP and UDP are valid transport protocols. Depending upon the application requirements, either one, or sometimes both, of these transport protocols can be used. Application developers must choose which transport protocol type is appropriate based on the requirements of the applications.

For some applications, segments must arrive in a very specific sequence to be processed successfully. With other applications, all data must be fully received before any of it is considered useful. In both of these instances, TCP is used as the transport protocol. For example, applications such as databases, web browsers, and email clients, require that all data that is sent arrives at the destination in its original condition. Any missing data could cause a corrupt communication that is either incomplete or unreadable. Therefore, these applications are designed to use TCP. The additional network overhead is considered to be required for these applications.

In other cases, an application can tolerate some data loss during transmission over the network, but delays in transmission are unacceptable. UDP is the better choice for these applications because less network overhead is required. UDP is preferable with applications, such as streaming audio, video, and Voice over IP (VoIP). Acknowledgments would slow down delivery and retransmissions are undesirable.

For example, if one or two segments of a video stream fail to arrive, it creates a momentary disruption in the stream. This may appear as distortion in the image, but may not even be noticeable to the user. On the other hand, the image in a streaming video would be greatly degraded if the destination device had to account for lost data and delay the stream while waiting for retransmissions. In this case, it is better to render the best video possible with the segments received, and forego reliability.

Internet radio is another example of an application that uses UDP. If some of the message is lost during its journey over the network, it is not retransmitted. If a few packets are missed, the listener might hear a slight break in the sound. If TCP were used and the lost packets were resent, the transmission would pause to receive them and the disruption would be more noticeable.

Refer to
Interactive Graphic
in online course.

7.1.1.8   Activity - TCP, UDP or Both

Refer to
Online Course
for Illustration

7.1.2   Introducing TCP and UDP

7.1.2.1   Introducing TCP

To really understand the differences between TCP and UDP, it is important to understand how each protocol implements specific reliability functions and how they track communications.

Transmission Control Protocol (TCP)

TCP was initially described in RFC 793. In addition to supporting the basic functions of data segmentation and reassembly, TCP, as shown in the figure, also provides:

- Connection-oriented conversations by establishing sessions

- Reliable delivery

- Ordered data reconstruction

- Flow control

Establishing a Session

TCP is a connection-oriented protocol. A connection-oriented protocol is one that negotiates and establishes a permanent connection (or session) between source and destination devices prior to forwarding any traffic. Session establishment prepares the devices to communicate with one another. Through session establishment, the devices negotiate the amount of traffic that can be forwarded at a given time, and the communication data between the two can be closely managed. The session is terminated only after all communication is completed.

Reliable Delivery

TCP can implement a method to ensure reliable delivery of the data. In networking terms, reliability means ensuring that each piece of data that the source sends arrives at the destination. For many reasons, it is possible for a piece of data to become corrupted, or lost completely, as it is transmitted over the network. TCP can ensure that all pieces reach their destination by having the source device retransmit lost or corrupted data.

Same-Order Delivery

Because networks may provide multiple routes that can have different transmission rates, data can arrive in the wrong order. By numbering and sequencing the segments, TCP can ensure that these segments are reassembled into the proper order.

Flow Control

Network hosts have limited resources, such as memory or bandwidth. When TCP is aware that these resources are overtaxed, it can request that the sending application reduce the rate of data flow. This is done by TCP regulating the amount of data the source transmits. Flow control can prevent the loss of segments on the network and avoid the need for retransmission.

Refer to **Online Course** for Illustration

7.1.2.2   Role of TCP

Once TCP establishes a session, it is then able to keep track of the conversation within that session. Because of the ability of TCP to track actual conversations, it is considered a stateful protocol. A stateful protocol is a protocol that keeps track of the state of the communication session. For example, when data is transmitted using TCP, the sender expects the destination to acknowledge that it has received the data. TCP tracks which information it has sent and which information has been acknowledged. If the data is not acknowledged, the sender assumes the data did not arrive and resends it. The stateful session begins with the session establishment and ends when the session is closed with session termination.

Note   Maintaining this state information requires resources that are not necessary for a stateless protocol, such as UDP.

TCP incurs additional overhead to gain these functions. As shown in the figure, each TCP segment has 20 bytes of overhead in the header encapsulating the application layer data. This is considerably more than a UDP segment, which only has 8 bytes of overhead. Extra overhead includes:

- **Sequence number (32 bits)** - Used for data reassembly purposes.
- **Acknowledgement number (32 bits)** - Indicates the data that has been received.
- **Header length (4 bits)** - Known as "data offset". Indicates the length of the TCP segment header.
- **Reserved (6 bits)** - This field is reserved for the future.
- **Control bits (6 bits)** - Includes bit codes, or flags, that indicate the purpose and function of the TCP segment.
- **Window size (16 bits)** - Indicates the number of segments that can be accepted at one time.
- **Checksum (16 bits)** - Used for error checking of the segment header and data.
- **Urgent (16 bits)** - Indicates if data is urgent.

Examples of applications that use TCP are web browsers, email, and file transfers.

Refer to
Online Course
for Illustration

7.1.2.3   Introducing UDP

User Datagram Protocol (UDP)

UDP is considered a best-effort transport protocol, described in RFC 768. UDP is a light-weight transport protocol that offers the same data segmentation and reassembly as TCP, but without TCP reliability and flow control. UDP is such a simple protocol, that it is usually described in terms of what it does not do compared to TCP.

As shown in the figure, the following features describe UDP:

- **Connectionless** - UDP does not establish a connection between the hosts before data can be sent and received.

- **Unreliable Delivery** - UDP does not provide services to ensure that the data will be delivered reliably. There are no processes within UDP to have the sender retransmit any data that is lost or is corrupted.

- **No Ordered Data Reconstruction** - Occasionally data is received in a different order than it was sent. UDP does not provide any mechanism for reassembling the data in its original sequence. The data is simply delivered to the application in the order that it arrives.

- **No Flow Control** - There are no mechanisms within UDP to control the amount of data transmitted by the source to avoid overwhelming the destination device. The source sends the data. If resources on the destination host become overtaxed, the destination host mostly likely drops data sent until resources become available. Unlike TCP, with UDP there is no mechanism for automatic retransmission of dropped data.

Refer to
Online Course
for Illustration

7.1.2.4   Role of UDP

Although UDP does not include the reliability and flow control mechanisms of TCP, as shown in the figure, UDP's low overhead data delivery makes it an ideal transport protocol for applications that can tolerate some data loss. The pieces of communication in UDP are called datagrams. These datagrams are sent as best effort by the transport layer protocol. A few applications that use UDP are Domain Name System (DNS), video streaming, and Voice over IP (VoIP).

One of the most important requirements for delivering live video and voice over the network is that the data continues to flow quickly. Video and voice applications can tolerate some data loss with minimal or no noticeable effect, and are perfectly suited to UDP.

UDP is a stateless protocol, meaning neither the client, nor the server, is obligated to keep track of the state of the communication session. As shown in the figure, UDP is not concerned with reliability or flow control. Data may be lost or received out of sequence without any UDP mechanisms to recover or reorder the data. If reliability is required when using UDP as the transport protocol, it must be handled by the application.

Refer to
Online Course
for Illustration

7.1.2.5   Separating Multiple Communications

The transport layer must be able to separate and manage multiple communications with different transport requirement needs. For example, consider a user connected to a network on an end device. The user is simultaneously receiving and sending email and instant messages, viewing websites, and conducting a Voice over IP (VoIP) phone call. Each of these applications is sending and receiving data over the network at the same time, despite different reliability requirements. Additionally, data from the phone call is not directed to the web browser, and text from an instant message does not appear in an email.

For reliability, users require that an email or web page be completely received and presented in full, for the information to be considered useful. Slight delays in loading the email or webpage are generally acceptable, as long as the final product is shown in its entirety and correctly. In this example, the network manages the resending or replacement of missing information, and does not display the final product until everything is received and correctly assembled.

In contrast, occasionally missing small parts of a telephone conversation might be considered acceptable. Even if some small parts of a few words are dropped, one can either infer the missing audio from the context of the conversation or ask the other person to repeat what was said. This is considered preferable to the incurred delays if the network were to manage and resend missing segments. In this example, the user, not the network, manages the resending or replacement of missing information.

As shown in the figure, for TCP and UDP to manage these simultaneous conversations with varying requirements, the TCP and UDP-based services must keep track of the various applications communicating. To differentiate the segments and datagrams for each application, both TCP and UDP have header fields that can uniquely identify these applications. These unique identifiers are the port numbers.

Refer to
Online Course
for Illustration

7.1.2.6   TCP and UDP Port Addressing

In the header of each segment or datagram, there is a source and destination port. The source port number is the number for this communication associated with the originating application on the local host. As shown in the figure, the destination port number is the number for this communication associated with the destination application on the remote host.

When a message is delivered using either TCP or UDP, the protocols and services requested are identified by a port number. A port is a numeric identifier within each segment that is used to keep track of specific conversations and destination services requested. Every message that a host sends contains both a source and destination port.

Destination Port

The client places a destination port number in the segment to tell the destination server what service is being requested. For example, port 80 refers to HTTP or web service. When a client specifies port 80 in the destination port, the server that receives the message knows that web services are being requested. A server can offer more than one service simultaneously. For example, a server can offer web services on port 80 at the same time that it offers FTP connection establishment on port 21.

Source Port

The source port number is randomly generated by the sending device to identify a conversation between two devices. This allows multiple conversations to occur simultaneously. In other words, a device can send multiple HTTP service requests to a web server at the same time. The separate conversations are tracked based on the source ports.

Refer to
Online Course
for Illustration

7.1.2.7   TCP and UDP Port Addressing (Cont.)

The source and destination ports are placed within the segment. The segments are then encapsulated within an IP packet. The IP packet contains the IP address of the source and destination. The combination of the source and destination IP addresses and the source and destination port numbers is known as a socket. The socket is used to identify the server and service being requested by the client. Every day thousands of hosts communicate with millions of different servers. Those communications are identified by the sockets.

It is the combination of the transport layer port number, and the network layer IP address of the host, that uniquely identifies a particular application process running on an individual host device. This combination is called a socket. A socket pair, consisting of the source and destination IP addresses and port numbers, is also unique and identifies the specific conversation between the two hosts.

A client socket might look like this, with 1099 representing the source port number: 192.168.1.5:1099

The socket on a web server might be: 192.168.1.7:80

Together, these two sockets combine to form a socket pair: 192.168.1.5:1099, 192.168.1.7:80

With the creation of sockets, communication endpoints are known so that data can move from an application on one host to an application on another. Sockets enable multiple processes running on a client to distinguish themselves from each other, and multiple connections to a server process to be distinguished from each other.

The source port of a client request is randomly generated. This port number acts like a return address for the requesting application. The transport layer keeps track of this port and the application that initiated the request so that when a response is returned, it can be forwarded to the correct application. The requesting application port number is used as the destination port number in the response coming back from the server.

Refer to
Online Course
for Illustration

7.1.2.8   TCP and UDP Port Addressing (Cont.)

The Internet Assigned Numbers Authority (IANA) assigns port numbers. IANA is a standards body that is responsible for assigning various addressing standards.

There are different types of port numbers, as shown in Figure 1:

- **Well-known Ports (Numbers 0 to 1023)** - These numbers are reserved for services and applications. They are commonly used for applications such as HTTP (web server), Internet Message Access Protocol (IMAP)/Simple Mail Transfer Protocol (SMTP) (email server) and Telnet. By defining these well-known ports for server applications, client applications can be programmed to request a connection to that specific port, and its associated service.

- **Registered Ports (Numbers 1024 to 49151)** - These port numbers are assigned to user processes or applications. These processes are primarily individual applications that a user has chosen to install, rather than common applications that would receive a well-known port number. When not used for a server resource, these ports may also be used dynamically selected by a client as its source port.

- **Dynamic or Private Ports (Numbers 49152 to 65535)** - Also known as ephemeral ports, these are usually assigned dynamically to client applications when the client initiates a connection to a service. The dynamic port is most often used to identify the client application during communication, whereas the client uses the well-known port to identify and connect to the service being requested on the server. It is uncommon for a client to connect to a service using a dynamic or private port (although some peer-to-peer file sharing programs do use these ports).

Figure 2 displays some common well-known and registered ports within TCP. Figure 3 displays common well-known and registered ports within UDP.

Using both TCP and UDP

Some applications may use both TCP and UDP (Figure 4). For example, the low overhead of UDP enables DNS to serve many client requests very quickly. Sometimes, however, sending the requested information may require the reliability of TCP. In this case, the well-known port number, 53, is used by both TCP and UDP with this service.

A current list of port numbers and the associated applications can be found on the IANA organizational website.

> Refer to
> **Online Course**
> for Illustration

7.1.2.9   TCP and UDP Port Addressing (Cont.)

Sometimes it is necessary to know which active TCP connections are open and running on a networked host. Netstat is an important network utility that can be used to verify those connections. Netstat lists the protocol in use, the local address and port number, the foreign address and port number, and the connection state.

Unexplained TCP connections can pose a major security threat, because they can indicate that something or someone is connected to the local host. Additionally, unnecessary TCP connections can consume valuable system resources, thus slowing down the host's performance. Netstat should be used to examine the open connections on a host when performance appears to be compromised.

Many useful options are available for the **netstat** command. Click the buttons in Figures 1 through 5 to see the different information output from the **netstat** command.

> Refer to
> **Online Course**
> for Illustration

7.1.2.10   TCP and UDP Segmentation

A previous chapter explained how protocol data units (PDUs) are built by passing data from an application down through the various layers to create a PDU that is then transmitted on the medium. At the destination host, this process is reversed until the data can be passed up to the application.

Some applications transmit large amounts of data, in some cases, many gigabytes. It would be impractical to send all of this data in one large piece. No other network traffic could be transmitted while this data was being sent. A large piece of data could take minutes or even hours to send. In addition, if there were any errors, the entire data file would be lost or have to be resent. Network devices would not have memory buffers large enough to store this much data while it is transmitted or received. The limit varies depending on the networking technology and specific physical medium being in use.

Dividing application data into segments both ensures that data is transmitted within the limits of the media and that data from different applications can be multiplexed on to the media.

TCP and UDP Handle Segmentation Differently

As shown in the figure, each TCP segment header contains a sequence number that allows the transport layer functions on the destination host to reassemble segments in the order in which they were transmitted. This ensures that the destination application has the data in the exact form the sender intended.

Although services using UDP also track the conversations between applications; they are not concerned with the order in which the information was transmitted or concerned with maintaining a connection. There is no sequence number in the UDP header. UDP is a simpler design and generates less overhead than TCP, resulting in a faster transfer of data.

Information may arrive in a different order than it was transmitted, because different packets may take different paths through the network. An application that uses UDP must tolerate the fact that data may not arrive in the order in which it was sent.

Refer to **Interactive Graphic** in online course.

7.1.2.11   Activity - Compare TCP and UDP Characteristics

Refer to **Online Course** for Illustration

7.2   TCP and UDP

7.2.1   TCP Communication

7.2.1.1   TCP Reliable Delivery

The key distinction between TCP and UDP is reliability. The reliability of TCP communication is obtained through the use of connection-oriented sessions. Before a host using TCP sends data to another host, TCP initiates a process to create a connection with the destination. This stateful connection enables the tracking of a session, or communication stream between the hosts. This process ensures that each host is aware of and prepared for the communication stream. A TCP conversation requires the establishment of a session between the hosts in both directions, as shown in the animation.

After a session has been established, and data transfer begins, the destination sends acknowledgements to the source for the segments that it receives. These acknowledgements form the basis of reliability within the TCP session. When the source receives an acknowledgement, it knows that the data has been successfully delivered and can quit tracking that data. If the source does not receive an acknowledgement within a predetermined amount of time, it retransmits that data to the destination.

Part of the additional overhead of using TCP is the network traffic generated by acknowledgements and retransmissions. The establishment of sessions creates overhead in the form of additional segments being exchanged. There is also additional overhead on the individual hosts created by the necessity to keep track of which segments are awaiting acknowledgement and by the retransmission process.

Refer to **Online Course** for Illustration

7.2.1.2   TCP Server Processes

Application processes run on servers. A single server may run multiple application processes at the same time. These processes wait until a client initiates communication with a request for information or other services.

Each application process running on the server is configured to use a port number, either by default or manually by a system administrator. An individual server cannot have two services assigned to the same port number within the same transport layer services. A host running a web server application and a file transfer application cannot have both configured to use the same port (for example, TCP port 8080). An active server application assigned to a specific port is considered to be open, which means that the transport layer accepts and processes segments addressed to that port. Any incoming client request addressed to the correct socket is accepted and the data is passed to the server application. There can be many simultaneous ports open on a server, one for each active server application. It is common for a server to provide more than one service at the same time, such as a web server and an FTP server.

One way to improve security on a server is to restrict server access to only those ports associated with the services and applications that should be accessible by authorized requestors.

Refer to Figures 1 through 5 to see the typical allocation of source and destination ports in TCP client/server operations.

Refer to
Online Course
for Illustration

7.2.1.3   TCP Connection Establishment and Termination

In some cultures, when two persons meet, they often greet each other by shaking hands. The act of shaking hands is understood by both parties as a signal for a friendly greeting. Connections on the network are similar. The first handshake requests synchronization. The second handshake acknowledges the initial synchronization request and synchronizes the connection parameters in the opposite direction. The third handshake segment is an acknowledgment used to inform the destination that both sides agree that a connection has been established.

When two hosts communicate using TCP, a connection is established before data can be exchanged. After the communication is completed, the sessions are closed and the connection is terminated. The connection and session mechanisms enable TCP's reliability function. See the figure for the steps to establish and terminate a TCP connection.

Hosts track each data segment within a session and exchange information about what data is received using the information in the TCP header. TCP is a full-duplex protocol, where each connection represents two one-way communication streams, or sessions. To establish the connection, the hosts perform a three-way handshake. Control bits in the TCP header indicate the progress and status of the connection. The three-way handshake:

- Establishes that the destination device is present on the network

- Verifies that the destination device has an active service and is accepting requests on the destination port number that the initiating client intends to use for the session

- Informs the destination device that the source client intends to establish a communication session on that port number

In TCP connections, the host client establishes the connection with the server. The three steps in TCP connection establishment are:

Step 1.   The initiating client requests a client-to-server communication session with the server.

Step 2.   The server acknowledges the client-to-server communication session and requests a server-to-client communication session.

Step 3.   The initiating client acknowledges the server-to-client communication session.

In the figure, click through buttons 1 through 3 to see the TCP connection establishment.

To understand the three-way handshake process, look at the various values that the two hosts exchange. Within the TCP segment header, there are six 1-bit fields that contain control information used to manage the TCP processes. Those fields are:

- **URG** - Urgent pointer field significant
- **ACK** - Acknowledgement field significant
- **PSH** - Push function
- **RST** - Reset the connection
- **SYN** - Synchronize sequence numbers
- **FIN** - No more data from sender

The ACK and SYN fields are relevant to our analysis of the three-way handshake.

Refer to **Online Course** for Illustration

7.2.1.4   TCP Three-way Handshake Analysis - Step 1

Using the output of protocol analysis software, such as Wireshark outputs, you can examine the operation of the TCP 3-way handshake:

Step 1: The initiating client requests a client-to-server communication session with the server.

A TCP client begins the three-way handshake by sending a segment with the synchronize sequence number (SYN) control flag set, indicating an initial value in the sequence number field in the header. This initial value for the sequence number, known as the initial sequence number (ISN), is randomly chosen and is used to begin tracking the flow of data from the client to the server for this session. The ISN in the header of each segment is increased by one for each byte of data sent from the client to the server as the data conversation continues.

As shown in the figure, output from a protocol analyzer shows the SYN control flag and the relative sequence number.

The SYN control flag is set and the relative sequence number is at 0. Although the protocol analyzer in the graphic indicates the relative values for the sequence and acknowledgement numbers, the true values are 32-bit binary numbers. The figure shows the four bytes represented in hexadecimal.

Refer to **Online Course** for Illustration

7.2.1.5   TCP Three-way Handshake Analysis - Step 2

Step 2: The server acknowledges the client-to-server communication session and requests a server-to-client communication session.

The TCP server must acknowledge the receipt of the SYN segment from the client to establish the session from the client to the server. To do so, the server sends a segment back to the client with the acknowledgement (ACK) flag set indicating that the acknowledgment number is significant. With this flag set in the segment, the client recognizes this as an acknowledgement that the server received the SYN from the TCP client.

The value of the acknowledgment number field is equal to the ISN plus 1. This establishes a session from the client to the server. The ACK flag remains set for the balance of the session. Recall that the conversation between the client and the server is actually two one-way sessions: one from the client to the server, and the other from the server to the client. In this second step of the three-way handshake, the server must initiate the response to the client. To start this session, the server uses the SYN flag in the same way that the client did. It sets the SYN control flag in the header to establish a session from the server to the client. The SYN flag indicates that the initial value of the sequence number field is in the header. This value is used to track the flow of data in this session from the server back to the client.

As shown in the figure, the protocol analyzer output shows that the ACK and SYN control flags are set and the relative sequence and acknowledgement numbers are displayed.

Refer to
Online Course
for Illustration

7.2.1.6   TCP Three-way Handshake Analysis - Step 3

Step 3: The initiating client acknowledges the server-to-client communication session.

Finally, the TCP client responds with a segment containing an ACK that is the response to the TCP SYN sent by the server. There is no user data in this segment. The value in the acknowledgment number field contains one more than the ISN received from the server. After both sessions are established between client and server, all additional segments exchanged in this communication will have the ACK flag set.

As shown in the figure, the protocol analyzer output shows the ACK control flag set and the relative sequence and acknowledgement numbers.

Security can be added to the data network by:

- Denying the establishment of TCP sessions
- Only allowing sessions to be established for specific services
- Only allowing traffic as a part of already established sessions

These security measures can be implemented for all TCP sessions or only for selected sessions.

Refer to
Online Course
for Illustration

7.2.1.7   TCP Session Termination Analysis

To close a connection, the Finish (FIN) control flag must be set in the segment header. To end each one-way TCP session, a two-way handshake is used, consisting of a FIN segment and an ACK segment. Therefore, to terminate a single conversation supported by TCP, four exchanges are needed to end both sessions, as shown in Figure 1.

Note   In this explanation, the terms client and server are used as a reference for simplicity, but the termination process can be initiated by any two hosts that have an open session:

Step 1.   When the client has no more data to send in the stream, it sends a segment with the FIN flag set.

Step 2.   The server sends an ACK to acknowledge the receipt of the FIN to terminate the session from client to server.

Step 3.   The server sends a FIN to the client, to terminate the server to client session.

Step 4.   The client responds with an ACK to acknowledge the FIN from the server.

When the client has no more data to transfer, it sets the FIN flag in the header of a segment. Next, the server end of the connection sends a normal segment containing data with the ACK flag set using the acknowledgment number, confirming that all the bytes of data have been received. When all segments have been acknowledged, the session is closed.

The session in the other direction is closed using the same process. The receiver indicates that there is no more data to send by setting the FIN flag in the header of a segment sent to the source. A return acknowledgement confirms that all bytes of data have been received and that session is, in turn, closed.

Refer to Figures 2 and 3 to see the FIN and ACK control flags set in the segment header, thereby closing a HTTP session.

It is also possible to terminate the connection by a three-way handshake. When the client has no more data to send, it sends a FIN to the server. If the server also has no more data to send, it can reply with both the FIN and ACK flags set, combining two steps into one. The client then replies with an ACK.

Refer to
Lab Activity
for this chapter

7.2.1.8   Lab - Using Wireshark to Observe the TCP 3-Way Handshake

In this lab, you will complete the following objectives:

- Part 1: Prepare Wireshark to Capture Packets
- Part 2: Capture, Locate, and Examine Packets

Refer to
Interactive Graphic
in online course.

7.2.1.9   Activity - TCP Connection and Termination Process

Refer to
Online Course
for Illustration

7.2.2   Reliability and Flow Control

7.2.2.1   TCP Reliability – Ordered Delivery

Resequencing Segments

When services send data using TCP, segments may arrive at their destination out of order. For the original message to be understood by the recipient, the data in these segments is reassembled into the original order. Sequence numbers are assigned in the header of each packet to achieve this goal.

During session setup, an initial sequence number (ISN) is set. This ISN represents the starting value for the bytes for this session that is transmitted to the receiving application. As data is transmitted during the session, the sequence number is incremented by the number of bytes that have been transmitted. This data byte tracking enables each segment to be uniquely identified and acknowledged. Missing segments can be identified.

Segment sequence numbers enable the reliability by indicating how to reassemble and reorder received segments, as shown in the figure.

The receiving TCP process places the data from a segment into a receiving buffer. Segments are placed in the proper sequence number order and passed to the application layer when reassembled. Any segments that arrive with non-contiguous sequence numbers are held for later processing. Then, when the segments with the missing bytes arrive, these segments are processed in order.

Refer to
Online Course
for Illustration

7.2.2.2   TCP Reliability – Acknowledgement and Window Size

Confirming Receipt of Segments

One of the functions of TCP is ensuring that each segment reaches its destination. The TCP services on the destination host acknowledge the data that it has received by the source application.

The sequence (SEQ) number and acknowledgement (ACK) number are used together to confirm receipt of the bytes of data contained in the transmitted segments. The SEQ number indicates the relative number of bytes that have been transmitted in this session, including the bytes in the current segment. TCP uses the ACK number sent back to the source to indicate the next byte that the receiver expects to receive. This is called expectational acknowledgement.

The source is informed that the destination has received all bytes in this data stream up to, but not including, the byte indicated by the ACK number. The sending host is expected to send a segment that uses a sequence number that is equal to the ACK number.

Remember, each connection is actually two one-way sessions. SEQ and ACK numbers are being exchanged in both directions.

In the example in the figure, the host on the left is sending data to the host on the right. It sends a segment containing 10 bytes of data for this session and a sequence number equal to 1 in the header.

The receiving host receives the segment at Layer 4 and determines that the sequence number is 1 and that it has 10 bytes of data. The host then sends a segment back to the host on the left to acknowledge the receipt of this data. In this segment, the host sets the ACK number to 11 to indicate that the next byte of data it expects to receive in this session is byte number 11. When the sending host receives this acknowledgement, it can now send the next segment containing data for this session starting with byte number 11.

Looking at this example, if the sending host had to wait for acknowledgement of receiving each 10 bytes, the network would have a lot of overhead. To reduce the overhead of these acknowledgements, multiple segments of data can be sent and acknowledged with a single TCP message in the opposite direction. This acknowledgement contains an ACK number based on the total number of bytes received in the session. For example, starting with a sequence number of 2000, if 10 segments of 1,000 bytes each were received, an ACK number of 12001 would be returned to the source.

The amount of data that a source can transmit before an acknowledgement must be received is called the window size, which is a field in the TCP header that enables the management of lost data and flow control.

Refer to
Online Course
for Illustration

7.2.2.3   TCP Reliability - Data Loss and Retransmission

Handling Segment Loss

No matter how well designed a network is, data loss occasionally occurs; therefore, TCP provides methods of managing these segment losses. Among these is a mechanism to retransmit segments with unacknowledged data.

A destination host service using TCP usually only acknowledges data for contiguous sequence bytes. If one or more segments are missing, only the data in the first contiguous sequence of bytes is acknowledged. For example, if segments with sequence numbers 1500 to 3000 and 3400 to 3500 were received, the ACK number would be 3001. This is because there are segments with the SEQ numbers 3001 to 3399 that have not been received.

When TCP at the source host has not received an acknowledgement after a predetermined amount of time, it returns to the last ACK number received and retransmits the data from that point forward. The retransmission process is not specified by the Request for Comments (RFC), but is left up to the particular implementation of TCP.

For a typical TCP implementation, a host may transmit a segment, put a copy of the segment in a retransmission queue, and start a timer. When the data acknowledgment is received, the segment is deleted from the queue. If the acknowledgment is not received before the timer expires, the segment is retransmitted.

Click the Play button in the figure to see the animation demonstrate the retransmission of lost segments.

Hosts today may also employ an optional feature called selective acknowledgements (SACKs). If both hosts support SACKs, it is possible for the destination to acknowledge bytes in discontinuous segments and the host would only need to retransmit the missing data.

Refer to
Online Course
for Illustration

7.2.2.4   TCP Flow Control – Window Size and Acknowledgements

Flow Control

TCP also provides mechanisms for flow control. Flow control helps maintain the reliability of TCP transmission by adjusting the rate of data flow between source and destination for a given session. Flow control is accomplished by limiting the amount of data segments forwarded at one time and by requiring acknowledgments of receipt prior to sending more.

To accomplish flow control, the first thing that TCP determines is the amount of data segments that the destination device can accept. The TCP header includes a 16-bit field called the window size. This is the number of bytes that the destination device of a TCP session is able to accept and process at one time. The initial window size is agreed upon during the session startup via the three-way handshake between source and destination. Once agreed upon, the source device must limit the amount of data segments sent to the destination device based on the window size. Only after the source device receives an acknowledgement that the data segments have been received, can it continue sending more data for the session.

During the delay in receiving the acknowledgement, the sender does not send any additional segments. In periods when the network is congested or the resources of the receiving host are strained, the delay may increase. As this delay grows longer, the effective transmission rate of the data for this session decreases. The slowdown in data transmission from each session helps reduce resource conflict on the network and destination device when multiple sessions are running.

See the figure for a simplified representation of window size and acknowledgements. In this example, the initial window size for a TCP session represented is set to 3000 bytes. When the sender has transmitted 3000 bytes, it waits for an acknowledgement of these bytes before transmitting more segments in this session. After the sender has received an acknowledgement from the receiver, the sender can transmit an additional 3000 bytes.

TCP uses window sizes to attempt to manage the rate of transmission to the maximum flow that the network and destination device can support, while minimizing loss and retransmissions.

Refer to
Online Course
for Illustration

7.2.2.5   TCP Flow Control - Congestion Avoidance

Reducing Window Size

Another way to control the data flow is to use dynamic window sizes. When network resources are constrained, TCP can reduce the window size to require that received segments be acknowledged more frequently. This effectively slows down the rate of transmission because the source waits for data to be acknowledged more frequently.

The receiving host sends the window size value to the sending host to indicate the number of bytes that it is prepared to receive. If the destination needs to slow down the rate of communication because of limited buffer memory, for example, it can send a smaller window size value to the source as part of an acknowledgement.

As shown in the figure, if a receiving host has congestion, it may respond to the sending host with a segment that specifies a reduced window size. In this figure, there was a loss of one of the segments. The receiver changed the window field in the TCP header of the returning segments in this conversation from 3,000 down to 1,500, which caused the sender to reduce the window size to 1,500.

After a period of transmission with no data losses or constrained resources, the receiver begins to increase the window field, which reduces the overhead on the network, because fewer acknowledgments must be sent. The window size continues to increase until there is data loss, which causes the window size to decrease.

This dynamic increasing and decreasing of window size is a continuous process in TCP. In highly efficient networks, window sizes may become very large because data is not lost. In networks where the underlying infrastructure is under stress, the window size likely remains small.

Refer to
Online Course
for Illustration

7.2.3   UDP Communication

7.2.3.1   UDP Low Overhead versus Reliability

UDP is a simple protocol that provides the basic transport layer functions. It has much lower overhead than TCP, because it is not connection-oriented and does not offer the sophisticated retransmission, sequencing, and flow control mechanisms that provide reliability.

This does not mean that applications that use UDP are always unreliable, nor does it mean that UDP is an inferior protocol. It simply means that these functions are not provided by the transport layer protocol and must be implemented elsewhere, if required.

Although the total amount of UDP traffic found on a typical network is often relatively low, key application layer protocols that use UDP include:

- Domain Name System (DNS)
- Simple Network Management Protocol (SNMP)
- Dynamic Host Configuration Protocol (DHCP)
- Routing Information Protocol (RIP)
- Trivial File Transfer Protocol (TFTP)

- IP telephony or Voice over IP (VoIP)
- Online games

Some applications, such as online games or VoIP, can tolerate some data loss. If these applications used TCP, they could experience large delays while TCP detects data loss and retransmits data. These delays would be more detrimental to the performance of the application than small data losses. Some applications, such as DNS, simply retry the request if no response is received; therefore, they do not need TCP to guarantee message delivery.

The low overhead of UDP makes it very desirable for such applications.

7.2.3.2   UDP Datagram Reassembly

Because UDP is connectionless, sessions are not established before communication takes place as they are with TCP. UDP is said to be transaction-based; that is, when an application has data to send, it simply sends the data.

Many applications that use UDP send small amounts of data that can fit in one segment. However, some applications send larger amounts of data that must be split into multiple segments. The UDP PDU is referred to as a datagram, although the terms segment and datagram are sometimes used interchangeably to describe a transport layer PDU.

When multiple datagrams are sent to a destination, they may take different paths and arrive in the wrong order. UDP does not track sequence numbers the way TCP does. UDP has no way to reorder the datagrams into their transmission order, as shown in the figure.

Therefore, UDP simply reassembles the data in the order that it was received and forwards it to the application. If the data sequence is important to the application, the application must identify the proper sequence and determine how the data should be processed.

Refer to
Online Course
for Illustration

7.2.3.3   UDP Server Processes and Requests

Like TCP-based applications, UDP-based server applications are assigned well-known or registered port numbers. When these applications or processes are running on a server, they accept the data matched with the assigned port number. When UDP receives a datagram destined for one of these ports, it forwards the application data to the appropriate application based on its port number.

7.2.3.4   UDP Client Processes

As with TCP, client/server communication is initiated by a client application that requests data from a server process. The UDP client process randomly selects a port number from the range of dynamic port numbers and uses this as the source port for the conversation. The destination port is usually the well-known or registered port number assigned to the server process.

Randomized source port numbers also help with security. If there is a predictable pattern for destination port selection, an intruder can more easily simulate access to a client by attempting to connect to the port number most likely to be open.

Because there is no session to be created with UDP, as soon as the data is ready to be sent and the ports identified, UDP can form the datagrams and pass them to the network layer to be addressed and sent on the network.

After a client has selected the source and destination ports, the same pair of ports is used in the header of all datagrams used in the transaction. For the data returning to the client from the server, the source and destination port numbers in the datagram header are reversed.

Scroll through the figures on the right to see details of UDP client processes.

Refer to
Lab Activity
for this chapter

7.2.3.5   Lab - Using Wireshark to Examine a UDP DNS Capture

In this lab, you will complete the following objectives:

- Part 1: Record a PC's IP Configuration Information

- Part 2: Use Wireshark to Capture DNS Queries and Responses

- Part 3: Analyze Captured DNS or UDP Packets

Refer to
Online Course
for Illustration

7.2.4   TCP or UDP, that is the Question

7.2.4.1   Applications that use TCP

Many applications require reliability and other services provided by TCP. These are applications that can tolerate some delay or performance loss due to the overhead imposed by TCP.

This makes TCP best suited for applications that need reliable transport and can tolerate some delay. TCP is a great example of how the different layers of the TCP/IP protocol suite have specific roles. Because the transport layer protocol TCP handles all tasks associated with segmenting the data stream into segments, reliability, flow control, and reordering of segments, it frees the application from having to manage any of this. The application can simply send the data stream to the transport layer and use the services of TCP.

As shown in the figure, some examples of well-known applications that use TCP include:

- Hypertext Transfer Protocol (HTTP)

- File Transfer Protocol (FTP)

- Simple Mail Transfer Protocol (SMTP)

- Telnet

Refer to
Online Course
for Illustration

7.2.4.2   Applications that use UDP

There are three types of applications that are best suited for UDP:

- Applications that can tolerate some data loss, but require little or no delay

- Applications with simple request and reply transactions

- Unidirectional communications where reliability is not required or can be handled by the application

Many video and multimedia applications, such as VoIP and Internet Protocol Television (IPTV) use UDP. These applications can tolerate some data loss with little or no noticeable effect. The reliability mechanisms of TCP introduce some delay that can be noticeable in the quality of the sound or video being received.

Other types of applications well suited for UDP are those that use simple request and reply transactions. This is where a host sends a request and may or may not receive a reply. These types of applications include:

- DHCP

- DNS - May also use TCP

- SNMP

- TFTP

Some applications handle reliability themselves. These applications do not need the services of TCP, and can better utilize UDP as the transport layer protocol. TFTP is one example of this type of protocol. TFTP has its own mechanisms for flow control, error detection, acknowledgements, and error recovery. It does not need to rely on TCP for those services.

Refer to
Lab Activity
for this chapter

7.2.4.3   Lab - Using Wireshark to Examine FTP and TFTP Captures

In this lab, you will complete the following objectives:

- Part 1: Identify TCP Header Fields and Operation Using a Wireshark FTP Session Capture

- Part 2: Identify UDP Header Fields and Operation Using a Wireshark TFTP Session Capture

Refer to
Online Course
for Illustration

7.3   Summary

Refer to
Lab Activity
for this chapter

7.3.1.1   Class Activity - We Need to Talk, Again - Game

We Need to Talk, Again

Note   It is important that the students have completed the Introductory Modeling Activity for this chapter. This activity works best in medium-sized groups of 6 to 8 students.

The instructor will whisper a complex message to the first student in a group. An example of the message might be "We are expecting a blizzard tomorrow. It should be arriving in the morning and school will be delayed two hours so bring your homework."

That student whispers the message to the next student in the group. Each group follows this process until all members of each group have heard the whispered message.

Here are the rules you are to follow:

- You can whisper the message in short parts to your neighbor AND you can repeat the message parts after verifying your neighbor heard the correct message.

- Small parts of the message may be checked and repeated again (clockwise OR counter-clockwise to ensure accuracy of the message parts) by whispering. A student will be assigned to time the entire activity.

- When the message has reached the end of the group, the last student will say aloud what she or he heard. Small parts of the message may be repeated (i.e., re-sent), and the process can be restarted to ensure that ALL parts of the message are fully delivered and correct.

- The Instructor will restate the original message to check for quality delivery.

Refer to **Packet Tracer Activity** for this chapter

7.3.1.2   Packet Tracer Simulation - TCP and UDP Communications

This simulation activity is intended to provide a foundation for understanding the TCP and UDP in detail. Simulation mode provides the ability to view the functionality of the different protocols.

As data moves through the network, it is broken down into smaller pieces and identified in some fashion so that the pieces can be put back together. Each of these pieces is assigned a specific name (protocol data unit [PDU]) and associated with a specific layer. Packet Tracer Simulation mode enables the user to view each of the protocols and the associated PDU. The steps outlined below lead the user through the process of requesting services using various applications available on a client PC.

This activity provides an opportunity to explore the functionality of the TCP and UDP protocols, multiplexing and the function of port numbers in determining which local application requested the data or is sending the data.

Refer to **Online Course** for Illustration

7.3.1.3   Summary

The transport layer provides transport-related services by:

- Dividing data received from an application into segments

- Adding a header to identify and manage each segment

- Using the header information to reassemble the segments back into application data

- Passing the assembled data to the correct application

UDP and TCP are common transport layer protocols.

UDP datagrams and TCP segments have headers added in front of the data that include a source port number and destination port number. These port numbers enable data to be directed to the correct application running on the destination computer.

TCP does not pass any data to the network until it knows that the destination is ready to receive it. TCP then manages the flow of the data and resends any data segments that are not acknowledged as being received at the destination. TCP uses mechanisms of handshaking, timers, acknowledgement messages, and dynamic windowing to achieve reliability. The reliability process, however, imposes overhead on the network in terms of much larger segment headers and more network traffic between the source and destination.

If the application data needs to be delivered across the network quickly, or if network bandwidth cannot support the overhead of control messages being exchanged between the source and the destination systems, UDP would be the developer's preferred transport layer protocol. Because UDP does not track or acknowledge the receipt of datagrams at the destination - it just passes received datagrams to the application layer as they arrive - and does not resend lost datagrams. However, this does not necessarily mean that the communication itself is unreliable; there may be mechanisms in the application layer protocols and services that process lost or delayed datagrams if the application has these requirements.

The application developer decides the transport layer protocol that best meets the requirements for the application. It is important to remember that the other layers all play a part in data network communications and influences its performance.

Go to the online course to take the quiz and exam.

Chapter 7 Quiz

This quiz is designed to provide an additional opportunity to practice the skills and knowledge presented in the chapter and to prepare for the chapter exam. You will be allowed multiple attempts and the grade does not appear in the gradebook.

Chapter 7 Exam

The chapter exam assesses your knowledge of the chapter content.

Your Chapter Notes

IP Addressing

8.0 IP Addressing

8.0.1.1 Introduction

Addressing is a key function of network layer protocols that enables data communication between hosts, regardless of whether the hosts are on the same network or on different networks. Both Internet Protocol version 4 (IPv4) and Internet Protocol version 6 (IPv6) provide hierarchical addressing for packets that carry data.

Designing, implementing and managing an effective IP addressing plan ensures that networks can operate effectively and efficiently.

This chapter examines in detail the structure of IP addresses and their application to the construction and testing of IP networks and subnetworks.

Refer to **Lab Activity** for this chapter

8.0.1.2 Class Activity –The Internet of Everything (IoE)

The Internet of Everything (IoE)

If nature, traffic, transportation, networking, and space exploration depend on digital information sharing, how will that information be identified from source to destination?

In this activity, you will begin to think about not only what will be identified in the IoE world, but how everything will be addressed in the same world!

- Read the blog/news source provided by John Chambers regarding the Internet of Everything - IoE - http://blogs.cisco.com/news/internet-of-everything-2. View the video halfway down the page.

- Next, venture to the IoE main page - http://www.cisco.com/web/tomorrow-starts-here/index.html. Click on a category that interests you.

- View the video, blog, or .pdf belonging to your IoE category of interest.

- Write 5 comments or questions about what you saw or read – share with the class.

Refer to
Online Course
for Illustration

8.1   IPv4 Network Addresses

8.1.1   IPv4 Address Structure

8.1.1.1   Binary Notation

To understand the operation of devices on a network, we need to look at addresses and other data the way devices do - in binary notation. Binary notation is a representation of information using only ones and zeros. Computers communicate using binary data. Binary data can be used to represent many different forms of data. For example, when typing letters on a keyboard, those letters appear on screen in a form that you can read and understand; however, the computer translates each letter to a series of binary digits for storage and transport. To translate those letters, the computer uses American Standard Code for Information Interchange (ASCII).

Using ASCII, the letter "A" is represented in bit form as: 01000001, while the lowercase letter "a" is represented in bit form as 01100001. Use the ASCII translator in Figure 1 to convert ASCII characters to binary.

While it is not generally necessary for people to concern themselves with binary conversion of letters, it is necessary to understand the use of binary for IP addressing. Each device on a network must be uniquely identified using a binary address. In IPv4 networks, this address is represented using a string of 32 bits (1s and 0s). At the network layer, the packets then include this unique identification information for both the source and destination systems. Therefore, in an IPv4 network, each packet includes a 32-bit source address and a 32-bit destination address in the Layer 3 header.

For most individuals, a string of 32 bits is difficult to interpret and even more difficult to remember. Therefore, we represent IPv4 addresses using dotted decimal format instead of binary. This means that we look at each byte (octet) as a decimal number in the range of 0 to 255. To understand how this works we need to have some skill in binary to decimal conversion.

Positional Notation

Learning to convert binary to decimal requires an understanding of the mathematical basis of a numbering system called positional notation. Positional notation means that a digit represents different values depending on the position the digit occupies. In a positional notation system, the number base is called the radix. In the base ten system, the radix is 10. In the binary system we use a radix of 2. The term radix and base can be used interchangeably. More specifically, the value that a digit represents is that value multiplied by the power of the base, or radix, represented by the position the digit occupies. Some examples will help to clarify how this system works.

For the decimal number 192, the value that the 1 represents is $1*10^2$ (1 times 10 to the power of 2). The 1 is in what we commonly refer to as the "100s" position. Positional notation refers to this position as the base^2 position because the base, or radix, is 10 and the power is 2. The 9 represents $9*10^1$ (9 times 10 to the power of 1). Positional notation for the decimal number 192 is shown in Figure 2.

Using positional notation in the base 10 number system, 192 represents:

$192 = (1 * 10^2) + (9 * 10^1) + (2 * 10^0)$

or

$192 = (1 * 100) + (9 * 10) + (2 * 1)$

Refer to
Online Course
for Illustration

8.1.1.2   Binary Number System

In IPv4, addresses are 32-bit binary numbers. However, for ease of use by people, binary patterns representing IPv4 addresses are expressed as dotted decimals. This is first accomplished by separating each byte (8 bits) of the 32-bit binary pattern, called an octet, with a dot. It is called an octet because each decimal number represents one byte or 8 bits.

The binary address:

```
11000000 10101000 00001010 00001010
```

is expressed in dotted decimal as:

192.168.10.10

In Figure 1, select each button to see how the 32-bit binary address is represented in dotted decimal octets.

But how are the actual decimal equivalents determined?

Binary Numbering System

In the binary numbering system, the radix is 2. Therefore, each position represents increasing powers of 2. In 8-bit binary numbers, the positions represent these quantities:

2^7 2^6 2^5 2^4 2^3 2^2 2^1 2^0

128 64 32 16 8 4 2 1

The base 2 numbering system only has two digits: 0 and 1.

When we interpret a byte as a decimal number, we have the quantity that position represents if the digit is a 1 and we do not have that quantity if the digit is a 0, as shown in Figure 1.

Figure 2 illustrates the representation of the decimal number 192 in binary. A 1 in a certain position means we add that value to the total. A 0 means we do not add that value. The binary number 11000000 has a 1 in the 2^7 position (decimal value 128) and a 1 in the 2^6 position (decimal value 64). The remaining bits are all 0 so we do not add the corresponding decimal values. The result of adding 128+64 is 192, the decimal equivalent of 11000000.

Here are two more examples:

Example 1: An octet containing all 1s: 11111111

A 1 in each position means that we add the value for that position to the total. All 1s means that the values of every position are included in the total, therefore, the value of all 1s in an octet is 255.

$128 + 64 + 32 + 16 + 8 + 4 + 2 + 1 = 255$

Example 2: An octet containing all 0s: 00000000

A 0 in each position indicates that the value for that position is not included in the total. A 0 in every position yields a total of 0.

0 + 0 + 0 + 0 + 0 + 0 + 0 + 0 = 0

A different combination of ones and zeros will yield a different decimal value.

Refer to
Online Course
for Illustration

8.1.1.3 Converting a Binary Address to Decimal

Each octet is made up of 8 bits and each bit has a value, either 0 or 1. The four groups of 8 bits have the same set of valid values in the range of 0 to 255 inclusive. The value of each bit placement, from right to left is 1, 2, 4, 8, 16, 32, 64, and 128.

Determine the value of the octet by adding the values of positions wherever there is a binary 1 present.

- If there is a 0 in a position, do not add the value.
- If all 8 bits are 0s, 00000000, the value of the octet is 0.
- If all 8 bits are 1s, 11111111, the value of the octet is 255 (128+64+32+16+8+4+2+1)
- If the 8 bits are mixed, the values are added together. For example, the octet 00100111 has a value of 39 (32+4+2+1).

So the value of each of the four octets can range from 0 to a maximum of 255.

Using the 32-bit IPv4 address, 11000000101010000000101000001010, convert the binary representation to dotted decimal using the following steps:

Step 1.   Divide the 32 bits into 4 octets.

Step 2.   Convert each octet to decimal.

Step 3.   Add a "dot" between each decimal.

Click Play in the figure to see how a binary address is converted to dotted decimal.

Refer to
Interactive Graphic
in online course.

8.1.1.4 Activity - Binary to Decimal Conversions

Refer to
Online Course
for Illustration

8.1.1.5 Converting from Decimal to Binary

In addition to being able to convert binary to decimal, it is also necessary to understand how to convert decimal to binary.

Because we represent IPv4 addresses using dotted decimal format, it is only necessary that we examine the process of converting 8-bit binary to the decimal values of 0 to 255 for each octet in an IPv4 address.

To begin the conversion process, we start by determining if the decimal number is equal to or greater than our largest decimal value represented by the most-significant bit. In the highest position, we determine if the octet number is equal to or greater than 128. If the octet number is smaller than 128, we place a 0 in the bit position for decimal value 128 and move to the bit position for decimal value 64.

If the octet number in the bit position for decimal value 128 is larger than or equal to 128, we place a 1 in the bit position for decimal value 128 and subtract 128 from the octet number being converted. We then compare the remainder of this operation to the next smaller value, 64. We continue this process for all the remaining bit positions.

Click through Figures 1-6 to see the process of converting 168 to the binary equivalent of 10101000.

Refer to
Online Course
for Illustration

8.1.1.6   Converting from Decimal to Binary (Cont.)

Follow the conversion steps in the figures to see how an IP address is converted to binary.

Figure 1: Convert 192 to binary.

Figure 2: Convert 168 to binary.

Figure 3: Convert 10 to binary.

Figure 4: Convert 10 to binary.

Figure 5: Combine the converted octets beginning with the first octet.

Refer to
Interactive Graphic
in online course.

8.1.1.7   Activity - Decimal to Binary Conversion Activity

Refer to
Interactive Graphic
in online course.

8.1.1.8   Activity - Binary Game

Refer to
Online Course
for Illustration

8.1.2   IPv4 Subnet Mask

8.1.2.1   Network Portion and Host Portion of an IPv4 Address

Understanding binary notation is important when determining if two hosts are in the same network. Recall that an IP address is a hierarchical address that is made up of two parts: a network portion and a host portion. But when determining the network portion versus the host portion, it is necessary to look, not at the decimal value, but at the 32-bit stream. Within the 32-bit stream, a portion of the bits makes up the network and a portion of the bits makes up the host.

The bits within the network portion of the address must be identical for all devices that reside in the same network. The bits within the host portion of the address must be unique to identify a specific host within a network. Regardless of whether the decimal numbers between two IPv4 addresses match up, if two hosts have the same bit-pattern in the specified network portion of the 32-bit stream, those two hosts will reside in the same network.

But how do hosts know which portion of the 32-bits is network and which is host? That is the job of the subnet mask.

When an IP host is configured, a subnet mask is assigned along with an IP address. Like the IP address, the subnet mask is 32 bits long. The subnet mask signifies which part of the IP address is network and which part is host.

The subnet mask is compared to the IP address from left to right, bit for bit. The 1s in the subnet mask represent the network portion; the 0s represent the host portion. As shown in Figure 1, the subnet mask is created by placing a binary 1 in each bit position that represents the network portion and placing a binary 0 in each bit position that represents the host portion. Note that the subnet mask does not actually contain the network or host portion of an IPv4 address, it just tells the computer where to look for these portions in a given IPv4 address.

Similar to IPv4 addresses, the subnet mask is represented in dotted decimal format for ease of use. The subnet mask is configured on a host device, in conjunction with the IPv4 address, and is required so the host can determine which network it belongs to. Figure 2 displays the valid subnet masks for an IPv4 octet.

Refer to
Online Course
for Illustration

8.1.2.2   Examining the Prefix Length

Network Prefixes

The prefix length is another way of expressing the subnet mask. The prefix length is the number of bits set to 1 in the subnet mask. It is written in "slash notation", a "/" followed by the number of bits set to 1. For example, if the subnet mask is 255.255.255.0, there are 24 bits set to 1 in the binary version of the subnet mask, so the prefix length is 24 bits or /24. The prefix and the subnet mask are different ways of representing the same thing - the network portion of an address.

Networks are not always assigned a /24 prefix. Depending on the number of hosts on the network, the prefix assigned may be different. Having a different prefix number changes the host range and broadcast address for each network.

The figures illustrate different prefixes using the same 10.1.1.0 address. Figure 1 illustrates /24 to /26 prefixes. Figure 2 illustrates /27 to /28 prefixes.

Notice that the network address could remain the same, but the host range and the broadcast address are different for the different prefix lengths. In the figures, you can see that the number of hosts that can be addressed on the network also changes.

8.1.2.3   IPv4 Network, Host and Broadcast Addresses

There are three types of addresses within the address range of each IPv4 network:

- Network address
- Host addresses
- Broadcast address

Network Address

The network address is a standard way to refer to a network. The subnet mask or the prefix length might also be used when referring to network address. For example, the network shown in Figure 1 could be referred to as the 10.1.1.0 network, the 10.1.1.0 255.255.255.0 network or the 10.1.1.0/24 network. All hosts in the 10.1.1.0/24 network will have the same network portion bits.

As shown in Figure 2, within the IPv4 address range of a network, the first address is reserved for the network address. This address has a 0 for each host bit in the host portion of the address. All hosts within the network share the same network address.

Host Address

Every end device requires a unique address to communicate on the network. In IPv4 addresses, the values between the network address and the broadcast address can be assigned to end devices in a network. As shown in Figure 3, this address has any combination of 0 and 1 bits in the host portion of the address but cannot contain all 0 bits or all 1 bits.

Broadcast Address

The IPv4 broadcast address is a special address for each network that allows communication to all the hosts in that network. To send data to all hosts in a network at once, a host can send a single packet that is addressed to the broadcast address of the network, and each host in the network that receives this packet will process its contents.

The broadcast address uses the highest address in the network range. This is the address in which the bits in the host portion are all 1s. All 1s in an octet in binary form, is equal to the number 255 in decimal form. Therefore, as shown in Figure 4, for the network 10.1.1.0/24, in which the last octet is used for the host portion, the broadcast address would be 10.1.1.255. Note that the host portion will not always be an entire octet. This address is also referred to as the directed broadcast.

Refer to **Online Course** for Illustration

8.1.2.4 First Host and Last Host Addresses

To ensure that all hosts within a network are assigned a unique IP address within that network range, it is important to identify the first host address and the last host address. Hosts within a network can be assigned IP addresses within this range.

First Host Address

As seen in Figure 1, the host portion of the first host address will contain all 0 bits with a 1 bit for the lowest order or right-most bit. This address is always one greater than the network address. In this example the first host address on the 10.1.1.0/24 network is 10.1.1.1. It is common in many addressing schemes to use the first host address for the router or default gateway address.

Last Host Address

The host portion of the last host address will contain all 1 bits with a 0 bit for the lowest order or right-most bit. This address is always one less than the broadcast address. As seen in Figure 2, the last host address on the 10.1.1.0/24 network is 10.1.1.254.

Refer to **Online Course** for Illustration

8.1.2.5 Bitwise AND Operation

When an IPv4 address is assigned to a device, that device uses the subnet mask to determine what network address the device belongs to. The network address is the address that represents all the devices on the same network.

When sending network data, the device uses this information to determine whether it can send packets locally, or if it must send the packets to a default gateway for remote delivery. When a host sends a packet, it compares the network portion of its own IP address to the network portion of the destination IP address, based on subnet masks. If the network bits match, both the source and destination host are on the same network and the packet can be delivered locally. If they do not match, the sending host forwards the packet to the default gateway to be sent on to the other network.

The AND Operation

ANDing is one of three basic binary operations used in digital logic. The other two are OR and NOT. While all three are used in data networks, AND is used in determining the network address. Therefore, our discussion here will be limited to logical AND. Logical AND is the comparison of two bits that yields the following results:

1 AND 1 = 1 (Figure 1)

0 AND 1 = 0 (Figure 2)

0 AND 0 = 0 (Figure 3)

1 AND 0 = 0 (Figure 4)

The IPv4 host address is logically ANDed, bit by bit, with its subnet mask to determine the network address to which the host is associated. When this bitwise ANDing between the address and the subnet mask is performed, the result yields the network address.

8.1.2.6   Importance of ANDing

Any address bit ANDed with a 1 bit value from the subnet mask will yield the original bit value from the address. So, a 0 (from the IPv4 address) AND 1 (from the subnet mask) is 0. 1 (from the IPv4 address) AND 1(from the subnet mask) is 1. Consequently, anything ANDed with a 0 yields a 0. These properties of ANDing are used with the subnet mask to "mask" the host bits of an IPv4 address. Each bit of the address is ANDed with the corresponding bit of the subnet mask.

Because all the bits of the subnet mask that represent host bits are 0s, the host portion of the resulting network address becomes all 0s. Recall that an IPv4 address with all 0s in the host portion represents the network address.

Likewise, all the bits of the subnet mask that indicate network portion are 1s. When each of these 1s is ANDed with the corresponding bit of the address, the resulting bits are identical to the original address bits.

As shown in the figure, the 1 bits in the subnet mask will result in the network portion of the network address having the same bits as the network portion of the host. The host portion of the network address will result in all 0s.

For a given IP address and its subnet, ANDing can be used to determine what subnetwork the address belongs to, as well as what other addresses belong to the same subnet. Remember that if two addresses are in the same network or subnetwork, they are considered to be local to each other and can therefore communicate directly with each other. Addresses that are not in the same network or subnetwork are considered to be remote to each other and must therefore have a Layer 3 device (like a router or Layer 3 switch) between them to communicate.

In network verification/troubleshooting, we often need to determine two hosts are on the same local network. We need to make this determination from the perspective of the network devices. Due to improper configuration, a host may see itself on a network that was not the intended one. This can create an operation that seems erratic unless diagnosed by examining the ANDing processes used by the host.

Refer to
Lab Activity
for this chapter

8.1.2.7   Lab - Using the Windows Calculator with Network Addresses

In this lab, you will complete the following objectives:

- Part 1: Access the Windows Calculator

- Part 2: Convert between Numbering Systems

- Part 3: Convert Host IPv4 Addresses and Subnet Masks into Binary

- Part 4: Determine the Number of Hosts in a Network Using Powers of 2

- Part 5: Convert MAC Addresses and IPv6 Addresses to Binary

Refer to
Lab Activity
for this chapter

8.1.2.8   Lab - Converting IPv4 Addresses to Binary

In this lab, you will complete the following objectives:

- Part 1: Convert IPv4 Addresses from Dotted Decimal to Binary

- Part 2: Use Bitwise ANDing Operation to Determine Network Addresses

- Part 3: Apply Network Address Calculations

Refer to
Interactive Graphic
in online course.

8.1.2.9   Activity - ANDing to Determine the Network Address

Refer to
Online Course
for Illustration

8.1.3   IPv4 Unicast, Broadcast, and Multicast

8.1.3.1   Assigning a Static IPv4 Address to a Host

Addresses for User Devices

In most data networks, the largest population of hosts includes the end devices such as PCs, tablets, smartphones, printers, and IP phones. Because this represents the largest number of devices within a network, the largest number of addresses should be allocated to these hosts. These hosts are assigned IP addresses from the range of available addresses in the network. These IP addresses can be assigned either statically or dynamically.

Static Assignment

With a static assignment, the network administrator must manually configure the network information for a host. Figure 1 shows the window for the network adapter properties. To configure a static IPv4 address, choose IPv4 on the network adapter screen, then key in the static address, subnet mask, and default gateway. Figure 2 shows the minimum static configuration: the host IP address, subnet mask, and default gateway.

There are several advantages to static addressing. For instance, they are useful for printers, servers, and other networking devices that do not change location often and need to be accessible to clients on the network based on a fixed IP address. If hosts normally access a server at a particular IP address, it would cause problems if that address changed. Additionally, static assignment of addressing information can provide increased control of network resources. For example, it is possible to create access filters based on traffic to and from a specific IP address. However, static addressing can be time-consuming to enter on each host.

When using static IP addressing, it is necessary to maintain an accurate list of the IP address assigned to each device. These are permanent addresses and are not normally reused.

Refer to
Online Course
for Illustration

8.1.3.2   Assigning a Dynamic IPv4 Address to a Host

Dynamic Assignment

On local networks it is often the case that the user population changes frequently. New users arrive with laptops and need a connection. Others have new workstations or other network devices, such as smart phones, that need to be connected. Rather than have the network administrator assign IP addresses for each workstation, it is easier to have IP addresses assigned automatically. This is done using a protocol known as Dynamic Host Configuration Protocol (DHCP), as shown in Figure 1.

DHCP enables the automatic assignment of addressing information such as IP address, subnet mask, default gateway, and other configuration information. The configuration of the DHCP server requires that a block of addresses, called an address pool, is used for assigning to the DHCP clients on a network. Addresses assigned to this pool should be planned so that they exclude any static addresses used by other devices.

DHCP is generally the preferred method of assigning IPv4 addresses to hosts on large networks because it reduces the burden on network support staff and virtually eliminates entry errors.

Another benefit of DHCP is that an address is not permanently assigned to a host but is only "leased" for a period of time. If the host is powered down or taken off the network, the address is returned to the pool for reuse. This feature is especially helpful for mobile users that come and go on a network.

If DCHP is enabled on a host device, the `ipconfig` command can be used to view the IP address information assigned by the DHCP server, as shown in Figure 2.

Refer to
Online Course
for Illustration

8.1.3.3   Unicast Transmission

In an IPv4 network, the hosts can communicate one of three ways:

- **Unicast** - The process of sending a packet from one host to an individual host
- **Broadcast** - The process of sending a packet from one host to all hosts in the network
- **Multicast** - The process of sending a packet from one host to a selected group of hosts, possibly in different networks

These three types of communication are used for different purposes in data networks. In all three cases, the IPv4 address of the originating host is placed in the packet header as the source address.

Unicast Traffic

Unicast communication is used for normal host-to-host communication in both a client/server and a peer-to-peer network. Unicast packets use the addresses of the destination device as the destination address and can be routed through an internetwork.

Play the animation to see an example of unicast transmission.

In an IPv4 network, the unicast addresses applied to an end device is referred to as the host address. For unicast communication, the addresses assigned to the two end devices are used as the source and destination IPv4 addresses. During the encapsulation process, the source host places its IPv4 address in the unicast packet header as the source address and the IPv4 address of the destination host in the packet header as the destination address. Regardless of whether the destination specified a packet is a unicast, broadcast or multicast; the source address of any packet is always the unicast address of the originating host.

Note   In this course, all communications between devices is unicast communication unless otherwise noted.

IPv4 host addresses are unicast addresses and are in the address range of 0.0.0.0 to 223.255.255.255. However, within this range are many addresses that are reserved for special purposes. These special purpose addresses will be discussed later in this chapter.

Refer to
Online Course
for Illustration

8.1.3.4   Broadcast Transmission

Broadcast Transmission

Broadcast traffic is used to send packets to all hosts in the network using the broadcast address for the network. With a broadcast, the packet contains a destination IP address with all ones (1s) in the host portion. This means that all hosts on that local network (broadcast domain) will receive and look at the packet. Many network protocols, such as DHCP, use broadcasts. When a host receives a packet sent to the network broadcast address, the host processes the packet as it would a packet addressed to its unicast address.

Some examples for using broadcast transmission are:

- Mapping upper layer addresses to lower layer addresses
- Requesting an address
- Unlike unicast, where the packets can be routed throughout the internetwork, broadcast packets are usually restricted to the local network. This restriction is dependent on the configuration of the gateway router and the type of broadcast. There are two types of broadcasts: directed broadcast and limited broadcast.

Directed Broadcast

A directed broadcast is sent to all hosts on a specific network. This type of broadcast is useful for sending a broadcast to all hosts on a non-local network. For example, for a host outside of the 172.16.4.0/24 network to communicate with all of the hosts within that network, the destination address of the packet would be 172.16.4.255. Although routers do not forward directed broadcasts by default, they may be configured to do so.

Limited Broadcast

The limited broadcast is used for communication that is limited to the hosts on the local network. These packets always use a destination IPv4 address 255.255.255.255. Routers do not forward a limited broadcast. For this reason, an IPv4 network is also referred to as a broadcast domain. Routers form the boundary for a broadcast domain.

As an example, a host within the 172.16.4.0/24 network would broadcast to all hosts in its network using a packet with a destination address of 255.255.255.255.

Play the animation to see an example of a limited broadcast transmission.

When a packet is broadcast, it uses resources on the network and causes every receiving host on the network to process the packet. Therefore, broadcast traffic should be limited so that it does not adversely affect performance of the network or devices. Because routers separate broadcast domains, subdividing networks with excessive broadcast traffic can improve network performance.

Refer to **Online Course** for Illustration

8.1.3.5   Multicast Transmission

Multicast Transmission

Multicast transmission is designed to conserve the bandwidth of an IPv4 network. It reduces traffic by allowing a host to send a single packet to a selected set of hosts that are part of a subscribing multicast group. To reach multiple destination hosts using unicast communication, a source host would need to send an individual packet addressed to each host. With multicast, the source host can send a single packet that can reach thousands of destination hosts. The internetwork's responsibility is to replicate the multicast flows in an efficient manner so that they reach only their intended recipients.

Some examples of multicast transmission are:

- Video and audio broadcasts
- Routing information exchange by routing protocols
- Distribution of software
- Remote gaming

Multicast Addresses

IPv4 has a block of addresses reserved for addressing multicast groups. This address range is 224.0.0.0 to 239.255.255.255. The multicast address range is subdivided into different types of addresses: reserved link local addresses and globally scoped addresses. One additional type of multicast address is the administratively scoped addresses, also called limited scope addresses.

The IPv4 multicast addresses 224.0.0.0 to 224.0.0.255 are reserved link local addresses. These addresses are to be used for multicast groups on a local network. A router connected to the local network recognizes that these packets are addressed to a link-local multicast group and never forwards them further. A typical use of reserved link-local addresses is in routing protocols using multicast transmission to exchange routing information.

The globally scoped addresses are 224.0.1.0 to 238.255.255.255. They may be used to multicast data across the Internet. For example, 224.0.1.1 has been reserved for the Network Time Protocol (NTP) to synchronize the time-of-day clocks of network devices.

Multicast Clients

Hosts that receive particular multicast data are called multicast clients. The multicast clients use services requested by a client program to subscribe to the multicast group.

Each multicast group is represented by a single IPv4 multicast destination address. When an IPv4 host subscribes to a multicast group, the host processes packets addressed to this multicast address and packets addressed to its uniquely allocated unicast address.

The animation demonstrates clients accepting multicast packets.

Refer to
Interactive Graphic
in online course.

8.1.3.6   Activity - Unicast, Broadcast, or Multicast

Refer to
Interactive Graphic
in online course.

8.1.3.7   Activity - Calculate the Network, Broadcast and Host Addresses

Refer to Packet
Tracer Activity
for this chapter

8.1.3.8   Packet Tracer - Investigate Unicast, Broadcast, and Multicast Traffic

This activity will examine unicast, broadcast, and multicast behavior. Most traffic in a network is unicast. When a PC sends an ICMP echo request to a remote router, the source address in the IP packet header is the IP address of the sending PC. The destination address in the IP packet header is the IP address of the interface on the remote router. The packet is sent only to the intended destination.

Using the `ping` command or the Add Complex PDU feature of Packet Tracer, you can directly ping broadcast addresses to view broadcast traffic.

For multicast traffic, you will view EIGRP traffic. EIGRP is used by Cisco routers to exchange routing information between routers. Routers using EIGRP send packets to multicast address 224.0.0.10, which represents the group of EIGRP routers. Although these packets are received by other devices, they are dropped at Layer 3 by all devices except EIGRP routers, with no other processing required.

Refer to
Online Course
for Illustration

8.1.4   Types of IPv4 Addresses

8.1.4.1   Public and Private IPv4 Addresses

Although most IPv4 host addresses are public addresses designated for use in networks that are accessible on the Internet, there are blocks of addresses that are used in networks that require limited or no Internet access. These addresses are called private addresses.

Private Addresses

The private address blocks are:

10.0.0.0 to 10.255.255.255 (10.0.0.0/8)

172.16.0.0 to 172.31.255.255 (172.16.0.0/12)

192.168.0.0 to 192.168.255.255 (192.168.0.0/16)

Private addresses are defined in RFC 1918, Address Allocation for Private Internets, and are sometimes referred to as RFC 1918 addresses. Private space address blocks, as shown in the figure, are used in private networks. Hosts that do not require access to the Internet can use private addresses. However within the private network, hosts still require unique IP addresses within the private space.

Hosts in different networks may use the same private space addresses. Packets using these addresses as the source or destination should not appear on the public Internet. The router or firewall device at the perimeter of these private networks must block or translate these addresses. Even if these packets were to make their way to the Internet, the routers would not have routes to forward them to the appropriate private network.

In RFC 6598, IANA reserved another group of addresses known as shared address space. Similar to RFC 1918 private address space, shared address space addresses are not globally routable. However, these addresses are intended only for use in service provider networks. The shared address block is 100.64.0.0/10.

Public Addresses

The vast majority of the addresses in the IPv4 unicast host range are public addresses. These addresses are designed to be used in the hosts that are publicly accessible from the Internet. Even within these IPv4 address blocks, there are many addresses that are designated for other special purposes.

Refer to Interactive Graphic in online course.

8.1.4.2 Activity - Pass or Block IPv4 Addresses

Refer to Online Course for Illustration

8.1.4.3 Special Use IPv4 Addresses

There are certain addresses that cannot be assigned to hosts. There are also special addresses that can be assigned to hosts, but with restrictions on how those hosts can interact within the network.

Network and Broadcast Addresses

As explained earlier, within each network the first and last addresses cannot be assigned to hosts. These are the network address and the broadcast address, respectively.

Loopback

One such reserved address is the IPv4 loopback address 127.0.0.1. The loopback is a special address that hosts use to direct traffic to themselves. The loopback address creates a shortcut method for TCP/IP applications and services that run on the same device to communicate with one another. By using the loopback address instead of the assigned IPv4 host address, two services on the same host can bypass the lower layers of the TCP/IP stack. You can also ping the loopback address to test the configuration of TCP/IP on the local host.

Although only the single 127.0.0.1 address is used, addresses 127.0.0.0 to 127.255.255.255 are reserved. Any address within this block will loop back to the local host. No address within this block should ever appear on any network.

Link-Local Addresses

IPv4 addresses in the address block 169.254.0.0 to 169.254.255.255 (169.254.0.0/16) are designated as link-local addresses. These addresses can be automatically assigned to the local host by the operating system in environments where no IP configuration is available. These might be used in a small peer-to-peer network or for a host that could not automatically obtain an address from a DHCP server.

Communication using IPv4 link-local addresses is only suitable for communication with other devices connected to the same network, as shown in the figure. A host must not send a packet with an IPv4 link-local destination address to any router for forwarding and should set the IPv4 time to live (TTL) for these packets to 1.

Link-local addresses do not provide services outside of the local network. However, many client/server and peer-to-peer applications will work properly with IPv4 link-local addresses.

TEST-NET Addresses

The address block 192.0.2.0 to 192.0.2.255 (192.0.2.0/24) is set aside for teaching and learning purposes. These addresses can be used in documentation and network examples.

Unlike the experimental addresses, network devices will accept these addresses in their configurations. You may often find these addresses used with the domain names example. com or example.net in RFCs, vendor, and protocol documentation. Addresses within this block should not appear on the Internet.

Experimental Addresses

The addresses in the block 240.0.0.0 to 255.255.255.254 are listed as reserved for future use (RFC 3330). Currently, these addresses can only be used for research or experimentation purposes, but cannot be used in an IPv4 network. Though, according to RFC 3330, they could, technically, be converted to usable addresses in the future.

Refer to **Online Course** for Illustration

8.1.4.4   Legacy Classful Addressing

Historically, RFC1700, Assigned Numbers, grouped the unicast ranges into specific sizes called class A, class B, and class C addresses. It also defined class D (multicast) and class E (experimental) addresses, as previously presented. The unicast address classes A, B, and C defined specifically-sized networks and specific address blocks for these networks. A company or organization was assigned an entire network from class A, class B, or class C address block. This use of address space is referred to as classful addressing.

Class A Blocks

A class A address block was designed to support extremely large networks with more than 16 million host addresses. Class A IPv4 addresses used a fixed /8 prefix with the first octet to indicate the network address. The remaining three octets were used for host addresses. All class A addresses required that the most significant bit of the high-order octet be a zero. This meant that there were only 128 possible class A networks, 0.0.0.0/8 to 127.0.0.0/8. Even though the class A addresses reserved one-half of the address space, because of their limit of 128 networks, they could only be allocated to approximately 120 companies or organizations.

Class B Blocks

Class B address space was designed to support the needs of moderate to large size networks with up to approximately 65,000 hosts. A class B IP address used the two high-order octets to indicate the network address. The other two octets specified host addresses. As with class A, address space for the remaining address classes needed to be reserved. For class B addresses, the most significant two bits of the high-order octet were 10. This restricted the address block for class B to 128.0.0.0/16 to 191.255.0.0/16. Class B had slightly more efficient allocation of addresses than class A because it equally divided 25% of the total IPv4 address space among approximately 16,000 networks.

Class C Blocks

The class C address space was the most commonly available of the historic address classes. This address space was intended to provide addresses for small networks with a maximum of 254 hosts. Class C address blocks used a /24 prefix. This meant that a class C network used only the last octet as host addresses with the three high-order octets used to indicate the network address. Class C address blocks set aside address space by using a fixed value of 110 for the three most significant bits of the high-order octet. This restricted the address block for class C from 192.0.0.0/24 to 223.255.255.0/24. Although it occupied only 12.5% of the total IPv4 address space, it could provide addresses to 2 million networks.

Figure 1 illustrates how these address classes are divided.

Limits to the Class-based System

Not all organizations' requirements fit well into one of these three classes. Classful allocation of address space often wasted many addresses, which exhausted the availability of IPv4 addresses. For example, a company that had a network with 260 hosts would need to be given a class B address with more than 65,000 addresses.

Even though this classful system was all but abandoned in the late 1990s, you will see remnants of it in networks today. For example, when you assign an IPv4 address to a computer, the operating system examines the address being assigned to determine if this address is a class A, class B, or class C. The operating system then assumes the prefix used by that class and makes the default subnet mask assignment.

Classless Addressing

The system in use today is referred to as classless addressing. The formal name is Classless Inter-Domain Routing (CIDR, pronounced "cider"). The classful allocation of IPv4 addresses was very inefficient, allowing for only /8, /16 or /24 prefix lengths, each from a separate address space. In 1993, the IETF created a new set of standards that allowed service providers to allocate IPv4 addresses on any address bit boundary (prefix length) instead of only by a class A, B, or C address.

The IETF knew that CIDR was only a temporary solution and that a new IP protocol would have to be developed to accommodate the rapid growth in the number of Internet users. In 1994, the IETF began its work to find a successor to IPv4, which eventually became IPv6.

Figure 2 shows the classful address ranges.

8.1.4.5   Assignment of IP Addresses

For a company or organization to have network hosts, such as web servers, accessible from the Internet, that organization must have a block of public addresses assigned. Remember that public addresses must be unique, and use of these public addresses is regulated and allocated to each organization separately. This is true for IPv4 and IPv6 addresses.

IANA and RIRs

Internet Assigned Numbers Authority (IANA) (http://www.iana.org) manages the allocation of IPv4 and IPv6 addresses. Until the mid-1990s, all IPv4 address space was managed directly by the IANA. At that time, the remaining IPv4 address space was allocated to various other registries to manage for particular purposes or for regional areas. These registration companies are called Regional Internet Registries (RIRs), as shown in the figure.

The major registries are:

- AfriNIC (African Network Information Centre) - Africa Region http://www.afrinic.net

- APNIC (Asia Pacific Network Information Centre) - Asia/Pacific Region http://www.apnic.net

- ARIN (American Registry for Internet Numbers) - North America Region http://www.arin.net

- LACNIC (Regional Latin-American and Caribbean IP Address Registry) - Latin America and some Caribbean Islands http://www.lacnic.net

- RIPE NCC (Reseaux IP Europeans) - Europe, the Middle East, and Central Asia http://www.ripe.net

ISPs

RIRs are responsible for allocating IP addresses to the Internet Service Providers (ISPs). Most companies or organizations obtain their IPv4 address blocks from an ISP. An ISP will generally supply a small number of usable IPv4 addresses (6 or 14) to their customers as a part of their services. Larger blocks of addresses can be obtained based on justification of needs and for additional service costs.

In a sense, the ISP loans or rents these addresses to the organization. If we choose to move our Internet connectivity to another ISP, the new ISP will provide us with addresses from the address blocks that have been provided to them, and our previous ISP returns the blocks loaned to us to their allocation to be loaned to another customer.

IPv6 addresses can be obtained from the ISP or in some cases directly from the RIR. IPv6 addresses and typical address block sizes will be discussed later in this chapter.

Refer to
Online Course
for Illustration

8.1.4.6   Assignment of IP Addresses (Cont.)

ISP Services

To get access to the services of the Internet, we have to connect our data network to the Internet using an Internet Service Provider (ISP).

ISPs have their own set of internal data networks to manage Internet connectivity and to provide related services. Among the other services that an ISP generally provides to its customers are DNS services, email services, and a website. Depending on the level of service required and available, customers use different tiers of an ISP.

ISP Tiers

ISPs are designated by a hierarchy based on their level of connectivity to the Internet backbone. Each lower tier obtains connectivity to the backbone via a connection to a higher tier ISP, as shown in the figures.

Tier 1

As shown in Figure 1, at the top of the ISP hierarchy are Tier 1 ISPs. These ISPs are large national or international ISPs that are directly connected to the Internet backbone. The customers of Tier 1 ISPs are either lower-tiered ISPs or large companies and organizations. Because they are at the top of Internet connectivity, they engineer highly reliable connections and services. Among the technologies used to support this reliability are multiple connections to the Internet backbone.

The primary advantages for customers of Tier 1 ISPs are reliability and speed. Because these customers are only one connection away from the Internet, there are fewer opportunities for failures or traffic bottlenecks. The drawback for Tier 1 ISP customers is its high cost.

Tier 2

As shown in Figure 2, Tier 2 ISPs acquire their Internet service from Tier 1 ISPs. Tier 2 ISPs generally focus on business customers. Tier 2 ISPs usually offer more services than the other two tiers of ISPs. These Tier 2 ISPs tend to have the IT resources to operate their own services such as DNS, email servers, and web servers. Other services that Tier 2 ISPs may offer include website development and maintenance, e-commerce/e-business, and VoIP.

The primary disadvantage of Tier 2 ISPs, as compared to Tier 1 ISPs, is slower Internet access. Because Tier 2 ISPs are at least one more connection away from the Internet backbone, they also tend to have lower reliability than Tier 1 ISPs.

Tier 3

As shown in Figure 3, Tier 3 ISPs purchase their Internet service from Tier 2 ISPs. The focus of these ISPs is the retail and home markets in a specific locale. Tier 3 customers typically do not need many of the services required by Tier 2 customers. Their primary need is connectivity and support.

These customers often have little or no computer or network expertise. Tier 3 ISPs often bundle Internet connectivity as a part of network and computer service contracts for their customers. While they may have reduced bandwidth and less reliability than Tier 1 and Tier 2 providers, they are often good choices for small to medium size companies.

Refer to **Interactive Graphic** in online course.

8.1.4.7   Activity - Public or Private IPv4 Addresses

Refer to **Lab Activity** for this chapter

8.1.4.8   Lab - Identifying IPv4 Addresses
In this lab, you will complete the following objectives:

- Part 1: Identify IPv4 Addresses
- Part 2: Classify IPv4 Addresses

Refer to **Online Course** for Illustration

8.2   IPv6 Network Addresses

8.2.1   IPv4 issues

8.2.1.1   The Need for IPv6
IPv6 is designed to be the successor to IPv4. IPv6 has a larger 128-bit address space, providing for 340 undecillion addresses. (That is the number 340, followed by 36 zeroes.) However, IPv6 is much more than just larger addresses. When the IETF began its development of a successor to IPv4, it used this opportunity to fix the limitations of IPv4 and include additional enhancements. One example is Internet Control Message Protocol version 6 (ICMPv6), which includes address resolution and address auto-configuration not found in ICMP for IPv4 (ICMPv4). ICMPv4 and ICMPv6 will be discussed later in this chapter.

Need for IPv6

The depletion of IPv4 address space has been the motivating factor for moving to IPv6. As Africa, Asia and other areas of the world become more connected to the Internet, there are not enough IPv4 addresses to accommodate this growth. On Monday, January 31, 2011, IANA allocated the last two /8 IPv4 address blocks to the Regional Internet Registries (RIRs). Various projections show that all five RIRs will have run out of IPv4 addresses between 2015 and 2020. At that point, the remaining IPv4 addresses will have been allocated to ISPs.

IPv4 has theoretical maximum of 4.3 billion addresses. RFC 1918 private addresses in combination with Network Address Translation (NAT) have been instrumental in slowing the depletion of IPv4 address space. NAT has limitations that severely impede peer-to-peer communications.

Internet of Things

The Internet of today is significantly different than the Internet of past decades. The Internet of today is more than email, web pages and file transfer between computers. The evolving Internet is becoming an Internet of things. No longer will the only devices accessing the Internet be computers, tablets and smart phones. The sensor-equipped, Internet-ready devices of tomorrow will include everything from automobiles and biomedical devices, to household appliances and natural ecosystems. Imagine a meeting at a customer site that is automatically scheduled on your calendar application, to begin an hour before you normally start work. This could be a significant problem, especially if you forget to check the calendar or adjust the alarm clock accordingly. Now imagine that the calendar application communicates this information directly to your alarm clock for you and to your automobile. Your car automatically warms up to melt the ice on the windshield before you enter the car and reroutes you to your meeting.

With an increasing Internet population, a limited IPv4 address space, issues with NAT and an Internet of things, the time has come to begin the transition to IPv6.

Refer to
Online Course
for Illustration

8.2.1.2   IPv4 and IPv6 Coexistence

There is not a single date to move to IPv6. For the foreseeable future, both IPv4 and IPv6 will coexist. The transition is expected to take years. The IETF has created various protocols and tools to help network administrators migrate their networks to IPv6. The migration techniques can be divided into three categories:

- **Dual Stack** – As shown in Figure 1, dual stack allows IPv4 and IPv6 to coexist on the same network. Dual stack devices run both IPv4 and IPv6 protocol stacks simultaneously.

- **Tunneling** – As shown in Figure 2, tunneling is a method of transporting an IPv6 packet over an IPv4 network. The IPv6 packet is encapsulated inside an IPv4 packet, similar to other types of data.

- **Translation** – As shown in Figure 3, Network Address Translation 64 (NAT64) allows IPv6-enabled devices to communicate with IPv4-enabled devices using a translation technique similar to NAT for IPv4. An IPv6 packet is translated to an IPv4 packet, and vice versa.

Refer to
Interactive Graphic
in online course.

8.2.1.3   Activity – IPv4 Issues and Solutions

Refer to
Online Course
for Illustration

8.2.2   IPv6 Addressing

8.2.2.1   Hexadecimal Number System

Unlike IPv4 addresses that are expressed in dotted decimal notation, IPv6 addresses are represented using hexadecimal values. You have seen hexadecimal used in the Packets Byte pane of Wireshark. In Wireshark, hexadecimal is used to represent the binary values within frames and packets. Hexadecimal is also used to represent Ethernet Media Access Control (MAC) addresses.

Hexadecimal Numbering

Hexadecimal ("Hex") is a convenient way to represent binary values. Just as decimal is a base ten numbering system and binary is base two, hexadecimal is a base sixteen system.

The base 16 numbering system uses the numbers 0 to 9 and the letters A to F. Figure 1 shows the equivalent decimal, binary, and hexadecimal values. There are 16 unique combinations of four bits, from 0000 to 1111. The 16 digit Hexadecimal is the perfect number system to use, because any four bits can be represented with a single hexadecimal value.

Understanding Bytes

Given that 8 bits (a byte) is a common binary grouping, binary 00000000 to 11111111 can be represented in hexadecimal as the range 00 to FF. Leading zeroes can be displayed to complete the 8-bit representation. For example, the binary value 0000 1010 is shown in hexadecimal as 0A.

Representing Hexadecimal Values

Note   It is important to distinguish hexadecimal values from decimal values regarding the characters 0 to 9.

Hexadecimal is usually represented in text by the value preceded by 0x (for example 0x73) or a subscript 16. Less commonly, it may be followed by an H, for example 73H. However, because subscript text is not recognized in command line or programming environments, the technical representation of hexadecimal is preceded with "0x" (zero X). Therefore, the examples above would be shown as 0x0A and 0x73 respectively.

Hexadecimal Conversions

Number conversions between decimal and hexadecimal values are straightforward, but quickly dividing or multiplying by 16 is not always convenient.

With practice, it is possible to recognize the binary bit patterns that match the decimal and hexadecimal values. Figure 2 shows these patterns for selected 8-bit values.

8.2.2.2   IPv6 Address Representation

IPv6 addresses are 128 bits in length and written as a string of hexadecimal values. Every 4 bits is represented by a single hexadecimal digit; for a total of 32 hexadecimal values. IPv6 addresses are not case sensitive and can be written in either lowercase or uppercase.

Preferred Format

As shown in Figure 1, the preferred format for writing an IPv6 address is x:x:x:x:x:x:x:x, with each "x" consisting of four hexadecimal values. When referring to 8 bits of an IPv4 address we use the term octet. In IPv6, a hextet is the unofficial term used to refer to a segment of 16 bits or four hexadecimal values. Each "x" is a single hextet, 16 bits or four hexadecimal digits.

Preferred format means the IPv6 address is written using all 32 hexadecimal digits. It does not necessarily mean it is the ideal method for representing the IPv6 address. In the following pages, we will see two rules to help reduce the number of digits needed to represent an IPv6 address.

Figure 2 has examples of IPv6 addresses in the preferred format.

Refer to **Online Course** for Illustration

8.2.2.3   Rule 1 - Omitting Leading 0s

The first rule to help reduce the notation of IPv6 addresses is any leading 0s (zeros) in any 16-bit section or hextet can be omitted. For example:

- 01AB can be represented as 1AB

- 09F0 can be represented as 9F0

- 0A00 can be represented as A00

- 00AB can be represented as AB

This rule only applies to leading 0s, NOT to trailing 0s, otherwise the address would be ambiguous. For example, the hextet "ABC" could be either "0ABC" or "ABC0".

The Figures 1 to 8 show several examples of how omitting leading 0s can be used to reduce the size of an IPv6 address. For each example the preferred format is shown. Notice how omitting the leading 0s in most examples results in a smaller address representation.

Refer to **Online Course** for Illustration

8.2.2.4   Rule 2 - Omitting All 0 Segments

The second rule to help reduce the notation of IPv6 addresses is that a double colon (::) can replace any single, contiguous string of one or more 16-bit segments (hextets) consisting of all 0s.

The double colon (::) can only be used once within an address, otherwise there would be more than one possible resulting address. When used with the omitting leading 0s technique, the notation of IPv6 address can often be greatly reduced. This is commonly known as the compressed format.

Incorrect address:

- 2001:0DB8::ABCD::1234

Possible expansions of ambiguous compressed addresses:

- 2001:0DB8::ABCD:0000:0000:1234

- 2001:0DB8::ABCD:0000:0000:0000:1234

- 2001:0DB8:0000:ABCD::1234

- 2001:0DB8:0000:0000:ABCD::1234

The Figures 1 to 7 show several examples of the how using the double colon (::) and omitting leading 0s can reduce the size of an IPv6 address.

Refer to
Interactive Graphic
in online course.

8.2.2.5   Activity - Practicing IPv6 Address Representations

Refer to
Online Course
for Illustration

8.2.3   Types of IPv6 Addresses

8.2.3.1   IPv6 Address Types

There are three types of IPv6 addresses:

- **Unicast** - An IPv6 unicast address uniquely identifies an interface on an IPv6-enabled device. As shown in the figure, a source IPv6 address must be a unicast address.

- **Multicast** - An IPv6 multicast address is used to send a single IPv6 packet to multiple destinations.

- **Anycast** - An IPv6 anycast address is any IPv6 unicast address that can be assigned to multiple devices. A packet sent to an anycast address is routed to the nearest device having that address. Anycast addresses are beyond the scope of this course.

Unlike IPv4, IPv6 does not have a broadcast address. However, there is an IPv6 all-nodes multicast address that essentially gives the same result.

Refer to
Online Course
for Illustration

8.2.3.2   IPv6 Prefix Length

Recall that the prefix, or network portion, of an IPv4 address can be identified by a dotted-decimal subnet mask or prefix length (slash notation). For example, an IP address of 192.168.1.10 with dotted-decimal subnet mask 255.255.255.0 is equivalent to 192.168.1.10/24.

IPv6 uses the prefix length to represent the prefix portion of the address. IPv6 does not use the dotted-decimal subnet mask notation. The prefix length is used to indicate the network portion of an IPv6 address using the IPv6 address/prefix length.

The prefix length can range from 0 to 128. A typical IPv6 prefix length for LANs and most other types of networks is /64. This means the prefix or network portion of the address is 64 bits in length, leaving another 64 bits for the interface ID (host portion) of the address.

Refer to
Online Course
for Illustration

8.2.3.3   IPv6 Unicast Addresses

An IPv6 unicast address uniquely identifies an interface on an IPv6-enabled device. A packet sent to a unicast address is received by the interface that is assigned that address. Similar to IPv4, a source IPv6 address must be a unicast address. The destination IPv6 address can be either a unicast or a multicast address.

There are six types of IPv6 unicast addresses.

Global unicast

A global unicast address is similar to a public IPv4 address. These are globally unique, Internet routable addresses. Global unicast addresses can be configured statically or assigned dynamically. There are some important differences in how a device receives its IPv6 address dynamically compared to DHCP for IPv4.

Link-local

Link-local addresses are used to communicate with other devices on the same local link. With IPv6, the term link refers to a subnet. Link-local addresses are confined to a single link. Their uniqueness must only be confirmed on that link because they are not routable beyond the link. In other words, routers will not forward packets with a link-local source or destination address.

Loopback

The loopback address is used by a host to send a packet to itself and cannot be assigned to a physical interface. Similar to an IPv4 loopback address, you can ping an IPv6 loopback address to test the configuration of TCP/IP on the local host. The IPv6 loopback address is all-0s except for the last bit, represented as ::1/128 or just ::1 in the compressed format.

Unspecified address

An unspecified address is an all-0s address represented in the compressed format as ::/128 or just :: in the compressed format. It cannot be assigned to an interface and is only be used as a source address in an IPv6 packet. An unspecified address is used as a source address when the device does not yet have a permanent IPv6 address or when the source of the packet is irrelevant to the destination.

Unique local

IPv6 unique local addresses have some similarity to RFC 1918 private addresses for IPv4, but there are significant differences as well. Unique local addresses are used for local addressing within a site or between a limited number of sites. These addresses should not be routable in the global IPv6. Unique local addresses are in the range of FC00::/7 to FDFF::/7.

With IPv4, private addresses are combined with NAT/PAT to provide a many-to-one translation of private-to-public addresses. This is done because of the limited availability of IPv4 address space. Many sites also use the private nature of RFC 1918 addresses to help secure or hide their network from potential security risks. However, this was never the intended use of these technologies and the IETF has always recommended that sites take the proper security precautions on their Internet facing router. Although, IPv6 does provide for site specific addressing, it is not intended to be used to help hide internal IPv6-enabled devices from the IPv6 Internet. IETF recommends that limiting access to devices should be accomplished using proper, best-practice security measures.

Note   The original IPv6 specification defined site-local addresses for a similar purpose, using the prefix range FEC0::/10. There were several ambiguities in the specification and site-local addresses were deprecated by the IETF in favor of unique local addresses.

IPv4 embedded

The last type of unicast address type is the IPv4 embedded address. These addresses are used to help transition from IPv4 to IPv6. IPv4 embedded addresses are beyond the scope of this course.

Refer to
Online Course
for Illustration

8.2.3.4   IPv6 Link-Local Unicast Addresses

An IPv6 link-local address enables a device to communicate with other IPv6-enabled devices on the same link and only on that link (subnet). Packets with a source or destination link-local address cannot be routed beyond the link from where the packet originated.

Unlike IPv4 link-local addresses, IPv6 link-local addresses have a significant role in various aspects of the network. The global unicast address is not a requirement; however, every IPv6-enabled network interface is required to have a link-local address.

If a link-local address is not configured manually on an interface, the device will automatically create its own without communicating with a DHCP server. IPv6-enabled hosts create an IPv6 link-local address even if the device has not been assigned a global unicast IPv6 address. This allows IPv6-enabled devices to communicate with other IPv6-enabled devices on the same subnet. This includes communication with the default gateway (router).

IPv6 link-local addresses are in the FE80::/10 range. The /10 indicates that the first 10 bits are 1111 1110 10xx xxxx. The first hextet has a range of 1111 1110 10**00 0000** (FE80) to 1111 1110 10**11 1111** (FEBF).

Figure 1 shows an example of communication using IPv6 link-local addresses.

Figure 2 shows the format of an IPv6 link-local address.

IPv6 link-local addresses are also used by IPv6 routing protocols to exchange messages and as the next-hop address in the IPv6 routing table. Link-local addresses are discussed in more detail in a later course.

Note   Typically, it is the link-local address of the router and not the global unicast address that is used as the default gateway for other devices on the link.

Refer to
Interactive Graphic
in online course.

8.2.3.5   Activity - Identify Types of IPv6 Addresses

Refer to
Online Course
for Illustration

8.2.4   IPv6 Unicast Addresses

8.2.4.1   Structure of an IPv6 Global Unicast Address

IPv6 global unicast addresses are globally unique and routable on the IPv6 Internet. These addresses are equivalent to public IPv4 addresses. The Internet Committee for Assigned Names and Numbers (ICANN), the operator for Internet Assigned Numbers Authority (IANA), allocates IPv6 address blocks to the five RIRs. Currently, only global unicast addresses with the first three bits of 001 or 2000::/3 are being assigned. This is only 1/8th of the total available IPv6 address space, excluding only a very small portion for other types of unicast and multicast addresses.

Note   The 2001:0DB8::/32 address has been reserved for documentation purposes, including use in examples.

Figure 1 shows the structure and range of a global unicast address.

A global unicast address has three parts:

- Global routing prefix
- Subnet ID
- Interface ID

Global Routing Prefix

The global routing prefix is the prefix, or network, portion of the address that is assigned by the provider, such as an ISP, to a customer or site. Currently, RIRs assign a /48 global routing prefix to customers. This includes everyone from enterprise business networks to individual households. This is more than enough address space for most customers.

Figure 2 shows the structure of a global unicast address using a /48 global routing prefix. /48 prefixes are the most common global routing prefixes assigned and will be used in most of the examples throughout this course.

For example, the IPv6 address 2001:0DB8:ACAD::/48 has a prefix that indicates that the first 48 bits (3 hextets) (2001:0DB8:ACAD) is the prefix or network portion of the address. The double colon (::) prior to the /48 prefix length means the rest of the address contains all 0s.

Subnet ID

The Subnet ID is used by an organization to identify subnets within its site.

Interface ID

The IPv6 Interface ID is equivalent to the host portion of an IPv4 address. The term Interface ID is used because a single host may have multiple interfaces, each having one or more IPv6 addresses.

Note   Unlike IPv4, in IPv6, the all-0s address can be assigned to a device because there are no broadcast addresses in IPv6. However, the all-0s address is reserved as a Subnet-Router anycast address, and should be assigned only to routers.

An easy way to read most IPv6 addresses is to count the number of hextets. As shown in Figure 3, in a /64 global unicast address the first four hextets are for the network portion of the address, with the fourth hextet indicating the Subnet ID. The remaining four hextets are for the Interface ID.

Refer to
Online Course
for Illustration

8.2.4.2   Static Configuration of a Global Unicast Address

Router Configuration

Most IPv6 configuration and verification commands in the Cisco IOS are similar to their IPv4 counterparts. In many cases the only difference is the use of `ipv6` in place of `ip` within the commands.

The `interface` command to configure an IPv6 global unicast address on an interface is **ipv6 address** *ipv6-address/prefix-length*.

Notice that there is not a space between *ipv6-address* and *prefix-length*.

The example configuration will use the topology shown in Figure 1 and these IPv6 subnets:

- 2001:0DB8:ACAD:0001:/64 (*or* 2001:DB8:ACAD:1::/64)
- 2001:0DB8:ACAD:0002:/64 (*or* 2001:DB8:ACAD:2::/64)
- 2001:0DB8:ACAD:0003:/64 (*or* 2001:DB8:ACAD:3::/64)

As shown in Figure 2, the commands required to configure the IPv6 global unicast address on the GigabitEthernet 0/0 interface of R1 would be:

`Router(config)#interface GigabitEthernet 0/0`

`Router(config-if)#ipv6 address 2001:db8:acad:1::1/64`

`Router(config-if)#no shutdown`

Host Configuration

Manually configuring the IPv6 address on a host is similar to configuring an IPv4 address.

As shown in Figure 3, the default gateway address configured for PC1 is 2001:DB8:ACAD:1::1, the global unicast address of the R1 GigabitEthernet interface on the same network.

Use the Syntax Checker in Figure 4 to configure the IPv6 global unicast address.

Just as with IPv4, configuring static addresses on clients does not scale to larger environments. For this reason, most network administrators in an IPv6 network will enable dynamic assignment of IPv6 addresses.

There are two ways in which a device can obtain an IPv6 global unicast address automatically:

- Stateless Address Autoconfiguration (SLAAC)
- DHCPv6

8.2.4.3   Dynamic Configuration of a Global Unicast Address using SLAAC

Stateless Address Autoconfiguration (SLAAC)

Stateless Address Autoconfiguration (SLAAC) is a method that allows a device to obtain its prefix, prefix length, and default gateway address information from an *IPv6 router* without the use of a DHCPv6 server. Using SLAAC, devices rely on the local router's ICMPv6 Router Advertisement (RA) messages to obtain the necessary information.

IPv6 routers periodically send out ICMPv6 Router Advertisement (RA) messages to all IPv6-enabled devices on the network. By default, Cisco routers send out RA messages every 200 seconds to the IPv6 all-nodes multicast group address. An IPv6 device on the network does not have to wait for these periodic RA messages. A device can send a Router Solicitation (RS) message to the router, using the IPv6 all-routers multicast group address. When an IPv6 router receives an RS message it will immediately respond with a router advertisement.

Even though an interface on a Cisco router can be configured with an IPv6 address, this does not make it an "IPv6 router". An IPv6 router is a router that:

■ Forwards IPv6 packets between networks

■ Can be configured with static IPv6 routes or a dynamic IPv6 routing protocol

■ Sends ICMPv6 RA messages

IPv6 routing is not enabled by default. To enable a router as an IPv6 router, the `ipv6 uni-cast-routing` global configuration command must be used.

Note   Cisco routers are enabled as IPv4 routers by default.

The ICMPv6 RA message contains the prefix, prefix length, and other information for the IPv6 device. The RA message also informs the IPv6 device how to obtain its addressing information. The RA message can contain one of the following three options, as shown in the figure:

■ **Option 1 - SLAAC Only** – The device should use the prefix, prefix-length, and default gateway address information contained in the RA message. No other information is available from a DHCPv6 server.

■ **Option 2 – SLAAC and DHCPv6** – The device should use the prefix, prefix-length, and default gateway address information in the RA message. There is other information available from a DHCPv6 server such as the DNS server address. The device will, through the normal process of discovering and querying a DHCPv6 server, obtain this additional information. This is known as stateless DHCPv6 because the DHCPv6 server does not need to allocate or keep track of any IPv6 address assignments, but only provide additional information such as the DNS server address.

■ **Option 3 – DHCPv6 only** – The device should not use the information in this RA message for its addressing information. Instead, the device will use the normal process of discovering and querying a DHCPv6 server to obtain all of its addressing information. This includes an IPv6 global unicast address, prefix length, a default gateway address, and the addresses of DNS servers. In this case, the DHCPv6 server is acting as a stateful DHCP server similar to DHCP for IPv4. The DHCPv6 server allocates and keeps track of IPv6 addresses so it does not assign the same IPv6 address to multiple devices.

Routers send ICMPv6 RA messages using the link-local address as the source IPv6 address. Devices using SLAAC use the router's link-local address as their default gateway address.

Refer to
Online Course
for Illustration

8.2.4.4   Dynamic Configuration of a Global Unicast Address using DHCPv6

DHCPv6

Dynamic Host Configuration Protocol for IPv6 (DHCPv6) is similar to DHCP for IPv4. A device can automatically receive its addressing information including a global unicast address, prefix length, default gateway address and the addresses of DNS servers using the services of a DHCPv6 server.

A device may receive all or some of its IPv6 addressing information from a DHCPv6 server depending upon whether option 2 (SLAAC and DHCPv6) or option 3 (DHCPv6 only) is specified in the ICMPv6 RA message. Additionally, the host OS may choose to ignore whatever is in the router's RA message and obtain its IPv6 address and other information directly from a DHCPv6 server.

Before deploying IPv6 devices in a network it is a good idea to first verify whether the host observes the options within the router's ICMPv6 RA message.

A device may obtain its IPv6 global unicast address dynamically and also be configured with multiple static IPv6 addresses on the same interface. IPv6 allows for multiple IPv6 addresses, belonging to the same IPv6 network, to be configured on the same interface.

A device may also be configured with more than one default gateway IPv6 address. For further information about how the decision is made regarding which address is used as a source IPv6 address or which default gateway address is used, refer to RFC 6724, Default Address Selection for IPv6.

The Interface ID

If the client does not use the information contained within the RA message and relies solely on DHCPv6, then the DHCPv6 server will provide the entire IPv6 global unicast address, including the prefix and the Interface ID.

However, if option 1 (SLAAC only) or option 2 (SLAAC with DHCPv6) is used, the client does not obtain the actual Interface ID portion of the address from this processes. The client device must determine its own 64-bit Interface ID, either by using the EUI-64 process or by generating a random 64-bit number.

Refer to
Online Course
for Illustration

8.2.4.5   EUI-64 Process or Randomly Generated

EUI-64 Process

IEEE defined the Extended Unique Identifier (EUI) or modified EUI-64 process. This process uses a client's 48-bit Ethernet MAC address, and inserts another 16 bits in the middle of the 48-bit MAC address to create a 64-bit Interface ID.

Ethernet MAC addresses are usually represented in hexadecimal and are made up of two parts:

- **Organizationally Unique Identifier (OUI)** – The OUI is a 24-bit (6 hexadecimal digits) vendor code assigned by IEEE.

- **Device Identifier** – The device identifier is a unique 24-bit (6 hexadecimal digits) value within a common OUI.

An EUI-64 Interface ID is represented in binary and is made up of three parts:

- 24-bit OUI from the client MAC address, but the 7th bit (the Universally/Locally (U/L) bit) is reversed. This means that if the 7th bit is a 0 it becomes a 1, and vice versa.

- The inserted 16-bit value FFFE (in hexadecimal)

- 24-bit Device Identifier from the client MAC address

The EUI-64 process is illustrated in Figure 1, using R1's GigabitEthernet MAC address of FC99:4775:CEE0.

Step 1. Divide the MAC address between the OUI and device identifier.

Step 2. Insert the hexadecimal value FFFE, which in binary is: 1111 1111 1111 1110.

Step 3. Convert the first 2 hexadecimal values of the OUI to binary and flip the U/L bit (bit 7). In this example the 0 in bit 7 is changed to a 1.

The result is an EUI-64 generated Interface ID of FE99:47FF:FE75:CEE0.

Note The use of the U/L bit and the reasons for reversing its value are discussed in RFC 5342.

The advantage of EUI-64 is the Ethernet MAC address can be used to determine the Interface ID. It also allows network administrators to easily track an IPv6 address to an end-device using the unique MAC address. However, this has caused privacy concerns among many users. They are concerned that their packets can be traced to the actual physical computer. Due to these concerns, a randomly generated Interface ID may be used instead.

Randomly Generated Interface IDs

Depending upon the operating system, a device may use a randomly generated Interface ID instead of using the MAC address and the EUI-64 process. For example, beginning with Windows Vista, Windows uses a randomly generated Interface ID instead of one created with EUI-64. Windows XP and previous Windows operating systems used EUI-64.

An easy way to identify that an address was more than likely created using EUI-64 is the FFFE located in the middle of the Interface ID, as shown in Figure 2.

After the Interface ID is established, either through the EUI-64 process or through random generation, it can be combined with an IPv6 prefix to create a global unicast address or a link-local address:

- **Global unicast address** – When using SLAAC, the device receives its prefix from the ICMPv6 RA and combines it with the Interface ID.

- **Link-local address** – A link-local prefix begins with FE80::/10. A device typically uses FE80::/64 as the prefix/prefix-length, followed by the Interface ID.

Refer to Online Course for Illustration

8.2.4.6 Dynamic Link-local Addresses

When using SLAAC (SLAAC only or SLAAC with DHCPV6), a device receives its prefix and prefix length from the ICMPv6 RA. Because the prefix of the address has been designated by the RA message, the device must provide only the Interface ID portion of its address. As stated previously, the Interface ID can be automatically generated using the EUI-64 process, or depending on the OS, randomly generated. Using the information from the RA message and the Interface ID, the device can establish its global unicast address.

After a global unicast address is assigned to an interface, the IPv6-enabled device will automatically generate its link-local address. IPv6-enabled devices must have, at a minimum, the link-local address. Recall that an IPv6 link-local address enables a device to communicate with other IPv6-enabled devices on the same subnet.

IPv6 link-local addresses are used for a variety of purposes including:

- A host uses the link-local address of the local router for its default gateway IPv6 address.

- Routers exchange dynamic routing protocol messages using link-local addresses.

- Routers' routing tables use the link-local address to identify the next-hop router when forwarding IPv6 packets.

A link-local address can be established dynamically or configured manually as a static link-local address.

Dynamically Assigned Link-Local Address

The link-local address is dynamically created using the FE80::/10 prefix and the Interface ID.

By default, Cisco IOS routers use EUI-64 to generate the Interface ID for all link-local address on IPv6 interfaces. For serial interfaces, the router will use the MAC address of an Ethernet interface. Recall that a link-local address must be unique only on that link or network. However, a drawback to using the dynamically assigned link-local address is its length, which makes it challenging to identify and remember assigned addresses.

Refer to **Online Course** for Illustration

8.2.4.7   Static Link-Local Addresses

Static Link-Local Address

Configuring the link-local address manually provides the ability to create an address that is recognizable and easier to remember.

Link-local addresses can be configured manually using the same interface command used to create IPv6 global unicast addresses but with an additional parameter:

```
Router(config-if)#ipv6 address link-local-address link-local
```

Figure 1 shows that a link-local address has a prefix within the range FE80 to FEBF. When an address begins with this hextet (16-bit segment) the link-local parameter must follow the address.

Figure 2 shows the configuration of a link-local address using the `ipv6 address interface` command. The link-local address FE80::1 is used to make it easily recognizable as belonging to router R1. The same IPv6 link-local address is configured on all of R1's interfaces. FE80::1 can be configured on each link because it only has to be unique on that link.

Similar to R1, router R2 would be configured with FE80::2 as the IPv6 link-local address on all of its interfaces

Refer to **Online Course** for Illustration

8.2.4.8   Verifying IPv6 Address Configuration

As shown in Figure 1, the command to verify the IPv6 interface configuration is similar to the command used for IPv4.

The `show interface` command displays the MAC address of the Ethernet interfaces. EUI-64 uses this MAC address to generate the Interface ID for the link-local address.

Additionally, the `show ipv6 interface brief` command displays abbreviated output for each of the interfaces. The [up/up] output on the same line as the interface indicates the Layer 1/Layer 2 interface state. This is the same as the Status and Protocol columns in the equivalent IPv4 command.

Notice that each interface has two IPv6 addresses. The second address for each interface is the global unicast address that was configured. The first address, the one that begins with FE80, is the link-local unicast address for the interface. Recall that the link-local address is automatically added to the interface when a global unicast address is assigned.

Also, notice that R1's Serial 0/0/0 link-local address is the same as its GigabitEthernet 0/0 interface. Serial interfaces do not have an Ethernet MAC addresses so Cisco IOS uses the MAC address of the first available Ethernet interface. This is possible because link-local interfaces only have to be unique on that link.

The link-local address of the router interface is typically the default gateway address for devices on that link or network.

As shown in Figure 2, the `show ipv6 route` command can be used to verify that IPv6 networks and specific IPv6 interface addresses have been installed in the IPv6 routing table. The `show ipv6 route` command will only display IPv6 networks, not IPv4 networks.

Within the route table, a C next to a route indicates that this is a directly connected network. When the router interface is configured with a global unicast address and is in the "up/up" state, the IPv6 prefix and prefix length is added to the IPv6 routing table as a connected route.

The IPv6 global unicast address configured on the interface is also installed in the routing table as a local route. The local route has a /128 prefix. Local routes are used by the routing table to efficiently process packets with a destination address of the router's interface address.

The `ping` command for IPv6 is identical to the command used with IPv4, except that an IPv6 address is used. As shown in Figure 3, the command is used to verify Layer 3 connectivity between R1 and PC1. When pinging a link-local address from a router, Cisco IOS will prompt the user for the exit interface. Because the destination link-local address can be on one or more of its links or networks, the router needs to know which interface to send the ping.

Use the Syntax Checker in Figure 4 to verify IPv6 address configuration.

Refer to
Online Course
for Illustration

8.2.5   IPv6 Multicast Addresses

8.2.5.1   Assigned IPv6 Multicast Addresses

IPv6 multicast addresses are similar to IPv4 multicast addresses. Recall that a multicast address is used to send a single packet to one or more destinations (multicast group). IPv6 multicast addresses have the prefix FF00::/8.

Note   Multicast addresses can only be destination addresses and not source addresses.

There are two types of IPv6 multicast addresses:

■ Assigned multicast

■ Solicited node multicast

Assigned Multicast

Assigned multicast addresses are reserved multicast addresses for predefined groups of devices. An assigned multicast address is a single address used to reach a group of devices running a common protocol or service. Assigned multicast addresses are used in context with specific protocols such as DHCPv6.

Two common IPv6 assigned multicast groups include:

■ **FF02::1 All-nodes multicast group** – This is a multicast group that all IPv6-enabled devices join. A packet sent to this group is received and processed by all IPv6 interfaces on the link or network. This has the same effect as a broadcast address in IPv4. The figure shows an example of communication using the all-nodes multicast address. An IPv6 router sends Internet Control Message Protocol version 6 (ICMPv6) RA messages to the all-node multicast group. The RA message informs all IPv6-enabled devices on the network about addressing information, such as the prefix, prefix length, and default gateway.

■ **FF02::2 All-routers multicast group** – This is a multicast group that all IPv6 routers join. A router becomes a member of this group when it is enabled as an IPv6 router with the `ipv6 unicast-routing` global configuration command. A packet sent to this group is received and processed by all IPv6 routers on the link or network.

IPv6-enabled devices send ICMPv6 Router Solicitation (RS) messages to the all-routers multicast address. The RS message requests an RA message from the IPv6 router to assist the device in its address configuration.

Refer to
Online Course
for Illustration

8.2.5.2   Solicited-Node IPv6 Multicast Addresses

A solicited-node multicast is similar to the all-nodes multicast address. Recall that the all-nodes multicast address is essentially the same thing as an IPv4 broadcast. All devices on the network must process traffic sent to the all-nodes address. To reduce the number of devices that must process traffic, use a solicited-node multicast address.

A solicited-node multicast address is an address that matches only the last 24 bits of the IPv6 global unicast address of a device. The only devices that need to process these packets are those devices that have these same 24 bits in the least significant, far right portion of their Interface ID.

An IPv6 solicited-node multicast address is automatically created when the global unicast or link-local unicast addresses are assigned. The IPv6 solicited-node multicast address is created by combining a special FF02:0:0:0:0:FF00::/104 prefix with the far right 24 bits of its unicast address.

The solicited-node multicast address consists of two parts:

■ **FF02:0:0:0:0:FF00::/104 multicast prefix** – This is the first 104 bits of the all solicited-node multicast address.

- **Least significant 24-bits** – These are the last or far right 24 bits of the solicited-node multicast address. These bits are copied from the far right 24 bits of the global unicast or link-local unicast address of the device.

It is possible that multiple devices will have the same solicited-node multicast address. Although rare, this can occur when devices have the same far right 24 bits in their Interface IDs. This does not create any problems because the device will still process the encapsulated message, which will include the complete IPv6 address of the device in question.

Refer to **Packet Tracer Activity** for this chapter

8.2.5.3   Packet Tracer - Configuring IPv6 Addressing

In this activity, you will practice configuring IPv6 addresses on a router, servers, and clients. You will also practice verifying your IPv6 addressing implementation.

Refer to **Lab Activity** for this chapter

8.2.5.4   Lab - Identifying IPv6 Addresses

In this lab, you will complete the following objectives:

- Part 1: Identify the Different Types of IPv6 Addresses
- Part 2: Examine a Host IPv6 Network Interface and Address
- Part 3: Practice IPv6 Address Abbreviation
- Part 4: Identify the Hierarchy of the IPv6 Global Unicast Address Network Prefix

Refer to **Lab Activity** for this chapter

8.2.5.5   Lab - Configuring IPv6 Addresses on Network Devices

In this lab, you will complete the following objectives:

- Part 1: Set Up Topology and Configure Basic Router and Switch Settings
- Part 2: Configure IPv6 Addresses Manually
- Part 3: Verify End-to-End Connectivity

Refer to **Online Course** for Illustration

8.3   Connectivity Verification

8.3.1   ICMP

8.3.1.1   ICMPv4 and ICMPv6 Messages

Although IP is not a reliable protocol, the TCP/IP suite does provide for messages to be sent in the event of certain errors. These messages are sent using the services of ICMP. The purpose of these messages is to provide feedback about issues related to the processing of IP packets under certain conditions, not to make IP reliable. ICMP messages are not required and are often not allowed within a network for security reasons.

ICMP is available for both IPv4 and IPv6. ICMPv4 is the messaging protocol for IPv4. ICMPv6 provides these same services for IPv6 but includes additional functionality. In this course, the term ICMP will be used when referring to both ICMPv4 and ICMPv6.

The types of ICMP messages, and the reasons why they are sent, are extensive. We will discuss some of the more common messages.

ICMP messages common to both ICMPv4 and ICMPv6 include:

- Host confirmation
- Destination or Service Unreachable
- Time exceeded
- Route redirection

Host Confirmation

An ICMP Echo Message can be used to determine if a host is operational. The local host sends an ICMP Echo Request to a host. If the host is available, the destination host responds with an Echo Reply. In the figure, click the Play button to see an animation the ICMP Echo Request/Echo Reply. This use of the ICMP Echo messages is the basis of the ping utility.

Destination or Service Unreachable

When a host or gateway receives a packet that it cannot deliver, it can use an ICMP Destination Unreachable message to notify the source that the destination or service is unreachable. The message will include a code that indicates why the packet could not be delivered.

Some of the Destination Unreachable codes for ICMPv4 are:

- 0 - net unreachable.
- 1 - host unreachable.
- 2 - protocol unreachable.
- 3 - port unreachable.

Note   ICMPv6 has similar but slightly different codes for Destination Unreachable messages.

Time Exceeded

An ICMPv4 Time Exceeded message is used by a router to indicate that a packet cannot be forwarded because the Time to Live (TTL) field of the packet was decremented to 0. If a router receives a packet and decrements the TTL field in the IPv4 packet to zero, it discards the packet and sends a Time Exceeded message to the source host.

ICMPv6 also sends a Time Exceeded message if the router cannot forward an IPv6 packet because the packet has expired. IPv6 does not have a TTL field; it uses the hop limit field to determine if the packet has expired.

Route Redirection

A router may use the ICMP Redirect Message to notify the hosts on a network that a better route is available for a particular destination. This message may only be used when the source host is on the same physical network as both gateways.

Both ICMPv4 and ICMPv6 use route redirection messages.

Refer to
Online Course
for Illustration

8.3.1.2 ICMPv6 Router Solicitation and Router Advertisement Messages

The informational and error messages found in ICMPv6 are very similar to the control and error messages implemented by ICMPv4. However, ICMPv6 has new features and improved functionality not found in ICMPv4.

ICMPv6 includes four new protocols as part of the Neighbor Discovery Protocol (ND or NDP):

- Router Solicitation message

- Router Advertisement message

- Neighbor Solicitation message

- Neighbor Advertisement message

Router Solicitation and Router Advertisement Messages

IPv6-enabled devices can be divided into two categories, routers and hosts. Router Solicitation and Router Advertisement messages are sent between hosts and routers.

- **Router Solicitation (RS) message:** When a host is configured to obtain its addressing information automatically using Stateless Address Autoconfiguration (SLAAC), the host will send an RS message to the router. The RS message is sent as an IPv6 all-routers multicast message.

- **Router Advertisement (RA) message:** RA messages are sent by routers to provide addressing information to hosts using SLAAC. The RA message can include addressing information for the host such as the prefix and prefix length. A router will send an RA message periodically or in response to an RS message. By default, Cisco routers send RA messages every 200 seconds. RA messages are sent to the IPv6 all-nodes multicast address. A host using SLAAC will set its default gateway to the link-local address of the router that sent the RA.

Refer to
Online Course
for Illustration

8.3.1.3 ICMPv6 Neighbor Solicitation and Neighbor Advertisement Messages

ICMPv6 Neighbor Discovery Protocol includes two additional message types, Neighbor Solicitation (NS) and Neighbor Advertisement (NA) messages.

Neighbor Solicitation and Neighbor Advertisement messages are used for:

- Address resolution

- Duplicate Address Detection (DAD)

Address Resolution

Address resolution is used when a device on the LAN knows the IPv6 unicast address of a destination but does not know its Ethernet MAC address. To determine the MAC address for the destination, the device will send an NS message to the solicited node address. The message will include the known (targeted) IPv6 address. The device that has the targeted IPv6 address will respond with a NA message containing its Ethernet MAC address.

Duplicate Address Detection

When a device is assigned a global unicast or link-local unicast address, it is recommended DAD is performed on the address to ensure that it is unique. To check the uniqueness of an address, the device will send a NS message with its own IPv6 address as the targeted IPv6 address. If another device on the network has this address it will respond with a NA message. This NA message will notify the sending device that the address is in use. If a corresponding NA message is not returned within a certain period of time, the unicast address is unique and acceptable for use.

Note DAD is not required, but RFC 4861 recommends that DAD is performed on unicast addresses.

Refer to **Online Course** for Illustration

8.3.2 Testing and Verification

8.3.2.1 Ping - Testing the Local Stack

Ping is a testing utility that uses ICMP echo request and echo reply messages to test connectivity between hosts. Ping works with both IPv4 and IPv6 hosts.

To test connectivity to another host on a network, an echo request is sent to the host address using the `ping` command. If the host at the specified address receives the echo request, it responds with an echo reply. As each echo reply is received, ping provides feedback on the time between when the request was sent and when the reply was received. This can be a measure of network performance.

Ping has a timeout value for the reply. If a reply is not received within the timeout, ping provides a message indicating that a response was not received. This usually indicates that there is a problem, but could also indicate that security features blocking ping messages have been enabled on the network.

After all the requests are sent, the ping utility provides a summary that includes the success rate and average round-trip time to the destination.

Pinging the Local Loopback

There are some special testing and verification cases for which we can use ping. One case is for testing the internal configuration of IPv4 or IPv6 on the local host. To perform this test, we ping the local loopback address of 127.0.0.1 for IPv4 (::1 for IPv6). Testing the IPv4 loopback is shown in the figure.

A response from 127.0.0.1 for IPv4, or ::1 for IPv6, indicates that IP is properly installed on the host. This response comes from the network layer. This response is not, however, an indication that the addresses, masks, or gateways are properly configured. Nor does it indicate anything about the status of the lower layer of the network stack. This simply tests IP down through the network layer of IP. If we get an error message, it is an indication that TCP/IP is not operational on the host.

Refer to **Online Course** for Illustration

8.3.2.2 Ping - Testing Connectivity to the Local LAN

You can also use ping to test the ability of a host to communicate on the local network. This is generally done by pinging the IP address of the gateway of the host. A ping to the gateway indicates that the host and the router interface serving as the gateway are both operational on the local network.

For this test, the gateway address is most often used, because the router is normally always operational. If the gateway address does not respond, a ping can be sent to the IP address of another host on the local network that is known to be operational.

If either the gateway or another host responds, then the local host can successfully communicate over the local network. If the gateway does not respond but another host does, this could indicate a problem with the router interface serving as the gateway.

One possibility is that the wrong gateway address has been configured on the host. Another possibility is that the router interface may be fully operational but have security applied to it that prevents it from processing or responding to ping requests.

Refer to
Online Course
for Illustration

8.3.2.3   Ping - Testing Connectivity to Remote

Ping can also be used to test the ability of a local host to communicate across an internetwork. The local host can ping an operational IPv4 host of a remote network, as shown in the figure.

If this ping is successful, the operation of a large piece of the internetwork can be verified. A successful ping across the internetwork confirms communication on the local network, the operation of the router serving as our gateway, and the operation of all other routers that might be in the path between the local network and the network of the remote host.

Additionally, functionality of the remote host can be verified. If the remote host could not communicate outside of its local network, it would not have responded.

Note   Many network administrators limit or prohibit the entry of ICMP messages into the corporate network; therefore, the lack of a ping response could be due to security restrictions.

Refer to
Online Course
for Illustration

8.3.2.4   Traceroute - Testing the Path

Ping is used to test connectivity between two hosts, but doesn't provide information about the details of devices between the hosts. Traceroute (tracert) is a utility generates a list of hops that were successfully reached along the path. This list can provide important verification and troubleshooting information. If the data reaches the destination, then the trace lists the interface of every router in the path between the hosts. If the data fails at some hop along the way, the address of the last router that responded to the trace can provide an indication of where the problem or security restrictions are found.

Round Trip Time (RTT)

Using traceroute provides round trip time for each hop along the path and indicates if a hop fails to respond. The round trip time is the time a packet takes to reach the remote host and for the response from the host to return. An asterisk (*) is used to indicate a lost or unreplied packet.

This information can be used to locate a problematic router in the path. If the display shows high response times or data losses from a particular hop, this is an indication that the resources of the router or its connections may be stressed.

IPv4 Time-to-Live (TTL) and IPv6 Hop Limit

Traceroute makes use of a function of the TTL field in IPv4 and the Hop Limit field in IPv6 in the Layer 3 headers, along with the ICMP time exceeded message.

Play the animation in the figure to see how Traceroute takes advantage of TTL.

The first sequence of messages sent from traceroute will have a TTL field value of 1. This causes the TTL to time out the IPv4 packet at the first router. This router then responds with an ICMPv4 message. Traceroute now has the address of the first hop.

Traceroute then progressively increments the TTL field (2, 3, 4...) for each sequence of messages. This provides the trace with the address of each hop as the packets timeout further down the path. The TTL field continues to be increased until the destination is reached or it is incremented to a predefined maximum.

Once the final destination is reached, the host responds with either an ICMP port unreachable message or an ICMP echo reply message instead of the ICMP time exceeded message.

Refer to **Packet Tracer Activity** for this chapter

8.3.2.5 Packet Tracer - Verifying IPv4 and IPv6 Addressing

IPv4 and IPv6 can coexist on the same network. From the command prompt of a PC there are some differences in the way commands are issued and in the way output is displayed.

Refer to **Packet Tracer Activity** for this chapter

8.3.2.6 Packet Tracer - Pinging and Tracing to Test the Path

There are connectivity issues in this activity. In addition to gathering and documenting information about the network, you will locate the problems and implement acceptable solutions to restore connectivity.

Refer to **Lab Activity** for this chapter

8.3.2.7 Lab - Testing Network Connectivity with Ping and Traceroute

In this lab, you will complete the following objectives:

- Part 1: Build and Configure the Network
- Part 2: Use Ping Command for Basic Network Testing
- Part 3: Use Tracert and Traceroute Commands for Basic Network Testing
- Part 4: Troubleshoot the Topology

Refer to **Packet Tracer Activity** for this chapter

8.3.2.8 Packet Tracer - Troubleshooting IPv4 and IPv6 Addressing

You are a network technician working for a company that has decided to migrate from IPv4 to IPv6. In the interim, they must support both protocols (dual stack). Three co-workers have called the help desk with problems and have received limited assistance. The help desk has escalated the matter to you, a Level 2 support technician.

Refer to
Online Course
for Illustration

8.4 Summary

Refer to
Lab Activity
for this chapter

8.4.1.1 Class Activity - The Internet of Everything...Naturally!

The Internet of Everything...Naturally!

In this chapter, you learned about how small to medium-sized businesses are connected to networks in groups. The Internet of Everything was also introduced in the beginning modeling activity.

For this activity, choose one of the following:

■ Online banking

■ World news

■ Weather forecasting/climate

■ Traffic conditions

Devise an IPv6 addressing scheme for the area you chose. Include in your addressing scheme how you would plan for:

■ Subnetting

■ Unicasts

■ Multicasts

■ Broadcasts

Keep a copy of your scheme to share with the class or learning community. Be prepared to explain:

■ How subnetting, unicasts, multicasts and broadcasts would be incorporated.

■ Where your addressing scheme could be used.

■ How small to medium-size businesses would be impacted by using your plan.

Refer to **Packet
Tracer Activity**
for this chapter

8.4.1.2 Packet Tracer – Skills Integration Challenge

Your company has won a contract to set up a small network for a restaurant owner. There are two restaurants near each other, and they all share one connection. The equipment and cabling is installed and the network administrator has designed the implementation plan. You job is implement the rest of the addressing scheme according to the abbreviated Addressing Table and verify connectivity.

Refer to
Online Course
for Illustration

8.4.1.3 Summary

IP addresses are hierarchical with network, subnetwork, and host portions. An IP address can represent a complete network, a specific host, or the broadcast address of the network.

Understanding binary notation is important when determining if two hosts are in the same network. The bits within the network portion of the IP address must be identical for all devices that reside in the same network. The subnet mask or prefix is used to determine the network portion of an IP address. IP addresses can be assigned either statically or dynamically. DHCP enables the automatic assignment of addressing information such as IP address, subnet mask, default gateway, and other configuration information.

IPv4 hosts can communicate one of three different ways: unicast, broadcast, and multicast. Also, blocks of addresses that are used in networks that require limited or no Internet access are called private addresses. The private IPv4 address blocks are: 10.0.0.0/8, 172.16.0.0/12, and 192.168.0.0/16.

The depletion of IPv4 address space is the motivating factor for moving to IPv6. Each IPv6 address has 128 bits verses the 32 bits in an IPv4 address. IPv6 does not use the dotted-decimal subnet mask notation. The prefix length is used to indicate the network portion of an IPv6 address using the following format: IPv6 address/prefix length.

There are three types of IPv6 addresses: unicast, multicast, and anycast. An IPv6 link-local address enables a device to communicate with other IPv6-enabled devices on the same link and only on that link (subnet). Packets with a source or destination link-local address cannot be routed beyond the link from where the packet originated. IPv6 link-local addresses are in the FE80::/10 range.

ICMP is available for both IPv4 and IPv6. ICMPv4 is the messaging protocol for IPv4. ICMPv6 provides the same services for IPv6 but includes additional functionality.

After it is implemented, an IP network needs to be tested to verify its connectivity and operational performance.

Go to the online course to take the quiz and exam.

Chapter 8 Quiz

This quiz is designed to provide an additional opportunity to practice the skills and knowledge presented in the chapter and to prepare for the chapter exam. You will be allowed multiple attempts and the grade does not appear in the gradebook.

Chapter 8 Exam

The chapter exam assesses your knowledge of the chapter content.

Your Chapter Notes

Subnetting IP Networks

9.0 Subnetting IP Networks

9.0.1.1 Introduction

Designing, implementing and managing an effective IP addressing plan ensures that networks can operate effectively and efficiently. This is especially true as the number of host connections to a network increases. Understanding the hierarchical structure of the IP address and how to modify that hierarchy in order to more efficiently meet routing requirements is an important part of planning an IP addressing scheme.

In the original IPv4 address, there are two levels of hierarchy: a network and a host. These two levels of addressing allow for basic network groupings that facilitate in routing packets to a destination network. A router forwards packets based on the network portion of an IP address; once the network is located, the host portion of the address allows for identification of the destination device.

However, as networks grow, with many organizations adding hundreds, and even thousands of hosts to their network, the two-level hierarchy is insufficient.

Subdividing a network adds a level to the network hierarchy, creating, in essence, three levels: a network, a subnetwork, and a host. Introducing an additional level to the hierarchy creates additional sub-groups within an IP network that facilities faster packet delivery and added filtration, by helping to minimize 'local' traffic.

This chapter examines, in detail, the creation and assignment of IP network and subnetwork addresses through the use of the subnet mask.

9.0.1.2 Class Activity - Call Me!

Call me!

Refer to **Lab Activity** for this chapter

In this chapter, you will be learning how devices can be grouped into subnets, or smaller network groups, from a large network.

In this modeling activity, you are asked to think about a number you probably use every day, a number such as your telephone number. As you complete the activity, think about how your telephone number compares to strategies that network administrators might use to identify hosts for efficient data communication.

Complete the two questions listed below and record your answers. Save the two sections in either hard- or soft-copy format to use later for class discussion purposes.

- Explain how your smartphone or landline telephone number is divided into identifying groups of numbers. Does your telephone number use an area code? An ISP identifier? A city, state, or country code?

■ In what ways does separating your telephone number into managed parts assist in contacting or communicating with others?

Refer to
Online Course
for Illustration

9.1 Subnetting an IPv4 Network

9.1.1 Network Segmentation

9.1.1.1 Reasons for Subnetting

In early network implementations, it was common for organizations to have all computers and other networked devices connected to a single IP network. All devices in the organization were assigned an IP address with a matching network ID. This type of configuration is known as a flat network design. In a small network, with a limited number of devices, a flat network design is not problematic. However, as the network grows, this type of configuration can create major issues.

Consider how on an Ethernet LAN, devices use broadcasts to locate needed services and devices. Recall that a broadcast is sent to all hosts on an IP network. The Dynamic Host Configuration Protocol (DHCP) is an example of a network service that depends on broadcasts. Devices send broadcasts across the network to locate the DHCP server. On a large network, this could create a significant amount of traffic slowing network operations. Additionally, because a broadcast is addressed to all devices, all devices must accept and process the traffic, resulting in increased device processing requirements. If a device must process a significant amount of broadcasts, it could even slow device operations. For reasons such as these, larger networks must be segmented into smaller sub-networks, keeping them localized to smaller groups of devices and services.

The process of segmenting a network, by dividing it into multiple smaller network spaces, is called subnetting. These sub-networks are called subnets. Network administrators can group devices and services into subnets that are determined by geographic location (perhaps the 3rd floor of a building), by organizational unit (perhaps the sales department), by device type (printers, servers, WAN), or any other division that makes sense for the network. Subnetting can reduce overall network traffic and improve network performance.

Note A subnet is equivalent to a network and these terms can be used interchangeably. Most networks are a subnet of some larger address block.

Refer to
Online Course
for Illustration

9.1.1.2 Communication Between Subnets

A router is necessary for devices on different networks to communicate. Devices on a network use the router interface attached to their LAN as their default gateway. Traffic that is destined for a device on a remote network will be processed by the router and forwarded toward the destination. To determine if traffic is local or remote, the router uses the subnet mask.

In a subnetted network space, this works exactly the same way. As shown in the figure, subnetting creates multiple logical networks from a single address block or network address. Each subnet is treated as a separate network space. Devices on the same subnet must use an address, subnet mask, and default gateway that correlates to the subnet that they are a part of.

Traffic cannot be forwarded between subnets without the use of a router. Every interface on the router must have an IPv4 host address that belongs to the network or subnet to which the router interface is connected.

Refer to
Online Course
for Illustration

9.1.2   IP Subnetting is FUNdamental

9.1.2.1   The Plan

As shown in the figure, planning network subnets requires examination of both the needs of an organization's network usage, and how the subnets will be structured. Doing a network requirement study is the starting point. This means looking at the entire network and determining the main sections of the network and how they will be segmented. The address plan includes deciding the needs for each subnet in terms of size, how many hosts per subnet, how host addresses will be assigned, which hosts will require static IP addresses and which hosts can use DHCP for obtaining their addressing information.

The size of the subnet involves planning the number of hosts that will require IP host addresses in each subnet of the subdivided private network. For example in a campus network design you might consider how many hosts are needed in the Administrative LAN, how many in the Faculty LAN and how many in the Student LAN. In a home network, a consideration might be done by the number of hosts in the Main House LAN and the number of hosts in the Home Office LAN.

As discussed earlier, the private IP address range used on a LAN is the choice of the network administrator and needs careful consideration to be sure that enough host address will be available for the currently known hosts and for future expansion. Remember the private IP address ranges are:

- 10.0.0.0 with a subnet mask of 255.0.0.0
- 172.16.0.0 with a subnet mask of 255.240.0.0
- 192.168.0.0 with a subnet mask of 255.255.0.0

Knowing your IP address requirements will determine the range or ranges of host addresses you implement. Subnetting the selected private IP address space will provide the host addresses to cover your network needs.

Public addresses used to connect to the Internet are typically allocated from a service provider. So while the same principles for subnetting would apply, this is not generally the responsibility of the organization's network administrator.

Refer to
Online Course
for Illustration

9.1.2.2   The Plan – Address Assignment

Create standards for IP address assignments within each subnet range. For example:

- Printers and servers will be assigned static IP addresses
- User will receive IP addresses from DHCP servers using /24 subnets
- Routers are assigned the first available host addresses in the range

Two very important factors that will lead to the determination of which private address block is required, are the number of subnets required and the maximum number of hosts needed per subnet. Each of these address blocks will allow you to appropriately allocate hosts based on the given size of a network and its required hosts currently and in the near future. Your IP space requirements will determine the range or ranges of hosts you implement.

In the upcoming examples you will see subnetting based on address blocks that have subnet masks of 255.0.0.0, 255.255.0.0, and 255.255.255.0.

> Refer to
> **Online Course**
> for Illustration

9.1.3   Subnetting an IPv4 Network

9.1.3.1   Basic Subnetting

Every network address has a valid range of host addresses. All devices attached to the same network will have an IPv4 host address for that network and a common subnet mask or network prefix.

The prefix and the subnet mask are different ways of representing the same thing - the network portion of an address.

IPv4 subnets are created by using one or more of the host bits as network bits. This is done by extending the mask to borrow some of the bits from the host portion of the address to create additional network bits. The more host bits borrowed, the more subnets that can be defined. For each bit borrowed, the number of subnetworks available is doubled. For example, if 1 bit is borrowed, 2 subnets can be created. If 2 bits, 4 subnets are created, if 3 bits are borrowed, 8 subnets are created, and so on. However, with each bit borrowed, fewer host addresses are available per subnet.

Bits can only be borrowed from the host portion of the address. The network portion of the address is allocated by the service provider and cannot be changed.

Note   In the examples in the figures, only the last octet is shown in binary because only bits from the host portion can be borrowed.

As shown in Figure 1, the 192.168.1.0/24 network has 24 bits in the network portion and 8 bits in the host portion, which is indicated with the subnet mask 255.255.255.0 or /24 notation. With no subnetting, this network supports a single LAN interface. If an additional LAN is needed, the network would need to be subnetted.

In Figure 2, 1 bit is borrowed from the most significant bit (leftmost bit) in the host portion, thus extending the network portion to 25 bits. This creates 2 subnets identified by using a 0 in the borrowed bit for the first network and a 1 in the borrowed bit for the second network. The subnet mask for both networks uses a 1 in the borrowed bit position to indicate that this bit is now part of the network portion.

As shown in Figure 3, when we convert the binary octet to decimal we see that the first subnet address is 192.168.1.0 and the second subnet address is 192.168.1.128. Because a bit has been borrowed, the subnet mask for each subnet is 255.255.255.128 or /25.

Refer to
Online Course
for Illustration

9.1.3.2   Subnets in Use

In the previous example, the 192.168.1.0/24 network was subnetted to create two subnets:

192.168.1.0/25

192.168.1.128/25

In Figure 1, notice that router R1 has two LAN segments attached to its GigabitEthernet interfaces. The subnets will be used for the segments attached to these interfaces. To serve as the gateway for devices on the LAN, each of the router interfaces must be assigned an IP address within the range of valid addresses for the assigned subnet. It is common practice to use the first or last available address in a network range for the router interface address.

The first subnet, 192.168.1.0/25, is used for the network attached to GigabitEthernet 0/0 and the second subnet, 192.168.1.128/25, is used for the network attached to GigabitEthernet 0/1. To assign an IP address for each of these interfaces, it is necessary to determine the range of valid IP addresses for each subnet.

The following are guidelines for each of the subnets:

- **Network address** - All 0 bits in the host portion of the address.

- **First host address** - All 0 bits plus a right-most 1 bit in the host portion of the address.

- **Last host address** - All 1 bits plus a right-most 0 bit in the host portion of the address.

- **Broadcast address** - All 1 bits in the host portion of the address.

As shown in Figure 2, the first host address for the 192.168.1.0/25 network is 192.168.1.1, and the last host address is 192.168.1.126. Figure 3 shows that the first host address for the 192.168.1.128/25 network is 192.168.1.129, and the last host address is 192.168.1.254.

To assign the first host address in each subnet to the router interface for that subnet, use the `ip address` command in interface configuration mode as shown in Figure 4. Notice that each subnet uses the subnet mask of 255.255.255.128 to indicate that the network portion of the address is 25 bits.

A host configuration for the 192.168.1.128/25 network is shown in Figure 5. Notice that the gateway IP address is the address configured on the G0/1 interface of R1, 192.168.1.129, and the subnet mask is 255.255.255.128.

Refer to
Online Course
for Illustration

9.1.3.3   Subnetting Formulas

Calculating Subnets

Use this formula to calculate the number of subnets:

2^n (where n = the number of bits borrowed)

As shown in Figure 1, for the 192.168.1.0/25 example, the calculation looks like this:

$2^1 = 2$ subnets

Calculating Hosts

Use this formula to calculate the number of hosts per network:

2^n (where n = the number of bits remaining in the host field)

As shown in Figure 2, for the 192.168.1.0/25 example, the calculation looks like this:

2^7 = 128

Because hosts cannot use the network address or broadcast address from a subnet, 2 of these addresses are not valid for host assignment. This means that each of the subnets has 126 (128-2) valid host addresses.

So in this example, borrowing 1 host bit toward the network results in creating 2 subnets, and each subnet can have a total of 126 hosts assigned.

9.1.3.4   Creating 4 Subnets

Consider an internetwork that requires three subnets.

Using the same 192.168.1.0/24 address block, host bits must be borrowed to create at least 3 subnets. Borrowing a single bit would only provide 2 subnets. To provide more networks, more host bits must be borrowed. Calculate the number of subnets created if 2 bits are borrowed using the formula 2^number of bits borrowed:

2^2 = 4 subnets

Borrowing 2 bits creates 4 subnets, as shown in Figure 1.

Recall that the subnet mask must change to reflect the borrowed bits. In this example, when 2 bits are borrowed, the mask is extended 2 bits into the last octet. In decimal, the mask is represented as 255.255.255.192, because the last octet is 1100 0000 in binary.

Host Calculation

To calculate the number of hosts, examine the last octet. After borrowing 2 bits for the subnet, there are 6 host bits remaining.

Apply the host calculation formula as shown in Figure 2.

2^6 = 64

But remember that all 0 bits in the host portion of the address is the network address, and all 1s in the host portion is a broadcast address. Therefore, there are only 62 host addresses that are actually available for each subnet.

As shown in Figure 3, the first host address for the first subnet is 192.168.1.1 and the last host address is 192.168.1.62. Figure 4 shows the ranges for subnets 0 - 2. Remember that each host must have a valid IP address within the range defined for that network segment. The subnet assigned to the router interface will determine which segment a host belongs to.

In Figure 5 a sample configuration is shown. In this configuration, the first network is assigned to the GigabitEthernet 0/0 interface, the second network is assigned to the GigabitEthernet 0/1 interface, and the third network is assigned to the Serial 0/0/0 network.

Again, using a common addressing plan, the first host address in the subnet is assigned to the router interface. Hosts on each subnet will use the address of the router interface as the default gateway address.

- PC1 (192.168.1.2/26) will use 192.168.1.1 (G0/0 interface address of R1) as its default gateway address

- PC2 (192.168.1.66/26) will use 192.168.1.65 (G0/1 interface address of R1) as its default gateway address

Note   All devices on the same subnet will have a host IPv4 address from the range of host addresses and will use the same subnet mask.

Refer to
Online Course
for Illustration

9.1.3.5   Creating 8 Subnets

Next, consider an internetwork that requires five subnets as shown in Figure 1.

Using the same 192.168.1.0/24 address block, host bits must be borrowed to create at least 5 subnets. Borrowing 3 bits would only provide 4 subnets as seen in the previous example. To provide more networks, more host bits must be borrowed. Calculate the number of subnets created if 3 bits are borrowed using the formula:

$2^3 = 8$ subnets

As shown in Figures 2 and 3, borrowing 3 bits creates 8 subnets. When 3 bits are borrowed, the subnet mask is extended 3 bits into the last octet (/27), resulting in a subnet mask of 255.255.255.224. All devices on these subnets will use the subnet mask 255.255.255.224 mask (/27).

Host Calculation

To calculate the number of hosts, examine the last octet. After borrowing 3 bits for the subnet, there are 5 host bits remaining.

Apply the host calculation formula:

$2^5 = 32$, but subtract 2 for the all 0s in the host portion (network address) and all 1s in the host portion (broadcast address).

The subnets are assigned to the network segments required for the topology as shown in Figure 4.

Again, using a common addressing plan, the first host address in the subnet is assigned to the router interface, as shown in Figure 5. Hosts on each subnet will use the address of the router interface as the default gateway address.

- PC1 (192.168.1.2/27) will use 192.168.1.1 address as its default gateway address.

- PC2 (192.168.1.34/27) will use 192.168.1.33 address as its default gateway address.

- PC3 (192.168.1.98/27) will use 192.168.1.97 address as its default gateway address.

- PC4 (192.168.1.130/27) will use 192.168.1.129 address as its default gateway address.

Refer to
Interactive Graphic
in online course.

9.1.3.6   Activity - Determining the Network Address - Basic

Refer to
Interactive Graphic
in online course.

9.1.3.7   Activity - Calculate the Number of Hosts - Basic

Refer to
Interactive Graphic
in online course.

9.1.3.8   Activity - Determining the Valid Addresses for Hosts - Basics

Refer to
Interactive Graphic
in online course.

9.1.3.9   Activity - Calculate the Subnet Mask

Refer to
Online Course
for Illustration

9.1.3.10   Creating 100 Subnets with a /16 prefix

In the previous examples, we considered an internetwork that required 3 subnets and one that required 5 subnets. To achieve the goal of creating four subnets we borrowed 2 bits from the 8 hosts bits available with an IP address that has a default mask of 255.255.255.0, or a /24 prefix. The resulting subnet mask was 255.255.255.192, and a total of 4 possible subnets were created. Applying the host calculation formula of 2^6-2, we determined that on each one of those 4 subnets we could have 62 host addresses to assign to nodes.

To acquire 5 subnets, we borrowed 3 bits from the 8 hosts bits available with an IP address that has a default mask of 255.255.255.0, or a /24 prefix. In borrowing those 3 bits from the host portion of the address, we left 5 hosts bits remaining. The resulting subnet mask was 255.255.255.224, with a total of 8 subnets create, and 30 host addresses per subnet.

Consider large organizations or campuses with an internetwork that requires 100 subnets. Just as in the previous examples, to achieve the goal of creating 100 subnets, we must borrow bits from the host portion of the IP address of the existing internetwork. As before, to calculate the number of subnets, we must look at the number of available host bits and use the subnet calculation formula 2^number of bits borrowed minus 2. Using the IP address of the last example, 192.168.10.0/24, we have 8 host bits; to create 100 subnets, we must borrow 7 bits.

Calculate the number of subnets if 7 bits are borrowed: 2^7=128 subnets.

However, borrowing 7 bits will leave just one remaining host bit and if we apply the host calculation formula, the result would be no hosts on these subnets. Calculate the number of hosts if one bit is remaining: 2^1=2, then subtract 2 for the network address and the network broadcast; the result 0 hosts (2^1-2=0).

In a situation requiring a larger number of subnets, an IP network is required that has more hosts bits to borrow from, such as an IP address with a default subnet mask of /16, or 255.255.0.0. Addresses that have a range of 128 - 191 in the first octet have a default mask of 255.255.0.0, or /16. Addresses in this range have 16 bits in the network portion and 16 bits in the host portion. These 16 bits are the bits that are available to borrow for creating subnets.

Using a new IP address of 172.16.0.0/16 address block, host bits must be borrowed to create at least 100 subnets. Starting from left to right with the first available host bit, we will borrow a single bit at a time until we reach the number of bits necessary to create 100 subnets. Borrowing 1 bit, we would create 2 subnets, borrowing 2 bits, we would create 4 subnets, 3 bits 8 subnets, and so on. Calculate the number of subnets created if 7 bits are borrowed using the formula 2^number of bits borrowed:

2^7 = 128 subnets

Borrowing 7 bits creates 128 subnets, as shown in the figure.

Recall that the subnet mask must change to reflect the borrowed bits. In this example, when 7 bits are borrowed, the mask is extended 7 bits into the third octet. In decimal, the mask is represented as 255.255.254.0, or a /23 prefix, because the third octet is 11111110 in binary and the fourth octet is 00000000 in binary. Subnetting will be done in the third octet, with the host bits in the third and fourth octets.

Refer to
Online Course
for Illustration

9.1.3.11 Calculating the Hosts

Host Calculation

To calculate the number of hosts, examine the third and fourth octet. After borrowing 7 bits for the subnet, there is one host bit remaining in the third octet and there are 8 host bits remaining in the fourth octet.

Apply the host calculation formula as shown in Figure 1.

$2^9 = 512$

But remember that all 0 bits in the host portion of the address is the network address, and all 1s in the host portion is a broadcast address. Therefore, there are only 510 host addresses that are actually available for each subnet.

As showing in Figure 2, the first host address for the first subnet is 172.16.0.1 and the last host address is 172.16.1.254. Remember that each host must have a valid IP address within the range defined for that network segment. The subnet assigned to the router interface will determine which segment a host belongs to.

Reminder:

Bits can only be borrowed from the host portion of the address. The network portion of the address is allocated by the service provider and cannot be changed. So organizations that required a significant number of subnets were required to communicate this need to their ISP so that the ISP would allocate an IP address with a default mask with enough bits to create the needed subnets.

Refer to
Online Course
for Illustration

9.1.3.12 Calculating the Hosts

There are some organizations, such as small service providers, that might need even more subnets than 100. Take for example, an organization that requires 1000 subnets. As always, in order to create subnets we must borrow bits from the host portion of the IP address of the existing internetwork. As before, to calculate the number of subnets it is necessary to look at the number of available hosts bits. A situation such as this requires that the IP address assigned by the ISP have enough host bits available to calculate 1000 subnets. IP addresses that have the range of 1-126 in the first octet have a default mask of 255.0.0.0 or /8. This means there are 8 bits in the network portion and 24 host bits available to borrow toward subnetting.

Using the 10.0.0.0/8 address block, host bits must be borrowed to create at least 1000 subnets. Starting from left to the right with the first available host bit we will borrow a single bit at a time until we reach the number of bits necessary to create 1000 subnets. Calculate the number of subnets created if 10 bits are borrowed using the formula 2^number of bits borrowed:

$2^{10} = 1024$ subnets

Borrowing 10 bits creates 1024 subnets, as shown in Figure 1.

Recall that the subnet mask must change to reflect the borrowed bits. In this example, when 10 bits are borrowed, the mask is extended 10 bits into the third octet. In decimal, the mask is represented as 255.255.192.0 or a /18 prefix, because the third octet of the subnet mask is 11000000 in binary and the fourth octet is 00000000 in binary. Subnetting will be done in the third octet, but don't forget about the host bits in the third and fourth octets.

Host Calculation

To calculate the number of hosts, examine the third and fourth octet. After borrowing 10 bits for the subnet, there are 6 host bits remaining in the third octet and 8 host bits remaining in the fourth octet. A total of 14 host bits remain.

Apply the host calculation formula as shown in Figure 2.

$2^{14} - 2 = 16382$

The first host address for the first subnet is 10.0.0.1 and the last host address is 10.0.63.254. Remember that each host must have a valid IP address within the range defined for that network segment. The subnet assigned to the router interface will determine which segment a host belongs to.

Note: All devices on the same subnet will have a host IPv4 address from the range of host addresses and will use the same subnet mask.

Refer to
Interactive Graphic
in online course.

9.1.3.13   Activity - Determining the Network Address - Advanced

Refer to
Interactive Graphic
in online course.

9.1.3.14   Activity - Calculating the Number of Hosts - Advanced

Refer to
Interactive Graphic
in online course.

9.1.3.15   Activity - Determining the Valid Addresses for Hosts - Advanced

Refer to
Online Course
for Illustration

9.1.4   Determining the Subnet Mask

9.1.4.1   Subnetting Based on Host Requirements

The decision about how many host bits to borrow to create subnets is an important planning decision. There are two considerations when planning subnets: the number of host addresses required for each network and the number of individual subnets needed. The animation shows the subnet possibilities for the 192.168.1.0 network. The selection of a number of bits for the subnet ID affects both the number of possible subnets and the number of host addresses in each subnet.

Notice that there is an inverse relationship between the number of subnets and the number of hosts. The more bits borrowed to create subnets the fewer host bits are available; therefore, fewer hosts per subnet. If more host addresses are needed, more host bits are required, resulting in fewer subnets.

Number of Hosts

When borrowing bits to create multiple subnets, you leave enough host bits for the largest subnet. The number of host addresses required in the largest subnet will determine how many bits must be left in the host portion. The formula 2^n (where n is the number the number of host bits remaining) is used to calculate how many addresses will be available on each subnet. Recall that 2 of the addresses cannot be used, so that the usable number of addresses can be calculated as 2^n-2.

Refer to
Online Course
for Illustration

9.1.4.2   Subnetting Network-Based Requirements

Sometimes a certain number of subnets is required, with less emphasis on the number of host addresses per subnet. This may be the case if an organization chooses to separate their network traffic based on internal structure or department setup. For example, an organization may choose to put all host devices used by employees in the Engineering department in one network, and all host devices used by management in a separate network. In this case, the number of subnets is most important in determining how many bits to borrow.

Recall the number of subnets created when bits are borrowed can be calculated using the formula 2^n (where n is the number of bits borrowed). There is no need to subtract any of the resulting subnets, as they are all usable.

The key is to balance the number of subnets needed and the number of hosts required for the largest subnet. The more bits borrowed to create additional subnets means fewer hosts available per subnet.

Refer to
Online Course
for Illustration

9.1.4.3   Subnetting to Meet Network Requirements

Every network within an organization is designed to accommodate a finite number of hosts. Basic subnetting requires enough subnets to accommodate the networks while also providing enough host addresses per subnet.

Some networks, such as point-to-point WAN links, require only two hosts. Other networks, such as a user LAN in a large building or department, may need to accommodate hundreds of hosts. Network administrators must devise the internetwork addressing scheme to accommodate the maximum number of hosts for each network. The number of hosts in each division should allow for growth in the number of hosts.

Determine the Total Number of Hosts

First, consider the total number of hosts required by the entire corporate internetwork. A block of addresses large enough to accommodate all devices in all the corporate networks must be used. These devices include end user devices, servers, intermediate devices, and router interfaces.

Consider the example of a corporate internetwork that must accommodate a total of 800 hosts in its five locations (see Figure 1). In this example, the service provider has allocated a network address of 172.16.0.0/22 (10 host bits). As shown in Figure 2, this will provide 1,022 host addresses, which will more than accommodate the addressing needs for this internetwork.

Refer to
Online Course
for Illustration

9.1.4.4   Subnetting To Meet Network Requirements, Cont.

Determine the Number and Size of the Networks

Next, consider the number of subnets required and the number of host addresses needed on each subnet. Based on the network topology consisting of 5 LAN segments and 4 internetwork connections between routers, 9 subnets are required. The largest subnet requires 40 hosts. When designing an addressing scheme, you should anticipate growth in both the number of subnets and the hosts per subnet.

The 172.16.0.0/22 network address has 10 host bits. Because the largest subnet requires 40 hosts, a minimum of 6 host bits should be borrowed. This is determined by using this formula: $2^6 - 2 = 62$ hosts. The 4 remaining host bits can be used to allocate subnets. Using the formula for determining subnets, this results in 16 subnets: $2^4 = 16$. Because the example internetwork requires 9 subnets this will meet the requirement and allow for some additional growth.

When 4 bits are borrowed the new prefix length is /26 with a subnet mask of 255.255.255.192.

As shown in Figure 1, using the /26 prefix length, the 16 subnet addresses can be determined. Only the subnet portion of the address is incremented. The original 22 bits of the network address cannot change and the host portion will contain all 0 bits.

Note   Notice that because the subnet portion is in both the third and fourth octets that one or both of these values will vary in the subnet addresses.

As shown in Figure 2, the original 172.16.0.0/22 network was a single network with 10 host bits providing 1,022 usable addresses to assign to hosts. By borrowing 4 host bits, 16 subnets (0000 through 1111) can be created. Each subnet has 6 host bits or 62 usable host addresses per subnet.

As shown in Figure 3, the subnets can be assigned to the LAN segments and router-to-router connections.

Refer to
Interactive Graphic
in online course.

9.1.4.5   Activity - Determining the Number of Bits to Borrow

Refer to **Packet Tracer Activity**
for this chapter

9.1.4.6   Packet Tracer - Subnetting Scenario 1

In this activity, you are given the network address of 192.168.100.0/24 to subnet and provide the IP addressing for the network shown in the topology. Each LAN in the network requires enough space for, at least, 25 addresses for end devices, the switch and the router. The connection between R1 to R2 will require an IP address for each end of the link.

Refer to **Packet Tracer Activity**
for this chapter

9.1.4.7   Packet Tracer - Subnetting Scenario 2

In this activity, you are given the network address of 172.31.1.0/24 to subnet and provide the IP addressing for the network shown in the topology. The required host addresses for each WAN and LAN link are labeled in the topology.

Refer to
Lab Activity
for this chapter

9.1.4.8   Lab - Calculating IPv4 Subnets

In this lab, you will complete the following objectives:

- Part 1: Determine IPv4 Address Subnetting
- Part 2: Calculate IPv4 Address Subnetting

Refer to
Lab Activity
for this chapter

9.1.4.9   Lab - Subnetting Network Topologies

In this lab, you will complete the following objectives:

Parts 1 to 5, for each network topology:

- Determine the number of subnets.

- Design an appropriate addressing scheme.

- Assign addresses and subnet mask pairs to device interfaces.

- Examine the use of the available network address space and future growth potential.

Refer to
Lab Activity
for this chapter

9.1.4.10   Lab - Researching Subnet Calculators

In this lab, you will complete the following objectives:

- Part 1: Review Available Subnet Calculators.

- Part 2: Perform Network Calculations Using a Subnet Calculator.

Refer to
Online Course
for Illustration

9.1.5   Benefits of Variable Length Subnet Masking

9.1.5.1   Traditional Subnetting Wastes Addresses

Using traditional subnetting, the same number of addresses is allocated for each subnet. If all the subnets have the same requirements for the number of hosts, these fixed size address blocks would be efficient. However, most often that is not the case.

For example, the topology shown in Figure 1 requires seven subnets, one for each of the four LANs and one for each of the three WAN connections between routers. Using traditional subnetting with the given address of 192.168.20.0/24, 3 bits can be borrowed from the host portion in the last octet to meet the subnet requirement of seven subnets. As shown in Figure 2, borrowing 3 bits creates 8 subnets and leaves 5 host bits with 30 usable hosts per subnet. This scheme creates the needed subnets and meets the host requirement of the largest LAN.

Although this traditional subnetting meets the needs of the largest LAN and divides the address space into an adequate number of subnets, it results in significant waste of unused addresses.

For example, only two addresses are needed in each subnet for the three WAN links. Because each subnet has 30 usable addresses, there are 28 unused addresses in each of these subnets. As shown in Figure 3, this results in 84 unused addresses (28x3).

Further, this limits future growth by reducing the total number of subnets available. This inefficient use of addresses is characteristic of traditional subnetting of classful networks.

Applying a traditional subnetting scheme to this scenario is not very efficient and is wasteful. In fact, this example is a good model for showing how subnetting a subnet can be used to maximize address utilization.

Subnetting a subnet, or using Variable Length Subnet Mask (VLSM), was designed to avoid wasting addresses.

Refer to
Online Course
for Illustration

9.1.5.2   Variable Length Subnet Masks (VLSM)

In all of the previous examples of subnetting, notice that the same subnet mask was applied for all the subnets. This means that each subnet has the same number of available host addresses.

As illustrated in Figure 1, traditional subnetting creates subnets of equal size. Each subnet in a traditional scheme uses the same subnet mask. As shown in Figure 2, VLSM allows a network space to be divided in unequal parts. With VLSM the subnet mask will vary depending on how many bits have been borrowed for a particular subnet, thus the "variable" part of the VLSM.

VLSM subnetting is similar to traditional subnetting in that bits are borrowed to create subnets. The formulas to calculate the number of hosts per subnet and the number of subnets created still apply. The difference is that subnetting is not a single pass activity. With VLSM, the network is first subnetted, and then the subnets are subnetted again. This process can be repeated multiple times to create subnets of various sizes.

Refer to
Online Course
for Illustration

9.1.5.3   Basic VLSM

To better understand the VLSM process, go back to the previous example.

In the previous example, shown in Figure 1, the network 192.168.20.0/24 was subnetted into eight equal sized subnets; seven of the eight subnets were allocated. Four subnets were used for the LANs and three subnets for the WAN connections between the routers. Recall that the wasted address space was in the subnets used for the WAN connections, because those subnets required only two usable addresses: one for each router interface. To avoid this waste, VLSM can be used to create smaller subnets for the WAN connections.

To create smaller subnets for the WAN links, one of the subnets will be divided. In Figure 2, the last subnet, 192.168.20.224/27, will be further subnetted.

Recall that when the number of needed host addresses is known, the formula 2^n-2 (where n equals the number of host bits remaining) can be used. To provide two usable addresses, 2 host bits must be left in the host portion.

$2^2 - 2 = 2$

Because there are 5 host bits in the 192.168.20.224/27 address space, 3 bits can be borrowed, leaving 2 bits in the host portion.

The calculations at this point are exactly the same as those used for traditional subnetting. The bits are borrowed and the subnet ranges are determined.

As shown in Figure 2, this VLSM subnetting scheme reduces the number addresses per subnet to a size appropriate for the WANs. Subnetting subnet 7 for WANs, allows subnets 4, 5, and 6 to be available for future networks, as well as several other subnets available for WANs.

Refer to
Online Course
for Illustration

9.1.5.4   VLSM in Practice

Using the VLSM subnets, the LAN and WAN segments can be addressed without unnecessary waste.

The hosts in each of the LANs will be assigned a valid host address with the range for that subnet and /27 mask. Each of the four routers will have a LAN interface with a /27 subnet and a one or more serial interfaces with a /30 subnet.

Using a common addressing scheme, the first host IPv4 address for each subnet is assigned to the LAN interface of the router. The WAN interfaces of the routers are assigned the IP addresses and mask for the /30 subnets.

Figures 1 - 4 show the interface configuration for each of the routers.

Hosts on each subnet will have a host IPv4 address from the range of host addresses for that subnet and an appropriate mask. Hosts will use the address of the attached router LAN interface as the default gateway address.

- Building A Hosts (192.168.20.0/27) will use router 192.168.20.1 address as the default gateway address.

- Building B Hosts (192.168.20.32/27) will use router 192.168.20.33 address as the default gateway address.

- Building C Hosts (192.168.20.64/27) will use router 192.168.20.65 address as the default gateway address.

- Building D Hosts (192.168.20.96/27) will use router 192.168.20.97 address as the default gateway address.

Refer to
Online Course
for Illustration

9.1.5.5   VLSM Chart

Address planning can also be accomplished using a variety of tools. One method is to use a VLSM chart to identify which blocks of addresses are available for use and which ones are already assigned. This method helps to prevent assigning addresses that have already been allocated. Using the network from the previous example, the VLSM chart can be used to plan address assignment.

Examining the /27 Subnets

As shown in Figure 1, when using traditional subnetting the first seven address blocks were allocated for LANs and WANs. Recall that this scheme resulted in 8 subnets with 30 usable addresses each (/27). While this scheme worked for the LAN segments, there were many wasted addresses in the WAN segments.

When designing the addressing scheme on a new network, the address blocks can be assigned in a way that minimizes waste and keeps unused blocks of addresses contiguous.

Assigning VLSM Address Blocks

As shown in Figure 2, in order to use the address space more efficiently, /30 subnets are created for WAN links. To keep the unused blocks of addresses together, the last /27 subnet was further subnetted to create the /30 subnets. The first 3 subnets were assigned to WAN links.

- .224 /30 host address range 225 to 226: WAN link between R1 and R2
- .228 /30 host address range 229 to 230: WAN link between R2 and R3
- .232 /30 host address range 233 to 234: WAN link between R3 and R4
- .236 /30 host address range 237 to 238: Available to be used
- .240 /30 host address range 241 to 242: Available to be used
- .244 /30 host address range 245 to 246: Available to be used
- .248 /30 host address range 249 to 250: Available to be used
- .252 /30 host address range 253 to 254: Available to be used

Designing the addressing scheme in this way leaves 3 unused /27 subnets and 5 unused /30 subnets.

Refer to
Interactive Graphic
in online course.

9.1.5.6   Activity - Practicing VLSM

Refer to
Online Course
for Illustration

9.2   Addressing Schemes

9.2.1   Structured Design

9.2.1.1   Planning to Address the Network

As shown in the figure, the allocation of network layer address space within the corporate network needs to be well designed. Address assignment should not be random. There are three primary considerations when planning address allocation.

- **Preventing Duplication of Addresses** - Each host in an internetwork must have a unique address. Without the proper planning and documentation, an address could be assigned to more than one host, resulting in access issues for both hosts.

- **Providing and Controlling Access** - Some hosts, such as servers, provide resources to internal hosts as well as to external hosts. The Layer 3 address assigned to a server can be used to control access to that server. If, however, the address is randomly assigned and not well documented, controlling access is more difficult.

- **Monitoring Security and Performance** - Similarly, the security and performance of network hosts and the network as a whole must be monitored. As part of the monitoring process, network traffic is examined for addresses that are generating or receiving excessive packets. If there is proper planning and documentation of the network addressing, problematic network devices can be easily found.

Assigning Addresses within a Network

Within a network, there are different types of devices, including:

- End user clients
- Servers and peripherals
- Hosts that are accessible from the Internet
- Intermediary devices
- Gateway

When developing an IP addressing scheme, it is generally recommended to have a set pattern of how addresses are allocated to each type of device. This benefits administrators when adding and removing devices, filtering traffic based on IP, as well as simplifies documentation.

Refer to
Online Course
for Illustration

9.2.1.2   Assigning Addresses to Devices

A network addressing plan might include using a different range of addresses within each subnet, for each type of device.

Addresses for Clients

Because of the challenges associated with static address management, end user devices often have addresses dynamically assigned, using Dynamic Host Configuration Protocol (DHCP). DHCP is generally the preferred method of assigning IP addresses to hosts on large networks because it reduces the burden on network support staff and virtually eliminates entry errors.

Another benefit of DHCP is that an address is not permanently assigned to a host but is only leased for a period of time. If we need to change the subnetting scheme of our network, we do not have to statically reassign individual host addresses. With DHCP, we only need to reconfigure the DHCP server with the new subnet information. After this has been done, the hosts only need to automatically renew their IP addresses.

Addresses for Servers and Peripherals

Any network resource, such as a server or a printer, should have a static IP address, as shown in the figure. The client hosts access these resources using the IP addresses of these devices. Therefore, predictable addresses for each these servers and peripherals are necessary.

Servers and peripherals are a concentration point for network traffic. There are many packets sent to and from the IPv4 addresses of these devices. When monitoring network traffic with a tool like Wireshark, a network administrator should be able to rapidly identify these devices. Using a consistent numbering system for these devices makes the identification easier.

Addresses for Hosts that are Accessible from Internet

In most internetworks, only a few devices are accessible by hosts outside of the corporation. For the most part, these devices are usually servers of some type. As with all devices in a network that provide network resources, the IP addresses for these devices should be static.

In the case of servers accessible by the Internet, each of these must have a public space address associated with it. Additionally, variations in the address of one of these devices will make this device inaccessible from the Internet. In many cases, these devices are on a network that is numbered using private addresses. This means that the router or firewall at the perimeter of the network must be configured to translate the internal address of the server into a public address. Because of this additional configuration in the perimeter intermediary device, it is even more important that these devices have a predictable address.

Addresses for Intermediary Devices

Intermediary devices are also a concentration point for network traffic. Almost all traffic within or between networks passes through some form of intermediary device. Therefore, these network devices provide an opportune location for network management, monitoring, and security.

Most intermediary devices are assigned Layer 3 addresses, either for the device management or for their operation. Devices, such as hubs, switches, and wireless access points do not require IPv4 addresses to operate as intermediary devices. However, if we must access these devices as hosts to configure, monitor, or troubleshoot network operation, they must have addresses assigned.

Because we must know how to communicate with intermediary devices, they should have predictable addresses. Therefore, their addresses are typically assigned manually.

Additionally, the addresses of these devices should be in a different range within the network block than user device addresses.

Address for the Gateway (Routers and Firewalls)

Unlike the other intermediary devices mentioned, routers and firewall devices have an IP address assigned to each interface. Each interface is in a different network and serves as the gateway for the hosts in that network. Typically, the router interface uses either the lowest or highest address in the network. This assignment should be uniform across all networks in the corporation so that network personnel will always know the gateway of the network no matter which network they are working on.

Router and firewall interfaces are the concentration point for traffic entering and leaving the network. Because the hosts in each network use a router or firewall device interface as the gateway out of the network, many packets flow through these interfaces. Therefore, these devices can play a major role in network security by filtering packets based on source and/or destination IP addresses. Grouping the different types of devices into logical addressing groups makes the assignment and operation of this packet filtering more efficient.

Refer to
Lab Activity
for this chapter

9.2.1.3   Lab - Designing and Implementing a Subnetted IPv4 Addressing Scheme

In this lab, you will complete the following objectives:

- Part 1: Design a Network Subnetting Scheme
- Part 2: Configure the Devices
- Part 3: Test and Troubleshoot the Network

Refer to
Lab Activity
for this chapter

9.2.1.4   Lab - Designing and Implementing a VLSM Addressing Scheme

In this lab, you will complete the following objectives:

- Part 1: Examine Network Requirements
- Part 2: Design the VLSM Address Scheme
- Part 3: Cable and Configure the IPv4 Network

Refer to **Packet Tracer Activity**
for this chapter

9.2.1.5   Packet Tracer - Designing and Implementing a VLSM Addressing Scheme

In this activity, you are given a network address to develop a VLSM addressing scheme for the network shown in the included topology.

9.3 Design Considerations for IPv6

9.3.1 Subnetting an IPv6 Network

9.3.1.1 Subnetting Using the Subnet ID

IPv6 subnetting requires a different approach than IPv4 subnetting. The primary reason is that with IPv6 there are so many addresses, that the reason for subnetting is completely different. An IPv6 address space is not subnetted to conserve addresses; rather, it is subnetted to support hierarchical, logical design of the network. While IPv4 subnetting is about managing address scarcity, IPv6 subnetting is about building an addressing hierarchy based on the number of routers and the networks they support.

Recall that an IPv6 address block with a /48 prefix has 16 bits for subnet ID, as shown in Figure 1. Subnetting using the 16 bit subnet ID yields a possible 65,536 /64 subnets and does not require borrowing any bits from the interface ID, or host portion of the address. Each IPv6 /64 subnet contains roughly eighteen quintillion addresses, obviously more than will ever be needed in one IP network segment.

Subnets created from the subnet ID are easy to represent because there is no conversion to binary required. To determine the next available subnet, just count up in hexadecimal. As shown in Figure 2, this means counting by hexadecimal in the subnet ID portion.

The global routing prefix is the same for all subnets. Only the subnet ID quartet is incremented for each subnet.

9.3.1.2 IPv6 Subnet Allocation

With over 65,000 subnets to choose from, the task of the network administrator becomes one of designing a logical scheme to address the network.

As shown in Figure 1, the example topology will require subnets for each LAN as well as for the WAN link between R1 and R2. Unlike the example for IPv4, with IPv6 the WAN link subnet will not be subnetted further. Although this may "waste" addresses, that is not a concern when using IPv6.

As shown in Figure 2, the allocation of 5 IPv6 subnets, with the subnet ID field 0001 through 0005 will be used for this example. Each /64 subnet will provide more addresses than will ever be needed.

As shown in Figure 3, each LAN segment and the WAN link is assigned a /64 subnet.

Similar to configuring IPv4, Figure 4 shows that each of the router interfaces has been configured to be on a different IPv6 subnet.

9.3.1.3 Subnetting into the Interface ID

Similar to borrowing bits from the host portion of an IPv4 address, with IPv6 bits can be borrowed from the interface ID to create additional IPv6 subnets. This is typically done for security reasons to create fewer hosts per subnet and not necessarily to create additional subnets.

When extending the subnet ID by borrowing bits from the interface ID, the best practice is to subnet on a nibble boundary. A nibble is 4 bits or one hexadecimal digit. As shown in the figure, the /64 subnet prefix is extended 4 bits or 1 nibble to /68. Doing this reduces the size of the interface ID by 4 bits, from 64 to 60 bits.

Subnetting on nibble boundaries means only using nibble aligned subnet masks. Starting at /64, the nibble aligned subnet masks are /68, /72, /76, /80, etc.

Subnetting on a nibble boundary creates subnets by using the additional hexadecimal value. In the example, the new subnet ID consists of the 5 hexadecimal values, ranging from 00000 through FFFFF.

It is possible to subnet within a nibble boundary, within a hexadecimal digit, but it is not recommended or even necessary. Subnetting within a nibble takes away the advantage easily determining the prefix from the interface ID. For example, if a /66 prefix length is used, the first two bits would be part of the subnet ID and the second two bits would be part of the interface ID.

Refer to **Packet Tracer Activity** for this chapter

9.3.1.4   Packet Tracer - Implementing a Subnetted IPv6 Addressing Scheme

Your network administrator wants you to assign five /64 IPv6 subnets to the network shown in the topology. Your job is to determine the IPv6 subnets, assign IPv6 addresses to the routers, and set the PCs to automatically receive IPv6 addressing. Your final step is to verify connectivity between IPv6 hosts.

Refer to **Online Course** for Illustration

9.4   Summary

Refer to **Lab Activity** for this chapter

9.4.1.1   Class Activity - Can you call me now?

Can you call me now?

Note   This activity may be completed individually or in small/large groups using Packet Tracer software.

You are setting up a dedicated, computer addressing scheme for patient rooms in a hospital. The switch will be centrally located in the nurses' station, as each of the five rooms will be wired so that patients can just connect to a RJ-45 port built into the wall of their room. Devise a physical and logical topology for only one of the six floors using the following addressing scheme requirements:

- There are six floors with five patient rooms on each floor for a total of thirty connections. Each room needs a network connection.
- Subnetting must be incorporated into your scheme.
- Use one router, one switch, and five host stations for addressing purposes.
- Validate that all PCs can connect to the hospital's in-house services.

Keep a copy of your scheme to share later with the class or learning community. Be prepared to explain how subnetting, unicasts, multicasts, and broadcasts would be incorporated, and where your addressing scheme could be used.

Refer to **Packet Tracer Activity** for this chapter

9.4.1.2   Packet Tracer - Skills Integration Challenge

As a network technician familiar with IPv4 and IPv6 addressing implementations, you are now ready to take an existing network infrastructure and apply your knowledge and skills to finalize the configuration. The network administrator has already configured some commands on the routers. **Do not to erase or modify those configurations**. Your task is to complete the IPv4 and IPv6 addressing scheme, implement IPv4 and IPv6 addressing, and verify connectivity.

Refer to **Online Course** for Illustration

9.4.1.3   Summary

As shown in the figure, the process of segmenting a network, by dividing it into to multiple smaller network spaces, is called subnetting.

Every network address has a valid range of host addresses. All devices attached to the same network will have an IPv4 host address for that network and a common subnet mask or network prefix. Traffic can be forwarded between hosts directly if they are on the same subnet. Traffic cannot be forwarded between subnets without the use of a router. To determine if traffic is local or remote, the router uses the subnet mask. The prefix and the subnet mask are different ways of representing the same thing - the network portion of an address.

IPv4 subnets are created by using one or more of the host bits as network bits. Two very important factors that will lead to the determination of the IP address block with the subnet mask, are the number of subnets required and the maximum number of hosts needed per subnet. There is an inverse relationship between the number of subnets and the number of hosts. The more bits borrowed to create subnets the fewer host bits are available; therefore fewer hosts per subnet.

The formula 2^n (where n is the number of host bits remaining) is used to calculate how many addresses will be available on each subnet. However, the network address and broadcast address within a range are not useable; therefore, to calculate the useable number of addresses the calculation 2^n-2 is required.

Subnetting a subnet, or using Variable Length Subnet Mask (VLSM) was designed to avoid wasting addresses.

IPv6 subnetting requires a different approach than IPv4 subnetting. An IPv6 address space is not subnetted to conserve addresses; rather it is subnetted to support hierarchical, logical design of the network. So, while IPv4 subnetting is about managing address scarcity, IPv6 subnetting is about building an addressing hierarchy based on the number of routers and the networks they support.

Careful planning is required to make best use of the available address space. Size, location, use, and access requirements are all considerations in the address planning process.

After it is implemented, an IP network needs to be tested to verify its connectivity and operational performance.

Go to the online
course to take the
quiz and exam.

Chapter 9 Quiz

This quiz is designed to provide an additional opportunity to practice the skills and knowledge presented in the chapter and to prepare for the chapter exam. You will be allowed multiple attempts and the grade does not appear in the gradebook.

Chapter 9 Exam

The chapter exam assesses your knowledge of the chapter content.

Your Chapter Notes

Application Layer

10.0 Application Layer

10.0.1.1 Introduction

We experience the Internet through the World Wide Web when streaming videos, playing online games, chatting with and emailing friends, and shopping for deals on web sites. Applications, such as the ones used to provide the services mentioned, provide the human interface to the underlying network. They enable us to send and receive data with relative ease. Typically we can access and use these applications without knowing how they work. However, for network professionals, it is important to know how an application is able to format, transmit and interpret messages that are sent and received across the network.

Visualizing the mechanisms that enable communication across the network is made easier if we use the layered framework of the OSI model.

In this chapter, we will explore the role of the application layer and how the applications, services, and protocols within the application layer make robust communication across data networks possible.

Refer to
Lab Activity
for this chapter

10.0.1.2 Class Activity - Application Investigation

What would happen if...

Your employer has decided to have IP telephones installed in your workplace resulting in the network being inoperable until next week.

Your work however, must continue. You have emails to send and quotes to write for your manager's approval. Because of possible security issues, you are not allowed to use personal or external computer systems, equipment, or off-site equipment and systems, to complete your corporate workload.

Your instructor may ask you to complete the questions from both scenarios below, or to choose one scenario (A. Emails, or B. Quote for Manager's Approval). Answer the questions fully for the scenario(s). Be prepared to discuss your answers in class.

A. Emails

- What method(s) can you use to send email communication?
- How could you send the same email to multiple recipients?
- How would you get a large attachment to multiple recipients, if necessary?
- Are these methods cost effective to your corporation?
- Do they violate any security policies of your corporation?

B. Quote for Manager's Approval

■ You have a desktop application software package installed on your computer. Will it be relatively easy to produce the quote your manager needs for the new contract due by the end of the week? What limitations will be experienced while trying to complete the quote?

■ How will you present the quote to your manager for approval? How do you think he or she will send the quote to the client for their approval?

■ Are these methods cost effective to your corporation? Justify your answer.

<table><tr><td>Refer to
Online Course
for Illustration</td></tr></table>

10.1   Application Layer Protocols

10.1.1   Application, Session and Presentation

10.1.1.1   OSI and TCP/IP Models Revisited

As shown in the figure, networking professionals use the OSI and TCP/IP models to communicate both verbally and in written technical documentation. As such, networking professional can use these models to describe the behavior of protocols and applications.

In the OSI model, data is passed from one layer to the next, starting at the application layer on the transmitting host, and proceeding down the hierarchy to the physical layer, and then passing over the communications channel to the destination host, where the data proceeds back up the hierarchy, ending at the application layer.

The application layer is the top layer of both the OSI and TCP/IP models. The TCP/IP application layer includes a number of protocols that provide specific functionality to a variety of end-user applications. The functionality of the TCP/IP application layer protocols fit roughly into the framework of the top three layers of the OSI model: application, presentation and session layers. The OSI model Layers 5, 6, and 7 are used as references for application software developers and vendors to produce products, such as web browsers that need to access networks.

<table><tr><td>Refer to
Online Course
for Illustration</td></tr></table>

10.1.1.2   Application Layer

The Application Layer

The application layer is closest to the end user. As shown in the figure, it is the layer that provides the interface between the applications we use to communicate and the underlying network over which our messages are transmitted. Application layer protocols are used to exchange data between programs running on the source and destination hosts. There are many application layer protocols and new protocols are always being developed. Some of the most widely known application layer protocols include Hypertext Transfer Protocol (HTTP), File Transfer Protocol (FTP), Trivial File Transfer Protocol (TFTP), Internet Message Access Protocol (IMAP), and Domain Name System (DNS) protocol.

Refer to
Online Course
for Illustration

10.1.1.3 Presentation and Session Layers

The Presentation Layer

The presentation layer has three primary functions:

- Formats, or presents, data from the source device into a compatible form for receipt by the destination device.

- Compression of the data in a way that can be decompressed by the destination device.

- Encryption of the data for transmission and the decryption of data upon receipt by the destination.

As shown in the figure, the presentation layer formats data for the application layer and it sets standards for file formats. Some well-known standards for video include QuickTime and Motion Picture Experts Group (MPEG). QuickTime is an Apple computer specification for video and audio, and MPEG is a standard for video and audio compression and coding.

Among the well-known graphic image formats that are used on networks are Graphics Interchange Format (GIF), Joint Photographic Experts Group (JPEG), and Portable Network Graphics (PNG) format. GIF and JPEG are compression and coding standards for graphic images. PNG was designed to address some of the limitations of the GIF format and to eventually replace it.

The Session Layer

As the name implies, functions at the session layer create and maintain dialogs between source and destination applications. The session layer handles the exchange of information to initiate dialogs, keep them active, and to restart sessions that are disrupted or idle for a long period of time.

Refer to
Online Course
for Illustration

10.1.1.4 TCP/IP Application Layer Protocols

While the OSI model separates the individual application, presentation, and session function, most widely known and implemented TCP/IP applications incorporate the functionality of all three layers.

The TCP/IP application protocols specify the format and control information necessary for many common Internet communication functions. Among these TCP/IP protocols are:

- **Domain Name System (DNS)** - This protocol resolves Internet names to IP addresses.

- **Telnet** - This is used to provide remote access to servers and networking devices.

- **Simple Mail Transfer Protocol (SMTP)** - This protocol transfers mail messages and attachments.

- **Dynamic Host Configuration Protocol (DHCP)** - A protocol used to assign an IP address, subnet mask, default gateway, and DNS server addresses to a host.

- **Hypertext Transfer Protocol (HTTP)** - This protocol transfers files that make up the web pages of the World Wide Web.

- **File Transfer Protocol (FTP)** - A protocol used for interactive file transfer between systems.

- **Trivial File Transfer Protocol (TFTP)** - This protocol is used for connectionless active file transfer.

- **Bootstrap Protocol (BOOTP)** - This protocol is a precursor to the DHCP protocol. BOOTP is a network protocol used to obtain IP address information during bootup.

- **Post Office Protocol (POP)** - A protocol used by email clients to retrieve email from a remote server.

- **Internet Message Access Protocol (IMAP)** - This is another protocol for email retrieval.

Application layer protocols are used by both the source and destination devices during a communication session. For the communications to be successful the application layer protocols implemented on the source and destination host must be compatible.

Refer to
Interactive Graphic
in online course.

10.1.1.5   Activity – Application Protocols and Standards

Refer to
Online Course
for Illustration

10.1.2   How Application Protocols Interact with End-User Applications

10.1.2.1   Peer-to-Peer Networks

When accessing information on a networking device, whether it is a PC, laptop, tablet, smartphone, or some other device connected to a network, the data may not be physically stored on the device. In this case, a request to access that information must be made to the device where the data resides. In the peer-to-peer (P2P) networking model, the data is accessed from a peer device without the use of a dedicated server.

The P2P network model involves two parts: P2P networks and P2P applications. Both parts have similar features, but in practice work quite differently.

P2P Networks

In a P2P network, two or more computers are connected via a network and can share resources (such as printers and files) without having a dedicated server. Every connected end device (known as a peer) can function as both a server and a client. One computer might assume the role of server for one transaction while simultaneously serving as a client for another. The roles of client and server are set on a per request basis.

An example is a simple home network with two computers, as shown in the figure. In this example, Peer2 has a printer attached to it directly by USB, and is setup to share the printer on the network so that Peer1 can print to it. Peer1 is set up to share a drive or folder on the network. This allows Peer2 to access and save files to the shared folder. In addition to sharing files, a network such as this one would allow users to enable networked games, or share an Internet connection.

P2P networks decentralize the resources on a network. Instead of locating data to be shared on dedicated servers, data can be located anywhere and on any connected device. Most of the current operating systems support file and print sharing without requiring additional server software. However, P2P networks do not use centralized user accounts or access servers to maintain permissions. Therefore, it is difficult to enforce security and access policies in networks containing more than just a few computers. User accounts and access rights must be set individually on each peer device.

Refer to
Online Course
for Illustration

10.1.2.2   Peer-to-Peer Applications

A peer-to-peer (P2P) application allows a device to act as both a client and a server within the same communication, as shown in the figure. In this model, every client is a server and every server a client. Both can initiate a communication and are considered equal in the communication process. However, P2P applications require that each end device provide a user interface and run a background service. When you launch a specific P2P application, it loads the required user interface and background services; afterward, the devices can communicate directly.

Some P2P applications use a hybrid system where resource sharing is decentralized, but the indexes that point to resource locations are stored in a centralized directory. In a hybrid system, each peer accesses an index server to get the location of a resource stored on another peer. The index server can also help connect two peers, but after connected, the communication takes place between the two peers without additional communication to the index server.

P2P applications can be used on P2P networks, client/server networks, and across the Internet.

Refer to
Online Course
for Illustration

10.1.2.3   Common P2P Applications

With P2P applications, each computer in the network running the application can act as a client or a server for the other computers in the network running the application. Common P2P applications include:

- eDonkey
- eMule
- Shareaza
- BitTorrent
- Bitcoin
- LionShare

Some P2P applications are based on the Gnutella protocol. They enable people to share files on their hard disks with others. As shown in the figure, Gnutella-compatible client software allows users to connect to Gnutella services over the Internet and to locate and access resources shared by other Gnutella peers. Many client applications are available for accessing the Gnutella network, including BearShare, Gnucleus, LimeWire, Morpheus, WinMX, and XoloX.

While the Gnutella Developer Forum maintains the basic protocol, application vendors often develop extensions to make the protocol work better with their application.

Many P2P applications do not use a central database to record all the files available on the peers. Instead, the devices on the network each tell the others what files are available when queried, and use the file sharing protocol and services to support locating resources.

Refer to
Lab Activity
for this chapter

10.1.2.4 Lab - Researching Peer-to-Peer File Sharing

In this lab, you will complete the following objectives:

- Part 1: Identify P2P Networks, File Sharing Protocols, and Applications

- Part 2: Research P2P File Sharing Issues

- Part 3: Research P2P Copyright Litigations

Refer to
Online Course
for Illustration

10.1.2.5 Client-Server Model

In the client-server model, the device requesting the information is called a client and the device responding to the request is called a server. Client and server processes are considered to be in the application layer. The client begins the exchange by requesting data from the server, which responds by sending one or more streams of data to the client. Application layer protocols describe the format of the requests and responses between clients and servers. In addition to the actual data transfer, this exchange may also require user authentication and the identification of a data file to be transferred.

One example of a client-server network is using an ISP's email service to send, receive and store email. The email client on a home computer issues a request to the ISP's email server for any unread mail. The server responds by sending the requested email to the client.

Although data is typically described as flowing from the server to the client, some data always flows from the client to the server. Data flow may be equal in both directions, or may even be greater in the direction going from the client to the server. For example, a client may transfer a file to the server for storage purposes. As shown in the figure, data transfer from a client to a server is referred to as an upload and data from a server to a client as a download.

Refer to
Online Course
for Illustration

10.2 Well-Known Application Layer Protocols and Services

10.2.1 Common Application Layer Protocols

10.2.1.1 Application Layer Protocols Revisited

There are dozens of application layer protocols, but on a typical day you probably use only five or six. Three application layer protocols that are involved in everyday work or play are:

- Hypertext Transfer Protocol (HTTP)

- Simple Mail Transfer Protocol (SMTP)

- Post Office Protocol (POP)

These application layer protocols make it possible to browse the web and send and receive email. HTTP is used to enable users to connect to web sites across the Internet. SMTP is used to enable users to send email. And POP is used to enable users to receive email.

The next few pages focus on these three application layer protocols.

Refer to
Online Course
for Illustration

10.2.1.2   Hypertext Transfer Protocol and Hypertext Markup Language

When a web address or uniform resource locator (URL) is typed into a web browser, the web browser establishes a connection to the web service running on the server using the HTTP protocol. URLs and Uniform Resource Identifier (URIs) are the names most people associate with web addresses.

The http://www.cisco.com/index.html URL is an example of a URL that refers to a specific resource; a web page named **index.html** on a server identified as **cisco.com**. Click each figure to see the steps used by HTTP.

Web browsers are the type of client application a computer uses to connect to the World Wide Web and access resources stored on a web server. As with most server processes, the web server runs as a background service and makes different types of files available.

To access the content, web clients make connections to the server and request the desired resources. The server replies with the resources and, upon receipt, the browser interprets the data and presents it to the user.

Browsers can interpret and present many data types (such as plain text or Hypertext Markup Language, the language in which web pages are constructed). Other types of data, however, may require another service or program, typically referred to as plug-ins or add-ons. To help the browser determine what type of file it is receiving, the server specifies what kind of data the file contains.

To better understand how the web browser and web client interact, we can examine how a web page is opened in a browser. For this example, use the http://www.cisco.com/index. html URL.

First, as shown in Figure 1, the browser interprets the three parts of the URL:

1. **http** (the protocol or scheme)

2. www.cisco.com (the server name)

3. **index.html** (the specific filename requested)

As shown in Figure 2, the browser then checks with a name server to convert www.cisco. com into a numeric address, which it uses to connect to the server. Using HTTP requirements, the browser sends a GET request to the server and asks for the **index.html** file. The server, as shown in Figure 3, sends the HTML code for this web page to the browser. Finally, as shown in Figure 4, the browser deciphers the HTML code and formats the page for the browser window.

Refer to
Online Course
for Illustration

10.2.1.3   HTTP and HTTPS

HTTP is used across the World Wide Web for data transfer and is one of the most used application protocols today. It was originally developed to simply publish and retrieve HTML pages; however the flexibility of HTTP has made it a vital application within distributed, collaborative information systems.

HTTP is a request/response protocol. When a client, typically a web browser, sends a request to a web server, HTTP specified the message types used for that communication. The three common message types are GET, POST, and PUT (see the figure).

GET is a client request for data. A client (web browser) sends the GET message to the web server to request HTML pages. When the server receives the GET request, it responds with a status line, such as HTTP/1.1 200 OK, and a message of its own. The message from the server may include the requested HTML file, if available, or it may contain an error or information message, such as "The location of the requested file has changed."

POST and PUT are used to upload data files to the web server. For example, when the user enters data into a form that is embedded within a web page (such as when completing an order request), the POST message is sent to the web server. Included within the POST message is the data that the user submitted in the form.

PUT uploads resources or content to the web server. For example, if a user attempts to upload a file or image to a website, a PUT message is sent from the client to the server with the attached file or image.

Although HTTP is remarkably flexible, it is not a secure protocol. The request messages send information to the server in plain text that can be intercepted and read. Similarly, the server responses, typically HTML pages, are also unencrypted.

For secure communication across the Internet, the HTTP Secure (HTTPS) protocol is used for accessing or posting web server information. HTTPS can use authentication and encryption to secure data as it travels between the client and server. HTTPS specifies additional rules for passing data between the application layer and the transport layer. HTTPS uses the same client request-server response process as HTTP, but the data stream is encrypted with Secure Socket Layer (SSL) before being transported across the network. HTTPS creates additional load and processing time on the server due to the encryption and decryption of traffic.

10.2.1.4   SMTP, POP, and IMAP

Refer to
Online Course
for Illustration

One of the primary services offered by an ISP is email hosting. Email has revolutionized how people communicate through its simplicity and speed. Yet to run on a computer or other end device, email requires several applications and services.

Email is a store-and-forward method of sending, storing, and retrieving electronic messages across a network. Email messages are stored in databases on mail servers. ISPs often maintain mail servers that support many different customer accounts.

Email clients communicate with mail servers to send and receive email. Mail servers communicate with other mail servers to transport messages from one domain to another. An email client does not communicate directly with another email client when sending email. Instead, both clients rely on the mail server to transport messages. This is true even when both users are in the same domain.

Email clients send messages to the email server configured in the application settings. When the server receives the message, it checks to see if the recipient domain is located on its local database. If it is not, it sends a DNS request to determine the IP address of the mail server for the destination domain. The email is then forwarded to the appropriate server.

Email supports three separate protocols for operation: Simple Mail Transfer Protocol (SMTP), Post Office Protocol (POP), and Internet Message Access Protocol (IMAP). The application layer process that sends mail, uses SMTP. This is the case if sending from a client to a server, as well as when sending from one server to another.

A client retrieves email, however, using one of two application layer protocols: POP or IMAP.

Refer to
Online Course
for Illustration

10.2.1.5   SMTP, POP, and IMAP (cont.)

Simple Mail Transfer Protocol (SMTP) transfers mail reliably and efficiently. For SMTP applications to work properly, the mail message must be formatted properly and SMTP processes must be running on both the client and server.

SMTP message formats require a message header and a message body. While the message body can contain any amount of text, the message header must have a properly formatted recipient email address and a sender address. Any other header information is optional.

When a client sends email, the client SMTP process connects with a server SMTP process on well-known port 25. After the connection is made, the client attempts to send the email to the server across the connection. When the server receives the message, it either places the message in a local account, if the recipient is local, or forwards the message using the same SMTP connection process to another mail server for delivery.

The destination email server may not be online or may be busy when email messages are sent. Therefore, SMTP spools messages to be sent at a later time. Periodically, the server checks the queue for messages and attempts to send them again. If the message is still not delivered after a predetermined expiration time, it is returned to the sender as undeliverable.

Refer to
Online Course
for Illustration

10.2.1.6   SMTP, POP, and IMAP (cont.)

Post Office Protocol (POP) enables a workstation to retrieve mail from a mail server. With POP, mail is downloaded from the server to the client and then deleted on the server.

The server starts the POP service by passively listening on TCP port 110 for client connection requests. When a client wants to make use of the service, it sends a request to establish a TCP connection with the server. When the connection is established, the POP server sends a greeting. The client and POP server then exchange commands and responses until the connection is closed or aborted.

Because email messages are downloaded to the client and removed from the server, there is not a centralized location where email messages are kept. Because POP does not store messages, it is undesirable for a small business that needs a centralized backup solution.

POP3 is desirable for an ISP, because it alleviates their responsibility for managing large amounts of storage for their email servers

Refer to
Online Course
for Illustration

10.2.1.7   SMTP, POP, and IMAP (cont.)

Internet Message Access Protocol (IMAP) is another protocol that describes a method to retrieve email messages. However, unlike POP, when the user connects to an IMAP-capable server, copies of the messages are downloaded to the client application. The original messages are kept on the server until manually deleted. Users view copies of the messages in their email client software.

Users can create a file hierarchy on the server to organize and store mail. That file structure is duplicated on the email client as well. When a user decides to delete a message, the server synchronizes that action and deletes the message from the server.

For small- to medium-sized businesses, there are many advantages to using IMAP. IMAP can provide long-term storage of email messages on mail servers and allows for centralized backup. It also enables employees to access email messages from multiple locations, using different devices or client software. The mailbox folder structure that a user expects to see is available for viewing regardless of how the user accesses the mailbox.

For an ISP, IMAP may not be the protocol of choice. It can be expensive to purchase and maintain the disk space to support the large number of stored emails. Additionally, if customers expect their mailboxes to be backed up routinely, that can further increase the costs to the ISP.

Refer to **Packet Tracer Activity** for this chapter

10.2.1.8   Packet Tracer - Web and Email

In this activity, you will configure HTTP and email services using the simulated server in Packet Tracer. You will then configure clients to access the HTTP and email services.

Refer to **Online Course** for Illustration

10.2.2   Providing IP Addressing Services

10.2.2.1   Domain Name Service

In data networks, devices are labeled with numeric IP addresses to send and receive data over networks. Most people cannot remember this numeric address. Domain names were created to convert the numeric address into a simple, recognizable name.

On the Internet, these domain names, such as http://www.cisco.com, are much easier for people to remember than 198.133.219.25, which is the actual numeric address for this server. If Cisco decides to change the numeric address of www.cisco.com, it is transparent to the user, because the domain name remains the same. The new address is simply linked to the existing domain name and connectivity is maintained. When networks were small, it was a simple task to maintain the mapping between domain names and the addresses they represented. As networks have grown and the number of devices increased, this manual system became unworkable.

The Domain Name System (DNS) was created for domain name to address resolution for these networks. DNS uses a distributed set of servers to resolve the names associated with these numbered addresses. Click the buttons in the figure to see the steps to resolve DNS addresses.

The DNS protocol defines an automated service that matches resource names with the required numeric network address. It includes the format for queries, responses, and data. The DNS protocol communications use a single format called a message. This message format is used for all types of client queries and server responses, error messages, and the transfer of resource record information between servers.

Figures 1 through 5 display the steps involved in DNS resolution.

Refer to **Online Course** for Illustration

10.2.2.2   DNS Message Format

A DNS server provides the name resolution using the *Berkeley Internet Name Domain* (BIND), or the name daemon, which is often called named (pronounced name-dee). BIND was originally developed by four students at the University of California Berkley in the early 1980s. As shown in the figure, the DNS message format used by BIND is the most widely used DNS format on the Internet.

The DNS server stores different types of resource records used to resolve names. These records contain the name, address, and type of record.

Some of these record types are:

- **A** - An end device address

- **NS** - An authoritative name server

- **CNAME** - The canonical name (or Fully Qualified Domain Name) for an alias; used when multiple services have the single network address, but each service has its own entry in DNS

- **MX** - Mail exchange record; maps a domain name to a list of mail exchange servers for that domain

When a client makes a query, the server's BIND process first looks at its own records to resolve the name. If it is unable to resolve the name using its stored records, it contacts other servers to resolve the name.

The request may be passed along to a number of servers, which can take extra time and consume bandwidth. After a match is found and returned to the original requesting server, the server temporarily stores the numbered address that matches the name in cache memory.

If that same name is requested again, the first server can return the address by using the value stored in its name cache. Caching reduces both the DNS query data network traffic and the workloads of servers higher up the hierarchy. The DNS Client service on Windows PCs optimizes the performance of DNS name resolution by also storing previously resolved names in memory. The **ipconfig /displaydns** command displays all of the cached DNS entries on a Windows computer system.

Refer to
Online Course
for Illustration

10.2.2.3   DNS Hierarchy

The DNS protocol uses a hierarchical system to create a database to provide name resolution. The hierarchy looks like an inverted tree with the root at the top and branches below (see the figure). DNS uses domain names to form the hierarchy.

The naming structure is broken down into small, manageable zones. Each DNS server maintains a specific database file and is only responsible for managing name-to-IP mappings for that small portion of the entire DNS structure. When a DNS server receives a request for a name translation that is not within its DNS zone, the DNS server forwards the request to another DNS server within the proper zone for translation.

Note   DNS is scalable because hostname resolution is spread across multiple servers.

The different top-level domains represent either the type of organization or the country of origin. Examples of top-level domains are:

- **.au** - Australia

- **.co** - Colombia

- **.com** - a business or industry

- **.jp** - Japan

- **.org** - a non-profit organization

After top-level domains are second-level domain names, and below them are other lower level domains. Each domain name is a path down this inverted tree starting from the root. For example, as shown in the figure, the root DNS server may not know exactly where the record for the email server, mail.cisco.com, is located, but it maintains a record for the .com domain within the top-level domain. Likewise, the servers within the .com domain may not have a record for mail.cisco.com, but they do have a record for the domain. The servers within the cisco.com domain have a record (a MX record to be precise) for mail. cisco.com.

DNS relies on this hierarchy of decentralized servers to store and maintain these resource records. The resource records list domain names that the server can resolve and alternative servers that can also process requests. If a given server has resource records that correspond to its level in the domain hierarchy, it is said to be authoritative for those records. For example, a name server in the cisco.netacad.net domain would not be authoritative for the mail.cisco.com record, because that record is held at a higher domain level server; specifically the name server in the cisco.com domain.

Refer to
Online Course
for Illustration

10.2.2.4   nslookup

DNS is a client/server service; however, it differs from the other client/server services. While other services use a client that is an application (such as web browser, email client), the DNS client runs as a service itself. The DNS client, sometimes called the DNS resolver, supports name resolution for other network applications and other services that need it.

When configuring a network device, we generally provide one or more DNS Server addresses that the DNS client can use for name resolution. Usually the Internet service provider (ISP) provides the addresses to use for the DNS servers. When a user's application requests to connect to a remote device by name, the requesting DNS client queries one of these name servers to resolve the name to a numeric address.

Computer operating systems also have a utility called nslookup that allows the user to manually query the name servers to resolve a given hostname. This utility can also be used to troubleshoot name resolution issues and to verify the current status of the name servers.

In the figure, when the `nslookup` command is issued, the default DNS server configured for your host is displayed. In this example, the DNS server is dns-sj.cisco.com which has an address of 171.70.168.183.

The name of a host or domain can be entered at the `nslookup` prompt. In the first query in the figure, a query is made for www.cisco.com. The responding name server provides the address of `198.133.219.25`.

The queries shown in the figure are only simple tests. The nslookup utility has many options available for extensive testing and verification of the DNS process. When finished, type `exit` to leave the nslookup utility.

Refer to
Online Course
for Illustration

10.2.2.5   Syntax Checker - DNS CLI Commands in Windows and UNIX

10.2.2.6   Dynamic Host Configuration Protocol

The Dynamic Host Configuration Protocol (DHCP) service enables devices on a network to obtain IP addresses and other information from a DHCP server. This service automates the assignment of IP addresses, subnet masks, gateway, and other IP networking parameters. This is referred to as dynamic addressing. The alternative to dynamic addressing is static addressing. When using static addressing, the network administrator manually enters IP address information on network hosts.

DHCP allows a host to obtain an IP address dynamically when it connects to the network. The DHCP server is contacted and an address requested. The DHCP server chooses an address from a configured range of addresses called a pool and assigns (leases) it to the host for a set period.

On larger local networks, or where the user population changes frequently, DHCP is preferred for address assignment. New users may arrive with laptops and need a connection; others may have new workstations that must be connected. Rather than have the network administrator assign IP addresses for each workstation, it is more efficient to have IP addresses assigned automatically using DHCP.

DHCP-distributed addresses are not permanently assigned to hosts, but are only leased for a period of time. If the host is powered down or taken off the network, the address is returned to the pool for reuse. This is especially helpful with mobile users that come and go on a network. Users can freely move from location to location and re-establish network connections. The host can obtain an IP address after the hardware connection is made, either via a wired or wireless LAN.

DHCP makes it possible to access the Internet using wireless hotspots at airports or coffee shops. When a wireless device enters a hotspot, the device DHCP client contacts the local DHCP server via a wireless connection, and the DHCP server assigns an IP address to the device.

As the figure shows, various types of devices can be DHCP servers when running DHCP service software. The DHCP server in most medium-to-large networks is usually a local dedicated PC-based server. With home networks, the DHCP server is usually located on the local router that connects the home network to the ISP. Local hosts receive IP address information directly from the local router. The local router receives an IP address from the DHCP server at the ISP.

DHCP can pose a security risk because any device connected to the network can receive an address. This risk makes physical security a determining factor of whether to use dynamic or manual addressing. Both dynamic and static addressing have a place in network design. Many networks use both DHCP and static addressing. DHCP is used for general purpose hosts, such as end user devices; static addressing is used for network devices, such as gateways, switches, servers, and printers.

10.2.2.7   DHCP Operation

Refer to **Online Course** for Illustration

Without DHCP, users have to manually input the IP address, subnet mask, and other network settings to join the network. The DHCP server maintains a pool of IP addresses and leases an address to any DHCP-enabled client when the client is powered on. Because the IP addresses are dynamic (leased), rather than static (permanently assigned), addresses no longer in use are automatically returned to the pool for reallocation. As shown in the figure, when a DHCP-configured device boots up or connects to the network, the client broadcasts a DHCP discover (DHCPDISCOVER) message to identify any available DHCP servers on the network. A DHCP server replies with a DHCP offer (DHCPOFFER) message, which offers a lease to the client. The offer message contains the IP address and subnet mask to be assigned, the IP address of the DNS server, and the IP address of the default gateway. The lease offer also includes the duration of the lease.

The client may receive multiple DHCPOFFER messages if there is more than one DHCP server on the local network; therefore, it must choose between them, and sends a DHCP request (DHCPREQUEST) message that identifies the explicit server and lease offer that the client is accepting. A client may also choose to request an address that it had previously been allocated by the server.

Assuming that the IP address requested by the client, or offered by the server, is still available, the server returns a DHCP acknowledgement (DHCPACK) message that acknowledges to the client that the lease is finalized. If the offer is no longer valid, perhaps due to a timeout or another client taking the lease, then the selected server responds with a DHCP negative acknowledgement (DHCPNAK) message. If a DHCPNAK message is returned, then the selection process must begin again with a new DHCPDISCOVER message being transmitted. After the client has the lease, it must be renewed prior to the lease expiration through another DHCPREQUEST message.

The DHCP server ensures that all IP addresses are unique (the same IP address cannot be assigned to two different network devices simultaneously). Using DHCP enables network administrators to easily reconfigure client IP addresses without having to manually make changes to the clients. Most Internet providers use DHCP to allocate addresses to their customers that do not require a static address.

Refer to **Packet Tracer Activity** for this chapter

10.2.2.8   Packet Tracer - DNS and DHCP

In this activity, you will configure and verify static IP addressing and DHCP addressing. You will then configure a DNS server to map IP addresses to the website names.

Refer to **Lab Activity** for this chapter

10.2.2.9   Lab - Observing DNS Resolution

In this lab, you will complete the following objectives:

■ Part 1: Observe the DNS Conversion of a URL to an IP Address

■ Part 2: Observe DNS Lookup Using the `nslookup` Command on a Web Site

■ Part 3: Observe DNS Lookup Using the `nslookup` Command on Mail Servers

Refer to **Online Course** for Illustration

10.2.3   Providing File Sharing Services

10.2.3.1   File Transfer Protocol

The File Transfer Protocol (FTP) is another commonly used application layer protocol. FTP was developed to allow for data transfers between a client and a server. An FTP client is an application that runs on a computer that is used to push and pull data from a server running an FTP daemon (FTPd).

As the figure illustrates, to successfully transfer data, FTP requires two connections between the client and the server, one for commands and replies, the other for the actual file transfer:

■ The client establishes the first connection to the server for control traffic, consisting of client commands and server replies.

■ The client establishes the second connection to the server for the actual data transfer. This connection is created every time there is data to be transferred.

The data transfer can happen in either direction. The client can download (pull) data from the server or, the client can upload (push) data to the server.

Refer to **Packet Tracer Activity** for this chapter

10.2.3.2   Packet Tracer - FTP

In this activity, you will configure FTP services. You will then use the FTP services to transfer files between clients and the server.

Refer to **Lab Activity** for this chapter

10.2.3.3   Lab - Exploring FTP

In this lab, you will complete the following objectives:

- Part 1: Use FTP from a Command Prompt

- Part 2: Download an FTP File Using WS_FTP LE

- Part 3: Use FTP in a Browser

Refer to **Online Course** for Illustration

10.2.3.4   Server Message Block

The Server Message Block (SMB) is a client/server file sharing protocol, developed by IBM in the late 1980s, to describe the structure of shared network resources, such as directories, files, printers, and serial ports. It is a request-response protocol.

The SMB protocol describes file system access and how clients can make requests for files. It also describes the SMB protocol interprocess communication. All SMB messages share a common format. This format uses a fixed-sized header, followed by a variable-sized parameter and data component.

SMB messages can:

- Start, authenticate, and terminate sessions

- Control file and printer access

- Allow an application to send or receive messages to or from another device

SMB file-sharing and print services have become the mainstay of Microsoft networking. With the introduction of the Windows 2000 software series, Microsoft changed the underlying structure for using SMB. In previous versions of Microsoft products, the SMB services used a non-TCP/IP protocol to implement name resolution. Beginning with Windows2000, all subsequent Microsoft products use DNS naming, which allows TCP/IP protocols to directly support SMB resource sharing, as shown in Figure 1. The SMB file exchange process between Windows PCs is shown in Figure 2.

Unlike the file sharing supported by File Transfer Protocol (FTP), clients establish a long-term connection to servers. After the connection is established, the user of the client can access the resources on the server as if the resource is local to the client host.

The LINUX and UNIX operating systems also provide a method of sharing resources with Microsoft networks using a version of SMB called SAMBA. The Apple Macintosh operating systems also support resource sharing using the SMB protocol.

Refer to
Online Course
for Illustration

10.3   The Message Heard Around the World

10.3.1   Move It!

10.3.1.1   The Internet of Things

The application layer is responsible for directly accessing the underlying processes that manage and deliver communication through the network. This layer serves as the source and destination of communications across data networks, regardless of the type of data network being used. In fact, advances in how we network are having a direct effect on the type of applications that are being developed.

Trends like bring your own device (BYOD), access anywhere, virtualization, and machine-to-machine (m2m) connections have made way to a new breed of applications. It is estimated that approximately 50 billion devices will be connected by 2020. In 2010 alone, more than 350,000 applications were developed with more than three million downloads. All of this leads to a world of intuitive connections between people, processes, data and things on the network.

Using smart-tagging and advanced connectivity to digitize unintelligent products - from bikes and bottles, to refrigerators and cars - and connect them to the Internet, will allow people and companies to interact in new and almost unimaginable ways. Objects will be able to collect, receive and send information to users and other connected objects. As shown in the figure, this new wave in Internet development is known as the Internet of Things!

Over 100 million vending machines, vehicles, smoke alarms, and other devices are already sharing information automatically today, a figure which market analysts at Berg Insight expect to rise to 360 million by 2016. Today, photocopiers with an M2M module can order fresh toner and paper automatically, or alert technicians to a fault - even telling them which parts to bring.

Refer to
Online Course
for Illustration

10.3.1.2   Message Travels Through a Network

The massive explosion of applications is due in large part to the genius of the layered approach for processing data through a network. Specifically, keeping the functionality of the application layer separate from the functionality of transporting the data, allows the application layer protocols to be changed and new applications to be developed, without the developer having to worry about the mechanics of getting the data across the network. That is the functionality of other layers and therefore, other developers.

As shown in the figure, when an application sends a request to a server application, the message is built by the application layer, but is then passed down through all the various layer functionalities on the client for delivery. As it moves through the stack each lower layer encapsulates the data with a header that contains the protocols of communication for that layer. These protocols, which are implemented on both the sending and receiving hosts, interact to provide end-to-end delivery of applications over the network.

Protocols like HTTP, for example, support the delivery of web pages to end devices. Now that we have learned all the various layers and their functionalities, we can follow a client request of a web page from the web server to see how each of these independent functionalities work fully, together.

Using the TCP/IP model, a complete communication process includes six steps:

Creation of the Data

The first step is the creation of data at the application layer of the originating source end device. In this case, after building the web client's request, known as an HTTP GET, that data will then be encoded, compressed, and encrypted if necessary. This is the job of the application layer protocol within the TCP/IP model – but this includes the functionality described by the application, presentation, and session layers of the OSI model. The application layer sends this data as a stream to the transport layer.

Segmentation and Initial Encapsulation

The next step is segmentation and encapsulation of the data as it passes down the protocol stack. At the transport layer, the HTTP GET message will be broken down into smaller more manageable pieces and each part of the message will have a transport layer header added to it. Inside the transport layer header are indicators on how to rebuild the message. Also included is an identifier, port number 80. This is used to tell the destination server that the message is destined for its web server application. A randomly generated source port is added as well, to ensure that the client can track return communication and forward it up to the correct client application.

Refer to **Online Course** for Illustration

10.3.1.3   Getting the Data to the End Device

Addressing

Next, address identifiers are added to the segments, as shown in the figure. Just as there are multiple layers of protocols that prepare the data for transmission to its destination, there are multiple layers of addressing to ensure its delivery. The role of the network layer is to add addressing that allows transfer of the data from the host that originates the data, to the host that uses it. The network layer accomplishes this by encapsulating each segment within an IP packet header. The IP packet header contains the IP addresses of the source and destination devices. (The IP address of the destination device is usually determined through an earlier application process known as domain name service.) The combination of the source and destination IP address, with the source and destination port number, is known as a socket. The socket is used to identify the server and service being requested by the client.

Refer to **Online Course** for Illustration

10.3.1.4   Getting the Data through the Internetwork

Preparing for Transportation

After IP addressing is added, the packet is passed to the network access layer for generation of the data onto the media, as shown in the figure. In order for this to occur, the network access layer must first prepare the packet for transmission by placing it into a frame with a header and trailer. This frame includes the host physical address of the source, as well as the physical address of the next hop on the path to the final destination. This is equivalent to the Layer 2, or data link layer, functionality of the OSI model. Layer 2 is concerned with the delivery of messages on a single local network. The Layer 2 address is unique on the local network and represents the address of the end device on the physical media. In a LAN using Ethernet, this address is called the Media Access Control (MAC) address. Once the network access layer has prepared the frame with source and destination addresses, it then encodes the frame into bits, and then into electrical pulses or flashes of light that are sent across the network media.

Transporting the Data

The data is transported through the internetwork, which consists of media and any intermediate devices. As the encapsulated message is transmitted across the network it may travel across several different media and network types. The network access layer specifies the techniques for getting the frame on and off each medium, otherwise known as the media access control method.

If the destination host is in the same network as the source host, the packet is delivered between the two hosts on the local media without the need for a router. However, if the destination host and source host are not in the same network, the packet may be carried across many networks, on many different media types, and through many routers. As it passes along the network, the information contained within the frame is not altered.

At the boundary of each local network, an intermediate network device, usually a router, de-encapsulate the frame to read the destination host address contained in the header of the packet. Routers use the network identifier portion of this address to determine which path to use to reach the destination host. Once the path is determined, the router encapsulates the packet in a new frame and sends it to the next hop on its way toward the destination end device

Refer to
Online Course
for Illustration

10.3.1.5   Getting the Data to the Right Application

Delivering the Data to the Correct Destination Application

Finally, at the destination end device, the frame is received. De-encapsulate and reassembly of the data occurs, as the data is passed up the stack in the destination device. The data is continually passed up the layers, from the network access layer to the network layer, to the transport layer, until it finally reaches the application layer and can then be processed. But how can the device be sure the correct application process is identified?

As shown in the figure, recall that at the transport layer, information contained in the PDU header identifies the specific process or service running on the destination host device that will act on the data. Hosts, whether they are clients or servers on the Internet, can run multiple network applications simultaneously. People using PCs often have an email client running at the same time as a web browser, an instant messaging program, some streaming media, and perhaps even a game. All these separately running programs are examples of individual processes.

Viewing a web page invokes at least one network process. Clicking a hyperlink causes a web browser to communicate with a web server. At the same time, in the background, an email client may be sending and receiving email, and a colleague or friend may be sending an instant message.

Think about a computer that has only one network interface on it. All the data streams created by the applications that are running on the PC enter and leave through that one interface, yet instant messages do not suddenly appear in the middle of word processor documents, nor do emails show up in the interface of a game.

This is because the individual processes running on the source and destination hosts communicate with each other. Each application or service is represented at Layer 4 by a port number. A unique dialogue between devices is identified with a pair of Layer 4 source and destination port numbers that are representative of the two communicating applications. When the data is received at the host, the port number is examined to determine which application or process is the correct destination for the data.

Refer to
Online Course
for Illustration

10.3.1.6   Warriors of the Net

An entertaining resource to help you visualize networking concepts is the animated movie "Warriors of the Net" by TNG Media Lab. Before viewing the video, there are a few things to consider. First, in terms of concepts you have learned in this chapter, think about when in the video you are on the LAN, on WAN, on intranet, on Internet; and what are end devices versus intermediate devices; how the OSI and TCP/IP models apply; what protocols are involved.

Second, while port numbers 21, 23, 25, 53, and 80 are referred to explicitly in the video, IP addresses are referred to only implicitly - can you see where? Where in the video might MAC addresses have been involved?

Finally, though all animations often have simplifications in them, there is one outright error in the video. About 5 minutes in, the statement is made "What happens when Mr. IP doesn't receive an acknowledgement, he simply sends a replacement packet." This is not a function of the Layer 3 Internet Protocol, which is an "unreliable", best effort delivery protocol, but rather a function of the transport layer TCP protocol.

Download the movie from http://www.warriorsofthe.net.

Refer to
Online Course
for Illustration

Refer to
Lab Activity
for this chapter

10.4   Summary

10.4.1.1   Class Activity - Make it happen!

Make it happen!

Refer to the modeling activity from the beginning of this chapter as the basis for this activity. Your IP telephones were installed in a half day vs. the full week originally anticipated. Your network has been restored to full capacity and network applications are available for your use. You have the same emails to answer and quotes to write for your manager's approval.

Use the same scenario you completed in the introduction modeling activity to answer the following questions:

A. Emails

- What method(s) can you use to send email correspondence now that the network is working?
- What format will your emails be sent over the network?
- How can you now send the same message to multiple recipients?
- How can you send the large attachments to multiple recipients using network applications?
- Would using network applications prove to be a cost-effective communication method for your corporation?

B. Quote for Manager's Approval

■ Because you have desktop application programs installed on your computer, will it be relatively easy to produce the quote your manager needs for the new contract due by the end of the week? Explain your answer.

■ When you finish writing the quote, how will you present it to your manager for approval? How will he or she send the quote to the client for their approval?

■ Is using network applications a cost-effective way to complete business transactions? Justify your answer.

Save a hard copy or an electronic copy of your answers. Be prepared to discuss your answers in class.

Refer to **Packet Tracer Activity** for this chapter

10.4.1.2   Packet Tracer Multiuser - Tutorial

The multiuser feature in Packet Tracer allows multiple point-to-point connections between multiple instances of Packet Tracer. This first Packet Tracer Multiuser (PTMU) activity is a quick tutorial demonstrating the steps to establish and verify a multiuser connection to another instance of Packet Tracer within the same LAN. Ideally, this activity is meant for two students. However, it can also be completed as a solo activity simply by opening the two separate files to create two separate instances of Packet Tracer on your local machine.

Refer to **Packet Tracer Activity** for this chapter

10.4.1.3   Packet Tracer Multiuser - Implement Services

In this multiuser activity, two students (players) cooperate to implement and verify services including DHCP, HTTP, Email, DNS and FTP. The server side player will implement and verify services on one server. The client side player will configure two clients and verify access to services.

Refer to **Online Course** for Illustration

10.4.1.4   Summary

The application layer is responsible for directly accessing the underlying processes that manage and deliver communication to the human network. This layer serves as the source and destination of communications across data networks. The application layer applications, services, and protocols enable users to interact with the data network in a way that is meaningful and effective.

■ Applications are computer programs with which the user interacts and which initiate the data transfer process at the user's request.

■ Services are background programs that provide the connection between the application layer and the lower layers of the networking model.

■ Protocols provide a structure of agreed-upon rules and processes that ensure services running on one particular device can send and receive data from a range of different network devices.

Delivery of data over the network can be requested from a server by a client, or between devices that operate in a P2P arrangement, where the client/server relationship is established, according to which device is the source and destination at that time. Messages are exchanged between the application layer services at each end device in accordance with the protocol specifications to establish and use these relationships.

Protocols like HTTP, for example, support the delivery of web pages to end devices. SMTP and POP support sending and receiving email. SMB and FTP enable users to share files. P2P applications make it easier for consumers to seamlessly share media in a distributed fashion. DNS resolves the human legible names used to refer to network resources into numeric addresses usable by the network. Clouds are remote upstream locations that store data and host applications so that users do not require as many local resources, and so that users can seamlessly access content on different devices from any location.

All of these elements work together, at the application layer. The application layer enables users to work and play over the Internet.

Go to the online course to take the quiz and exam.

Chapter 10 Quiz

This quiz is designed to provide an additional opportunity to practice the skills and knowledge presented in the chapter and to prepare for the chapter exam. You will be allowed multiple attempts and the grade does not appear in the gradebook.

Chapter 10 Exam

The chapter exam assesses your knowledge of the chapter content.

Your Chapter Notes

It's a Network

11.0   It's a Network

11.0.1.1   Introduction

Up to this point in the course, we have considered the services that a data network can provide to the human network, examined the features of each layer of the OSI model and the operations of TCP/IP protocols, and looked in detail at Ethernet, a universal LAN technology. The next step is to learn how to assemble these elements together in a functioning network that can be maintained.

Refer to
Lab Activity
for this chapter

11.0.1.2   Class Activity – Did You Notice...?

Did You Notice...?

Note   Students can work singularly, in pairs, or the full classroom can complete this activity together.

Take a look at the two networks in the diagram. Visually compare and contrast the two networks. Make note of the devices used in each network design. Since the devices are labeled, you already know what types of end devices and intermediate devices are on each network.

But how are the two networks different? Is it just that there are more devices present on Network B than on Network A?

Select the network you would use if you owned a small to medium-sized business. Be able to justify your selected network based on cost, speed, ports, expandability, and manageability.

Refer to
Online Course
for Illustration

11.1   Create and Grow

11.1.1   Devices in a Small Network

11.1.1.1   Small Network Topologies

The majority of businesses are small businesses. It is not surprising then that the majority of networks are small networks.

With small networks, the design of the network is usually simple. The number and type of devices on the network are significantly reduced compared to that of a larger network. The network topologies for small networks typically involve a single router and one or more switches. Small networks may also have wireless access points (possibly built into the router) and IP phones. As for connection to the Internet, normally a small network has a single WAN connection provided by DSL, cable, or an Ethernet connection.

Managing a small network requires many of the same skills as those required for managing a larger one. The majority of work is focused on maintenance and troubleshooting of existing equipment, as well as securing devices and information on the network. The management of a small network is either done by an employee of the company or a person contracted by the company, depending on the size of the business and the type of business.

A typical small-business network is shown in the figure.

Refer to
Online Course
for Illustration

11.1.1.2   Device Selection for a Small Network

In order to meet user requirements, even small networks require planning and design. Planning ensures that all requirements, cost factors, and deployment options are given due consideration.

One of the first design considerations when implementing a small network is the type of intermediate devices to use to support the network. When selecting the type of intermediate devices, there are a number of factors that need to be considered, as shown in the figure.

Cost

Cost is typically one of the most important factors when selecting equipment for a small business network. The cost of a switch or router is determined by its capacity and features. The device capacity includes the number and types of ports available and the backplane speed. Other factors that impact the cost are network management capabilities, embedded security technologies, and optional advanced switching technologies. The expense of cable runs required to connect every device on the network must also be considered. Another key element affecting cost consideration is how much redundancy to incorporate into the network – this includes devices, ports per device, and copper or fiber-optic cabling.

Speed and Types of Ports/Interfaces

Choosing the number and type of ports on a router or switch is a critical decision. Questions to be asked include: "Do we order just enough ports for today's needs, or do we consider growth requirements?", "Do we require a mixture of UTP speeds?", and "Do we require both UTP and fiber ports?"

Newer computers have built-in 1 Gbps NICs. 10 Gbps ports are already included with some workstations and servers. While it is more expensive, choosing Layer 2 devices that can accommodate increased speeds allows the network to evolve without replacing central devices.

Expandability

Networking devices come in both fixed and modular physical configurations. Fixed configurations have a specific number and type of ports or interfaces. Modular devices have expansion slots that provide the flexibility to add new modules as requirements evolve. Most modular devices come with a basic number of fixed ports as well as expansion slots. Switches are available with special additional ports for optional high-speed uplinks. Also, because routers can be used for connecting different numbers and types of networks, care must be taken to select the appropriate modules and interfaces for the specific media.

Questions to be considered include: "Do we order devices with upgradable modules?", and "What type of WAN interfaces, if any, are required on the router(s)?"

Operating System Features and Services

Depending on the version of the operating system, a network device can support certain features and services, such as:

- Security
- QoS
- VoIP
- Layer 3 switching
- NAT
- DHCP

Routers can be expensive based on interfaces and features needed. Additional modules, such as fiber-optics, increase the cost of the network devices.

Refer to
Online Course
for Illustration

11.1.1.3   IP Addressing for a Small Network

When implementing a small network, it is necessary to plan the IP addressing space. All hosts within an internetwork must have a unique address. Even on a small network, address assignment within the network should not be random. Rather the IP addressing scheme should be planned, documented and maintained based on the type of device receiving the address.

Examples of different types of devices that will factor into the IP design are:

- End devices for users
- Servers and peripherals
- Hosts that are accessible from the Internet
- Intermediary devices

Planning and documenting the IP addressing scheme helps the administrator to track device types. For example, if all servers are assigned a host address between ranges of 50-100, it is easy to identify server traffic by IP address. This can be very useful when troubleshooting network traffic issues using a protocol analyzer.

Additionally, administrators are better able to control access to resources on the network based on IP address when a deterministic IP addressing scheme is used. This can be especially important for hosts that provide resources to the internal network as well as to the external network. Web servers or e-commerce servers play such a role. If the addresses for these resources are not planned and documented, the security and accessibility of the devices are not easily controlled. If a server has a random address assigned, blocking access to this address is difficult and clients may not be able to locate this resource.

Each of these different device types should be allocated to a logical block of addresses within the address range of the network.

Click the buttons in the figure to see the method for assignment.

Refer to
Online Course
for Illustration

11.1.1.4   Redundancy in a Small Network

Another important part of network design is reliability. Even small businesses often rely on their network heavily for business operation. A failure of the network can be very costly. In order to maintain a high degree of reliability, redundancy is required in the network design. Redundancy helps to eliminate single points of failure. There are many ways to accomplish redundancy in a network. Redundancy can be accomplished by installing duplicate equipment, but it can also be accomplished by supplying duplicate network links for critical areas, as shown in the figure.

The smaller the network, the less the chance that redundancy of equipment will be affordable. Therefore, a common way to introduce redundancy is through the use of redundant switch connections between multiple switches on the network and between switches and routers.

Also, servers often have multiple NIC ports that enable redundant connections to one or more switches. In a small network, servers typically are deployed as web servers, file servers, or email servers.

Small networks typically provide a single exit point toward the Internet via one or more default gateways. With one router in the topology, the only redundancy in terms of Layer 3 paths is enabled by utilizing more than one inside Ethernet interface on the router. However, if the router fails, the entire network loses connectivity to the Internet. For this reason, it may be advisable for a small business to pay for a least-cost option account with a second service provider for backup.

Refer to
Online Course
for Illustration

11.1.1.5   Design Considerations for a Small Network

Users expect immediate access to their emails and to the files that they are sharing or updating. To help ensure this availability, the network designer should take the following steps:

Step 1. Secure file and mail servers in a centralized location.

Step 2. Protect the location from unauthorized access by implementing physical and logical security measures.

Step 3. Create redundancy in the server farm that ensures if one device fails, files are not lost.

Step 4. Configure redundant paths to the servers.

In addition, modern networks often use some form of voice or video over IP for communication with customers and business partners. This type of converged network is implemented as an integrated solution or as an additional form of raw data overlaid onto the IP network. The network administrator should consider the various types of traffic and their treatment in the network design. The router(s) and switch(es) in a small network should be configured to support real-time traffic, such as voice and video, in a distinct manner relative to other data traffic. In fact, a good network design will classify traffic carefully according to priority, as shown in the figure. Traffic classes could be as specific as:

- File transfer
- Email
- Voice

- Video

- Messaging

- Transactional

In the end, the goal for a good network design, even for a small network, is to enhance productivity of the employees and minimize network downtime.

Refer to
Online Course
for Illustration

11.1.1.6   Identifying Devices in a Small Network

Refer to
Online Course
for Illustration

11.1.2   Protocols in a Small Network

11.1.2.1   Common Applications in a Small Network

The network is only as useful as the applications that are on it. As shown in the figure, within the application layer, there are two forms of software programs or processes that provide access to the network: network applications and application layer services.

Network Applications

Applications are the software programs used to communicate over the network. Some end-user applications are network-aware, meaning that they implement application layer protocols and are able to communicate directly with the lower layers of the protocol stack. Email clients and web browsers are examples of this type of application.

Application Layer Services

Other programs may need the assistance of application layer services to use network resources, like file transfer or network print spooling. Though transparent to an employee, these services are the programs that interface with the network and prepare the data for transfer. Different types of data, whether text, graphics, or video, require different network services to ensure that they are properly prepared for processing by the functions occurring at the lower layers of the OSI model.

Each application or network service uses protocols, which define the standards and data formats to be used. Without protocols, the data network would not have a common way to format and direct data. In order to understand the function of various network services, it is necessary to become familiar with the underlying protocols that govern their operation.

Refer to
Online Course
for Illustration

11.1.2.2   Common Protocols in a Small Network

Most of a technician's work, in either a small or a large network, will in some way be involved with network protocols. Network protocols support the applications and services used by employees in a small network. Common network protocols include:

- DNS

- Telnet

- IMAP, SMTP, POP (email)

- DHCP

- HTTP

- FTP

Click the servers in the figure for a brief description of the network services each provides.

These network protocols comprise the fundamental tool set of a network professional. Each of these network protocols defines:

- Processes on either end of a communication session
- Types of messages
- Syntax of the messages
- Meaning of informational fields
- How messages are sent and the expected response
- Interaction with the next lower layer

Many companies have established a policy of using secure versions of these protocols whenever possible. These protocols are HTTPS, SFTP, and SSH.

Refer to **Online Course** for Illustration

11.1.2.3   Real-Time Applications for a Small Network

In addition to the common network protocols described previously, modern businesses, even small ones, typically utilize real-time applications for communicating with customers and business partners. While a small company may not be able to justify the cost of an enterprise Cisco Telepresence solution, there are other real-time applications, as shown in Figure 1, that are affordable and justifiable for small business organizations. Real-time applications require more planning and dedicated services (relative to other types of data) to ensure priority delivery of voice and video traffic. This means that the network administrator must ensure the proper equipment is installed in the network and that the network devices are configured to ensure priority delivery. Figure 2 shows elements of a small network that support real-time applications.

Infrastructure

To support the existing and proposed real-time applications, the infrastructure must accommodate the characteristics of each type of traffic. The network designer must determine whether the existing switches and cabling can support the traffic that will be added to the network. Cabling that can support gigabit transmissions should be able to carry the traffic generated and not require any changes to the infrastructure. Older switches may not support Power over Ethernet (PoE). Obsolete cabling may not support the bandwidth requirements. The switches and cabling would need to be upgraded to support these applications.

VoIP

VoIP is implemented in an organization that still uses traditional telephones. VoIP uses voice-enabled routers. These routers convert analog voice from traditional telephone signals into IP packets. After the signals are converted into IP packets, the router sends those packets between corresponding locations. VoIP is much less expensive than an integrated IP telephony solution, but the quality of communications does not meet the same standards. Voice and video over IP solutions for small businesses can be realized, for example, with Skype and non-enterprise versions of Cisco WebEx.

IP Telephony

In IP telephony, the IP phone itself performs voice-to-IP conversion. Voice-enabled routers are not required within a network with an integrated IP telephony solution. IP phones use a dedicated server for call control and signaling. There are now many vendors with dedicated IP telephony solutions for small networks.

Real-time Applications

To transport streaming media effectively, the network must be able to support applications that require delay-sensitive delivery. Real-Time Transport Protocol (RTP) and Real-Time Transport Control Protocol (RTCP) are two protocols that support this requirement. RTP and RTCP enable control and scalability of the network resources by allowing quality of service (QoS) mechanisms to be incorporated. These QoS mechanisms provide valuable tools for minimizing latency issues for real-time streaming applications.

Refer to
Online Course
for Illustration

11.1.3   Growing to Larger Networks

11.1.3.1   Scaling a Small Network

Growth is a natural process for many small businesses, and their networks must grow accordingly. A network administrator for a small network will either work reactively or proactively, depending on the leaders of the company, which often include the network administrator. Ideally, the network administrator has enough lead time to make intelligent decisions about growing the network in-line with the growth of the company.

To scale a network, several elements are required:

- **Network documentation** - physical and logical topology
- **Device inventory** - list of devices that use or comprise the network
- **Budget** - itemized IT budget, including fiscal year equipment purchasing budget
- **Traffic analysis** - protocols, applications, and services and their respective traffic requirements should be documented

These elements are used to inform the decision-making that accompanies the scaling of a small network.

Refer to
Online Course
for Illustration

11.1.3.2   Protocol Analysis of a Small Network

Supporting and growing a small network requires being familiar with the protocols and network applications running over the network. While the network administrator will have more time in a small network environment to individually analyze network utilization for each network-enabled device, a more holistic approach with some type of software- or hardware-based protocol analyzer is recommended.

As shown in the figure, protocol analyzers enable a network professional to quickly compile statistical information about traffic flows on a network.

When trying to determine how to manage network traffic, especially as the network grows, it is important to understand the type of traffic that is crossing the network as well as the current traffic flow. If the types of traffic are unknown, the protocol analyzer will help identify the traffic and its source.

To determine traffic flow patterns, it is important to:

■ Capture traffic during peak utilization times to get a good representation of the different traffic types.

■ Perform the capture on different network segments, because some traffic will be local to a particular segment.

Information gathered by the protocol analyzer is analyzed based on the source and destination of the traffic as well as the type of traffic being sent. This analysis can be used to make decisions on how to manage the traffic more efficiently. This can be done by reducing unnecessary traffic flows or changing flow patterns altogether by moving a server, for example.

Sometimes, simply relocating a server or service to another network segment improves network performance and accommodates the growing traffic needs. At other times, optimizing the network performance requires major network redesign and intervention.

Refer to **Online Course** for Illustration

11.1.3.3 Evolving Protocol Requirements

In addition to understanding changing traffic trends, a network administrator must also be aware of how network use is changing. As shown in the figure, a network administrator in a small network has the ability to obtain in-person IT "snapshots" of employee application utilization for a significant portion of the employee workforce over time. These snapshots typically include information such as:

■ OS + OS Version

■ Non-Network Applications

■ Network Applications

■ CPU Utilization

■ Drive Utilization

■ RAM Utilization

Documenting snapshots for employees in a small network over a period of time will go a long way toward informing the network administrator of evolving protocol requirements and associated traffic flows. For example, it may be that some employees are using off-site resources such as social media in order to better position a company with respect to marketing. When they began working for the company, these employees may have focused less on Internet-based advertising. This shift in resource utilization may require the network administrator to shift network resource allocations accordingly.

It is the responsibility of the network administrator to track network utilization and traffic flow requirements, and implement network modifications in order to optimize employee productivity as the network and business grow.

Refer to
Online Course
for Illustration

11.2   Keeping the Network Safe

11.2.1   Network Device Security Measures

11.2.1.1   Categories of Threats to Network Security

Whether wired or wireless, computer networks are essential to everyday activities. Individuals and organizations alike depend on their computers and networks. Intrusion by an unauthorized person can result in costly network outages and loss of work. Attacks to a network can be devastating and can result in a loss of time and money due to damage or theft of important information or assets.

Intruders can gain access to a network through software vulnerabilities, hardware attacks or through guessing someone's username and password. Intruders who gain access by modifying software or exploiting software vulnerabilities are often called hackers.

After the hacker gains access to the network, four types of threats may arise:

- Information theft
- Identity theft
- Data loss/manipulation
- Disruption of service

Click the images in the figure to see more information.

Even in small networks, it is necessary to consider security threats and vulnerabilities when planning a network implementation.

Refer to
Online Course
for Illustration

11.2.1.2   Physical Security

When you think of network security, or even computer security, you may imagine attackers exploiting software vulnerabilities. An equally important vulnerability is the physical security of devices, as shown in the figure. An attacker can deny the use of network resources if those resources can be physically compromised.

The four classes of physical threats are:

- **Hardware threats** - physical damage to servers, routers, switches, cabling plant, and workstations
- **Environmental threats** - temperature extremes (too hot or too cold) or humidity extremes (too wet or too dry)
- **Electrical threats** - voltage spikes, insufficient supply voltage (brownouts), unconditioned power (noise), and total power loss
- **Maintenance threats** - poor handling of key electrical components (electrostatic discharge), lack of critical spare parts, poor cabling, and poor labeling

Some of these issues must be dealt with in an organizational policy. Some of them are subject to good leadership and management in the organization.

Refer to
Online Course
for Illustration

11.2.1.3   Types of Security Vulnerabilities

Three network security factors are vulnerability, threat, and attack.

Vulnerability is the degree of weakness which is inherent in every network and device. This includes routers, switches, desktops, servers, and even security devices.

Threats include the people interested and qualified in taking advantage of each security weakness. Such individuals can be expected to continually search for new exploits and weaknesses.

Threats are realized by a variety of tools, scripts, and programs to launch attacks against networks and network devices. Typically, the network devices under attack are the endpoints, such as servers and desktop computers.

There are three primary vulnerabilities or weaknesses:

- Technological, as shown in Figure 1
- Configuration, as shown in Figure 2
- Security policy, as shown in Figure 3

All three of these vulnerabilities or weaknesses can lead to various attacks, including malicious code attacks and network attacks.

Refer to
Interactive Graphic
in online course.

11.2.1.4   Activity – Security Threats and Vulnerabilities

Refer to
Online Course
for Illustration

11.2.2   Vulnerabilities and Network Attacks

11.2.2.1   Viruses, Worms, and Trojan Horses

Malicious code attacks include a number of types of computer programs that were created with the intention of causing data loss or damage. The three main types of malicious code attacks are viruses, Trojan horses, and worms.

A virus is malicious software that is attached to another program to execute a particular unwanted function on a workstation. An example is a program that is attached to command.com (the primary interpreter for Windows systems) and deletes certain files and infects any other versions of command.com that it can find.

A Trojan horse is different only in that the entire application was written to look like something else, when in fact it is an attack tool. An example of a Trojan horse is a software application that runs a simple game on a workstation. While the user is occupied with the game, the Trojan horse mails a copy of itself to every address in the user's address book. The other users receive the game and play it, thereby spreading the Trojan horse to the addresses in each address book.

Viruses normally require a delivery mechanism, a vector, such as a zip file or some other executable file attached to an email, to carry the virus code from one system to another. The key element that distinguishes a computer worm from a computer virus is that human interaction is required to facilitate the spread of a virus.

Worms are self-contained programs that attack a system and try to exploit a specific vulnerability in the target. Upon successful exploitation of the vulnerability, the worm copies its program from the attacking host to the newly exploited system to begin the cycle again. The anatomy of a worm attack is as follows:

- **The enabling vulnerability** - A worm installs itself by exploiting known vulnerabilities in systems, such as naive end users who opens unverified executable attachments in emails.

- **Propagation mechanism** - After gaining access to a host, a worm copies itself to that host and then selects new targets.

- **Payload** - After a host is infected with a worm, the attacker has access to the host, often as a privileged user. Attackers could use a local exploit to escalate their privilege level to administrator.

Refer to
Online Course
for Illustration

11.2.2.2   Reconnaissance Attacks

In addition to malicious code attacks, it is also possible for networks to fall prey to various network attacks. Network attacks can be classified into three major categories:

- **Reconnaissance attacks** - the unauthorized discovery and mapping of systems, services, or vulnerabilities

- **Access attacks** - the unauthorized manipulation of data, system access, or user privileges

- **Denial of service** - the disabling or corruption of networks, systems, or services

Reconnaissance Attacks

External attackers can use Internet tools, such as the nslookup and whois utilities, to easily determine the IP address space assigned to a given corporation or entity. After the IP address space is determined, an attacker can then ping the publicly available IP addresses to identify the addresses that are active. To help automate this step, an attacker may use a ping sweep tool, such as fping or gping, which systematically pings all network addresses in a given range or subnet. This is similar to going through a section of a telephone book and calling each number to see who answers.

Click each type of reconnaissance attack tool to see an animation of the attack.

11.2.2.3   Access Attacks

Access Attacks

Access attacks exploit known vulnerabilities in authentication services, FTP services, and web services to gain entry to web accounts, confidential databases, and other sensitive information. An access attack allows an individual to gain unauthorized access to information that they have no right to view. Access attacks can be classified into four types. One of the most common types of access attacks is the password attack. Password attacks can be implemented using a packet sniffer to yield user accounts and passwords that are transmitted as clear text. Password attacks can also refer to repeated attempts to log in to a shared resource, such as a server or router, to identify a user account, password, or both. These repeated attempts are called dictionary attacks or brute-force attacks.

Click the buttons in the figure to see examples of access attacks.

Refer to
Online Course
for Illustration

11.2.2.4   DoS Attacks

Denial of Service

DoS attacks are the most publicized form of attack and also among the most difficult to eliminate. Even within the attacker community, DoS attacks are regarded as trivial and considered bad form, because they require so little effort to execute. But because of their ease of implementation and potentially significant damage, DoS attacks deserve special attention from security administrators.

DoS attacks take many forms. Ultimately, they prevent authorized people from using a service by consuming system resources.

Click the buttons in the figure to see examples of DoS and DDoS attacks.

Refer to
Interactive Graphic
in online course.

11.2.2.5   Activity – Types of Attack

Refer to
Lab Activity
for this chapter

11.2.2.6   Lab - Researching Network Security Threats

In this lab, you will complete the following objectives:

■ Part 1: Explore the SANS Website

■ Part 2: Identify Recent Network Security Threats

■ Part 3: Detail a Specific Network Security Threat

Refer to
Online Course
for Illustration

11.2.3   Mitigating Network Attacks

11.2.3.1   Backup, Upgrade, Update, and Patch

Antivirus software can detect most viruses and many Trojan horse applications and prevent them from spreading in the network. Antivirus software can be deployed at the user level and at the network level.

Keeping up to date with the latest developments in these sorts of attacks can also lead to a more effective defense against these attacks. As new virus or Trojan applications are released, enterprises need to keep current with the latest versions of antivirus software as well.

Worm attack mitigation requires diligence on the part of system and network administration staff. The following are the recommended steps for worm attack mitigation:

■ **Containment** - Contain the spread of the worm within the network. Compartmentalize uninfected parts of the network.

■ **Inoculation** - Start patching all systems and, if possible, scanning for vulnerable systems.

■ **Quarantine** - Track down each infected machine inside the network. Disconnect, remove, or block infected machines from the network.

■ Treatment - Clean and patch each infected system. Some worms may require complete core system reinstallations to clean the system.

The most effective way to mitigate a worm attack is to download security updates from the operating system vendor and patch all vulnerable systems. This is difficult with uncontrolled user systems in the local network. Administering numerous systems involves the creation of a standard software image (operating system and accredited applications that are authorized for use on client systems) that is deployed on new or upgraded systems. However, security requirements change and already deployed systems may need to have updated security patches installed.

One solution to the management of critical security patches is to create a central patch server that all systems must communicate with after a set period of time, as shown in the figure. Any patches that are not applied to a host are automatically downloaded from the patch server and installed without user intervention.

Refer to
Online Course
for Illustration

11.2.3.2   Authentication, Authorization, and Accounting

Authentication, authorization, and accounting (AAA, or "triple A") network security services provide the primary framework to set up access control on a network device. AAA is a way to control who is permitted to access a network (authenticate), what they can do while they are there (authorize), and to watch the actions they perform while accessing the network (accounting). AAA provides a higher degree of scalability than the console, AUX, VTY, and privileged EXEC authentication commands alone.

Authentication

Users and administrators must prove that they are who they say they are. Authentication can be established using username and password combinations, challenge and response questions, token cards, and other methods. For example: "I am user 'student'. I know the password to prove that I am user 'student'."

In a small network, local authentication is often used. With local authentication, each device maintains its own database of username/password combinations. However, when there are more than a few user accounts in a local device database, managing those user accounts becomes complex. Additionally, as the network grows and more devices are added to the network, local authentication becomes difficult to maintain and does not scale. For example, if there are 100 network devices, all user accounts must be added to all 100 devices.

For larger networks, a more scalable solution is external authentication. External authentication allows all users to be authenticated through an external network server. The two most popular options for external authentication of users are RADIUS and TACACS+:

■ RADIUS is an open standard with low use of CPU resources and memory. It is used by a range of network devices, such as switches, routers, and wireless devices.

■ TACACS+ is a security mechanism that enables modular authentication, authorization, and accounting services. It uses a TACACS+ daemon running on a security server.

Authorization

After the user is authenticated, authorization services determine which resources the user can access and which operations the user is allowed to perform. An example is, "User 'student' can access host serverXYZ using Telnet only."

Accounting

Accounting records what the user does, including what is accessed, the amount of time the resource is accessed, and any changes that were made. Accounting keeps track of how network resources are used. An example is, "User 'student' accessed host serverXYZ using Telnet for 15 minutes."

The concept of AAA is similar to the use of a credit card. The credit card identifies who can use it, how much that user can spend, and keeps account of what items the user spent money on, as shown in the figure.

Refer to
Online Course
for Illustration

11.2.3.3   Firewalls

In addition to protecting individual computers and servers attached to the network, it is important to control traffic traveling to and from the network.

A firewall is one of the most effective security tools available for protecting internal network users from external threats. A firewall resides between two or more networks and controls the traffic between them and also helps prevent unauthorized access. Firewall products use various techniques for determining what is permitted or denied access to a network. These techniques are:

- **Packet filtering** - Prevents or allows access based on IP or MAC addresses.

- **Application filtering** - Prevents or allows access by specific application types based on port numbers.

- **URL filtering** - Prevents or allows access to websites based on specific URLs or keywords.

- **Stateful packet inspection (SPI)** - Incoming packets must be legitimate responses to requests from internal hosts. Unsolicited packets are blocked unless permitted specifically. SPI can also include the capability to recognize and filter out specific types of attacks such as denial of service (DoS).

Firewall products may support one or more of these filtering capabilities. Additionally, firewalls often perform Network Address Translation (NAT). NAT translates an internal IP address or group of IP addresses into an outside, public IP address that is sent across the network. This allows internal IP addresses to be concealed from outside users.

Firewall products come packaged in various forms, as shown in the figure.

- **Appliance-based firewalls** - An appliance-based firewall is a firewall that is built-in to a dedicated hardware device known as a security appliance.

- **Server-based firewalls** - A server-based firewall consists of a firewall application that runs on a network operating system (NOS) such as UNIX or Windows.

- **Integrated firewalls** - An integrated firewall is implemented by adding firewall functionality to an existing device, such as a router.

- **Personal firewalls** - Personal firewalls reside on host computers and are not designed for LAN implementations. They may be available by default from the OS or may come from an outside vendor.

Refer to
Online Course
for Illustration

11.2.3.4 Endpoint Security

A secure network is only as strong as its weakest link. The high-profile threats most often discussed in the media are external threats, such as Internet worms and DoS attacks. But securing the internal network is just as important as securing the perimeter of a network. The internal network is made up of network endpoints, some of which are shown in the figure. An endpoint, or host, is an individual computer system or device that acts as a network client. Common endpoints are laptops, desktops, servers, smart phones, and tablets. If users are not practicing security with their endpoint devices, no amount of security precautions will guarantee a secure network.

Securing endpoint devices is one of the most challenging jobs of a network administrator, because it involves human nature. A company must have well-documented policies in place and employees must be aware of these rules. Employees need to be trained on proper use of the network. Policies often include the use of antivirus software and host intrusion prevention. More comprehensive endpoint security solutions rely on network access control.

Endpoint security also requires securing Layer 2 devices in the network infrastructure to prevent against Layer 2 attacks such as MAC address spoofing, MAC address table overflow attacks, and LAN storm attacks. This is known as attack mitigation.

Refer to
Online Course
for Illustration

11.2.4 Securing Devices

11.2.4.1 Introduction to Securing Devices

Part of network security is securing actual devices, including end devices and intermediate devices, such as network devices.

When a new operating system is installed on a device, the security settings are set to the default values. In most cases, this level of security is inadequate. For Cisco routers, the Cisco AutoSecure feature can be used to assist securing the system, as described in the figure. There are some simple steps that should be taken that apply to most operating systems:

- Default usernames and passwords should be changed immediately.

- Access to system resources should be restricted to only the individuals that are authorized to use those resources.

- Any unnecessary services and applications should be turned off and uninstalled, when possible.

All devices should be updated with security patches as they become available. Often, devices shipped from the manufacturer have been sitting in a warehouse for a period of time and do not have the most up-to-date patches installed. It is important, prior to implementation, to update any software and install any security patches.

Refer to
Online Course
for Illustration

11.2.4.2 Passwords

To protect network devices, it is important to use strong passwords. Here are standard guidelines to follow:

- Use a password length of at least 8 characters, preferably 10 or more characters. A longer password is a better password.

- Make passwords complex. Include a mix of uppercase and lowercase letters, numbers, symbols, and spaces, if allowed.

- Avoid passwords based on repetition, common dictionary words, letter or number sequences, usernames, relative or pet names, biographical information, such as birth-dates, ID numbers, ancestor names, or other easily identifiable pieces of information.

- Deliberately misspell a password. For example, Smith = Smyth = 5mYth or Security = 5ecur1ty.

- Change passwords often. If a password is unknowingly compromised, the window of opportunity for the attacker to use the password is limited.

- Do not write passwords down and leave them in obvious places such as on the desk or monitor.

The figure shows examples of strong and weak passwords.

On Cisco routers, leading spaces are ignored for passwords, but spaces after the first character are not ignored. Therefore, one method to create a strong password is to use the space bar in the password and create a phrase made of many words. This is called a pass phrase. A pass phrase is often easier to remember than a simple password. It is also longer and harder to guess.

Administrators should ensure that strong passwords are used across the network. One way to accomplish this is to use the same "brute force" attack tools that attackers use as a way to verify password strength.

Refer to
Online Course
for Illustration

11.2.4.3   Basic Security Practices

When implementing devices, it is important to follow all security guidelines set by the organization. This includes naming devices in a fashion that allows for easy documentation and tracking, but also maintains some form of security. It is not wise to provide too much information about the use of the device in the hostname. There are many other basic security measures that should be taken.

Additional Password Security

Strong passwords are only as useful as they are secret. There are several steps that can be taken to help ensure that passwords remain secret. Using the global configuration command `service password-encryption` prevents unauthorized individuals from viewing passwords in plaintext in the configuration file, as shown in the figure. This command causes the encryption of all passwords that are unencrypted.

Additionally, to ensure that all configured passwords are a minimum of a specified length, use the `security passwords min-length` command in global configuration mode.

Another way hackers learn passwords is simply by brute-force attacks, trying multiple passwords until one works. It is possible to prevent this type of attack by blocking login attempts to the device if a set number of failures occur within a specific amount of time.

```
Router(config)# login block-for 120 attempts 3 within 60
```

This command will block login attempts for 120 seconds, if there are three failed login attempts within 60 seconds.

Banners

A banner message is similar to a no trespassing sign. They are important in order to be able to prosecute, in a court of law, anyone that accesses the system inappropriately. Be sure banner messages comply with security policies for the organization.

```
Router(config)# banner motd #message#
```

Exec Timeout

Another recommendation is setting executive timeouts. By setting the exec timeout, you are telling the Cisco device to automatically disconnect users on a line after they have been idle for the duration of the exec timeout value. Exec timeouts can be configured on console, vty, and aux ports.

```
Router(config)# line vty 0 4
Router(config-vty)# exec-timeout 10
```

This command will disconnect users after 10 minutes.

Refer to
Online Course
for Illustration

11.2.4.4   Enable SSH

Remote access via SSH

The legacy protocol to manage devices remotely is Telnet. Telnet is not secure. Data contained within a Telnet packet is transmitted unencrypted. Using a tool like Wireshark, it is possible for someone to "sniff" a Telnet session and obtain password information. For this reason, it is highly recommended to enable SSH on devices for secure remote access. It is possible to configure a Cisco device to support SSH using four steps, as shown in the figure.

Step 1.   Ensure that the router has a unique host name, and then configure the IP domain name of the network using the `ip domain-name` domain-name command in global configuration mode.

Step 2.   One-way secret keys must be generated for a router to encrypt SSH traffic. The key is what is actually used to encrypt and decrypt data. To create an encryption key, use the `crypto key generate rsa general-keys modulus` modulus-size command in global configuration mode. The specific meaning of the various parts of this command are complex and out of scope for this course, but for now, just note that the modulus determines the size of the key and can be configured from 360 bits to 2048 bits. The larger the modulus, the more secure the key, but the longer it takes to encrypt and decrypt information. The minimum recommended modulus length is 1024 bits.

```
Router(config)# crypto key generate rsa general-keys modulus 1024
```

Step 3.   Create a local database username entry using the `username` name `secret` secret global configuration command.

Step 4.   Enable vty inbound SSH sessions using the line vty commands `login local` and `transport input ssh`.

The router SSH service can now be accessed using an SSH client software.

Refer to
Lab Activity
for this chapter

11.2.4.5   Lab - Accessing Network Devices with SSH

In this lab, you will complete the following objectives:

- Part 1: Configure Basic Device Settings

- Part 2: Configure the Router for SSH Access

- Part 3: Examine a Telnet Session with Wireshark

- Part 4: Examine a SSH Session with Wireshark

- Part 5: Configure the Switch for SSH Access

- Part 6: SSH from the CLI on the Switch

Refer to
Lab Activity
for this chapter

11.2.4.6   Lab - Securing Network Devices

In this lab, you will complete the following objectives:

- Part 1: Configure Basic Device Settings

- Part 2: Configure Basic Security Measures on the Router

- Part 3: Configure Basic Security Measures on the Switch

Refer to
Online Course
for Illustration

11.3   Basic Network Performance

11.3.1   Ping

11.3.1.1   Interpreting Ping Results

After the network has been implemented, a network administrator must be able to test the network connectivity to ensure that it is operating appropriately. Additionally, it is a good idea for the network administrator to document the network

The `Ping` Command

Using the `ping` command is an effective way to test connectivity. The test is often referred to as testing the protocol stack, because the `ping` command moves from Layer 3 of the OSI model to Layer 2 and then Layer 1. Ping uses the ICMP protocol to check for connectivity.

The `ping` command will not always pinpoint the nature of a problem, but it can help to identify the source of the problem, an important first step in troubleshooting a network failure.

The `ping` command provides a method for checking the protocol stack and IPv4 address configuration on a host as well as testing connectivity to local or remote destination hosts, as shown in the figure. There are additional tools that can provide more information than `ping`, such as Telnet or Trace, which will be discussed in more detail later.

IOS Ping Indicators

A ping issued from the IOS will yield one of several indications for each ICMP echo that was sent. The most common indicators are:

- ! - indicates receipt of an ICMP echo reply message

- . - indicates a time expired while waiting for an ICMP echo reply message

- U - an ICMP unreachable message was received

The "!" (exclamation mark) indicates that the ping completed successfully and verifies Layer 3 connectivity.

The "." (period) can indicate problems in the communication. It may indicate that a connectivity problem occurred somewhere along the path. It may also indicate that a router along the path did not have a route to the destination and did not send an ICMP destination unreachable message. It also may indicate that ping was blocked by device security.

The "U" indicates that a router along the path did not have a route to the destination address or that the ping request was blocked and responded with an ICMP unreachable message.

Testing the Loopback

The `ping` command is used to verify the internal IP configuration on the local host. Recall that this test is accomplished by using the `ping` command on a reserved address called the loopback (127.0.0.1). This verifies the proper operation of the protocol stack from the network layer to the physical layer - and back - without actually putting a signal on the media.

`Ping` commands are entered at a command line.

Enter the `ping loopback` command with this syntax:

```
C:\> ping 127.0.0.1
```

The reply from this command would look something like this:

```
Reply from 127.0.0.1: bytes=32 time<1ms TTL=128
Reply from 127.0.0.1: bytes=32 time<1ms TTL=128
Reply from 127.0.0.1: bytes=32 time<1ms TTL=128
Reply from 127.0.0.1: bytes=32 time<1ms TTL=128
Ping statistics for 127.0.0.1:
Packets: Sent = 4, Received = 4, Lost = 0 (0% loss),
Approximate round trip times in milli-seconds:
Minimum = 0ms, Maximum = 0ms, Average = 0ms
```

The result indicates that four 32 byte test packets were sent and were returned from host 127.0.0.1 in a time of less than 1 ms. TTL stands for Time-to-Live and defines the number of hops that the ping packet has remaining before it will be dropped.

Refer to
Online Course
for Illustration

11.3.1.2   Extended Ping

The Cisco IOS offers an "extended" mode of the ping command. This mode is entered by typing ping in privileged EXEC mode, without a destination IP address. A series of prompts are then presented as shown in the example below. Pressing Enter accepts the indicated default values. The example below illustrates how to force the source address for a ping to be 10.1.1.1 (see R2 in the figure); the source address for a standard ping would be 209.165.200.226. By doing this, the network administrator can verify remotely (from R2) that R1 has the route 10.1.1.0/24 in its routing table.

R2# **ping**

Protocol [ip]:

Target IP address: **192.168.10.1**

Repeat count [5]:

Datagram size [100]:

Timeout in seconds [2]:

Extended commands [n]: **y**

Source address or interface: **10.1.1.1**

Type of service [0]:

Set DF bit in IP header? [no]:

Validate reply data? [no]:

Data pattern [0xABCD]:

Loose, Strict, Record, Timestamp, Verbose[none]:

Sweep range of sizes [n]:

Type escape sequence to abort.

Sending 5, 100-byte ICMP Echos to 192.168.10.1, timeout is 2 seconds:

!!!!!

Success rate is 100 percent (5/5), round-trip min/avg/max = 36/97/132 ms

Entering a longer timeout period than the default allows for possible latency issues to be detected. If the ping test is successful with a longer value, a connection exists between the hosts, but latency may be an issue on the network.

Note that entering "y" to the "Extended commands" prompt provides more options that are useful in troubleshooting.

11.3.1.3 Network Baseline

Refer to
Online Course
for Illustration

One of the most effective tools for monitoring and troubleshooting network performance is to establish a network baseline. A baseline is a process for studying the network at regular intervals to ensure that the network is working as designed. A network baseline is more than a single report detailing the health of the network at a certain point in time. Creating an effective network performance baseline is accomplished over a period of time. Measuring performance at varying times (Figures 1 and 2) and loads will assist in creating a better picture of overall network performance.

The output derived from network commands can contribute data to the network baseline.

One method for starting a baseline is to copy and paste the results from an executed ping, trace, or other relevant command into a text file. These text files can be time stamped with the date and saved into an archive for later retrieval.

An effective use of the stored information is to compare the results over time (Figure 3). Among items to consider are error messages and the response times from host to host. If there is a considerable increase in response times, there may be a latency issue to address.

The importance of creating documentation cannot be emphasized enough. Verification of host-to-host connectivity, latency issues, and resolutions of identified problems can assist a network administrator in keeping a network running as efficiently as possible.

Corporate networks should have extensive baselines; more extensive than we can describe in this course. Professional-grade software tools are available for storing and maintaining baseline information. In this course, we only cover some basic techniques and discuss the purpose of baselines.

Best practices for baseline processes can be found here.

Capturing `ping` command output can also be completed from the IOS prompt, as shown in Figure 4.

Refer to **Online Course** for Illustration

11.3.2   Tracert

11.3.2.1   Interpreting Tracert Messages

A trace returns a list of hops as a packet is routed through a network. The form of the command depends on where the command is issued. When performing the trace from a Windows computer, use `tracert`. When performing the trace from a router CLI, use `traceroute`, as shown in Figure 1.

Like `ping` commands, `trace` commands are entered in the command line and take an IP address as the argument.

Assuming that the command will be issued from a Windows computer, we use the `tracert` form:

```
C:\> tracert 10.1.0.2
Tracing route to 10.1.0.2 over a maximum of 30 hops
1  2 ms  2 ms  2 ms  10.0.0.254
2  *  *  *  Request timed out.
3  *  *  *  Request timed out.
4  ^C
```

The only successful response was from the gateway on Router A. Trace requests to the next hop timed out, meaning that the next hop router did not respond. The trace results indicate that the failure is therefore in the internetwork beyond the LAN.

Capturing the traceroute output can also be done from the router prompt, as shown in Figure 2.

Refer to **Packet Tracer Activity** for this chapter

11.3.2.2   Packet Tracer - Test Connectivity with Traceroute

This activity is designed to help you troubleshoot network connectivity issues using commands to trace the route from source to destination. You are required to examine the output of `tracert` (the Windows command) and `traceroute` (the IOS command) as packets traverse the network and determine the cause of a network issue. After the issue is corrected, use the `tracert` and `traceroute` commands to verify the completion.

Refer to **Lab Activity** for this chapter

11.3.2.3   Lab - Testing Network Latency with Ping and Traceroute

In this lab, you will complete the following objectives:

- Part 1: Use Ping to Document Network Latency
- Part 2: Use Traceroute to Document Network Latency

Refer to
Online Course
for Illustration

11.3.3 Show Commands

11.3.3.1 Common show Commands Revisited

The Cisco IOS CLI `show` commands display relevant information about the configuration and operation of the device.

Network technicians use `show` commands extensively for viewing configuration files, checking the status of device interfaces and processes, and verifying the device operational status. The `show` commands are available whether the device was configured using the CLI or Cisco Configuration Professional.

The status of nearly every process or function of the router can be displayed using a `show` command. Some of the more popular show commands are:

■ `show running-config` (Figure 1)

■ `show interfaces` (Figure 2)

■ `show arp` (Figure 3)

■ `show ip route` (Figure 4)

■ `show protocols` (Figure 5)

■ `show version` (Figure 6)

Click the buttons in the figure to see more information about the `show` commands.

Refer to
Online Course
for Illustration

11.3.3.2 Viewing Router Settings with the show version Command

After the startup configuration file is loaded and the router boots successfully, the `show version` command can be used to verify and troubleshoot some of the basic hardware and software components used during the bootup process. The output from the `show version` command includes:

■ The Cisco IOS software version being used.

■ The version of the system bootstrap software, stored in ROM memory that was initially used to boot the router.

■ The complete filename of the Cisco IOS image and where the bootstrap program located it.

■ Type of CPU on the router and amount of RAM. It may be necessary to upgrade the amount of RAM when upgrading the Cisco IOS software.

■ The number and type of physical interfaces on the router.

■ The amount of NVRAM. NVRAM is used to store the startup-config file.

■ The amount of flash memory on the router. It may be necessary to upgrade the amount of flash when upgrading the Cisco IOS software.

■ The currently configured value of the software configuration register in hexadecimal.

Click Play in the figure to see an animation about identification of these features of the show version output.

The configuration register tells the router how to boot up. For example, the factory default setting for the configuration register is 0x2102. This value indicates that the router attempts to load a Cisco IOS software image from flash and loads the startup configuration file from NVRAM. It is possible to change the configuration register and, therefore, change where the router looks for the Cisco IOS image and the startup configuration file during the bootup process. If there is a second value in parentheses, it denotes the configuration register value to be used during the next reload of the router.

Click the Note icon at the bottom right corner of the figure to obtain more information about the configuration register.

Refer to
Online Course
for Illustration

11.3.3.3   Viewing Switch Settings with the show version Command

The `show version` command on a switch displays information about the currently loaded software version, along with hardware and device information. Some of the information displayed by this command is:

- **Software version** - IOS software version

- **Bootstrap version** - Bootstrap version

- **System up-time** - Time since last reboot

- **System restart info** - Method of restart (e.g., power cycle, crash)

- **Software image name** - IOS filename

- **Switch platform and processor type** - Model number and processor type

- **Memory type (shared/main)** - Main processor RAM and shared packet I/O buffering

- **Hardware interfaces** - Interfaces available on the switch

- **Configuration register** - Sets bootup specifications, console speed setting, and related parameters.

The figure shows a sample of typical `show version` output displayed by a switch.

Refer to **Packet
Tracer Activity**
for this chapter

11.3.3.4   Packet Tracer - Using show Commands

This activity is designed to reinforce the use of router `show` commands. You are not required to configure, but rather examine the output of several `show` commands.

Refer to
Online Course
for Illustration

11.3.4   Host and IOS Commands

11.3.4.1   ipconfig Command Options

As shown in Figure 1, the IP address of the default gateway of a host can be viewed by issuing the `ipconfig` command at the command line of a Windows computer.

A tool to examine the MAC address of our computer is `ipconfig /all`. Note that in Figure 2, the MAC address of the computer is now displayed along with a number of details regarding the Layer 3 addressing of the device. Try using this command.

In addition, the manufacturer of the network interface in the computer can be identified through the OUI portion of the MAC address. This can be researched on the Internet.

The DNS Client service on Windows PCs optimizes the performance of DNS name resolution by storing previously resolved names in memory, as well. The `ipconfig /displaydns` command displays all of the cached DNS entries on a Windows computer system.

Refer to
Online Course
for Illustration

11.3.4.2   arp Command Options

The `arp` command enables the creation, editing, and display of mappings of physical addresses to known IPv4 addresses. The `arp` command is executed from the Windows command prompt.

To execute an `arp` command, at the command prompt of a host, enter:

```
C:\host1> arp -a
```

As shown in the figure the `arp -a` command lists all devices currently in the ARP cache of the host, which includes the IPv4 address, physical address, and the type of addressing (static/dynamic), for each device.

The cache can be cleared by using the `arp -d` command in the event the network administrator wants to repopulate the cache with updated information.

Note   The ARP cache only contains information from devices that have been recently accessed. To ensure that the ARP cache is populated, ping a device so that it will have an entry in the ARP table.

Refer to
Online Course
for Illustration

11.3.4.3   show cdp neighbors Command Options

Examine the output from the `show cdp neighbors` commands in Figure 1, with the topology in Figure 2. Notice that R3 has gathered some detailed information about R2 and the switch connected to the Fast Ethernet interface on R3.

CDP is a Cisco-proprietary protocol that runs at the data link layer. Because CDP operates at the data link layer, two or more Cisco network devices, such as routers that support different network layer protocols, can learn about each other even if Layer 3 connectivity does not exist.

When a Cisco device boots up, CDP starts up by default. CDP automatically discovers neighboring Cisco devices running CDP, regardless of which Layer 3 protocol or suites are running. CDP exchanges hardware and software device information with its directly connected CDP neighbors.

CDP provides the following information about each CDP neighbor device:

- **Device identifiers** - For example, the configured host name of a switch
- **Address list** - Up to one network layer address for each protocol supported
- **Port identifier** - The name of the local and remote port-in the form of an ASCII character string such as ethernet0
- **Capabilities list** - For example, whether this device is a router or a switch
- **Platform** - The hardware platform of the device; for example, a Cisco 1841 series router

The `show cdp neighbors detail` command reveals the IP address of a neighboring device. CDP will reveal the neighbor's IP address regardless of whether or not you can ping the neighbor. This command is very helpful when two Cisco routers cannot route across their shared data link. The `show cdp neighbors detail` command will help determine if one of the CDP neighbors has an IP configuration error.

For network discovery situations, knowing the IP address of the CDP neighbor is often all the information needed to Telnet into that device.

For obvious reasons, CDP can be a security risk. Because some IOS versions send out CDP advertisements by default, it is important to know how to disable CDP.

To disable CDP globally, use the global configuration command `no cdp run`. To disable CDP on an interface, use the interface command `no cdp enable`.

Refer to
Online Course
for Illustration

11.3.4.4   Using the show ip interface brief Command

In the same way that commands and utilities are used to verify a host configuration, commands can be used to verify the interfaces of intermediate devices. The Cisco IOS provides commands to verify the operation of router and switch interfaces.

Verifying Router Interfaces

One of the most frequently used commands is the `show ip interface brief` command. This command provides a more abbreviated output than the `show ip interface` command. It provides a summary of the key information for all the network interfaces on a router.

Figure 1 shows the topology that is being used in this example.

On Figure 2, click the R1 button. The `show ip interface brief` output displays all interfaces on the router, the IP address assigned to each interface, if any, and the operational status of the interface.

According to the output, the FastEthernet 0/0 interface has an IP address of 192.168.254.254. The last two columns in this line show the Layer 1 and Layer 2 status of this interface. The `up` in the Status column shows that this interface is operational at Layer 1. The `up` in the Protocol column indicates that the Layer 2 protocol is operational.

Also notice that the Serial 0/0/1 interface has not been enabled. This is indicated by `administratively down` in the Status column.

As with any end device, we can verify Layer 3 connectivity with the `ping` and `traceroute` commands. In this example, both the `ping` and `trace` commands show successful connectivity.

Verifying the Switch Interfaces

On Figure 2, click the S1 button. The `show ip interface brief` command can also be used to verify the status of the switch interfaces. The IP address for the switch is applied to a VLAN interface. In this case, the Vlan1 interface is assigned an IP address of 192.168.254.250 and has been enabled and is operational.

The output also shows that the FastEthernet0/1 interface is down. This indicates that either, no device is connected to the interface, or that the device that is connected to this interface has a network interface that is not operational.

In contrast, the output shows that the FastEthernet0/2 and FastEthernet0/3 interfaces are operational. This is indicated by both the Status and Protocol being shown as **up**.

The switch can also test its Layer 3 connectivity with the **show ip interface brief** and **traceroute** commands. In this example, both the **ping** and **trace** commands show successful connectivity.

It is important to keep in mind that an IP address is not required for a switch to perform its job of frame forwarding at Layer 2. An IP address is only necessary if the switch will be managed over the network using Telnet or SSH. If the network administrator plans to remotely connect to the switch from a location outside of the local LAN, then a default gateway must also be configured.

Refer to
Interactive Graphic
in online course.

11.3.4.5   Activity – Show Commands

Refer to
Lab Activity
for this chapter

11.3.4.6   Lab - Using the CLI to Gather Network Device Information.pdf

In this lab, you will complete the following objectives:

- Part 1: Set Up Topology and Initialize Devices
- Part 2: Configure Devices and Verify Connectivity
- Part 3: Gather Network Device Information

Refer to
Online Course
for Illustration

11.4   Managing IOS Configuration Files

11.4.1   Router and Switch File Systems

11.4.1.1   Router File Systems

In addition to implementing and securing a small network, it is also the job of the network administrator to manage configuration files. Managing the configuration files is important for purposes of backup and retrieval in the event of a device failure.

The Cisco IOS File System (IFS) provides a single interface to all the file systems a router uses, including:

- Flash memory file systems
- Network file systems (TFTP and FTP)
- Any other endpoint for reading or writing data such as NVRAM, the running configuration, ROM, and others

With Cisco IFS, all files can be viewed and classified (image, text file, and so forth), including files on remote servers. For example, it is possible to view a configuration file on a remote server to verify that it is the correct configuration file before loading the file on the router.

Cisco IFS allows the administrator to move around to different directories and list the files in a directory, and to create subdirectories in flash memory or on a disk. The directories available depend on the device.

The Figure 1 displays the output of the `show file systems` command, which lists all of the available file systems on a Cisco 1941 router, in this example. This command provides useful information such as the amount of available and free memory, the type of file system, and its permissions. Permissions include read only (ro), write only (wo), and read and write (rw), shown in the Flags column of the command output.

Although there are several file systems listed, of interest to us will be the tftp, flash, and nvram file systems.

Notice that the flash file system also has an asterisk preceding it. This indicates that flash is the current default file system. The bootable IOS is located in flash; therefore, the pound symbol (#) is appended to the flash listing indicating that it is a bootable disk.

The Flash File System

Figure 2 lists the content of the current default file system, which in this case is flash as was indicated by the asterisks preceding the listing in the previous figure. There are several files located in flash, but of specific interest is the last listing. This is the name of the current Cisco IOS file image that is running in RAM.

The NVRAM File System

To view the contents of NVRAM, you must change the current default file system using the `cd` (change directory) command, as shown in Figure 3. The `pwd` (present working directory) command verifies that we are viewing the NVRAM directory. Finally, the `dir` (directory) command lists the contents of NVRAM. Although there are several configuration files listed, of specific interest is the startup-configuration file.

Refer to
Online Course
for Illustration

11.4.1.2   Switch File Systems

With the Cisco 2960 switch flash file system, you can copy configuration files, and archive (upload and download) software images.

The command to view the file systems on a Catalyst switch is the same as on a Cisco router: `show file systems`, as shown in the figure.

Many basic UNIX commands are supported on Cisco switches and routers: `cd` for changing to a file system or directory, `dir` to display directories on a file system, and `pwd` to display the working directory.

Refer to
Online Course
for Illustration

11.4.2   Back up and Restore Configuration files

11.4.2.1   Backing up and Restoring using Text Files

Backup Configurations with Text Capture (Tera Term)

Configuration files can be saved/archived to a text file using Tera Term.

As shown in the figure, the steps are:

Step 1.   On the File menu, click **Log**.

Step 2.   Choose the location to save the file. Tera Term will begin capturing text.

Step 3. After capture has been started, execute the `show running-config` or `show startup-config` command at the privileged EXEC prompt. Text displayed in the terminal window will be directed into the chosen file.

Step 4. When the capture is complete, select **Close** in the Tera Term: Log window.

Step 5. View the file to verify that it was not corrupted.

Restoring Text Configurations

A configuration can be copied from a file to a device. When copied from a text file and pasted into a terminal window, the IOS executes each line of the configuration text as a command. This means that the file will require editing to ensure that encrypted passwords are in plain text and that non-command text such as "--More--" and IOS messages are removed. This process is discussed in the lab.

Further, at the CLI, the device must be set at the global configuration mode to receive the commands from the text file being pasted into the terminal window.

When using Tera Term, the steps are:

Step 1. On the File menu, click **Send** file.

Step 2. Locate the file to be copied into the device and click **Open**.

Step 3. Tera Term will paste the file into the device.

The text in the file will be applied as commands in the CLI and become the running configuration on the device. This is a convenient method for manually configuring a router.

Refer to
Online Course
for Illustration

11.4.2.2   Backing up and Restoring using TFTP

Backup Configurations with TFTP

Copies of configuration files should be stored as backup files in the event of a problem. Configuration files can be stored on a Trivial File Transfer Protocol (TFTP) server or a USB drive. A configuration file should also be included in the network documentation.

To save the running configuration or the startup configuration to a TFTP server, use either the `copy running-config tftp` or `copy startup-config tftp` command as shown in the figure. Follow these steps to back up the running configuration to a TFTP server:

Step 1. Enter the `copy running-config tftp` command.

Step 2. Enter the IP address of the host where the configuration file will be stored.

Step 3. Enter the name to assign to the configuration file.

Step 4. Press Enter to confirm each choice.

Restoring Configurations with TFTP

To restore the running configuration or the startup configuration from a TFTP server, use either the `copy tftp running-config` or `copy tftp startup-config` command. Use these steps to restore the running configuration from a TFTP server:

Step 1. Enter the `copy tftp running-config` command.

Step 2. Enter the IP address of the host where the configuration file is stored.

Step 3. Enter the name to assign to the configuration file.

Step 4. Press Enter to confirm each choice.

Refer to
Online Course
for Illustration

11.4.2.3   Using USB Ports on a Cisco Router

The Universal Serial Bus (USB) storage feature enables certain models of Cisco routers to support USB flash drives. The USB flash feature provides an optional secondary storage capability and an additional boot device. Images, configurations, and other files can be copied to or from the Cisco USB flash memory with the same reliability as storing and retrieving files using the Compact Flash card. In addition, modular integrated services routers can boot any Cisco IOS Software image saved on USB flash memory.

Cisco USB flash modules are available in 64MB, 128 MB, and 256MB versions.

To be compatible with a Cisco router, a USB flash drive must be formatted in a FAT16 format. If that is not the case, the show file systems command will display an error indicating an incompatible file system.

Here is an example of the use of the dir command on a USB file system:

Router# dir usbflash0:

Directory of usbflash0:/

1 -rw- 30125020 Dec 22 2032 05:31:32 +00:00 c3825-entservicesk9-mz.123-14.T

63158272 bytes total (33033216 bytes free)

Ideally, USB flash can hold multiple copies of the Cisco IOS and multiple router configurations. The USB flash allows an administrator to easily move and copy those IOS files and configurations from router to router, and many times, the copying process can take place several times faster than it would over a LAN or WAN. Note that the IOS may not recognize the proper size of the USB flash, but that does not necessarily mean that the flash is unsupported. Additionally, the USB ports on a router are usually USB 2.0, as shown in the figure.

Refer to
Online Course
for Illustration

11.4.2.4   Backing up and Restoring using a USB

Backup Configurations with a USB flash drive

When backing up to a USB port, it is a good idea to issue the `show file systems` command to verify that the USB drive is there and confirm the name, as shown in Figure 1.

Next, use the `copy run usbflash0:/` command to copy the configuration file to the USB flash drive. Be sure to use the name of the flash drive, as indicated in the file system. The slash is optional but indicates the root directory of the USB flash drive.

The IOS will prompt for the filename. If the file already exists on the USB flash drive, the router will prompt for overwrite, as seen in Figure 2.

Use the `dir` command to see the file on the USB drive and use the `more` command to see the contents, as seen in Figure 3.

Restore Configurations with a USB flash drive

In order to copy the file back, it will be necessary to edit the USB R1-Config file with a text editor to make it a valid config file; otherwise, there are a lot of entries that are invalid commands and no interfaces will be brought up.

```
R1# copy usbflash0:/R1-Config running-config
Destination filename [running-config]?
```

Refer to **Packet Tracer Activity** for this chapter

11.4.2.5   Packet Tracer - Backing up Configuration Files

This activity is designed to show how to restore a configuration from a backup and then perform a new backup. Due to an equipment failure, a new router has been put in place. Fortunately backup configuration files have been saved to a Trivial File Transfer Protocol (TFTP) Server. You are required to restore the files from the TFTP Server to get the router back online with as little down time as possible.

Refer to **Lab Activity** for this chapter

11.4.2.6   Lab - Managing Router Configuration Files with Tera Term

In this lab, you will complete the following objectives:

■ Part 1: Configure Basic Device Settings

■ Part 2: Use Terminal Emulation Software to Create a Backup Configuration File

■ Part 3: Use a Backup Configuration File to Restore a Router

Refer to **Lab Activity** for this chapter

11.4.2.7   Lab - Managing Device Configuration Files Using TFTP, Flash, and USB

In this lab, you will complete the following objectives:

■ Part 1: Build the Network and Configure Basic Device Settings

■ Part 2: (Optional) Download TFTP Server Software

■ Part 3: Use TFTP to Back Up and Restore the Switch Running Configuration

■ Part 4: Use TFTP to Back Up and Restore the Router Running Configuration

■ Part 5: Back Up and Restore Running Configurations Using Router Flash Memory

■ Part 6: (Optional) Use a USB Drive to Back Up and Restore the Running Configuration

Refer to **Lab Activity** for this chapter

11.4.2.8   Lab - Researching Password Recovery Procedures

In this lab, you will complete the following objectives:

■ Part 1: Research the Configuration Register

■ Part 2: Document the Password Recovery Procedure for a Specific Cisco Router

11.5   Integrated Routing Services

11.5.1   Integrated Router

11.5.1.1   Multi-Function Device

The use of networking is not limited to small businesses and large organizations.

Another environment that is increasingly taking advantage of networking technology is the home. Home networks are being used to provide connectivity and Internet sharing among multiple personal computers systems and laptops throughout the house. They also allow individuals to take advantage of various services such as print sharing to a network printer, centralized storage of photos, music, and movies on a network attached storage (NAS) appliance; as well as allowing other end user devices, such as tablet computers, cell phones, and even home appliances, such as a television, to have access to Internet services.

A home network is very similar to a small-business network. However, most home networks, and many small business networks, do not require high-volume devices, such as dedicated routers and switches. Smaller scale devices, as long as they provide the same functionality of routing and switching, are all that are required. For this reason, many home and small business networks utilize the service of a multi-function device.

For the purpose of this course, multi-function devices will be referred to as integrated routers.

An integrated router is like having several different devices connected together. For example, the connection between the switch and the router still occurs, but it occurs internally. When a packet is forwarded from one device to another on the same local network, the integrated switch will automatically forward the packet to the destination device. If a packet is forwarded to a device on a remote network, however, the integrated switch will then forward the packet to the internal router connection. The internal router will then determine the best path and forward the packet out accordingly.

Most integrated routers offer both wired switching capabilities and wireless connectivity, and serve as the access point (AP) in the wireless network, as shown in Figure 1. Wireless connectivity is a popular, flexible, and cost-effective way for homes, and businesses alike, to provide network services to end devices.

Figures 2 and 3 list some common advantages and considerations for using wireless.

In addition to supporting routing, switching and wireless connectivity, many additional features may be available on an integrated router, including: DHCP service, a firewall, and even network attached storage services.

11.5.1.2   Types of Integrated Routers

Integrated routers can range from small devices designed for home office and small business applications to more powerful devices that can support enterprise branch offices.

An example of this type of integrated router is a Linksys wireless router, as shown in the figure. This type of integrated router is simple in design and does not typically have separate components. This reduces the cost of the device. However, in the event of a failure, it is not possible to replace any single failed component. As such, they create a single point of failure, and are not optimized for any one function.

Another example of an integrated router is the Cisco integrated services router or ISR. The Cisco ISR product family offers a wide range of products, including those designed for small office and home office environments as well as those designed for larger networks. Many of the ISRs offer modularity and have separate components for each function, such as a switch component and a router component. This enables individual components to be added, replaced, and upgraded as necessary.

All integrated routers allow for basic configuration settings such as passwords, IP addresses, and DHCP settings, which are the same whether the device is being used to connect wired or wireless hosts. However, if using the wireless functionality, additional configuration parameters are required, such as setting the wireless mode, SSID, and the wireless channel.

Refer to
Online Course
for Illustration

11.5.1.3   Wireless Capability

Wireless Mode

The wireless mode refers to setting the IEEE 802.11 wireless standard that the network will use. There are four amendments to the IEEE 802.11 standard that describe different characteristics for wireless communications; they are 802.11a, 802.11b, 802.11g, and 802.11n. Figure 1 lists more information about each standard.

Most integrated wireless routers support 802.11b, 802.11g, and 802.11n. The three technologies are compatible, but all devices on the network must operate at the same standard common to all devices. For example: If an 802.11n router is connected to a laptop with 802.11n, the network would function as an 802.11n standard. However, add an 802.11b wireless printer to the network. Both the router and the laptop will revert to using the slower 802.11b standard for all communications. Therefore, keeping older wireless devices on the network will make the entire network slow down. It is important to keep that in mind when deciding whether or not to keep older wireless devices.

Service Set Identifier (SSID)

There may be many other wireless networks in your area. It is important that the wireless devices connect to the correct WLAN. This is done using a Service Set Identifier (SSID).

The SSID is a case-sensitive, alpha-numeric name for your home wireless network. The name can be up to 32-characters in length. The SSID is used to tell wireless devices which WLAN they belong to and with which other devices they can communicate. Regardless of the type of WLAN installation, all wireless devices in a WLAN must be configured with the same SSID in order to communicate.

Wireless Channel

Channels are created by dividing up the available RF spectrum. Each channel is capable of carrying a different conversation. This is similar to the way that multiple television channels are transmitted across a single medium. Multiple APs can function in close proximity to one another as long as they use different channels for communication.

Refer to
Online Course
for Illustration

11.5.1.4   Basic Security of Wireless

Security measures should also be planned and configured before connecting the AP to the network or ISP.

As shown in Figure 1, some of the more basic security measures include:

- Change default values for the SSID, usernames, and passwords
- Disable broadcast SSID
- Configure encryption using WEP or WPA

Encryption is the process of transforming data so that even if it is intercepted it is unusable.

Wired Equivalency Protocol (WEP)

WEP is an advanced security feature that encrypts network traffic as it travels through the air. WEP uses pre-configured keys to encrypt and decrypt data, as shown in Figure 2.

A WEP key is entered as a string of numbers and letters and is generally 64 bits or 128 bits long. In some cases, WEP supports 256 bit keys as well. To simplify creating and entering these keys, many devices include a Passphrase option. The passphrase is an easy way to remember the word or phrase used to automatically generate a key.

In order for WEP to function, the AP, as well as every wireless device allowed to access the network must have the same WEP key entered. Without this key, devices will not be able to understand the wireless transmissions.

There are weaknesses within WEP, including the use of a static key on all WEP enabled devices. There are applications available to attackers that can be used to discover the WEP key. These applications are readily available on the Internet. Once the attacker has extracted the key, they have complete access to all transmitted information.

One way to overcome this vulnerability is to change the key frequently. Another way is to use a more advanced and secure form of encryption known as Wi-Fi Protected Access (WPA).

Wi-Fi Protected Access (WPA)

WPA also uses encryption keys from 64 bits up to 256 bits. However, WPA, unlike WEP, generates new, dynamic keys each time a client establishes a connection with the AP. For this reason, WPA is considered more secure than WEP because it is significantly more difficult to crack.

There are several other security implementations that can be configured on a wireless AP, including MAC address filtering, authentication, and traffic filtering. However, those security implementations are beyond the scope of this course.

Refer to
Online Course
for Illustration

11.5.2   Configuring the Integrated Router

11.5.2.1   Configuring the Integrated Router

A Linksys wireless router is a common device used in home and small business networks, and will be used in this course to demonstrate basic configurations of an integrated router. A typical Linksys device offers five to eight Ethernet ports for wired connectivity, in addition to acting as a wireless access point. The Linksys device also acts as both a DHCP server and a mini-webserver that supports a web based graphical user interface (GUI).

Accessing and Configuring a Linksys Router

Initially access the router by cabling a computer to one of the router's LAN Ethernet ports, as shown in the figure. Once cabled, the connecting device will automatically obtain IP addressing information, including a default gateway address, from the integrated router. The default gateway address is the IP address of the Linksys device. Check the computer network settings using the `ipconfig /all` command to obtain this address. You can now type that IP address into a web browser on the computer to access the web-based configuration GUI.

The Linksys device has a default configuration that allows switching and basic routing services. It is also configured, by default, as a DCHP server. Basic configuration tasks, such as changing the default username and password, changing the default Linksys IP address, and even default DHCP IP address ranges, should be conducted before the AP is connected to a live network.

Refer to **Online Course** for Illustration

11.5.2.2   Enabling Wireless

To enable wireless connectivity, the wireless mode, SSID, RF channel, and any desired security encryption mechanism must be configured.

First, select the correct wireless mode, as shown in the figure. When selecting the mode, or wireless standard, each mode includes a certain amount of overhead. If all devices on the network use the same standard, selecting the mode associated with that standard limits the amount of overhead incurred. It also increases security by not allowing devices with different standards to connect. However, if devices using different standards need access to the network, mixed mode must be selected. Network performance will decrease due to the additional overhead of supporting all modes.

Next, set the SSID. All devices that wish to participate in the WLAN must use the same SSID. For security purposes, the default SSID should be changed. To allow easy detection of the WLAN by clients, the SSID is broadcast by default. It is possible to disable the broadcast feature of the SSID. If the SSID is not broadcast; wireless clients will need to have this value manually configured.

The choice of RF channel used for the integrated router must be made relative to the other wireless networks around it.

Adjacent wireless networks must use non-overlapping channels in order to optimize throughput. Most access points now offer a choice to allow the router to automatically locate the least congested channel.

Finally, select the encryption mechanism that you prefer and enter a key or passphrase.

Refer to **Online Course** for Illustration

11.5.2.3   Configure a Wireless Client

Configure a Wireless Client

A wireless host, or client, is defined as any device that contains wireless NIC and wireless client software. This client software allows the hardware to participate in the WLAN. Devices include: some smart phones, laptops, desktop PCs, printers, televisions, game systems, and tablet computers.

In order for a wireless client to connect to the WLAN, the client configuration settings must match that of the wireless router. This includes the SSID, security settings, and channel information (if the channel was manually set). These settings are specified in the client software.

The wireless client software used can be software integrated into the device operating system, or can be a stand-alone, downloadable, wireless utility software specifically designed to interact with the wireless NIC.

Once the client software is configured, verify the link between the client and the AP.

Open the wireless link information screen to display information such as: the connection data rate, connection status, and wireless channel used, as shown in the figure. The Link Information feature, if available, displays the current signal strength and quality of the wireless signal.

In addition, to verifying the wireless connection status, verify that data can actually be transmitted. One of the most common tests for verifying successful data transmission is the ping test. If the ping is successful, data transmission is possible.

Refer to Packet Tracer Activity for this chapter

11.5.2.4   Packet Tracer - Configuring a Linksys Router

In this activity, you will configure a Linksys wireless router, allowing remote access to wireless clients as well as connectivity with WPA security.

Refer to Online Course for Illustration

11.6   Summary

Refer to Lab Activity for this chapter

11.6.1.1   Capstone Project - Design and Build a Small Business Network

Capstone Project

Design and Build a Small Business Network

Use Packet Tracer and a word processing application to complete this activity – 2-3 students per group.

Design and build a network from scratch.

- Your design must include a minimum of one router, one switch, and one PC.
- Fully configure the network - use IPv4 or IPv6 (subnetting must be included as a part of your addressing scheme).
- Verify the network using at least five `show` commands.
- Secure the network using SSH, secure passwords, and console passwords (minimum).

Create a rubric to use for peer grading – or your Instructor may choose to use the rubric provided with this activity.

Present your Capstone Project to the class – be able to answer questions from your peers and Instructor!

Refer to **Packet Tracer Activity** for this chapter

11.6.1.2   Packet Tracer - Skills Integration Challenge

The network administrator has asked you to prepare [[R1Name]] for deployment. Before it can be connected to the network, security measures must be enabled.

Refer to **Online Course** for Illustration

11.6.1.3   Summary

In order to meet user requirements, even small networks require planning and design, as shown in the figure. Planning ensures that all requirements, cost factors, and deployment options are given due consideration. An important part of network design is reliability, scalability, and availability.

Supporting and growing a small network requires being familiar with the protocols and network applications running over the network. Protocol analyzers enable a network professional to quickly compile statistical information about traffic flows on a network. Information gathered by the protocol analyzer is analyzed based on the source and destination of the traffic as well as the type of traffic being sent. This analysis can be used by a network technician to make decisions on how to manage the traffic more efficiently. Common network protocols include: DNS, Telnet, SMTP, POP, DHCP, HTTP, and FTP.

It is a necessity to consider security threats and vulnerabilities when planning a network implementation. All network devices must be secured. This includes routers, switches, end user devices, and even security devices. Networks need to be protected from malicious software such as viruses, Trojan horses, and worms. Antivirus software can detect most viruses and many Trojan horse applications and prevent them from spreading in the network. The most effective way to mitigate a worm attack is to download security updates from the operating system vendor and patch all vulnerable systems.

Networks must also be protected from network attacks. Network attacks can be classified into three major categories: reconnaissance, access attacks, and denial of service. There are several ways to protect a network from network attacks.

■ Authentication, authorization, and accounting (AAA, or "triple A") network security services provide the primary framework to set up access control on a network device. AAA is a way to control who is permitted to access a network (authenticate), what they can do while they are there (authorize), and to watch the actions they perform while accessing the network (accounting).

■ A firewall is one of the most effective security tools available for protecting internal network users from external threats. A firewall resides between two or more networks and controls the traffic between them and also helps prevent unauthorized access.

■ To protect network devices, it is important to use strong passwords. Also, when accessing network devices remotely, it is highly recommended to enable SSH instead of the unsecured telnet.

After the network has been implemented, a network administrator must be able to monitor and maintain network connectivity. There are several commands available toward this end. For testing network connectivity to local and remote destinations, commands such as `ping`, `telnet`, and `traceroute` are commonly used.

On Cisco IOS devices, the `show version` command can be used to verify and troubleshoot some of the basic hardware and software components used during the bootup process. To view information for all network interfaces on a router, the `show ip inter-face` command is used. The `show ip interface brief` can also be used to view a more abbreviated output than the `show ip interface` command. Cisco Discovery Protocol (CDP) is a Cisco-proprietary protocol that runs at the data link layer. Because CDP operates at the data link layer, two or more Cisco network devices, such as routers that support different network layer protocols, can learn about each other even if Layer 3 connectivity does not exist.

Cisco IOS configuration files such as startup-config or running-config should be archived. These files can be saved to a text file or stored on a TFTP server. Some models of routers also have an USB port and a file can be backed up to a USB drive. If needed, these files can be copied to the router and or switch from the TFTP server or USB drive.

The use of networking is not limited to small businesses and large organizations. Another environment that is increasingly taking advantage of networking technology is the home. A home network is very similar to a small-business network. However, most home networks (and many small business networks) do not require high-volume devices, such as dedicated routers and switches. Instead, most home networks use a single multi-function device. For the purpose of this course, multi-function devices will be referred to as integrated routers. Most integrated routers offer both wired switching capabilities and wireless connectivity, and serve as the access point (AP) in the wireless network. To enable wireless connectivity, the wireless mode, SSID, RF channel, and any desired security encryption mechanism must be configured.

Go to the online
course to take the
quiz and exam.

Chapter 11 Quiz

This quiz is designed to provide an additional opportunity to practice the skills and knowledge presented in the chapter and to prepare for the chapter exam. You will be allowed multiple attempts and the grade does not appear in the gradebook.

Chapter 11 Exam

The chapter exam assesses your knowledge of the chapter content.

Your Chapter Notes